by

THE
LETTERS AND
PAPERS OF

CHAIM
WEIZMANN

YAD CHAIM WEIZMANN

This publication programme was initiated by Meyer W. Weisgal (1894–1977), Chancellor of the Weizmann Institute of Science and Chairman of the Weizmann National Memorial (Yad Chaim Weizmann). He was General Editor of the Weizmann Letters and Papers 1968–77.

Associate Editor NEHAMA A. CHALOM

ISRAEL UNIVERSITIES PRESS

Executive Editor GEOFFREY WIGODER
Administrative Manager MEIRA BENOUDIZ

Staff Editor, R.J.M. DENNERSTEIN; *Biographical Research and Indexer,* YEHUDA BLUMENFELD; *Research Assistant,* ELISSA COHEN; *Translator,* DON DANEMAN

Chaim Weizmann speaking in New York, 1942.

The Letters and
Papers of

Chaim Weizmann

GENERAL EDITOR

BARNET LITVINOFF

═══

VOLUME XX · SERIES A
July 1940–January 1943

Editor: MICHAEL J. COHEN

TRANSACTION BOOKS • RUTGERS UNIVERSITY
ISRAEL UNIVERSITIES PRESS • JERUSALEM

1979

Transaction Books, Rutgers University, New Brunswick, N.J.
ISBN   0   87855   260   X

Israel Universities Press, P.O. Box 7145, Jerusalem
ISBN   0   7065   1319   3

Library of Congress Catalog No. 74-35 4485

CONTENTS

ILLUSTRATIONS

ACKNOWLEDGEMENTS

The cooperation of the following is gratefully acknowledged:

Shaul Avigur (deceased), Kvutsat Kinneret, Israel.
Yehuda Benari, Jabotinsky Institute, Tel Aviv.
Mrs. K. F. Campbell, Library and Records Dept., British Foreign and Commonwealth Office, London.
Dr. Nathan Kaganoff, American Jewish Historical Society, Brandeis University, U.S.A.
Menahem Kaufman, Jerusalem.
Mrs. Sylvia Landress, Zionist Archives, New York.
Harry Sabel (deceased) and Dr. Paul Jacobi, Jewish National Fund, Jerusalem.
Dr. Max Sulzbacher, London.
Albert S. Lyons, M.D., Mount Sinai Medical Centre, New York.
Central Zionist Archives, Jerusalem.
Public Record Office, London.
Ben-Gurion Archives, Sde Boker.
Menahem Kedem, Kiryat Motzkin.

INTRODUCTION

The two and a half years covered by this volume of the Letters and Papers of Chaim Weizmann introduce a period of unparalleled tragedy for the Jewish people, with, ironically, the Zionist movement in deep conflict with Great Britain, for most of the time the only Power actively engaged in the struggle against Jewry's enemy, Adolf Hitler.

Despite ever-increasing evidence of Nazi intentions towards the Jews, British immigration policy as regards Palestine remained tied to the rigidly-enforced limits set by the White Paper issued by the Chamberlain Government in May 1939. The arrival without prior authorization of refugees twice led (from October 1939 to March 1940, and again from October 1940 to June 1941) to a total ban on certificated entry. The doors of Palestine virtually remained sealed even after the first authenticated news of the 'Final Solution' reached the West, in mid-1942. By the beginning of 1943, the extermination of a people in the Nazi death-machine had begun, yet nearly half the White Paper immigration quota of 75,000 remained unused. (During 1935, the peak year for Jewish immigration into Palestine, some 60,000 Jews had entered in a single year.)

For Weizmann himself, this period was marked by his frustration both as a political leader and a scientist, and embraced a direct challenge to his stewardship of the Zionist movement. It was also marked by deep personal grief. He was a man older than his years witnessing the disappearance of the world with which he was familiar, and all that it represented. As a consequence he was to suffer an almost complete breakdown of health.

Weizmann refused to believe that the 'true spirit' of England would not one day emerge. He was convinced that the presence of such trusted friends as Winston Churchill and Leopold Amery in the Cabinet would bring about a change in political attitudes, once war conditions had passed from the Middle East. In fact, his approach was anachronistic and his estimation of his own potential influence outdated. He harboured hopes of repeating his 'scientist-statesman' role of World War I. In place of acetone, one might read oil and synthetic rubber. And he intended this time to make an overt claim for his 'reward'—a definite undertaking to establish a Jewish State. However, he was unable to achieve his anticipated *tour de force*. The British remembered only too well the lessons of World War I, and, furthermore, the oil companies, particularly in America, had a vested interest in blocking his scientific initiatives.

The volume opens in the shadow of major disasters for British military fortunes: June 1940 had seen the entry of Italy into the war, and the fall of France. What until then had been essentially a European conflict now extended to the Middle East, and the *Yishuv* (the Jews in Palestine) could expect to be actively involved. Earlier Zionist offers to organize a specifically Jewish formation to join the struggle received added relevance and urgency as Italian armies began to concentrate on the Egyptian frontier and advance into British Somaliland. Indeed, Zionist expectations were high, for on 3 September 1940 Churchill agreed to a draft plan to mobilize Jews to fight in Palestine and in the Middle East, and details were soon agreed between the Zionists and the government departments concerned. Weizmann envisaged, in the first instance, a Jewish Division of 10,000 men, 3,000 of whom were to be mobilized in Palestine, the rest to come from the United States. Despite the officials' warnings that such a force would lead to political embarrassment for Great Britain, the Cabinet gave its approval to the scheme, though insisting upon complete secrecy until after the Presidential Election in the United States on 5 November 1940.

In the meantime, opposition to the proposed force in the Foreign Office and Colonial Office gathered momentum, and could have been immediately decisive were it not for the emotional tidal wave engendered by the *Patria* disaster (see below), which made this an inopportune moment for inflicting further political setbacks on the Zionists. Moreover, Churchill had given his personal support to the scheme, and he was not alone in the Government to appreciate the strength of the Jewish claim to the right of self-defence in Palestine.

Thus, concurrently with the Zionist initiative, pressure increased for some compensatory gesture to the Arabs. It was contended that the Government would incur their odium with the creation of a Jewish army, and this called for implementation of the 'constitutional clauses' laid down in the 1939 White Paper but suspended because the Government did not wish to relinquish control over Palestine during the war. These clauses provided for the appointment of Palestinian Ministers from the local communities, in the proportion of two Arabs to each Jew. In July 1940 a British officer, Colonel S.F. Newcombe, had, under the auspices of the Ministry of Information, conducted talks with the ex-Mufti of Jerusalem and the Iraqi Foreign Minister Nuri Said in Baghdad which led him to claim that implementation of the constitutional clauses would bring the support of the Mufti's Husseini faction to the British war effort, while the Iraqi Government would supply two Divisions for service in Libya. Newcombe's belief in the wisdom of such a course inspired this observation from Weizmann: 'In your memorandum all the British statesmen concerned with Palestinian affairs up to 1939— Mr. Lloyd George, Lord Balfour, Lord Curzon, Mr. Churchill, Mr. Amery, etc.—appear as nitwits, and myself the villain of the piece. It is only Mr. Malcolm MacDonald at the Palestine Conference (so aptly renamed by you the "Arab Conference") who sees the light. This reminds me of the fond Scottish mother who, seeing her son's regiment march past, observed, "they are all out of step, except our Jock".' No. 70
(2 Dec. 1940)

Following the American Presidential Election, negotiations between Weizmann and the Government were resumed and on the last day of 1940 a Commander was selected for the proposed Division. The Zionists had hoped that the command would go to Orde Wingate, but the latter's outspoken sympathy for the Jewish cause debarred him.

To Weizmann, nothing now remained for discussion except the technical details of the scheme, but the government departments concerned began to impose conditions which threatened to deprive the plan of much of the moral value it held for the Jewish people and the Zionist movement. In particular, Weizmann was incensed at the deletion of all mention of himself and the Jewish Agency as initiators and organizers of the project. Further, the Government was insistent about requiring a guarantee from recruits that their countries of origin would receive them back after the war. Lord Lloyd, the Colonial Secretary, stated that this proviso had been inserted because 'the Revisionists had been saying that the Jews were going to use the force to "gate-crash" into Palestine.' In a heated argument with Anthony Eden, newly-appointed Foreign Secretary, in January 1941, Weizmann, in a typical outburst, declared that the Jews had no intention of using backdoors after the war; the clamour for Palestine would be taken up by sixteen millions, and at least two millions of these would need to immigrate there. Doubtless such outbursts could have served only to reinforce Eden's strong feelings against the Zionist plans.

Soon, the hard-pressed Middle East Command added its objections to the weight of governmental opinion against the Jewish Force. General Wavell warned in February, 1941, that the raising of a Jewish army might well incite the Arabs to rebellion, at a time when his forces were over-stretched on three fronts. Churchill therefore bowed to the view of the new Colonial Secretary, Lord Moyne, that consideration of the Jewish Division scheme be postponed for a further six months, insisting all the while that the sole reason for postponement was lack of equipment. The Prime Minister himself received the Jewish leader and took the occasion to reassure him that this in no sense constituted a reversal of policy, and he 'would not let the Jews down'. Weizmann appears to have accepted this at face value, and telegraphed the head of the Jewish Agency's Political Department in Jerusalem, Moshe Shertok, to consider practical measures which would hasten formation of the Division when the scheme was resumed.

The negotiations had taken place against a backcloth of deepening gloom over the fate of European Jewry, with the Baltic States occupied by the Soviet Union and the Balkans newly under German domination. Appeals for exceptions to the immigration policy were met by refusals from a Government torn between its humanitarian sense and its fear of jeopardizing its paramountcy in the Arab world. Only in the case of the *Patria* disaster at the end of November 1940, in which some 240 Jewish refugees from Austria, Czechoslovakia and Danzig lost their lives, was mercy shown. Apparently it was through Weizmann's personal appeal to Lord Halifax, still Foreign Secretary, that permission was given for the survivors of the ill-fated ship to remain in Palestine. Further exceptions were ruled out by a decision not to facilitate immigration of aliens from enemy, or enemy-occupied, territories other than those already fortunate enough to be in possession of certificates.

With Britain determined not to incur Arab wrath, the Zionist movement turned to the great centre of free Jewry in the United States. Weizmann, particularly, felt that much political capital could be gained out of the alleged influence of American Jewry on the Administration, both as serving notice on the British Government that support for Zionism was part of America's price for strengthening Britain's hand in the war, and because American support for the Zionist platform would be of the greatest significance when the Great Powers came to settling the fate of the Middle East. He set off for his second war-time visit to the United States in March, 1941. Three months in the country, however, did not convince him that American Jewry would be quickly mobilised to a common, Zionist-orientated front. As he commented to Justice Felix Frankfurter:

No. 152
(21 June
1941)

'Somehow Zionists remain outside the mainstream of Jewish life and have not reached out beyond a narrow compass'. He also made mention of 'the waste of a certain amount of energy which is expended on undue friction inside the machine'. As regards the structure of the American-Jewish community in general, Weizmann was painfully reminded of the situation in pre-war Germany. The Zionist movement, as yet without a clear, crystallized programme, did not occupy the central position in the American-Jewish community which Weizmann wanted for it. On the contrary: 'There is a certain part of Jewish bourgeoisie—rich, quasi-powerful, loud, vulgar, pulling weight far in excess of their numbers, ostentatious—who, in the eyes of the Gentiles, they and almost they alone represent Jewry, and this is the grave danger. . . The Gentiles somehow expect the Jews always to be united. . . And the moment a group of Jews, however small, proclaims an opinion which happens to differ from ours, it somehow affects the minds of the statesmen more deeply than both the nature of the views and the character of the exponents would justify. The British Government, and particularly that of Palestine, have always made good use of such an opposition, and are likely to do so in the future in an increased measure.'

The dangers were compounded, in Weizmann's opinion, because the officials of the Near Eastern Division at the State Department were 'not one iota different from the Colonial Office officials'. And President Roosevelt himself, despite his 'great sympathy for the Zionist cause', could not help being influenced as a consequence. This had already been demonstrated when Roosevelt accepted the British pretext of lack of equipment for the postponement of the Army project. Weizmann was now convinced that the main reason for the postponement was 'political, and bound up with the appeasement of the Arabs'. In his opinion, the Zionist movement would have to embark on a great publicity campaign, similar to that mounted prior to the issue of the Balfour Declaration, in order to prepare the ground for a future favourable settlement.

Weizmann's apprehensions were increased when Eden, in a much-publicized speech at the Mansion House in London, declared that his Government would encourage any Arab initiative towards union in the Middle East. Weizmann regarded the speech as an 'inkling of the shape of things to come', especially in its 'one grave and significant omission—the Jews and Palestine'. In a message cabled to Churchill's secretary from the United States, he warned that the speech would have adverse effect in the United States. He notified Jan Smuts, the South African statesman and Zionist sympathizer, of the 'complete neglect of the Jewish people as an active factor in the Middle East', and expressed the somewhat far-fetched idea that Eden's declaration might one day be seized on by the Arabs in the same way that they had in 1919 seized on ambiguous British undertakings given during World War I. *[No. 146 (30 May 1941)]* *[No. 170 (15 Aug. 1941)]*

According to Weizmann, the role of the Zionist movement in rousing the American Administration against British policy was crucial. He described a British myth that had to be exploded in a letter to his devoted aide in New York, Meyer W. Weisgal: 'Our opponents in the Cabinet maintain the following point of view: it is true that in the last war the Jews of U.S.A. played an important *[No. 196 (14 Oct. 1941)]* part and contributed greatly towards the entry of America into the war. But things have changed. The Jews are deeply divided with regard to Zionism. The American Government did nothing when the White Paper was issued and is therefore indifferent to the question of Palestine. We need not take America into consideration, and can pursue our policy of placating the Arabs'.

With America's entry in the war at the end of 1941, Weizmann himself began lobbying the Administration in the name of Zionism's contribution to the Allied cause, and despite his allegiance to Great Britain he had no scruples about personally pressing for American intervention to persuade the British to change their Middle East policy. He was now a bitterly disappointed man, for in October, 1941, he was informed of the final abandonment of the 'Jewish Division' scheme.

He had demanded of Lord Moyne a definite and final answer regarding the fate of the scheme on his return to London, in August 1941, and he had addressed a final appeal to the Prime Minister. His No. 182 letter reviewed the ironic tragedy of the Jews' situation—their posi-(10 Sept. tion in Palestine, where British fortunes could literally mean a matter 1941) of life and death, and in Europe, 'tortured by Hitler as no nation has ever been in modern times'—yet permitted to serve 'only under humiliating limitations and conditions'. Weizmann absolved Churchill himself from responsibility for this policy, which had sacrificed the Jews 'in order to win over the Mufti of Jerusalem and his friends who were serving Hitler in the Middle East'. The letter deftly played on Churchill's known preoccupation with American aid. In the United States, Weizmann claimed, forces were finely balanced, and the 'one big ethnic group. . . willing to stand, to a man, for Great Britain [is] the five million American Jews'. Weizmann intimated that American Jewry awaited a British gesture, such as the formation of the Jewish Division, before they would tip the scales decisively in Britain's favour, inferring, quite wrongly, that this had been the case in World War I.

But for all Churchill's sympathy, he was out-voted within his Cabinet. The War Office doubted the military benefits that would accrue, and the Foreign Office now insisted that the announcement of the formation of any Jewish Force include specific reassurance to the Arabs that it would *not* be used in the Middle East. Moyne rightly pointed out that the new conditions would render the scheme unpalatable to the Jews. The Cabinet therefore decided definitely to reject the scheme—once more officially on the grounds of lack of equipment.

Weizmann's first public revelation of the negotiations and their outcome, in November 1941, came as a shock to the Zionist rank

and file. The initial Cabinet agreement to the scheme had been regarded by a former Minister, the strongly pro-Zionist Walter Elliot,
as 'Weizmann's greatest achievement since the Balfour Declaration'.
The reversal was proportionately disappointing, and the greatest
blow to the Weizmann school of Zionism since the 1939 White
Paper. The Government's decision to form a Palestine Regiment
during the retreat in the Western Desert in the summer of 1942 did
not compensate for this setback, for the regiment merely grouped
together those battalions already in service, without giving them a
separate Jewish identity or allowing them a full combat role as a
regiment of the line.

The British rejection of the Division scheme marked the end of an
era in Zionist, and in Weizmann's own, strategy. There were those,
like David Ben-Gurion, chairman of the Executive of the Jewish
Agency, who abandoned further hope in Great Britain, placing all
faith in the United States. Weizmann himself was emotionally unable to sever his affinity to London. But he did appreciate that the
centre of gravity of Zionist work must now pass to the United
States, and he was to spend over a year on his next momentous visit
there, from April 1942 until May 1943.

The failure of the Jewish Division negotiations precipitated a
direct clash between Weizmann and Ben-Gurion. The latter had
long been suspicious of Weizmann's penchant for Britain and its
'Establishment', and already in 1940 he had begun to boycott
meetings of the Jewish Agency Executive in London, considering its
members to be too much under Weizmann's influence. Ben-Gurion
felt that Weizmann was too remote from the realities of Palestine
itself. During the negotiations on the Army scheme, he had warned
that he could only ask Palestinians to enlist if it was understood
that they were to be employed in the defence of their country. On
the other hand, Weizmann and his circle in London believed that
they should seize on whatever concessions could be wrung from the
Government, even without an immediate undertaking as to the
theatre of operations of the force. Ben-Gurion charged Weizmann
with weakness, and a failure to consult.

The Zionist President was now to pay a heavy price for having
staked his political career on the Anglo-Zionist connection. Despite
a plea from Dr. Stephen Wise that internal feuds be laid aside in
times of crisis (Egypt, and therefore Palestine, was at the time under
the gravest threat from Rommel's armies), Ben-Gurion insisted that
the American Zionists consider and take action on his accusations
against Weizmann. But he was over-estimating his strength among
them, for the Americans refused. He therefore warned that he would
press the Jewish Agency Executive in Jerusalem and Zionist General

Council (the Actions Committee) to demand Weizmann's resignation as leader of the movement. Declaring that he personally was unwilling to continue working with Weizmann, Ben-Gurion ignored a proposal to establish a branch of the Jewish Agency Executive in New York. A deadlock ensued, and remained unbroken with the termination of this volume, with the two leaders following their divergent paths.

The personal conflict between Weizmann and Ben-Gurion found its political expression in their differing interpretations of the Biltmore Programme, adopted by a meeting of Zionist leaders in May 1942 at the Biltmore Hotel, New York. The Biltmore resolutions, which did not become official Zionist policy until the end of that year and were not adopted officially by American Jewry until mid-1943, spoke of Jewish Agency control over immigration into Palestine, and the eventual establishment there of a Jewish Commonwealth. This programme was based on an article written by Weizmann the previous January for the American journal *Foreign Affairs*. Weizmann himself regarded the resolutions as a long-term goal, without specific timetable, and to be implemented if possible within the framework of the traditional partnership with Great Britain. On the other hand, Ben-Gurion seized on the Biltmore resolutions as the instrument with which the movement would embark on a direct clash with the British Mandatory. He did not believe that Britain would ever agree to the establishment of a Jewish State in Palestine, in any form. He saw the solution to the plight of European Jewry in the mass migration of two million Jews to Palestine in one great operation. Weizmann regarded Ben-Gurion's interpretation as a tactical ploy in the struggle for the leadership of the movement, calculated to demonstrate the victory of his own policy, as against Weizmann's moderate formulation of the same aims. Ben-Gurion's proposal, fantastic though it might be, took official Zionism away from the path along which the other had directed it for a generation, and towards full confrontation with the Mandatory. (It was perhaps an instinctive, more representative reaction to the confirmation of the scale of Nazi genocide which reached the United States on the eve of Ben-Gurion's departure for Jerusalem.)

Meanwhile, Weizmann's 'gradualist' programme of political pressure exerted through powerful connections could not succeed while American Jewry remained divided. The need for this unity was all No. 195 the more urgent, given 'the temporary obliteration of something (13 Oct. like eight million Jews in Europe'. During his 1941 visit to the United 1941) States Weizmann had initiated talks between representatives of the various groups there in an attempt to arrive at some common, 'minimum' Zionist-orientated programme. The net result then had been the formation of a working committee of Zionists and non-Zionists, in an attempt to reach a consensus. Negotiations began tardily and continued intermittently, though the prospect looked promising while the American Jewish Committee was headed by Maurice Wertheim. But there soon arose an opposition group within his own ranks, headed by Judge Joseph Proskauer, which forced his resignation. Negotiations between the two streams in American Jewry consequently reached a stalemate.

Weizmann had earlier made a similar unsuccessful effort in London to reconcile the Anglo-Jewish leadership to the Zionist movement. The talks proceeded in both countries throughout 1942, but the results were meagre, and Weizmann remained pessimistic. He wrote: 'It is all like 1917 in England. . . history repeats itself'. No. 364 (8 Jan. 1943)

As in World War I, the struggle between the nations created new outlets and demands for Weizmann's scientific skills. Two of the most critical problems for the Allies were the supply of oil and rubber. The former was concentrated most accessibly for Great Britain in the Arab Middle East. The latter was at a premium following Japanese successes in Southeast Asia during the winter of 1941–42, especially when the United States entered the conflict unprepared at the end of 1941. Weizmann believed that he had the answer to both problems, in the work he was doing on grain fermentation from mid-1940 in his Government-sponsored laboratory in London.

In September 1940 Lloyd had intimated to Weizmann that at the root of the Government's Palestine policy lay the fear that Britain would one day be totally dependent on the Arabs for its oil. Weizmann had retorted that 'he could make the Empire flow with oil', No. 47 (27 Sept. 1940) from sources within the Empire itself. Weizmann was concurrently negotiating with Amery at the India Office to exploit the Indian Government's expected surpluses of molasses likewise through his own fermentation process. At the interview with the Colonial Secretary, Weizmann alluded to the link between his own work on acetone during World War I and the Balfour Declaration. This time, Weizmann insisted, there would be no ambiguity; he wanted Palestine. Once more he helped condemn his own aspirations with untimely, over-revealing remarks.

At the end of 1940 Weizmann was simultaneously negotiating the details of the Jewish Division scheme and discussing his own scientific contribution to the Imperial cause. The Government's retraction, early in 1941, from its agreement to raise the Division also militated against Weizmann's proposals for solving the fuel problem. In January, 1942, the Ministry of Supply pronounced its official, negative verdict on Weizmann's process for the manufacture of aromatic fuels, offering in meagre recompense to recommend the process to the appropriate authorities in the United States. Undoubtedly, the oil cartels must have seen here a threat to their interests, but one cannot rule out Weizmann's declared political motive as a factor in the rejection.

The by-products of this process were important in the production of synthetic rubber, a problem on which much effort and money was being expended, primarily by the large American oil companies. But on his arrival in 1942 Weizmann was alarmed at what he regarded as the totally inadequate measures to produce the quantities of rubber now needed following American entry into the war. Vast sums had been given to the oil industry to produce synthetic rubber, but appreciable quantities were not expected from this source for at least 18 months. The solution, in his opinion, lay in his own fermentation process, which could exploit the huge American grain surpluses now lying unused.

Weizmann devoted much of his first interview with President Roosevelt, on 7 July 1942, to expounding his fermentation process. Perhaps he felt that only after he had made his scientific contribution to the war effort would his political demands carry real weight. As for Palestine, Weizmann had for the present to accept the President's reluctance to press the British over the Jewish Division issue. He had, in the meantime, a calculated scale of priorities and, like a No. 323 chemical experiment, events had to take their proper course: 'The (18 Aug. scientific work has opened many avenues for me which, as you will 1942) probably gather, I am not neglecting to use for our own affairs. They may prove decisive at the opportune time'. But he found himself in the midst of a struggle between the oil concerns and the National Farmers' Union, each seeking lucrative Government subsidies. Roosevelt followed Weizmann's advice and appointed a governmental committee to investigate his process for the production of synthetic rubber. However, for reasons which are not entirely clear, it advised against adoption of his ideas.

Weizmann's disappointments in the scientific field were not confined solely to his dealings with the British and American governments. His own beloved contribution to Palestine, the Daniel Sieff Research Institute at Rehovot, suffered from his prolonged war-time absence from Palestine. His scientific staff did not live up to his No. 193 expectations: 'I have now received the reports of the various scien-(13 Oct. tists, and I am sorry to have to tell you that they have made me 1941) thoroughly unhappy. The results are very meagre, and I cannot for the life of me understand how so much time can have been spent on so little'.

He therefore notified the Administrative Director of the Institute, Benjamin Bloch, of his intention to cut down on staff and budget for the duration of the war. Of course, much of the trouble was due to his inability to exert personal control over the Institute's affairs, and being compelled to rely on unpredictable war-time communication. One cannot avoid the impression that Weizmann's disappointment was an overflow in part also from his own inter-connected political and private misfortunes.

The Weizmanns suffered a tragic loss in February, 1942, when their younger son Michael was reported missing on a flying mission. They were informed of the news at Bristol Aerodrome, on the point of their departure for the United States, and postponed their journey for some weeks, in the vain hope of news of their son's safety. The tragedy marked both parents indelibly. Undoubtedly, it contributed to Chaim Weizmann's breakdown and lengthy incapacitation from August to November 1942, requiring long convalescence, while his wife's suffering caused her ill-health that gave him permanent anxiety.

Thus bleakly did the year 1943 begin. In Weizmann's report to his London colleague Mrs. Blanche ('Baffy') Dugdale, he summarized the political constellation as he saw it. He attacked Ben-Gurion's thesis that the movement must look solely to the United States for its political future: 'It is quite true that America will No. 364 arise as a very great force in the world... but whether the United (8 Jan. States, after the war, will take an interest in Middle East politics, 1943) or whether it will again retire from continental and European entanglements—this is a very moot question... in view of the present [isolationist] tendencies... it would be a great mistake to discount Great Britain and to over-emphasise the importance of America for our cause'.

After the war, Weizmann believed, British colonial enterprise would concern itself with the development of Africa, where the war had enabled a consolidation of its position to that of paramount power. Palestine, situated 'across the Canal', might well fit in with the Imperial scheme of colonial development. He regarded the scheme propounded by the American soil expert, Walter Lowdermilk, for the extensive irrigation of Palestine under a 'Jordan Valley Authority' as providing the key to the future absorption of at least four million people. This project might also win over liberal America to Zionism and demonstrate the chauvinism of Arab nationalism.

Yet to Weizmann the future for Zionism was without promise unless the schisms within Jewry could be healed. He saw his two main tasks before leaving the United States to be: to convince the State Department of the justice of the Zionist programme; and to organize a democratic conference of American Jews, which might end the domination of the 'self-perpetuating group of plutocrats of the American Jewish Committee'.

In both these tasks, political and human factors outside Weizmann's own control would affect the degree of success he was to achieve in the crucial last two years of the war, years in which the nations' thoughts turned to a new world order. And above all, the Jewish psyche during these years would be profoundly affected by the gradual realisation of the full dimensions of the Nazi 'Final Solution' to the Jewish problem.

MICHAEL J. COHEN

LIST OF LETTERS

Reference should be made to the General Introduction to the Series, published in Volume I, for explanations on the structure of the Zionist Organization and associated institutions. A concise Weizmann Chronology will be found on pp. xxxvi–xxxvii of Volume I.

ABBREVIATIONS

C.O.	Colonial Office
C.Z.A.	Central Zionist Archives, Jerusalem
E.Z.F.	English Zionist Federation
F.O.	Foreign Office
H.W.	Handwritten
J.A.	Jewish Agency
J.D.C.	(American Jewish) Joint Distribution Committee
J.N.F.	Jewish National Fund *(Keren Kayemet L'Israel)*
J.T.A.	Jewish Telegraphic Agency
K.H.	*Keren Hayesod* (Palestine Foundation Fund)
Or. Copy	Original Copy
Premier	Prime Minister's Files
P.R.O.	Public Record Office, London
T.	Telegram
T. and E.	*Trial and Error,* the autobiography of Chaim Weizmann (London 1949 edition)
T.W.	Typewritten
U.J.A.	United Jewish Appeal
U.P.A.	United Palestine Appeal
V.W.	Vera Weizmann
W.	Chaim Weizmann
W.A.	Weizmann Archives, Rehovot
W.I.Z.O.	Women's International Zionist Organization
W.O.	War Office
(W.)Z.O.	(World) Zionist Organization
Z.O.A.	Zionist Organization of America

[As this volume opens, Chaim Weizmann is resident in London, having returned in March, 1940, from his first war-time visit to the United States. He is engaged on scientific research which he hopes will lead to the laboratory production of motor fuels. The fall of France in June, 1940, isolated Britain in its struggle against Germany and brought Italy into the war, an act that posed immediate threat to the British position in the Middle East, including Palestine. The first letter illustrates anxiety for relatives of his wife Vera, who were resident in Paris.]

1. To Lucio Thomo Feteira,[1] Lisbon.
English: Or. Copy. T.W.: W.A.

London, 1 July 1940

My dear Mr. Feteira,
I telegraphed to you today as follows:
"Shall be most grateful if you can enquire about my family Mr. J. Blumenfeld[2] who may be at Villa Torriano La Croix Department Var France. If possible send someone to see them, shall pay all expenses. Most gratefully.
Weizmann Dorchester Hotel."
I hope you will remember me. We used to meet fairly often at the Aviza Hotel, together with Mr. Kramarsky[3] and you had planned to take me to Coimbra, but the weather was not good. I am writing now to ask your help in a personal matter.
My wife's sister and her husband, M. and Mme. J. Blumenfeld (French citizens), were in France, at La Rochelle near Bordeaux, on the 14th June. Since then we have heard nothing of them. They have a small property at La Croix (Var) called Villa Torriano, and it is quite possible that the family is there, but I cannot establish any contact with them. I thought you might perhaps be kind enough to do so on my behalf; if they are in La Croix, perhaps one of our Portuguese friends could go over and see them and find out what their intentions are. Naturally everything would have to be handled with the greatest discretion. I shall be most grateful for anything you may be kind enough to do to help me in this matter, and remain, with many thanks in advance, and kind regards,[4]

Very sincerely yours,

1. [1] Consul for Paraguay at Lisbon
    [2] Joseph Blumenfeld (Biog. Index, Vol. V). Chemical engineer, married to Rachel Khatzman, sister of V.W. Engaged in industrial application and marketing of W.'s chemical discoveries. The Blumenfelds lived in Paris, and had fled on its occupation.
    [3] Siegfried Kramarsky (1893–1961). Banker. B. Germany, moved to Netherlands 1923, and to New York 1940. He and his wife were close friends of the Weizmanns.
    [4] W. received a telegram from Blumenfeld 17 July 1940 (W.A.) stating that he was at the Hotel Crillon, Avignon (see also No. 20).

2. To Harold Macmillan,[1] London.   *London, 1 July 1940*
English: Or. Copy. T.W.: W.A.

Dear Mr. Macmillan,

In connection with Mr. Leo Herrmann's[2] departure for Palestine with a view to organizing work there for the Ministry of Supply, I would like to say that there is another gentleman here, Dr. Benjamin Bloch,[3] who is the administrative head of the Daniel Sieff Research Institute in Rehovot, of which I am the Director, who must also go out as soon as possible, by the same route, in order to assist Herrmann and others on the chemical side. The Institute is playing a leading part in the development of the chemical industry in Palestine, and the presence there of Dr. Bloch at the earliest possible moment is, I feel sure, indispensable for the success of the effort.

I would therefore like to ask that Dr. Bloch may be given the same facilities as have been accorded to Mr. Herrmann with the Ministry of Shipping, with a view to his leaving here on July 11th.[4]

I have mentioned the matter to Mr. Amery who wishes to have the services of the Institute in certain chemical matters arising in connection with India, and told him that I should be writing to you about it—a suggestion in which he concurred.[5]

I also mentioned the matter to your secretary on the telephone this morning.

With many thanks in advance, I am

Yours very sincerely,
Ch. W.

2. [1] Biog. Index, Vol. XIX. He was then Parliamentary Secretary, Ministry of Supply.

[2] Biog. Index, Vol. VI. He was K.H. Secretary-General, and was to obtain from Palestine such supplies as textiles and general stores—munitions were specifically excluded (Macmillan to W., 2 July 1940, W.A.).

[3] Biog. Index, Vol. XVII. Physicist. Administrative Director and Vice-President of Executive of Sieff Research Institute, and later of Weizmann Institute of Science.

[4] The Ministry of Supply arranged a passage for Bloch on a Union Castle ship to South Africa, and a priority flight from Durban to Cairo. This was the usual war-time route to Palestine from June 1940 following the collapse of France.

[5] Leopold S. Amery (Biog. Index, Vol. VIII). Secretary of State for India. Friend of W., strongly pro-Zionist. He and W. had discussed Jewish offers of a military role 9 June 1940. Amery had also sought W.'s help in providing experts for an aircraft factory in India, and in supplying from Palestine drugs difficult to obtain there (see also Amery to W., 24 July, W.A.; Nos. 17, 18).

3. To Sir Archibald Sinclair,[1] London.   *London, 2 July 1940*

English: Or. Copy. T.W.: W.A.

We naturally warmly welcome the call which we understand has been made by the Air Officer commanding the R.A.F. in Palestine for Palestinians and other citizens to volunteer for service in the R.A.F., and do not doubt that suitable candidates will apply from among our people in Palestine.

I should like, however, in this connection, to ask you the following questions:

1) Has any decision been reached concerning the proposal for a Jewish Air Squadron in Palestine transmitted to you in a letter from Namier[2] on May 27th, and acknowledged by you the following day?[3]

2) Would it be possible for Palestinians resident in this country to enlist for service with the R.A.F. in Palestine? There are a number of suitable candidates available—students of engineering, etc.

3) Would other Jews, citizens of allied countries (Polish, Czechoslovak, Dutch, etc.) be allowed to enlist here in the same way for the R.A.F. in Palestine?[4]

Ch. W.

4. To Albert K. Epstein,[1] Chicago.   *London, 3 July 1940*

English: Or. Copy. T.W.: W.A.

My dear A. K.,

Very many thanks for your letter of June 17th, which came into my hands three days ago.[2] You can scarcely imagine how incongruous it seems to receive such a letter at a time when we are fighting for our lives, and do not know from one hour to another what may

---

3. [1] Later Viscount Thurso (Biog. Index, Vol. XIX). Secretary of State for Air 1940–45.

  [2] Lewis Namier (Biog. Index, Vol. XIV). A historian, he was Political Adviser to Jewish Agency Executive in London 1938–45.

  [3] This exchange of letters untraced.

  [4] Replying 8 July 1940 (W.A.), Sinclair stated that a final decision on a Jewish Air Squadron had not yet been reached, and he was consulting the Air Officer Commanding, Palestine. He was making enquiries regarding the other questions (see also Nos. 13, 29).

4. [1] Biog. Index, Vol. XVII. Manufacturer of chemical products; active American Zionist and friend of W.

  [2] This (W.A.) concerned rifts within the American Zionist movement, and dissatisfaction occasioned by the appointment of Meyer W. Weisgal (Biog. Index, Vol. X; d. 1977) to act as W.'s U.S. representative. Epstein claimed that the American commercial community had little faith in Weisgal's business acumen.

happen to us—when absolutely everything, including the fate of Palestine, is at stake.[3] Please don't misunderstand me: I am not objecting to your letter; only it seems to have come from a world which for us has completely disappeared. I am aghast when I read the American papers to see the kind of problem which seems to occupy men's minds and attention there. Whether it is the "Goldman Plan"[4]—whatever that may be—or whether this, that or the other person is elected President of the American Zionist Organization, seem to be questions agitating a world of shadows which has no relation to the grim realities which to-day face humanity at large and the Jews in particular.

I should have thought that whatever differences may have existed before, and however grave they may at the time have appeared, all such disputes would by now have been sunk in the common effort, and everyone would be "stripped for action" to try and save whatever can be saved from the hurricane which is breaking over our heads. But it seems that the Jews are just as incurably complacent as many of their neighbours, and equally heedless of the warnings and signs of the times. Then, when catastrophe reaches their gates, they will start up perplexed and wondering, as though something totally unexpected had happened.

Now as to the points you raise in your letter, although—as I have said—they seem to me to be utterly irrelevant in the changed circumstances. But as you have thought it necessary to put them to me, I would like to give you my point of view as clearly as I can.

1) The matter of my project[5] was not left in the hands of Weisgal and his associates. When I left New York a Committee was in existence there consisting of responsible Zionists, including Mr. Szold[6] and representatives of the *Keren Hayesod*. Weisgal's part in the matter was that he rendered me great service in helping me to establish contacts with all kinds and conditions of people with whom the others had no relations whatsoever. He was of great assistance in this way; he worked long days and evenings to do it, and whatever

---

[3] Italy had declared war 10 June; France surrendered 22 June.

[4] Epstein's letter had informed W. that Rabbi Solomon Goldman (Biog. Index, Vol. XVIII) was being canvassed for re-election as President of Z.O.A., his two-year term of office having just expired. Goldman's 'plan' was 'to recruit more members, to re-organize the Z.O.A. and lead American Zionism out of its stagnation.' Epstein stated that his own associates would willingly help, but they were antagonized by such 'Old Guard' leaders as Rabbi Stephen Wise, Louis Lipsky, Maurice Karpf and Maurice Hexter. See also Meyer Weisgal, *So Far. . .* (London 1971), pp. 165 ff.

[5] W.'s 'project' was the launching of a major development loan for Zionist undertakings in Palestine through the K.H.—see Vol. XIX.

[6] Robert Szold (Biog. Index, Vol. IX; d. 1977). A lawyer, he was engaged in various economic activities for Palestine.

small success I had was certainly due in no small measure to him. I would like to make it clear that he had no desire or ambition to deal with the financial side of the project. He was perfectly satisfied to act as my personal representative and friend, and the others were fully cognisant of the position. Goldman certainly knew all about it. What may have happened after my departure I do not know, but this was the position as I left it. It seems to me that there is a sort of Kabal against Weisgal who—I must emphasise—had no desire whatever to mix in financial matters. This was left entirely to the Committee which was in existence at that time, and should have functioned perfectly constitutionally.

2) I am amazed to read in paragraph 2 of your letter that Kaufman[7] did not want to take the Chairmanship of the Committee because of Weisgal. I spent a whole week in Florida with Kaufman. Weisgal was there with me the whole time. Kaufman was much more enthusiastic about the loan than I was myself, and consistently reproached me with not working fast enough, and being too hesitant. If he had had any objections to Weisgal, it would have been the simplest thing in the world for him to ask me just what was Weisgal's role in the business, and to express his doubts if he had any. But he never breathed a word of this kind. He accepted the Chairmanship, fixed a time to go over to New York to discuss things with our colleagues there and make further arrangements, and was most insistent that I should return to America as soon as possible in order to complete the work begun under such favourable auspices.

I do not know who are the "associates of Mr. Weisgal" to whom you refer. I suppose they can only be the group of Zionist leaders who have been in the Movement these forty years. I never heard that Kaufman raised any objections to them, and in fact it was Wise[8] who arranged with Kaufman my stay in Florida, as I did not then know Kaufman at all. Why Kaufman should have changed his mind a fortnight after I left I do not know, and I do not care to investigate. But he was perfectly free to choose his own Committee, and to insist on working with men able to carry such a project through successfully. I hardly think anyone could have put obstacles in his way; certainly not myself. My repeated appeals to Kaufman since my return here have met with vague and unconvincing replies, and I hear now, for the first time, that Weisgal was apparently the obstacle, which—forgive me for being blunt—seems to me to be quite ridicu-

---

[7] Edmund I. Kaufman (1886–1950). President of Z.O.A. June 1940 to Sept. 1941; co-founder of U.J.A.

[8] Dr. Stephen Wise (Biog. Index, Vol. VII). Reform rabbi; President of American Zionist Emergency Council 1940.

lous and even fantastic. Weisgal had no ambitions whatsoever, and would certainly not have stood in the way. I cannot help feeling that there must have been some other reasons which I cannot fathom, or properly assess, from here.

3) As for Dr. Ish-Zahav's[9] attitude, this is also one of those riddles which I may hope to solve one day—if I live. He worked intimately with me throughout my stay in America until the last ten days. Weisgal took great care that he should be kept fully informed of every step we took and every move we made. Ish-Zahav promised to come to Florida, but did not appear. He then promised to come to New York for a few days before my departure, but again did not come—even to say goodbye. Somebody suggested that he felt peeved about something. But my own conscience is entirely clear on that score. I have, however, since heard that Ish-Zahav got from somewhere the impression that I was supporting the candidature of Lipsky[10] as against his own for the forthcoming elections. I have studiously avoided mixing myself up in any of these internal matters, and I am sure that no word or act of mine would, by any stretch of the imagination, have been interpreted in any such sense. Throughout the many years of my Presidency of the Zionist Organization I have made it a golden rule never to intervene in any way in local Zionist politics, however important they might be. (My life would not have been worth an hour's purchase otherwise.) I am shocked by the behaviour of Ish-Zahav; I have always treated him with the greatest kindness and consideration, and hoped that he would continue his fruitful activities in the same spirit in which he began them on his election.

4) Whether Kaufman should be a candidate for the presidency of the Z.O.A. is not for me to say. He was certainly a most desirable person to head the Loan Committee, and had he proved successful in that, his leadership of the Movement in America might have followed as a natural consequence. He is a charming man, possessed of great qualities; but whether he has the patience, the knowledge and experience, or the training, to conduct a democratic Movement like ours I do not know. It is one thing to be the head of a financial corporation; quite another to guide a Movement of millions of people, with all the currents and cross-currents that develop in it!

Looking back on my last stay in America, which gave me a great deal of encouragement and hope for a better future, I am saddened by the thought that all this effort has been to some extent undone

[9] Hebr.: 'man of gold', i.e., Goldman.
[10] Louis Lipsky (Biog. Index, Vol. VI). Long-time friend of W., a veteran Zionist. Vice-President and Chairman of Governing Council of American Jewish Congress 1934–45.

by events of which I know little and care less. But in view of the world-shaking upheaval now taking place, all this does seem rather unreal. This may be my last letter to you, and I can only conclude it by expressing the hope that American Jewry will prove itself worthy of the terrible responsibility which rests upon it.

As regards ourselves, we shall go on fighting, and we are confident of victory. When that victory comes, we shall have to build a new world. If we survive the storm, we shall have to adapt ourselves to the new conditions then to be created. Whether we, who have carried the Movement thus far along its course, happen to survive or not is perhaps irrelevant. But that you people, who will have to carry on after us, should still be wasting your time in petty politics of this kind adds greatly to the pain and anguish which are our daily bread. Is it really so impossible for American Jewry to unite? What can it matter who presides at meetings so long as he knows what he has to do? *Everything* is at stake to-day, and 3,000 miles of water will not save American Jewry or America itself, if they refuse to take the right decisions now.

I have no plans at present. I believe my place is here. If there should be any change, I shall of course let you know at once. As regards my personal affairs, the fate of my family in France is still unknown to me, and I am at a loss to know how to find out about them, or how to get in touch with them if they are still alive.[11] We live here from hour to hour, and every minute of sunshine and fresh air, and relative tranquillity, is a gift for which we are thankful to God who is trying us so severely. If we emerge from this ordeal into what I hope may be better days, we shall go forward along the road to redemption. I hope American Jewry may be animated by the same spirit; if it is not, then it will perish, unhonoured and unsung. This must not happen. My last word to you is a prayer that you may rise above all the petty bitternesses of the day, and devote yourselves body and soul to maintaining what we have achieved in Palestine, which is now in mortal danger, to fortifying the structure there, and strengthening the internal life of the Community.

Every conceivable effort of American Jewry should be devoted towards helping the Allies in this struggle—which is our struggle. If the battle here should be lost, there will be no hope for you, and very little for America as a whole. This should therefore be the guiding principle of your lives, and everything else must, for the time being, take second place.

Affectionately yours,

---

[11] See Nos. 1, 20.

P.S. While this letter was being typed, I heard the news of Kaufman's election to the Z.O.A. Presidency. I have just cabled to him, and need only add here that I wish him the greatest possible success in the heavy task he has undertaken, and trust that he may lead American Jewry in the right paths and to the fulfilment of its great mission. Let me also express my personal hope that he may be loyally supported by everybody, and that his task will not be made unnecessarily difficult for him.

5. To Richard Austin Butler,[1] London.   *London, 4 July 1940*
English: Or. Copy. T.W.: W.A.

Dear Mr. Butler,

I am writing to you about the question of our archives and our personnel, which Mr. Namier discussed with you on June 25th; yesterday he saw Mr. Vincent Massey[2] about them. Mr. Massey, who was agreeable to communicate about these matters with his Government, asked us to obtain an official letter from the Foreign Office which would serve him as a basis.

I therefore wish to re-state in writing the points which Mr. Namier put before you:

1) We should like to send off to Canada part of our London archives, in parcels sealed by us, and after that by the Foreign Office, to remain in Canada for safekeeping. As under these seals the documents would not be accessible to anybody, I take it that the ordinary censorship regulations could be waived. Arrangements would have to be made with the Canadian Government for the reception and preservation of these parcels.

2) Should things take so grave a turn that the British Government themselves would decide to evacuate to Canada, our office would naturally wish to follow. Certain non-political branches might even conveniently be transferred earlier—the European continent has ceased to exist for us, and these branches could more conveniently carry on their work from the American end, with American Jewry as its base; but we want the centre of every branch of our organization to remain within the British Empire, and would therefore ask for visas for Canada which would enable our people to proceed there whenever required. If all our employees were British, the

---

5. [1] B. 1902. Cons. M.P. Under-Secretary of State at F.O. 1938–41. Later held most senior Cabinet posts except Prime Minister. Created Lord Butler 1965.
[2] 1887–1967. High Commissioner for Canada in London 1935–46.

matter would naturally be much simpler; they would require merely exit visas from this country, while at the other end, the Canadian Zionist Organization would assume financial responsibility for them. But a certain number of them are foreigners (German, Austrian, Polish and Swiss). Therefore the question of their Canadian visas requires early attention. I include a list of these employees and their families.[3]

Yours very sincerely,
Ch. W.

6. To Lord Chetwode,[1] [London?].   *London, 5 July 1940*
English: Or. Copy. T.W.: W.A.

Dear Lord Chetwode,
 You were good enough to give me permission to write to you with regard to Mrs. Weizmann,[2] who is anxious to help in some way in the emergency.
 She is a British subject (we have both been naturalized for the last thirty years), took her medical degree at the Victoria University, Manchester, and was in practice there for several years before the last war. Besides being a fully qualified medical woman, she has done a great deal of social work, in Palestine, in England and in America, is an excellent organizer, and speaks—in addition to English—French, a certain amount of German, and Russian (her native language, as it is mine).
 If you can suggest any work in which her training and experience could be utilised she would be only too delighted to give full-time service in a voluntary capacity.[3]
 With renewed thanks for your kindness, I am

Very sincerely yours,
Ch. W.

---

[3] Following further correspondence, the documents were despatched under seal and without examination by the censors, and arrived in Canada late Sept. A visa was requested only for Felix Rosenblueth (later Pinhas Rosen) of the Zionist Executive. See Butler to W., 6 July; W.–F.O. exchange, 30 July, 3 Aug.; Minutes of Executive meeting, 16 Aug. 1940—all in W.A.

6. [1] Field-Marshal Sir Philip Chetwode (1869–1950). In 1917–18 commanded Army Corps which took part in conquest of Palestine and Syria; Chairman of Executive of Red Cross and St. John Joint War Organization 1940–47.
 [2] Vera Weizmann (née Khatzman)—Biog. Index, Vol. I.
 [3] No reply traced. For her war service, see V.W.'s memoirs *The Impossible Takes Longer* (London 1967), pp. 180, 183, 190–91; see also No. 24.

[On 29 August 1939, W. had suggested that the Zionist movement set aside its political differences with the British Government, and in a letter to the Prime Minister, Neville Chamberlain, he offered the full potential of the Jewish people in the coming struggle against Nazi Germany, their common enemy. In his reply, the Prime Minister declined 'at this stage' to discuss the offer in detail. The subject assumed urgency with the entry of Italy into the war and the threat to Palestine itself. In September, 1940, Haifa was bombed four times by Italian aircraft, while Italian armies advanced across the Western Desert to Egypt. Although the Allied forces under Wavell inflicted heavy losses on the Italians in January, 1941, the threat to Egypt (and consequently Palestine) was renewed by Rommel in the summers of 1941 and 1942. The war in the Middle East brought home the need to organize the Jews of Palestine for some form of self-defence against invasion. Thus W.'s diplomatic efforts during the period of this volume centred on the demand for a Jewish Division, for which Palestinian Jewry was to raise 3,000 of the 10,000 men required.]

7. To Lord Chetwode, [London?].   *London, 6 July 1940*
English: Or. Copy. T.W.: W.A.

Dear Field Marshal Chetwode,

With reference to our conversation last Wednesday, I would like to sort out the facts for you as briefly as I can:

Since the beginning of the war we have been anxious to cooperate with H.M. Government, and have offered to place at their disposal all the available man-power in Palestine and to enlist young Jews to fight in Jewish units on the side of the Allies wherever such enlistment is possible. There is no need for me to recapitulate here all the disappointments and frustrations which this simple proposal has brought us. For various reasons—chief among them the fear lest the Arabs might take umbrage—the proposal has even now not been accepted. During Mr. MacDonald's[1] term of office there was some definite obstruction from his Department, and even now Lord Lloyd[2] still feels that the carrying of our proposals into effect would be fraught with dangers.

The position in the Middle East and Egypt changes from day to day. But I think that there is now perhaps a better prospect of the realization of our aims than there has been hitherto. To-day, however, with the Germans occupying practically the whole of Europe, the possibilities of recruitment are limited, in effect, to Palestine itself and America.

We are therefore reduced to two suggestions: first, the creation

---

7. [1] Malcolm MacDonald (Biog. Index, Vol. XIV). Colonial Secretary 1938–40; Minister of Health 1940–41.

[2] Biog. Index, Vol. XIV. Colonial Secretary May 1940—Feb. 1941.

of a nucleus in Palestine, and secondly the organization of a force in the United States, South Africa, and possibly also in South America.

In Palestine we have some 22,000 partially trained men, who have had experience as supernumerary police during the riots.[3] They are sturdy and reliable people, and could be easily and rapidly militarised to form a substantial force. I am told that one great difficulty is the lack of equipment for them. But surely there must now be a great deal of equipment available in Syria—where it is probably going begging. This last point is of great urgency and importance, and needs to be taken up immediately. Mittelhauser's[4] army is disintegrating, and it is quite possible that weapons may fall into the hands of rebellious Arabs who will use them to fight us and to fight the British.

So far as America is concerned, I am told that recruitment there is perfectly possible. I may be going over myself shortly. If I do, it will be with two objects in mind: (a) to accelerate the process of recruitment and training of such a force (the training would presumably be done in Canada), and (b) to use what influence I have with the Jewish community (which plays an important part in the industrial life of the country) to help to speed up production.

I would also like to put in hand the training of pilots. There are hundreds of young Jewish pilots flying in the commercial air lines of America, who would be very willing to fight for Great Britain, and would be excellent material.

But it is essential that the Government should come to some sort of decision on these points. At present they are full of doubts and hesitations, and if they do agree to anything they do it piecemeal, and leave the whole situation blurred and unsatisfactory.

I have tried to set out the position as briefly as I can, as I do not want to weary you with details. The crux of the whole matter is speed and decision.

Thanking you again for anything you may be able to do to clear up this matter, and to help in the realisation of our proposals, I remain,[5]

Very sincerely yours,

Ch. W.

---

[3] The Arab riots of 1936–39.

[4] Gen. Eugène D. Mittelhauser (1873–1949). In May 1940 succeeded Weygand at Beirut as commander of French forces in Levant.

[5] No reply traced.

8. To Lord Lloyd, London. *London, 12 July 1940*
English: Or. Copy. T.W.: W.A.

Dear Lord Lloyd,
   I have to acknowledge receipt of your letter of July 4th concerning the actions of certain British policemen early in March, and the murder of Menahem Prives on March 2nd.[1]
   The Jewish Agency cannot accept the conclusions put forward by the High Commissioner on these matters, nor acquiesce in outrages and murder committed by the police remaining unpunished.
   We deeply regret your refusal to reopen the enquiry. Present circumstances naturally make us unwilling to discuss the subject in public, but I must reserve to the Agency the right to publish the entire correspondence about it as soon as this can be done without injury to our common cause.[2]

Yours very sincerely,
Ch. W.

9. To Moshe Shertok,[1] Jerusalem. *London, 15 July 1940*
English: Code: T.: W.A.

Saw Haining[2] today about cadres. He promised Wavell[3] will go ahead and has cabled him instructions. You should make all preparations.[4]

Weizmann

---

8. [1] The death of Menahem Prives was the climax to a series of violent demonstrations in Palestine against the enactment of the Land Laws section of the 1939 White Paper, at the end of Feb. 1940. Prives was among the demonstrators in Jerusalem who were treated roughly by the police, and subsequently died in hospital of a fractured skull (see Report by Bernard Joseph to the Chief Secretary of the Palestine Government, in C.Z.A. Pol/30/40). Lloyd's letter of 4 July 1940 (W.A.) quoted the tribute paid by Sir Harold MacMichael, the High Commissioner, to the 'restraint and firmness shown in general by the forces of public security in somewhat exacting circumstances.' Prives' death had been investigated officially by MacMichael, who was satisfied that complaints against the police had been greatly exaggerated. A Court of Enquiry had been unable to ascertain the precise circumstances in which Prives' injuries had been sustained and Lloyd refused to ask MacMichael to institute further proceedings, judicial or otherwise (see Vol. XIX).
   [2] See also No. 205.

9. [1] Biog. Index, Vol. XVI. Head of J.A. Political Department. As Sharett, Israel's first Minister for Foreign Affairs 1948–53, and Prime Minister 1953–55.
   [2] Gen. Sir Robert Haining (Biog. Index). Vice-Chief of Imperial General Staff 1940–41.
   [3] Gen. Sir Archibald Wavell (Biog. Index). Then C.-in-C. Middle East.
   [4] On 21 June, Shertok reported to J.A. Executive in Jerusalem that David Ben-Gurion

10. To W. D. H. Danby,[1] London.   *London, 16 July 1940*
English: Or. Copy. T.W.: W.A.

My dear Mr. Danby,
    I would like to sum up as briefly as I can the gist of our conversation to-day.
    (i) Journey to America: I should like to discuss rather more fully the aims and objects of this trip with Lord Lloyd and also, if at all possible, with the Prime Minister,[2] before actually leaving. I outlined to you my own conception of the aims of such a visit, and need not go over them in detail here.
    (ii) As soon as a definite decision is taken as regards the best date for my departure, we shall have to settle the best way of proceeding. As things stand at present, it seems to me that the Clipper[3] is both safer and quicker than any other route, and as the Clipper is probably fairly heavily booked up, it would need some assistance on your part before I could obtain one or two seats. (I am not yet sure whether Mrs. Weizmann will wish to accompany me, or whether I shall go alone.)
    (iii) With regard to the approximate date of my departure, the following consideration occurs to me. August is the worst month for New York: it is very hot, and everyone is away. If I were to leave here, say, at latest in a month's time, I could first of all set my laboratory work in proper order before I leave, and secondly, arrive in New York about the second half of August, which would give me a couple of weeks to make my plans on the spot and be ready to start work in the first days of September, when people begin to come back from their holidays. Unless some other considerations occur to us meanwhile, this would seem to be the most appropriate date.

---

had obtained permission from Lloyd to train Jewish officers. On 5 July the Palestine Government officially informed the Agency that it would agree to Jewish mobilization, as follows: 550 transport drivers for the route to Iraq; 500 men for R.A.F., of whom 150 would be drivers and the rest ground staff; and a further 660 for a Labour Brigade, presumably to construct fortifications. By the end of July, some 1,000 Jews had been mobilized in Palestine. There were no specific instructions given to train officers to lead the prospective Jewish Force. Officers would be chosen as required from those men recruited for general purposes (see J.A. Executive Minutes, C.Z.A. Vol. 32). During negotiations with the W.O. on the formation of the Jewish Division, in Jan. 1941, the Agency Executive was informed that a Military Board would be appointed to select Palestinian recruits for training as officers and N.C.O.'s. Col. Frederick Kisch was to be the J.A. representative on the Board (see Namier Note of 27 Jan. 1941, W.A.).

10. [1] Secretary at C.O.
   [2] Winston S. Churchill (Biog. Index, Vol. X).
   [3] I.e., the flying-boat on the transatlantic route.

Moreover, it should be easier to secure accommodation on the Clipper for a date a month hence if we try to make the reservations now.

(iv) One of the objects of such a visit would, as you know, be recruiting. I had a long talk with General Haining to-day on this subject, and we reached the following conclusions: he thinks that recruiting of cadres in Palestine—meaning by this three or four hundred young men for training as officers and N.C.O.'s— might be begun at once, and believes that General Wavell is favourably disposed towards such a project. I urged General Haining to send General Wavell a message asking him to proceed with this recruiting forthwith. It occurs to me that it would be of the utmost importance if the Secretary of State would agree to send a similar message to the High Commissioner.[4] I do not know what are the present relations between the High Commissioner and the Jewish Agency in Palestine; I believe they have greatly improved of late. But I am quite certain that a word from the Secretary of State would speed matters up very considerably.

(v) The same applies to another subject on which I touched in our talk this morning. You know that the Ministry of Supply has agreed to utilise the industrial resources of Palestine for war purposes, and that two men have recently gone out on behalf of the Ministry for this purpose. They are now on their way to Palestine, and if all goes well, should arrive there in about a week's time. One of the institutions destined to play a very important part in this endeavour is the Research Institute of which I am the (at present) absent Director. The administrative head of this Institute,[5] who is at present in this country, will be leaving on the 25th July for Palestine. I would be very grateful if word could be sent to the High Commissioner asking him to regard the Institute as an organization of national importance. We have several times been approached by the India Office and asked either to send chemists out to India from the Institute to supervise the manufacture of drugs there, or to make certain types of drugs ourselves, in Palestine, both for local consumption, and also for Egypt and the surrounding countries. On the latter work we are at present engaged, and there can be little doubt that the Institute will play an increasingly important part in the development of Palestine's chemical resources as time goes on. My request for its recognition as an organization of national importance is therefore not merely a matter of form, but one whose grant would be of real service to the war effort.

(vi) A minor point which we raised to-day was that of the grant

---

[4] Sir Harold MacMichael (Biog. Index, Vol. XVIII).
[5] Bloch.

of exit permits, etc. I hardly think I need trouble you about this. Both Mrs. Weizmann and myself have American visas which are, I think, still valid, and no doubt the exit permits could easily be obtained. The main trouble will, I believe, be that of transport.

(vii) Another matter which arises in connection with my departure is that of the position of my elder son, Benjamin.[6] He is now serving with the 83rd Light A.A. Battery (Oakwood House, Maidstone Road, Chatham). But he is also entered for the Field Security Police, has been interviewed by their people, and stands, I believe, a good chance of acceptance there. The day before yesterday, General Spears[7] (or someone from his office) rang me up and made further enquiries about my son, and it seems quite likely that he may be asked to join the F.S.P. for which his qualifications as a linguist—he speaks fluently French, Spanish and Russian, and is British-born—probably make him more suitable than for gunnery. I know, too, that he is rather keen on the work. As you were kind enough to say that you knew General Spears, perhaps you might bear the matter in mind.[8] I am quite content to wait to hear from the F.S.P. in the ordinary course, and would not press the matter in any way at present. But if the time of my departure approaches without having heard anything definite from the F.S.P., I may perhaps trouble you again.

(viii) Lastly, we agreed that you would kindly try and arrange for me to have a quiet talk with the Secretary of State towards the end of the week, at which we might go into the matter more fully.[9]

Please forgive the length of this letter—I have tried to be as short as I can—and believe me to be,

Yours very sincerely,
Ch. W.

[6] Biog. Index, Vol. V.

[7] (Sir) Edward Spears (1886–1973). Then head of British Mission to Gen. de Gaulle, he was transferred to Syria and Lebanon in July, 1941, and became British Minister to Republic of Syria and Lebanon 1942–44.

[8] Replying 9 Aug. (W.A.), Danby stated that he was making enquiries at W.O. regarding Benjamin W., who was later invalided out of the army.

[9] At a meeting with W. 25 July (report in W.A.), Lloyd proposed raising Jewish forces on a parity basis with Arabs in Palestine, possibly 2,000 men from each community. Alternatively, he proposed conscription, which W. rejected. Further, W. stated that he might be able to obtain arms in Syria and U.S. Lloyd expressed interest, and held out the possibility of government finance for purchases. On 29 July a Ministerial Committee on Military Policy in the Middle East agreed to recruitment of 1,000 Jews and 1,000 Arabs under the parity rule (Minutes in P.R.O., Cab 95/2, also in Premier 4.32/6). On 6 Aug. Eden told the Commons that 'arrangements have now been made, as the outcome of a recent decision, to form a number of Palestine Companies of the British Army' (Hansard). Ben-Gurion described this scheme as 'letting down the Jews of Palestine and leaving them to be destroyed by invaders and Arabs' (his memorandum, 7 Aug. 1940, in W.A.). When W. met Lloyd again on 7 Aug., the latter

11. To Sir Robert Haining, London.   *London, 16 July 1940*
English: Or. Copy. T.W.: W.A.

Dear General Haining,

Following up our conversation of July 15th, I have cabled to Mr. Shertok[1] (through official channels in Government code) asking him to proceed with the selection of suitable candidates for cadres of Jewish officers and N.C.O.'s for Jewish units in His Majesty's fighting forces in the Middle East. May I ask you once more to send instructions to General Wavell to take the necessary measures.[2]

Yours very sincerely,

Ch. W.

12. To the Manager, Alexandra Hotel, London.

English: Or. Copy. T.W.: W.A.   *London, 23 July 1940*

Dear Sir,

In continuation of our telephone conversation, I wish to express my gratitude for the permission you have kindly given to the members of my staff at the Grosvenor Laboratory (25 Grosvenor Crescent Mews) to use your air-raid shelter in case of need.[1]

I am, dear Sir,

Yours faithfully,

Ch. W.

expressed indignation that W. should have meanwhile appealed directly to the P.M. (see No. 23). Lloyd claimed that the W.O. was resisting the idea of a specifically Jewish army, although he personally could agree to the raising of units *outside* Palestine, and the parity scheme was therefore the best in the circumstances. Although the Government had called for 1,000 men from each community, Lloyd was prepared to call for another 3,000 from each, or even 5,000. W. expressed anxiety over possible trouble from mixing the two communities in the same units. As to arms from Syria, Lloyd reported on a Shertok-MacMichael discussion which had clarified that it had been possible to obtain arms in Syria following the French collapse, and in the ensuing chaos a few hundred rifles had reached Palestine. The situation in Syria had now tightened up and it was difficult to get arms—report in W.A. See also No. 31, and ns. there.

11. [1] See No. 9.

[2] Replying 18 July (W.A.), Haining corrected the impression that he had in any way agreed to such a proposal. He understood that Wavell was contemplating the formation of Palestine units, both Jewish and Arab, as garrison companies, and he himself would take no further action in the matter. Haining emphasized that any recruiting that W. intended in U.S.A. in no way concerned the W.O.

12. [1] W. had been appointed 15 July as Honorary Chemical Adviser to Herbert Morrison, Minister of Supply. His laboratory worked on the production of aromatics from mineral oils (yielding benzene and toluene), and the production of anti-knock fuels from grain fermentation. By-products of his fermentation processes later became important for the production of synthetic rubber.

13. To Sir Hugh Seeley,[1] London.   *London, 23 July 1940*
English: Or. Copy. T.W.: W.A.

Dear Sir Hugh Seeley,
I wish to confirm in writing the request made to you by Mr. Namier.
1) That Palestinian Jews, besides being recruited for the ground forces of the R.A.F., should also be trained as pilots. The personnel of the Aviron Company[2] might serve as a beginning. I understand that they have over 40 members who have obtained their "A" licence, including 20 who have had a considerable amount of advanced training.
2) That suitable Palestinians now in this country should be allowed to enlist here for the R.A.F. in Palestine. I enclose a first list of candidates.
Should it be desired to enlist Jews from neutral countries for service with the R.A.F. in Palestine, I feel sure that a good many could be made available.[3]

Yours sincerely,
Ch. W.

14. To Rebecca D. Sieff,[1] London.   *London, 24 July 1940*
English: Or. Copy. T.W.: W.A.

Dear Mrs. Sieff,
Thank you for your letter of the 19th July.[2] I am enclosing a copy of my letter of 1st July to Mr. Osbert Peake, from which you will see that I dealt only with the children whom it is hoped eventually to send to Palestine on *Youth Aliyah* certificates.[3] The Jewish

---

13. [1] Later Lord Sherwood (1898–1970). Lib. M.P. 1923–41; Parliamentary Private Secretary at Air Ministry 1940–41; Under-Secretary of State at Air Ministry 1941–45.
[2] *Aviron* (Hebr.: aeroplane). Company formed 1936 which pioneered Jewish aviation in Palestine, becoming nucleus of Israel Air Force in 1948.
[3] See also No. 29.

14. [1] Wife of Israel Moses Sieff (Biog. Index, Vol. VI). Founding-President of British and world W.I.Z.O.,1924, until her death in 1966.
[2] Untraced.
[3] Osbert Peake (1897–1966; 1st Viscount Ingleby, 1955). Cons. M.P.; Under-Secretary of State at Home Office 1939–44. W.'s letter to him (W.A.) indicated that the organization for settlement of young refugees in Palestine (*Youth Aliyah*) had 410 German children in training camps in England, and proposed that those over the age of 16 should not be interned but placed in a special camp under J.A. responsibility. W. further asked Peake whether the Home Office could provide a permanent site for such a camp. This letter was acknowledged by the Home Office the following day, with assurance that the issue would be dealt with (W.A.). No further relevant correspondence traced. For *Youth Aliyah* see also No. 60.

Agency is constantly receiving representations urging it to take up the problem both of *Haluzim*[4] and of children at present in training in this country for immigration to Palestine, and we felt that the Agency, which has some standing in the matter, should take what action it could to prevent people from being interned. When the *Youth Aliyah* informed us of the internment of their trainees over sixteen years of age, we thought it might be useful if, in addition to the action being taken on—as we understood—similar lines by your Council and other bodies, the Agency also approached the Home Office direct. As you rightly say, the more pressure brought to bear on the authorities by influential quarters, the more likely we are to succeed in what is, after all, our common aim—to enable the refugees to continue their training here without the constant fear of sudden internment.

Very sincerely yours,

Ch. W.

15. To Christopher Eastwood,[1] London.   *London, 25 July 1940*
English: Or. Copy. T.W.: W.A.

Dear Eastwood,

As my telephone conversation with Lord Lloyd was interrupted this evening, I am venturing to send in the attached brief *Aide Memoire* of the various points remaining to be settled. I shall be very grateful if you will pass it on.

Yours very sincerely,

Ch. W.

AIDE MEMOIRE

As our telephone conversation was interrupted I am venturing to send you, as an *aide-memoire,* the following brief enumeration of the points which we discussed yesterday, but as to which we reached no conclusion. I hope that it may be possible for us to complete the discussion shortly, so as to achieve some positive results which would be extremely helpful for my visit to America.

1) My departure for America: As understood between Mr. B.B.[2] and myself, it seems advisable that I leave about the third week of

---

[4] Hebr.: pioneers.

15. [1] B. 1905. Private Secretary to Lloyd (Colonial Secretary 1940–41) and Lord Moyne (Colonial Secretary 1941–42).

[2] Brendan Bracken (1901–58). Newspaper proprietor; Cons. M.P., 1929–51; Parliamentary Private Secretary to Winston Churchill 1940–41; Minister of Information 1941–45. Designated by Churchill as his liaison with the Zionists.

August, the reason being that very little can be done in America in August, and moreover, it would give me a chance of setting my laboratory work here in proper order, so that it may continue uninterrupted during my absence.

2) Jewish Units: This question has been fully gone into, and the arguments pro and con discussed. We are still most anxious that Jewish Units should be established in Palestine, and we sincerely believe that we could also be useful in encouraging the enlistment of loyal Arabs, so that a considerable force might result.[3]

3) Arms: (Syria and South America).[4]

4) Conscription: I believe that the proclamation of conscription in Palestine would be fraught with very grave dangers.

5) Cadre: The training of some three or four hundred young Jews as a cadre for the Jewish Units could be done in Egypt or Rhodesia and anywhere else convenient; I cannot see that it can possibly cause any trouble.[5]

Ch.W.

[Please forgive the above brief—and I fear rather casual—notes: they are merely meant to refresh your memory.]

16. To Leopold S. Amery, London.   *London, 26 July 1940*
English: Or. Copy. T.W.: W.A.

My dear Amery,

I am sorry that you should have been worried by Mr. Abrahams—and in a matter of so little importance.[1]

I did not promise that I would send a cable to Mr. Jabotinsky[2] in support of his scheme. Nor would I care to be mixed up with any of his activities, in America or elsewhere.[3] I did see Mr. Abrahams,

---

[3] See No. 10, n. 9; No. 31.

[4] See No. 10, n. 9; No. 26.

[5] The cadres scheme was not taken up by W.O. or Wavell (see No. 9, n. 4; No. 23).

16. [1] Abraham Abrahams (1897–1955). London Secretary of the New Zionist (Revisionist) Organization, which Jabotinsky had formed by secession from W.Z.O. 1935. Abrahams had written to Amery, claiming W.'s support for his organization's scheme for the 'Unification of the Jewish effort for the Jewish Army project' (see Amery to W., 24 July 1940, W.A.). Amery wrote of his reluctance to become involved in the scheme, since the P.M. was already taking a direct interest in W.'s negotiations, and the Colonial Secretary was apprehensive about the 'Palestinian aspect' of any Jewish Army scheme.

[2] Ze'ev Vladimir Jabotinsky (Biog. Index, Vol. IV). Journalist, soldier, leader of Revisionist movement.

[3] On 12 May 1940, Jabotinsky forwarded to Churchill his scheme for a Jewish army to

and told him that if and when I went to America, I would try to get into touch with Mr. Jabotinsky, and a telegram was sent to the latter to that effect.

My negotiations with Lord Lloyd are still going on, and seem now to give some promise of giving concrete results—but I am afraid they may be prejudiced if Mr. Jabotinsky's organization continues to interfere.

I can only repeat that I am deeply sorry that you should have been worried.

Yours ever,
Ch. W.

17. To Sir Harold MacMichael, Jerusalem.   *London, 26 July 1940*
English: Or. Copy. T.W.: W.A.

Dear Sir Harold,

I take the liberty of writing to you in connection with the effort we are making in Palestine to develop the manufacture of drugs. The position is briefly as follows:

You may have heard that we are building a small plant in Rehovot in connection with the Sieff Institute: we expect that it will be capable of producing some two or three tons of drugs a year. This manufacturing plant will be kept entirely separate from the Institute, which is, and will remain, a purely scientific research institution. We have made all our arrangements for the new enterprise, and I really believe it can be of service in supplying a number of drugs at present unobtainable in the open market by reason of the emergency.

Dr. Bloch, who carries this letter, is the Administrative Head of the Institute, of which—as you know—I am the Scientific Director.

be formed in Palestine under Allied High Command. Churchill forwarded this to the C.O., which gave its verdict that such schemes were designed to gain the Jews recognition as a nation with a seat at any peace conference, and the consequent conversion of Palestine into a Jewish State, in reward for Jewish military assistance during the war. Lloyd attacked the Revisionist leadership, its methods, and its political goal of a Jewish State on both sides of the Jordan. The C.O. recommended negotiation with W. alone (see notes on Jabotinsky's scheme in P.R.O. Premier 4/51/9, and F.O. 371/24566 E2044/187/31). The New Zionist Organization approached the Government again in Nov. 1940, and in response to C.O. enquiries, the W.O. replied: 'We have committed ourselves to Dr. Weizmann and must stick to him. Our information is that the New Zionists are non-cooperative and imbued with one single aim, the domination of New Zionism over Jewry' (see W.O. to Martin, Churchill's Private Secretary, 12 Nov. 1940, in P.R.O. Premier, 4/5/9). There is no evidence of any cooperation between W. and Jabotinsky, who died the following week, on this issue. See also Vol. XIX, No. 290, n. 2.

He will be in a position to give you any further details which you may desire to have with regard to the various types of drugs which we hope to supply, and to the practical arrangements made to speed up production.

Both the Ministry of Supply and the India Office here are much interested in seeing this work go forward as quickly as possible. I enclose a letter from the India Office,[1] and have had a number of conversations with the authorities at the Ministry of Supply on the same subject. I may perhaps add, in parenthesis, that I am myself at present engaged on work for the Ministry of Supply, to which I am Honorary Chemical Adviser, and that they have placed a laboratory at my disposal here.

The plant which we have put up in Rehovot cannot lay claim to be a large-scale manufacturing establishment capable of supplying the ever growing needs of the military authorities in the vast territories of the Near and Middle East. It is simply a pilot plant, designed to produce a certain limited quantity of certain drugs, the idea being that when it has been working for some time, and we have been able to test out various methods of production, we shall be prepared to send our chemists to give the benefit of the experience thus gained in other establishments in Palestine and abroad, should this be desired. We should simply be pioneers and not large-scale manufacturers, which would be out of place for people connected with a purely scientific institution.

I am troubling you with these details in the hope that we may enjoy the friendly encouragement of yourself and your administration, since it is not easy in these days to carry on such an enterprise successfully without official approval and support.[2]

Yours very sincerely,
Ch. W.

---

17. [1] See. No. 2, n. 5.

[2] MacMichael received the letter late Sept. 1940. His reply, 20 Sept. (W.A.), spoke of misunderstanding on the part of the India Office and the Government of India regarding the scale of production contemplated and the precise function of the Sieff Institute. MacMichael noted that the Sieff Institute was to confine itself to research, and that the separate pilot plant was to produce only a limited quantity of drugs. He also noted that it would take some 4–5 months before machinery and equipment could be installed. MacMichael estimated that the expected 2–3 tons production per annum would suffice for the needs of Palestine, and in part for India. See also No. 18.

18. To Isaac Magasanik, Harold Davies and Frieda Goldschmidt,[1]
Rehovot. London, 26 July 1940

English: T.W./H.W.: W.A.

My dear Friends,

Though this letter is addressed to the members of the Executive Committee, it is also meant for all my colleagues and co-workers at the Daniel Sieff Institute.

I can hardly tell you how deep is my regret that circumstances over which I have no control have forced me to stay away from the Institute for so long. My regret is all the deeper since it is difficult for me at present to foretell how soon it may become possible for me to satisfy my ardent desire to return to Rehovot. But like everybody else, I am living in hope, and can only trust that my hope may be fulfilled in the not very distant future.

Dr. Bloch is leaving here, after a prolonged stay, tomorrow. His presence in London has been most useful and valuable for the future of the Institute, but I know that he is very anxious to get back, and that no one regrets more than he does that his stay here should have had to be prolonged beyond the limits which he had set for it. The main reason has been the complexity of the business which we had to settle, and the difficulties which arise in present circumstances in trying to despatch any sort of business quickly.

Dr. Bloch will report to you personally about what he has been doing here, and what he has achieved—and I believe his achievements are of no mean importance. To set out the main points briefly (I must leave a detailed report to him):

(i) We have settled the constitution of the Institute, so that after registration in Palestine it will become a legal personality.

(ii) We have founded the Palestine Pharmaceutical Products Company, which will at once undertake at Rehovot the manufacture of a limited quantity of drugs, and will serve as a pioneer for much larger developments.

(iii) We have entered into a contract with a very respectable and important firm in England, who will cooperate with us in the development of this industry in Palestine and the Near East.[2]

(iv) We have secured the support and sympathy both of the

18. [1] Magasanik (1885–1941): Chemist, b. Poland, studied in Germany and Switzerland, went to Palestine 1927, employed at Agricultural Experimental Station, Rehovot, and was from 1932 director of its chemical department. Davies (Biog. Index, Vol. V): Chemist, W.'s personal assistant at Daniel Sieff Institute from 1935, and in charge of financial affairs. Miss Goldschmidt (1899–1971): Chemist at Sieff Institute from 1934.

[2] The company was Genatosan—see No. 238, n. 2.

India Office and the Ministry of Supply here for this new enterprise.

The new Company is, of course, only a beginning; but if it develops successfully, as I hope it may, it can render great service to the cause for which we are all fighting, and later on to the general development of Palestine and the neighbouring countries. Modest as the beginning is at present—and I feel that modesty is essential in such things—I think it bears within it the germ of a promise for the future, not only for the pharmaceutical industry, but for the chemical industry generally. I know I can rely on your wholehearted cooperation in this undertaking, in the same spirit which has animated the Institute from its foundation up till now.

In spite of the trying times through which we are living, and of the great financial stringency which prevails almost everywhere (and especially in Palestine, as I know well), I was able while in America to secure additional financial support for the Institute, so that your work need not suffer from lack of funds. In fact, the Budget for 1940 is on a more generous scale than in previous years. Again I must leave it to Dr. Bloch to tell you the details, and will only say that there is every prospect of your being able to continue and extend your work with redoubled energy.

I realise that we are undertaking an important new task, but I believe you will agree that it is an attractive one, both from the scientific and from the technical point of view; I feel that it will call forth your best and fullest endeavours.

In conclusion, I would say again how sorry I am not to be with you to initiate this new period in the development of the Institute, and not to see the opening of the new buildings. But I am sure you will understand.

I wish you every success and good fortune; we are all passing through grim days, but not for one moment am I assailed by any doubt that we shall ultimately win through, however hard and stony the road to victory may be. And with the wish that the same spirit of confidence and determination may live and grow among you, I send you my warmest greetings and hearty *Shalom*.

Yours ever,

Ch. Weizmann

P.S. Please convey my kindest regards to Professor Neuberg;[3] I

---

[3] Gustav Embden Carl Neuberg (1877–1956). Biochemist; Professor at Berlin University; Director of Institute of Biochemistry at Kaiser Wilhelm Institute, Berlin, 1920–38; Professor of Biochemistry at Hebrew University 1940–41; Professor at New York University until 1950. W., as chairman of Board of Governors of Hebrew University, refers here to Neuberg's professorial appointment there.

am particularly sorry to have missed greeting him personally at the beginning of his work with us. Dr. Bloch brings him personal messages from me.

Dr. Bloch will explain to you that Dr. Bergmann[4] will stay on here. We have a Lab and are both working for the Government.

Ch. W.

My love to my sister[5] and to the family.

19. To the Palestine Building Syndicate, Ltd.,[1] Tel Aviv.

London, 26 July 1940

English: Or. Copy. T.W.: W.A.

Dear Sirs,

    I write to acknowledge receipt of your letter of June 6th,[2] and to point out that, according to information which I have received from Dr. Landsberg[3] and Mr. Erich Mendelsohn,[4] all your accounts with regard to my house in Rehovot have been settled, with the exception of a final account of £P.31, which is still with Dr. Landsberg, awaiting your final receipt. I can only suggest, therefore, that you should accept this sum in final settlement.

I am, dear Sirs,
Yours faithfully,
Ch. W.

20. To Lucio Thomo Feteira, Lisbon.   *London, 4 August 1940*

English: Or. Copy. T.W.: W.A.

My dear Mr. Feteira,

    I was delighted to receive your telegram with the information about my relatives in Avignon, and can scarcely find words to thank

[4] Ernst David Bergmann (Biog. Index, Vol. XVI). W.'s scientific deputy at Sieff Institute and his close collaborator in all scientific undertakings.

[5] W.'s sister Anna (Biog. Index, Vol. I) was a chemist at Sieff Institute.

19. [1] The Syndicate, a private enterprise established 1934, was liquidated 1972.

[2] W.A. This suggested appointment of an arbitrator to decide on the final account for the construction of W.'s house in Rehovot, completed 1937.

[3] Alfred Abraham Landsberg (Biog. Index, Vol. XII). Lawyer, friend of W. from 1924. Settled in Palestine 1932; founder and director of RASSCO (building contractors). W.'s adviser and attorney in construction of his home at Rehovot.

[4] Eric Mendelsohn (1887–1953). The celebrated German architect lived in Palestine 1934–41, and designed the Schocken Library and Anglo-Palestine Bank in Jerusalem, and the Hadassah Hospital on Mount Scopus, as well as W.'s house.

you for your very great kindness, and for all the trouble which you have taken in making contact with them.[1] All I can say at present is that I hope it may be given to me to see you again before very long, so that I may express to you personally my heartfelt gratitude and appreciation.

I wonder whether you could find out, through your friend, from my brother-in-law what his intentions are? Is he doing any work in France, or is he preparing to emigrate? I would be very much obliged if discreet enquiry could be made on this point. Then we can see what we can do to help.[2]

With very kind regards, and renewed thanks,

I am,

Very sincerely yours,

Ch. W.

21. To Lewis Ruskin,[1] Chicago.   *London, 4 August 1940*
English: Or. Copy. T.W.: W.A.

My dear Lewis,

I was delighted to receive your note of the 22nd July,[2] containing your interesting report of your conversation with Harry Hopkins.[3] I am also very glad to hear that you have linked up with John Hertz.[4] I remember very well the dinner party at his house, and our talk there; I found him a very interesting and intelligent man.

I can quite understand that people are a little shy just now of giving money for Palestine. But I am personally so convinced that we shall all emerge victorious from this struggle, and that Palestine is destined to play a very big part in that victory, that this faith sus-

---

20. [1] See No. 1.

[2] Telegram dated 31 July (W.A.). Feteira further undertook to help procure passage for the family to U.S. W. informed Feteira 19 Sept. (W.A.) that he had obtained American visas for the Blumenfelds. See Nos. 150, 303.

21. [1] B. 1905. Manufacturing chemist; Chief of Supply, Planning and Control, Military Planning Division, U.S. Army Quartermaster Corps 1942–44; Vice-President, Weizmann Institute of Science; Chairman, Chaim Weizmann Research Foundation in U.S.; Chairman, Budget Committee, Jewish Welfare Fund.

[2] This (W.A.) related news of fund-raising for Sieff Institute. Further, Ruskin reported that Harry Hopkins ('Roosevelt's greatest friend') had told him of his optimism, shared by the President, of England's ability to resist invasion, and that U.S. assistance in the autumn would be of a magnitude to safeguard her cause.

[3] 1890–1946. U.S. Secretary of Commerce 1938–40; Member U.S. War Production Board; Chairman, Munitions Assignments Board; Special Adviser to President Roosevelt.

[4] Banker, partner in Lehman Bros., New York, from 1934; head of Yellow Cab Company of Chicago.

tains me through the temporary anxiety caused by the general situation in the world today. The same faith strengthens us to continue our work, both here and in Palestine, undeterred by speculations as to the future, which are anyway quite useless. You may know that for the time being I am working in a Laboratory here, and have Dr. Bergmann with me. Dr. Bloch, on the other hand, left last week for Palestine, and should arrive there in a fortnight or so. He has done a great deal of useful work during his stay here, namely:

(1) We have founded the Palestine Pharmaceutical Products Company, Limited, with a small capital of £5,000 contributed by Mr. Marks[5] for the purpose of helping to build up the chemical industry in Palestine. We have already established excellent relations with the neighbouring countries, and shall probably have more customers than we can supply. But we shall not be in a hurry to increase production in the Daniel Wolf Laboratory.[6] We shall need six months or so to acquire experience of manufacture on a semi-large scale, and then we can expand if the need arises. It may well be that we may be called upon to set up similar establishments, under very good auspices, in some of the neighbouring countries. In other words, we shall probably be pioneering for a year or so before we launch out into really large-scale production. But a start is being made now, and I hope it will prove successful.

(2) In order to enable the Institute to carry out the above-described operations, it has had to acquire a legal personality. With the assistance of some legal talent here, Dr. Bloch has prepared, and has taken with him to Palestine, a draft constitution for the Institute, which, after being adapted to the requirements of Palestine law, will be registered in that country. The Institute will be controlled by a Governing Board on which the Founders will have a forty per cent representation and other Donors sixty per cent. For the time being the Board is to consist of ten members. We would accordingly be honoured if you and Mr. N[ate] Shapero[7] would represent the Weizmann Research Foundation on it. Other representatives will be Bloch and myself, Professor Selig Brodetsky[8] on behalf of the

[5] Simon Marks (Lord Marks of Broughton, Biog. Index, Vol. VI). Philanthropist. W.'s close friend and Zionist collaborator; Chairman, Marks and Spencer Ltd.; President, Joint Palestine Appeal from its inception.

[6] Chemistry laboratory at Sieff Institute, named after Dutch benefactor, as to whom, see Nos. 36, 48.

[7] Nate Samuel Shapero, b. 1892. Detroit merchant; President, Weizmann Research Foundation.

[8] Biog. Index, Vol. VI. He was then head of Political Dept. of J.A. in London, and President of Board of Deputies of British Jews.

English Zionist Federation and some British Donors, one South African (probably Mr. Harry Lourie, Arthur's father[9]), since they have been regular contributors since the inception of the Institute, and finally four representatives of "the Family"—Mr. Sieff,[10] Mr. Marks, Mr. Sacher,[11] and Mr. Louis Green[12] in Palestine, who built the Institute for us.

I think it is quite a good arrangement, though it can of course be modified or supplemented at the first meeting of the Board. When this first meeting can take place, no one can say at present. As soon as the constitution is ready, we shall send you a copy. But without waiting for that, perhaps you would be kind enough, on receipt of this letter, to telegraph me whether you and Mr. Shapero are prepared to accept membership of the Board? Dr. Bloch is named as the Managing Director of the Institute, and myself as Scientific Director for life. According to the constitution as drafted, the conduct of affairs rests with the two of us, though naturally the Board lays down the general principles of policy. I think you will find the constitution to be modelled on those of great Institutes like the Lister Institute here and the Pasteur in Paris.

(3) The Palestine Pharmaceutical Products Company has entered into an arrangement with a distinguished British company for the processing and sale of the drugs produced in our laboratory. I shall let you know the details of this arrangement as soon as they have been fully worked out.

I would be grateful if you would be so kind as to inform other friends like the Epsteins of the contents of this letter, as this would save me some duplicate correspondence. I hope the information given here will help you in your work; you may be sure I shall do my best to supplement it from time to time, and to keep it up to date.

With every good wish to you personally, to Mr. Shapero, and to Josef,[13] I remain,

Affectionately yours,

Ch. W.

[9] Harry Lourie (1875–1960). B. Latvia, settled 1895 in South Africa, where he was an industrialist and prominent Zionist. His son Arthur (Biog. Index, Vol. XVII; d. 1978) transferred that year from J.A. headquarters in London to become Executive Secretary of American Zionist Emergency Council, and subsequently a senior Israeli diplomat.

[10] Israel Moses Sieff (Lord Sieff of Brimpton, Biog. Index, Vol. VI). Succeeded Marks as Chairman of Marks and Spencer Ltd.; likewise W.'s close friend and Zionist collaborator. 'The Family' refers to the Sieff, Marks and Sacher families, all inter-connected by marriage, and among the world's leading Zionist benefactors.

[11] Harry Sacher (Biog. Index, Vol. V). Journalist; an early intimate of W. at Manchester. In private legal practice in Jerusalem in 1920s and on Zionist Executive.

[12] 1870–1947. Engineer, honorary technical adviser to Hebrew University 1925–47.

[13] Josef Cohn (Biog. Index, Vol. XIX). Acted in U.S. on behalf of Sieff Institute.

22. To Joanna Jabotinsky,[1] London.   *London, 5 August 1940*
English: T.: C.Z.A. A/87.

Executive of the Jewish Agency and Zionist Organization are shocked by the terrible loss you have sustained. All Zionists mourn with you the loss of a great champion of our national aim. Our sincerest sympathy goes out to you. May you find some consolation in the eminent services he rendered to his people.[2]

Chaim Weizmann

23. To Winston S. Churchill, London.   *London, 6 August 1940*
English: Or. Copy. T.W.: W.A.

Dear Mr. Prime Minister,

Loth as I am to take up your time, the moment has come[1] when I feel compelled to lay before you the claim of Palestine Jewry to the right of self-defence in the present situation in the Middle East, and the request of Jews outside Palestine to be allowed to form Jewish units for service with the British Army. I have pressed the mobilisation of Jewish resources and man-power on the Government ever since the beginning of the war. Although in the past three months goodwill and a desire for cooperation have been manifest, the results are not yet apparent, and I should be grateful if you would allow me to put our request before you personally.

In addressing myself to you, I would urge these requests not only on grounds of British interests, and on account of the strong wish of Palestinian Jewry to be allowed to contribute its maximum war effort to the British cause, but I speak also as the mouth-piece of half-a-million Jews whose homes, families, and future are bound up with the defence of the Middle East, and of Palestine in particular.

In a war of the magnitude now proceeding, it is impossible to say what the strategic dispositions of the British fleets and armies may be before victory is attained. Should it come to a temporary withdrawal from Palestine—a contingency which we hope will never arise—the Jews of Palestine would be exposed to wholesale

---

22. [1] Joanna Jabotinsky (1884–1949). Wife of Vladimir Jabotinsky.

[2] Jabotinsky died in New York 3 Aug. 1940. A cable of sympathy, signed Vera and Chaim W., was sent 6 Aug. (W.A.).

23. [1] On 4 Aug. 1940, the Italians began their advance from Abyssinia into British Somaliland. W.'s letter had been drafted 22 July, but was sent only after the Italian advance had begun, and following Eden's announcement on the formation of mixed Palestine Companies. (See No. 10, n. 9.)

massacre at the hands of the Arabs, encouraged and directed by the Nazis and Fascists. This possibility reinforces the demand for our elementary human right to bear arms, which should not normally be denied to the loyal citizens of a country at war. Palestinian Jewry can furnish a force of 50,000 men, all of them in the prime of their strength—no negligible force if properly trained, armed, and led. If Palestine be invaded and the Jewish community be destroyed for lack of the means of self-defence, a grave responsibility will attach to the British Government which refused them.

I hope within a short time to set forth for America. But I do not conceal from you that both my own internal strength and the good-will of those whom I hope to influence would be immeasurably reinforced if I could leave England assured that the point of view which I propose to put before you has received recognition, and is being followed by definite action by the British authorities.[2]

Yours sincerely,
Ch. W.

24. To Harold Nicolson,[1] London.   *London, 6 August 1940*
English: Or. Copy. T.W.: W.A.

Dear Mr. Nicolson,

I am writing this note on behalf of Mrs. Weizmann, who is most anxious to offer full-time service, in an honorary capacity, to the war effort, but has so far not succeeded in finding a place where she can be useful.

She is a fully qualified doctor (Geneva and Manchester); she speaks fluently English (of course), French, and Russian, and has a quite good knowledge of German. Earlier in the war she served for three months as Liaison Officer at Aliens Tribunal No. 1, and I believe acquitted herself very well in a difficult job. We think she could perhaps help either with the foreign press, or with foreign visitors to this country, or elsewhere in the Ministry where her languages would stand her in good stead. I do not know whether you can make any

---

[2] Churchill forwarded this letter to Lloyd, who seems to have resented W.'s 'going over his head' (see No. 10, n. 9). Churchill notified Wavell 12 Aug. that he did not 'consider that proper use is being made of the large forces in Palestine. The essence of the situation depends upon arming the Jewish colonists sufficiently to enable them to undertake their own defence, so that if necessary for a short time the whole of Palestine can be left to very small British forces.' See Churchill, *The Second World War* (London 1949), Vol. II, p. 377.

24. [1] 1886–1968. Author and diplomat; Parliamentary Secretary to Ministry of Information 1940–41.

suggestions as to how she could be useful, but we should both be very grateful for any advice you may feel able to give.[2]
With kind regards, I am,
Yours very sincerely,
Ch. W.

25. To Sir Arthur Wauchope,[1] Edinburgh.   *London, 15 August 1940*
English: Or. Copy. T.W.: W.A.

Dear Sir Arthur,

I have tried several times to reach you on the telephone since my arrival in London, and only learned to-day that you are in Edinburgh until the end of the month. I cannot leave, however, without sending you a line to say that I am very sorry indeed to have missed you—there are so many things about Palestine I would have wished to discuss with you, since I believe that even in the midst of war you will not have forgotten us, any more than we have forgotten you.

I know, too, that you would understand how ardently we desire to be given means of defending ourselves, and taking our proper part in the defence of Palestine, and in the defeat of Hitler, and how much we fear that by the time a formal decision has been taken by authority, it will already be too late.

I hope to leave early next week for America—en route for Palestine!—and to be back home within six weeks or so, by Trans-Pacific Air Route. Who knows whether and when we shall meet again? In case we do not, I would like you to know that the deep affection and respect which you inspired in us all in Palestine lives on, and will follow you wherever you may be. No doubt you do know this already—and I hope I may be forgiven for being so un-English as to say it!

I know that Mr. Shertok and all my colleagues in Jerusalem would wish to join me in sending you our warmest regards and good wishes, and in the hope that we may all meet again, when victory is won, in a happier world.[2]
Very sincerely yours,

---

[2] Nicolson replied 7 Aug. (W.A.) discouragingly. V.W. was not in fact employed by the Government—see No. 6, n. 3.

25. [1] Biog. Index, Vol. XV. High Commissioner for Palestine and Transjordan 1931–38.
[2] They did not in fact meet.

26. To Meyer W. Weisgal, New York.   *London, 15 August 1940*
English: T.: W.A.

Would be grateful if you could make discreet enquiries possibility acquiring military equipment all kinds including ammunition in South America. Goldmann[1] should be able indicate persons to be approached. Essential act quickly obtain considerable quantities. Goldmann should perhaps fly down view ensuring speedy acquisition. If reply rapid, positive could provide necessary finance.[2]

Weizmann

27. To David Ben-Gurion,[1] London.   *London, 19 August 1940*
English: Or. Copy. T.W.: W.A.

Dear Ben-Gurion,
I understand that you will shortly be leaving for Palestine, via America. I therefore consider it necessary to ask you most urgently to attend a meeting of the Executive on any morning before you leave which may be arranged as mutually convenient for us.[2]

Yours sincerely,
Ch. W.

28. To W. D. H. Danby, London.   *London, 20 August 1940*
English: Or. Copy. T.W.: W.A.

My dear Danby,
This is just a note to remind you of two points:
(i) I have not yet had a copy of my handwritten letter to

26. [1] Nahum Goldmann (Biog. Index, Vol. XII). Representative of J.A. in Washington during W.W.II.
[2] W. had intimated to Lloyd that arms might be available from South America (see No. 10, n. 9) when he had been informed of the postponement of formation of a Jewish Division on grounds of insufficient equipment. Weisgal telegraphed W. 4 Sept. (W.A.) that Goldmann required more precise information before embarking on such a mission. See No. 36.

27. [1] Biog. Index, Vol. IX. Chairman of J.A. Executive; first Prime Minister and Defence Minister of State of Israel.
[2] The J.A. Executive meeting took place 21 Aug. 1940, and W. sought Ben-Gurion's approval, which was given, for a scheme suggested by the Minister of Labour, Ernest Bevin, to overcome the 'parity' limitation on Jewish recruitment. Bevin had proposed to W. that Jewish Palestinians mobilized beyond the number of Arabs should be enlisted into a Jewish army to be formed outside Palestine. The Zionists canvassed the idea widely. W. saw Lloyd George and Amery; Namier saw R. Barrington-Ward of *The Times*. Bevin himself succeeded in convincing Lloyd (Minutes in W.A.).

Shuckburgh.¹ I now have all the material for the memorandum on supplies promised to the Secretary of State, with the exception of this letter. As soon as I have a copy of it, I shall draw up the memorandum, and either bring or send it in to the Secretary of State.²

(ii) Could you let me know whether the Secretary of State has written to the War Office with regard to the training of cadres? At our last conversation it was agreed that, taking as a basis a force of 10,000 Jewish volunteers outside Palestine, the number of officers and N.C.O.'s required should be estimated, and that number selected from among suitable candidates in Palestine. It is for the War Office to determine both the numbers required and the place of training—whether Egypt, Kenya, or elsewhere. As soon as I hear that a letter to this effect has gone to the War Office, I would go and see them about it.

I look forward to hearing from you shortly with regard to a meeting with the Secretary of State.³

With kind regards, I am,
Very sincerely yours,
Ch. W.

29. To Sir Archibald Sinclair, London.   *London, 20 August 1940*
English: Or. Copy. T.W.: W.A.

I learn from a letter from Sir Hugh Seeley to Namier that Seeley has given to you my letter of July 23rd.¹

I hope to start for America on September 21st, or possibly even on the 14th if the booking on the Clipper can be advanced; and in America I hope to be able, among other things, to start a Jewish Fund for purchasing Spitfires for the R.A.F. If an air squadron of Palestinian Jews was started, this would give the greatest possible encouragement to such a fund, which, in turn, would be extremely useful for pro-British propaganda in the States and Canada.

28. ¹ Sir John Shuckburgh (Biog. Index, Vol. X). Deputy Under-Secretary of State, C.O., 1931–42; head of its Middle Eastern department from 1937. W.'s letter untraced.
² See No. 31, n. 2.
³ Danby replied the same day that he would later notify W. when his interview with Lloyd was arranged (W.A.). Lloyd subsequently informed Ben-Gurion that he favoured a scheme to train some 2–300 men from Palestine as cadres (interview 26 Aug. 1940, W.A.). See No. 31, n. 1.

29. ¹ See No. 13.

I should be very grateful if you could spare me a quarter of an hour for a talk this week or next.[2]

Yours very sincerely,
Ch. W.

30. To J. Cameron, London.
English: Or. Copy. T.W.: W.A.

London, 22 August 1940

c/o Messrs. Fitzpatrick Graham,[1]

My dear Cameron,

I beg to enclose the Income Tax Return, duly signed.

For your information and that of the authorities, I would like to point out the following:

As you know, since 1931 I have been carrying out research work on my own account on several subjects:

(i) in connection with foodstuffs,
(ii) in connection with fuels,
(iii) in connection with the cracking of petrol residues.

As regards (iii), the work was done mainly, as you know, at the Featherstone Laboratories, but also in collaboration with my brother-in-law, Blumenfeld, in Paris, and in my Rehovot Laboratory. The work on (i) and (ii) was almost entirely done at the Featherstone Laboratories. So that from 1931 until the death of Mr. Adam[2] I had been paying rent, rates, patent fees, the cost of chemicals, and the salaries of Davies, and later Sulzbacher[3] and a lab-boy. I think a conservative estimate of the average expenditure would be in the neighbourhood of £700 a year.

Some of these researches are now beginning to bear fruit. For instance, I have sold a licence to a subsidiary company of Bovril Limited, which will in due course begin the manufacture of a food-

[2] Replying 24 Aug. (W.A.), Sinclair stated that he had raised the question of an air squadron of Palestinian Jews with Air Officer Commanding, Palestine, and was awaiting a response. He expressed interest in W.'s idea of raising Jewish funds in America to buy Spitfires. In a discussion with W. 16 Sept. (record in W.A.), Sinclair went into details of training of Jewish pilots in U.S. and Palestine. He reported that Air Officer Commanding in Palestine wished prospective pilots there to have initial training with Aviron Company, and proceed to advanced training with R.A.F. from April, 1941. Sinclair wished to leave the size of the force open for future discussion, as he still awaited Cabinet authority. But further negotiations were suspended pending the Jewish Army negotiations. See No. 203.

30. [1] W.'s accountants.
[2] Matthew Atkinson Adam (Biog. Index, Vol. VIII). W.'s patent agent.
[3] Max Sulzbacher, b. 1901. Chemist who had worked with W. in London from 1934.

stuff in accordance with my patents. They have paid me an advance of £400 to cover some of the expenses previously incurred. In addition, Petrocarbon Limited, which is taking over the patents connected with the cracking processes, has paid me an advance of £1,000 towards expenses, of which roughly £252 belong to me (see attached account). I should say that this £252 should be credited to cover a part of the expenses incurred by me in the past eight years. When any really substantial income begins to come in from royalties on these inventions, I would like to feel that I would get some relief in respect of the considerable expenditure incurred by me during the same period.

I should add that as long as the war lasts, there will be no income from the fuel or cracking processes, as I have placed the results of all this work unreservedly at the disposal of the Government, for whom I am at present working in laboratories provided by the Ministry of Supply at the above address.

With kind regards, I am,
Very sincerely yours,

31. To Lord Lloyd, London.   *London, 25 August 1940*
English: Or. Copy. T.W.: W.A.

Dear Lord Lloyd,

In accordance with my promise[1] I am sending you herewith a memorandum on the supplies which could be obtained from Palestine.[2]

With kind regards, I am,
Very sincerely yours,
Ch. W.

31. [1] Lloyd had informed W. 23 Aug. 1940 of his agreement to the mobilization of separate (rather than mixed) units in Palestine, stipulating a maximum of 500 from each community, because of the paucity of likely Arab recruits and the shortage of equipment. He agreed to Bevin's idea that Jews recruited in excess of the number of Arabs might join a Jewish army outside Palestine. The possible appointment of Orde Wingate to command the prospective army was raised (W.'s report to J.A. Political Advisory Committee, 27 Aug. 1940, C.Z.A. Z4/302/24).

[2] The memorandum, with copies to Amery and Macmillan, concerned Palestine's capacity to manufacture materials required for the production of explosives, aviation fuels, lubricating oils and poisonous gases, small arms and ammunition, pharmaceuticals, bandages and precision instruments. The establishment of repair workshops was discussed, and the utilisation of some 600 Jewish engineers and chemists in Palestine not currently employed in their professions. Lloyd informed W. (17 Sept., W.A.) that the W.O. favoured acquisition of drugs for military purposes, but the Ministry of Supply opposed manufacture of supplies in Palestine. W. requested Macmillan, 26 Sept. 1940 (W.A.), to convene a meeting between himself

32. To John S. Stopford,[1] Manchester.   *London, 2 September 1940*
English: Or. Copy. T.W.: W.A.

My dear Vice-Chancellor,
I learn from Namier that you and the University have acceded to the request put to you by Lord Lloyd, and have released him for a further period.[2] May I thank you most warmly for doing so? We very much appreciate your action; it makes it much easier for me to leave for America at this time.

Yours sincerely,
Ch. W.

33. To Sir John G. Dill,[1] London.   *London, 3 September 1940*
English: Or. Copy. T.W.: W.A.

Dear General Dill,
I have just seen the Prime Minister.[2] I submitted to him the enclosed proposals, with which he expressed his full agreement. I asked whether I might go to see you in order to discuss the details, and the implementing of these proposals, and he gave me permission to do so.
I should therefore be grateful to you for letting me know when it would be convenient for you to see me.[3]

Yours very sincerely,
Ch. Weizmann

and the Ministers concerned with their experts to arrive at some conclusion in the matter, commenting: 'My memorandum seems to have been left to its bureaucratic fate.'

32. [1] Later Lord Stopford (1888–1961). Vice-Chancellor of University of Manchester 1934–56.
[2] Namier had been released in 1939 by the university on C.O. recommendation for service with the J.A. and its Political Advisory Committee. He continued in this capacity throughout the war.

33. [1] 1881–1944, Chief of Imperial General Staff May 1940–Dec. 1941; G.O.C. Palestine 1936–37; Field-Marshal 1941. In Dec. 1941 appointed British Representative on Combined Chiefs of Staff Committee, Washington.
[2] See W.'s report to J.A. Political Advisory Committee, 4 Sept. (W.A.). Bracken, Herbert Morrison, Robert Boothby (Parliamentary Secretary at Ministry of Food) and Sir Walter Layton (Ministry of Supply) were also present. Following a general discussion of the war situation, Churchill told W. that he had informed the W.O. of his support for a Jewish Army. Bracken felt that this should have a Jewish commander, whereupon W. mentioned Wingate.
[3] The War Minister, Anthony Eden, received W. 9 Sept., and expressed surprise at not being informed previously about negotiations for a Jewish Army. He wondered whether this was due to his reputation as an anti-Zionist. W. replied that he did not know Eden's views on

ENCLOSURE

I. Recruitment of greatest possible number of Jews in Palestine for fighting services, to be formed into Jewish Battalions or larger formations.

II. The Colonial Office insists on an approximate parity in the number of Jews and of Arabs recruited for specific Jewish and Arab units in Palestine. As Jewish recruitment in Palestine is certain to yield much larger numbers than Arab, the excess of Jews to be sent for training to Egypt or anywhere else in the Middle East.

III. Officers' Cadres, sufficient for a Jewish Division in the first instance, to be picked immediately from Jews from Palestine, and trained in Egypt.

IV. "Jewish Desert Unit."

V. Jewish military units to be formed in England from foreign Jews in England, and volunteers from other countries, for service in the Middle East or elsewhere.

34. To Ernest Bevin,[1] London.   *London, 4 September 1940*
English: Or. Copy. T.W.: W.A.

My dear Bevin,

I was very glad to hear that you are now fully recovered from your indisposition, and would like to send you a word at once to let you know that the suggestion you were good enough to make when we met at the House (about the training of Jews enlisting in Palestine in excess of the Arabs enlisting in some other part of Africa or the Near East) has met with a very favourable reception,

the subject, as the latter had never before received him, even when Eden was Foreign Secretary during the discussions over partition. Eden stated that it had been decided to form one Jewish and one Arab battalion. He understood the request for cadres and for recruiting in Palestine, but not that of a 'Desert Force' (Pt. IV of W.'s Proposals), and claimed that the Army lacked sufficient instructors and equipment. W. replied that he might raise equipment in U.S. Dill then joined the meeting, and stated that Wingate was going to Palestine. W. expressed surprise, as Lloyd had objected to such a proposition. In the course of the discussion, W. and Dill agreed that Wingate should organize a striking force of about 3,000 men, to work on the pattern of the Night Squads in Palestine that had guarded the oil pipeline in 1938. Eden then said that they would have to consult Halifax, Foreign Secretary, as well as Lloyd, on the political implication of the whole issue—record of meeting in W.A.

34. [1] Biog. Index.

and seems likely to provide a way of settling the difficulties raised
by the Colonial Office.

I am most grateful to you, not only for making this suggestion,
but also for the interest you have so kindly shown in the whole
matter and for bringing it to the notice of the Prime Minister, whom
I had the pleasure of seeing yesterday, and who seems to approve.[2]

With all good wishes, I remain,

Yours very sincerely,

Ch. W.

35. To Brendan Bracken, London.   *London, 5 September 1940*
English: Or. Copy. T.W.: W.A.

My dear B. B.,

You will have noted that in the proposals which I submitted to the
Prime Minister, Number 4 was given a mere heading: "Jewish
'Desert Unit'." I did not enter into detail, as this is a technical
military problem with which neither I nor any of my colleagues
are fit to deal.

I understand that Orde Wingate[1] has discussed with you his
ideas on desert forces. Such a unit would, in my opinion, form the
best beginning for a Jewish fighting force, and we would like it to
be commanded by Wingate. He knows our people, was highly
successful in dealing with them, and has our complete confidence.

For all these reasons I would wish that he could be brought
officially into our negotiations with the War Office as soon as
possible. Can you suggest any way of doing it? I should be most
grateful if you helped us in this matter, to which I attach the greatest
importance.[2]

Yours ever,

[2] See No. 33, n. 2.

35. [1] Biog. Index, Vol. XVIII. As a junior officer in Palestine 1936–39, he had organized and
led the special Night Squads composed of Jews and led by British officers, whose main task
was to defend the Iraq Petroleum Company pipeline against Arab bands. See also C. Sykes,
Orde Wingate (London 1959).

[2] See No. 33, n. 3; No. 38, n. 1.

36. To Meyer Weisgal, New York.   *London, 5 September 1940*
English: T.: W.A.

Shall telegraph Kaufman few days time.[1] Regarding South American matter please contact Daniel Wolf Savoy Plaza, who came on same mission. Make no arrangements till further notice.[2] Love.

Weizmann

37. To David Ben-Gurion, London.   *London, 9 September 1940*
English: Or. Copy. T.W.: W.A.

Personal

My dear Ben-Gurion,

I was very much surprised not to see you here to-day when we had a discussion preliminary to my seeing the Secretary for War and the C.I.G.S.[1]

You will remember that you asked me for an opportunity of discussing these matters, and I replied that I was prepared to have such a discussion, as I always am. Being terribly rushed on Wednesday, I asked Miss May[2] to ring you up and say we had better leave our talk until after the appointment with Dill was actually fixed— not, as you seem to have understood, until after the interview. The latter could obviously not have been reasonable. The appointment with Dill was fixed on Friday afternoon for Monday afternoon, September 9th, at 4.30 p.m., and I was looking forward to seeing you and other members of the Political Department before it. I asked Miss May to inform you that we would be having a meeting at 12.15, and I would have liked also to have a discussion with you personally—in fact I was holding myself free for it.

---

36. [1] Weisgal wished W. to notify Kaufman and the American Zionist Emergency Commitee officially of his arrival date in U.S.—cable, 4 Sept. (W.A.).

[2] W. informed a J.A. Executive meeting, 6 Sept. (Minutes in W.A.) that should Eden raise the equipment problem at their meeting (see No. 33, n. 3), he would counter with the mission of Daniel Wolf to Argentina to purchase a million rifles. The British Embassy in Washington were advising caution in the matter of arms purchases (Weisgal to W., 9 Sept., W.A.), but Weisgal favoured action—see his cable of 25 Sept. quoted in No. 48.

37. [1] Refers to a meeting of J.A. Political Committee, where W. reported that Wingate had advised the Zionists to request a Jewish Desert Force of 3,000 men, primarily from Palestine, so, Wingate had claimed, 'the Jews could do what the Arabs had failed to do under Lawrence' (Minutes in W.A.). Ben-Gurion was then expressing his displeasure at W.'s handling of the Army question by boycotting the meetings of the Executive—see Introduction; also N. Rose, Ed. *Baffy: The Diaries of Blanche Dugdale* (London 1973) p. 174.

[2] Doris H. May (Biog. Index, Vol. XV). W.'s secretary 1929–48.

I have discussed the whole matter fully in the course of the week-end with Wingate, and I understand you had also had a talk with him on the same subject.

Yours very sincerely,

Ch. W.

38. To Sir John G. Dill, London.   *London, 10 September 1940*
English: Or. Copy. T.W.: W.A.

Dear General Dill,

Our talk yesterday opened up a number of important technical military questions, with which I, as a layman, am not qualified to deal. But as Major Wingate was mentioned as the officer best fitted to take charge of a Jewish Fighting Force, may I venture to say that it would be a great help to me if you saw fit to call him in and give him your views now, so that the main lines of development could be settled before I go to America. I expect to leave London in eight or nine days, and the technical discussions may possibly raise some points with which I may have to deal.[1]

Yours very sincerely,

Ch. W.

39. To Viscount Halifax,[1] London.   *London, 10 September 1940*
English: Or. Copy. T.W.: W.A.

Dear Lord Halifax,

I have seen the Prime Minister and the Secretary for War, who told me that he had received a letter from you about our affairs. I am grateful to you. I would much like to have an opportunity of telling you about these conversations, and at the same time to take leave of you before going to America, which I expect to do in eight or nine days from now.[2]

Yours very sincerely,

Ch. W.

38. [1] Circumstances changed after 17 Sept., when Dill informed W. that he had received Wingate and hoped for a meeting with W. before the latter's departure for U.S. For W. reported to J.A. Executive 19 Sept. that Wingate's service was now requested by Wavell, to whom he was in fact seconded, and he went on to lead a successful guerilla campaign in Ethiopia. Dill nevertheless expressed the hope that Wingate would command the Jewish Army once the scheme was under way. See Dill to W., 17 Sept.; J.A. Executive Minutes, 19 Sept. (W.A.); Sykes, *op. cit.* In the event, Wingate was transferred direct from the Middle East to assume command of Chindit forces in Burma, where he met his death.

39. [1] Biog. Index, Vol. XVIII. Foreign Secretary 1938–40, then Ambassador to U.S.

[2] A meeting was effected Dec. 1940, as W.'s departure was delayed (see No. 75).

40. To Stephen Wise, New York.   *London, 11 September 1940*
English: T.: W.A.

Understand Leon Blum[1] in deadly danger. Only chance saving him if intervention higher quarters. Please use full weight your influence immediately.[2]

Weizmann

41. To Sir John Dill, London.   *London, 16 September 1940*
English: Or. Copy. T.W.: W.A.

Dear Sir John,

When I had the pleasure of seeing you last, and attempted to express my thanks for your kindness in our affairs, you said that I should not try to thank you until I had heard the decision of the authorities. As you know, there was a formal meeting on Friday last at which the Secretary for War, the Colonial Secretary, and a representative of the Foreign Office were present, and the decision reached was then communicated to me.[1] I see that the project submitted by us to the Government has been accepted practically in its entirety, and I cannot help feeling that your great influence must have had very much to do with this favourable decision. I would

---

40. [1] Biog. Index, Vol. XI. Three times French Premier. W. had frequently consulted him on Zionist matters.

[2] Wise was personally close to Roosevelt, but any efforts that may have been made on behalf of Blum were unsuccessful. He was interned by the Vichy Government that month on grounds that he constituted a danger to the security of the French State. His brilliant defence at his trial at Riom confounded both the Germans and the Vichy authorities, and the former suspended the trial. But he passed the rest of the war in imprisonment.

41. [1] Meeting of 13 Sept.: W. with Eden, Lloyd, and Baggallay, Head of F.O. Middle Eastern Department representing Halifax (W.'s report to J.A. Executive, 16 Sept., in C.Z.A. Z4/302/24). Eden produced a written draft scheme, accepting W.'s proposals in their entirety. He indicated that as the principal Ministers concerned were all agreed, he foresaw no Cabinet difficulty. The only criticism was likely to come from the P.M. who might consider the scheme too modest. Replying to a query from Eden, W. stated that in the first instance he envisaged a force of 10,000 men, of whom some 3,000–4,000 would come from Palestine, and 5,000–6,000 from U.S. They could be trained in Kenya or the Sudan. Eden proposed training them in England, where equipment was already available. Lloyd wanted a guarantee that American recruits would be allowed home after the war (because Americans would technically be breaking the laws of neutrality; the U.S. did not enter the war until Dec. 1941), and warned against a Jewish Army being given political connotation. See also No. 44. In reporting the outcome, W. averred to the Executive that the recent bombing of Tel Aviv had accelerated the Government's decision. At the same meeting, Ben-Gurion insisted that Palestinians be deployed only in the defence of Palestine.

therefore like to thank you now, most heartily, for all you have done to help. I can only express the hope that you may find us worthy of this great mark of confidence. We shall endeavour to produce the best men we can, and I trust that they may be able to contribute something towards a final victory.

Perhaps I may still have an opportunity of expressing my thanks personally when I come—if you permit—to take leave of you before my departure for America.

I would also like to remind you, if I may, that Wingate is still in this country, but may be leaving any day now. As he will be going to the Middle East,[2] I think you agreed that it might be useful if you could give him your views before he goes.

Once more with heartfelt thanks and kind regards, I am

Very sincerely yours,

Ch. W.

42. To Meyer W. Weisgal, New York.   *London, 17 September 1940*
English: T.: W.A.

Sorry trouble you again but important developments here demand postponement my trip three weeks or month. Could you kindly try transfer my booking to date towards end October. Shall wire again soon.[1] Love.

Weizmann

43. To Mikhail Weizmann,[1] Haifa.   *London, 21 September 1940*
English: H.W.: W.A.

The Dorchester Hotel, Park Lane,
London, W.
Sept. 21st. 40.

My dear Chilik,

This is only a line to let you know that we are all well. We are all bearing up under the "strafing" which Hitler is meting out to

---

[2] See No. 38, n. 1.

42. [1] The 'important developments' were the Government's (as yet unofficial) acceptance in principle of the Jewish Army scheme, for which W. was awaiting Cabinet confirmation, and about which he was optimistic—see Rose, *op. cit.*, p. 175. In fact, due to the protraction of negotiations, W. did not leave for the U.S. until Feb. 1941.

43. [1] Biog. Index, Vol. I. W.'s youngest brother. Agronomist. Engaged in industry, and development of Tel Mond.

London; there is a great deal of destruction and misery but fundamentally the position remains unchanged and Hitler's dream of subduing England is more remote from realization than ever. I have had to postpone my trip to the U.S.A. for a few weeks and expect to go by the end of October.

Michael[2] is well in the R.A.F., Benji has had a tough time in Anti-Aircraft; he will now be getting some leave.

I hope that your work is going well and that Feivel[3] and the others are alright. Give my love to the people in Tel Aviv and Rehovot and you can always telegraph to me if anything is required.

With very much love to all of you,

Chaim

[Both the Zionists and certain non-Palestinian Arab leaders believed that the 'Palestine problem' might be reduced to manageable proportions if placed within the larger context of an Arab Federation. In 1936 W. had discussed such a proposal with Nuri es Said of Iraq, who promoted the concept in the hope of giving his country a leading role in the Arab world. Ben-Gurion, during the same year, conducted talks with George Antonius (Secretary of the Arab Higher Committee of Palestine) on an autonomous Jewish unit within a 'Greater Syria' federation. However, nothing came of these negotiations. (See, *inter alia,* Volumes XVII and XVIII; records of meetings in C.Z.A.; and Ben-Gurion's *My Talks with Arab Leaders,* Jerusalem 1967.) Since the partition proposal in 1937 favoured some federative scheme for the Middle East, within which a Jewish State in Palestine would play its role, W. openly advocated this idea at the St. James's Conference in 1939. Such schemes aroused the suspicions of the Wahhabi ruler of Saudi Arabia Ibn Saud, the traditional rival of the Hashemite rulers of Iraq and Transjordan. The British Government was caught in a dilemma. On the one hand, they had no wish to alienate Ibn Saud; on the other, certain figures in the Government, in particular Lord Moyne, believed that the solution to the Palestine conflict might lie in federation: 'It is just conceivable that the Arabs, if they wished to secure the disappearance of the Mandate and the participation of Palestine in an Arab Federation, might be willing to acquiesce in a greater degree of Jewish penetration than would be otherwise contemplated' (Joint memorandum of Foreign and Colonial Office, Dec. 1941, in P.R.O. Cab. 95/1). The Government sounded both Arabs and Jews on the question of federation, but the Arabs would not concede to Palestine the degree of autonomy contemplated by the Zionists, especially as regards immigration.]

44. To Moshe Shertok, Jerusalem. *London, 22 September 1940*
English: Copy. T.W.: W.A.

My dear Moshe,

As you see, I have not left for the U.S.A. yet. The reasons for the

---

[2] Michael Weizmann (Biog. Index, Vol. VII). W.'s younger son.

[3] Feivel Weizmann (Biog. Index, Vol. I). W.'s eldest brother; employed by I.C.I., Palestine.

postponement are manifold. Firstly I don't feel justified in leaving London just now, when the crisis is at its height; I should not have a minute's peace when I got into the security of New York. Secondly, there have been important developments in the last ten days, which now require my presence here for a few weeks longer.

The Government has at last agreed to the formation of a Jewish Army on the same basis, and I believe with the same status, as the Czech or Polish Army. Its size to begin with is to be about 10,000, assuming that 4,000 would come from Palestine and another 6,000 from the rest of the world, America in particular. This number would include the cadres which, as you know, would also come from Palestine. They are to be trained and organized *here,* and when ready would return to the Middle East. Transport does not seem to be a difficulty, as empty ships are returning from Egypt (through the Mediterranean) in considerable numbers. The P.M., whom I have seen about a fortnight ago, is heartily in favour of it, so are—I must add—all the other members of the Cabinet, including Beaverbrook[1] and Halifax. With the latter I have had a long talk about the political future of Palestine on the lines of a Jewish entity within the framework of an Arab Confederation.[2] Lord Halifax has assured me that he considers such a solution a fair one, and that Lord Lloyd's mind is moving in the same direction.

On Friday, September 13th, at 3.30, a meeting took place at the W.O. with Mr. Eden in the chair, and in the presence of Lloyd and of a representative of the F.O. (Mr. Baggallay, head of the Middle Eastern Department). Mr. Eden then communicated to me officially that the Government has decided to proceed with the organization of a Jewish Army, and he used the expression: "on the same lines and with the same status as our other allies, the Poles and Czechs." Towards the end of the meeting, Lord Lloyd remarked in a somewhat jocular tone: "This thing has no political implications." I took up the challenge and repeated what I had said to Lord Halifax, and what the latter had said to me, which Mr. Baggallay confirmed. Lloyd said at the end that he thinks we could settle the problem satisfactorily.

The matter of the Army will come before the Cabinet very soon, and I expect an official intimation one of these days. We shall then have to set to work.

B.G. has gone to the U.S.A., and after having done some preliminary work there, will proceed to Palestine. I intend to leave for the States at the end of October. As you have no doubt heard and read,

---

44. [1] Lord Beaverbrook (Biog. Index, Vol. XI). Then Minister of Aircraft Production.
    [2] Record of W.'s conversation with Halifax untraced.

we are having a somewhat tough time here. Hitler has set his heart—
or whatever he may have as an equivalent of such an organ—on the
destruction of London. Speaking quite objectively, I would like
to say that this bombardment entails a considerable amount of
hideous destruction, and a great deal of misery to thousands of
people, but it makes very little impression on the military situation.
It may well be that the enemy is misinformed, and that he misreads
the situation. I hope so, at any rate! So far our work has not been
impeded; I am regularly in the office and in the Lab. where a fair
amount of interesting work is proceeding. Michael is doing well
in the R.A.F. Benji has had a pretty harassing time in a Kentish
A.A. Battery, and I hope that he may soon get some leave, when
he will recover from the shock. At present he is in a hospital. I saw
him yesterday, and hope that he may come home for some time.
We are all getting used to the new forms of life, ברוך ד׳ יום יום,[3] when
one lives from day to day without really trying to look ahead beyond
a very limited compass!

I am afraid that the storm may be approaching your shores soon,
but somehow I am confident that things will go fairly right there.
A good deal will turn on the attitude of Syria, and the de Gaulle
people, with whom I am in touch, are anxious for our cooperation.
I know that you are mindful of all that.[4]

Orde Wingate has gone to Egypt as a staff officer to Wavell. So
far I have not succeeded in retaining him definitely as an organizer
of the Jewish Army, although I'm not without hope in this respect.
The C.I.G.S., who has been most helpful in the whole matter, thinks
that Orde might come back when the thing is going there.[5] A great
deal will depend upon his relations with Wavell. I have impressed
that upon Orde repeatedly; he must try and work in with W[avell],
just as Lawrence did with Allenby.[6] You must go to Egypt and see
to that. Then work at this end will be much easier. Orde won't reach
Egypt for another three weeks from now.

---

[3] 'Blessed be the Lord, day by day.' (Psalms 68:20).

[4] W. informed J.A. Executive 22 Aug. that a French contact was arranging for him to meet
de Gaulle, with the object of the Zionists obtaining ammunition from French Forces in Syria,
in return for which they would arrange for de Gaulle to broadcast his cause to Syria from
Palestine. On 8 Oct. W. reported that progress was unsatisfactory, but subsequently two
officers of the de Gaulle Committee evidently gave W. satisfactory assurances (Executive
meeting, 12 Nov. 1940, W.A.).

[5] Wingate resented his posting to Egypt. He asked W. to intervene with the C.I.G.S.,
which W. felt himself unable to do—see Rose, *op. cit.*, pp. 175–76.

[6] T.E. Lawrence (Biog. Index, Vol. IX). As British liaison officer with the Arab Revolt led
by Emir Feisal he served with Gen. Edmund Allenby, Commander of the British Army that
conquered Palestine and Syria in 1917–18.

Give my love to everybody at the office, and to my family in Haifa, Tel Aviv and Rehovot. I hope that all is well with you and your family.

Ever yours affectionately,

Ch. W.

45. To Vera Weizmann, Southampton. *London, 23 September 1940*
English: H.W.: W.A.

Sept. 23, 40.

Verochka darling,

I was glad to hear your voice on the 'phone and to know that you are comfortably established in S'Hampton. I hope that you will have peace and that our Benji will soon be free.[1]

As already mentioned there is a cheque for £25 for you from Burton and a nice letter from Goodenday with a promise of 15 dozens stockings.[2]

My day was as usual, things in the lab are going fairly well. I was by myself for lunch and dinner. Nurse[3] has not shown up, as she returned late from her home and probably did not venture out to come here while the raid is on.

The Germans arrived with their usual punctuality, but so far things are comparatively quiet.

I am seeing Lloyd tomorrow and Major Taylor;[4] shall probably be seeing Haining this week. Have been to Harborow's this morning. The destruction in Old Bond Street is hideous and the poor people were standing about watching it with very sad faces.

In the office nothing new. Ben-Gurion has gone off, and so—an irritant less.

Poor Ida and her husband (Olden)[5] perished on the torpedoed boat yesterday; they were on their way to the U.S.A. to start a new chapter and came to an abrupt tragic end.

Miriam[6] telephoned to inquire about you; they are still in the country; Baffy[7] sends her best love.

---

45. [1] Benjamin W. had served in an anti-aircraft battery in Kent. After six months' service, he was hospitalized near Southampton with shell-shock, and invalided out of the army (*T. and E.*, p. 517).

[2] These were probably contributions by the industrialists Montague Burton and John Goodenday for the welfare committee for Jewish soldiers that V.W. headed.

[3] Jessica Usher, in the Weizmann family service.

[4] Unidentified.

[5] Daughter of W.'s long-time Zionist colleague George Halpern, to whom W. sent a cable of sympathy 24 Sept. 1940 (W.A.).

[6] Probably Mrs. Simon Marks.

[7] I.e., Mrs. Blanche (Edgar) Dugdale (Biog. Index, Vol. XIII). She worked closely with W. as a political adviser and facilitated his contacts with British public figures.

I have posted your letter and telephoned Mrs. Duffie;[8] shall see to it that Nurse sends off the parcel for Benji as soon as she comes in tomorrow.

H.G. Wells has sent me his new little book about Noah.[9] You remember he talked about it when he was here. It's amusing. We tried to reach Tounya[10] but without success; shall try again tomorrow.

My fondest love to Maidie[11] and Benji; tell Benji to be more cheerful; but above all he must get thoroughly well.

I hear that de Gaulle is in Dakar and I understand that Larminat[12] has gone to Syria. I hope they succeed.

I enclose a letter from Walter [Elliot] which will interest you.[13]

Good night my dears and may God be with you all.

Best love
Chaim

46. To Sir John Shuckburgh, London.   *London, 26 September 1940*
English: Or. Copy. T.W.: W.A.

Dear Sir John,

There are two points arising out of my talk with Lord Lloyd on Tuesday, September 24th on which I should like to give some additional information:[1]

1) I was unable to tell Lord Lloyd off-hand the ages of the five key officials for whom we desire to secure exemption from military service. They are as follows:

Mr. M. Pearlman	...29
Mr. L. Bakstansky	...36
Mr. S. Temkin	...38

---

[8] Unidentified.

[9] H.G. Wells (1866–1946). Novelist and thinker. His *All Aboard for Ararat* (London 1940).

[10] Unidentified.

[11] Wife of Benjamin W.

[12] René Marie Edgar de Larminat (1895–1962). Chief of Staff, French Forces in Levant until 1940; joined de Gaulle 1940; High Commissioner for Free French in Africa 1940–41; Commander French army in Tripoli 1942. Larminat and de Gaulle were on missions which aimed to prevent French colonies from submitting to Metropolitan (Vichy) France.

[13] See Elliot to W., 22 Sept. (W.A.): 'I hear you have succeeded in getting a Jewish Army. Second in time, but only in time, to the Balfour Declaration. Great historic achievement'.

46. [1] The talk had concerned exemptions from military service for Zionist officials, and consultation with the Jews should Britain hold talks with the Arabs. Further, W. stated that he would require release of the '43' (see No. 73, n. 1) for the cadre scheme and because of the inadequate air raid precautions in Tel Aviv.

Mr. I. J. Linton   . . . 40
Mr. H. Shine   . . . 44[2]

You will see that all except the first are well over the age at which men are usually exempted in the various reserved occupations, and are not likely to be called up in the near future. They are senior officials of the Jewish Agency and the Zionist Federation, and in the case of Mr. Linton and Mr. Bakstansky, occupy key positions in the two organizations.

The immediate problem, however, is that of Mr. Pearlman, our Press Officer, and the Editor of the *Zionist Review,* who has already registered, and whose calling up has been temporarily postponed. On August 6th Dr. Brodetsky wrote to Mr. Downie giving the reasons why we were anxious to retain the services of Mr. Pearlman. A further reason is now the propaganda for the recruiting of Jewish units, and it would involve us in great inconvenience to have to change the Editor of the *Zionist Review* at this juncture. I understand that under existing regulations, Mr. Pearlman would have had a claim to exemption as an Editor had he been six months older.

2) My second point concerns the conversion of 100 capitalist and student immigration certificates out of the current Schedule into 100 Category C (Labour) certificates.[3] I attach a copy of the note which I left with Lord Lloyd.[4]

We are anxious to obtain the certificates as quickly as possible, as there are grave risks that later on the Soviet authorities may refuse to allow these people to leave the Baltic countries. One hundred certificates may seem a very small contribution towards meeting the catastrophe which has struck the Jews in these countries, but it at least gives us the opportunity of saving a certain

---

[2] Moshe (Maurice) Pearlman, b. 1911: author, journalist. Director of J.A. Press Office 1938–40; commissioned in British Army 1940–46; emigrated to Palestine 1948, as Director of Information Services at P.M.'s office; director, Israel Broadcasting Service 1952–56. Lavy Bakstansky (Biog. Index): General Secretary, E.Z.F. 1930–71. Shlomo Temkin, b. 1902: Secretary, E.Z.F. Education Department 1933–42; R.A.F. 1942–46; director, E.Z.F. Office in Israel from 1950. Ivor Joseph Linton (Biog. Index, Vol. XIX): then J.A. Political Secretary in London. Harry Shine, b. 1896: member Board of Deputies of British Jews; Executive Director, Joint Palestine Appeal.

[3] The Churchill White Paper of 1922 adumbrated the principle of immigration into Palestine according to the 'economic absorptive capacity' of the country, as determined by the administration. Accordingly, the Palestine Government issued bi-annual quotas of immigration certificates for labour immigrants. 'Capitalist' immigrants, bringing their own minimum capital, were not restricted. A limited quota was allowed for students. The J.A. wished to convert altogether 600 'capitalist' and 'student' certificates unused because of the German conquest of Western Europe to 'labour' certificates for Jews in Baltic countries—see W. to Lloyd, 29 Aug. (P.R.O. CO 733/415 75985/39).

[4] This contained information sent by Shertok, 30 Aug., to the effect that notable Zionist leaders in the Baltic States were being interned in Central Russia and Siberia (copy in W.A.); Russia had occupied the Baltic States in June 1940.

number of the Zionist leaders from Poland who have managed to escape to Lithuania, as well as a few from Lithuania and Latvia.[5]

With kind regards, I am,

Very sincerely yours,

47. To Lord Lloyd, London.   *London, 27 September 1940*
English: Or. Copy. T.W.: W.A.

My dear Lord Lloyd,

Here is the brief "Child's Guide" to the oil question for which you asked me.[1] I think you do not want to be worried with technical details.

The man most competent to understand the whole problem and give a definite opinion on the project which I am ready to submit, together with all the experimental data, is Sir Harold Hartley.[2] If he approves, then I think the Ministry of Petrol could go forward at once. If Sir Harold would do me the honour of paying me a visit at my laboratory, he could convince himself as to the result of the experiments, and see the figures.

As you know, I may be going away towards the end of next month, but I and my team have been pressing on with this work almost incessantly so as to bring it to a stage at which it could safely be left to the technical people to complete it. I believe that stage has now been reached.

I have nothing to add. You yourself are well able to judge of the importance of the matter, and to bring me, if you think fit, into touch with Sir Harold Hartley, to whom I mentioned the process when I met him some weeks ago. I had the impression then that he was interested.

With kind regards, I am,

Very sincerely yours,

Ch. W.

[5] Lloyd replied 21 Oct. (W.A.) refusing the request for the 100 certificates, quoting the High Commissioner's objections on economic grounds. Further, Lloyd doubted whether the Soviet authorities would permit prospective immigrants to leave the former Baltic States. He also refused to exempt Pearlman from military service.

47. [1] Presumably at their interview on 24 Sept. On 20 Dec. 1940 W. reported that Lloyd had advised him three days earlier that within 30 years American sources of oil would dry up, reducing Britain to dependence for oil from Arab lands. W. had replied that for some years he had been working on the production of oil from sugar, and claimed that he 'could make the Empire flow with oil' from sources within the Empire itself. But this time, continued W. (referring to his role as scientist and Zionist leader during W.W.I), there would be no ambiguity: he wanted Palestine. See report to Smaller Zionist Actions Committee (C.Z.A. Z4/302/24).

[2] 1878–1972. Chemist, Chairman of Fuel Research Board, 1932–47.

OIL

1) The world's production of crude oil may be estimated at some 300,000,000 tons, of which the United States produces some 190,000,000 tons.

2) The maximum potential output of the U.S.A. of 96 octane spirit by various processes has been estimated by Dr. Egloff (the leading American authority in this matter) at about 6,000,000 tons per annum, provided all suitable materials were used for this purpose. To this should be added another 2,000,000 tons from other sources, made by new methods which are, I fear, still in the experimental stage. Assuming that these new methods will work on a technical scale, the maximum potential production of the U.S.A. of high-quality gasolene would be increased to about 8,000,000 tons per annum. But I am afraid that this is still a theoretical figure, and not nearly that amount is actually being produced. In order to reach an output of 8,000,000 tons a year, very expensive and complicated plant would have to be erected, and this would take a considerable time.

3) In the opinion of the experts, the actual U.S.A. production of high-octane fuel would be entirely inadequate for the joint requirements of Great Britain and the United States, particularly if our Air Force is to be increased substantially beyond its present size. During a period of offensive air action, we would presumably have to maintain daily in the air some 2,500 or 3,000 planes in the various theatres of war. I think this is not an over-estimate.

4) It may be assumed that 2,500 or 3,000 planes in the air daily would consume something like 350,000 tons of high-class oil per month—probably equal to the total monthly world production to-day. In other words, in order to keep in the air an offensive Air Force, provision should be made at once for the opening-up of new sources of high-octane fuel, both as reserves, and as alternative sources of supply in case maximum production in America cannot be achieved, or can only be achieved slowly and at very high cost.

5) Without going into technical details, I would submit that such alternative sources can be found, and that production is possible from materials available within the British Empire, e.g., in Canada, India, the West Indies, and other places. The method of production is comparatively simple, and it can be carried out within reasonable time.

6) I could undertake to discuss the whole question with Sir Harold Hartley, who is, I believe, a leading expert on fuel, to whom I mentioned the matter some time ago, and we could plan together whatever action may be necessary.

Ch. W.

48. To Lord Lloyd, London.   *London, 27 September 1940*
English: Or. Copy. T.W.: W.A.

Personal and Secret

My dear Lord Lloyd,

Thank you for your encouraging letter of the 17th September.[1] I am afraid I have been rather slow in acknowledging it, and hope you will forgive the delay.

May I take this opportunity of informing you of a telegram which I have just received from America, and of which the relevant part reads as follows:

> "We all agree extraordinary opportunity now through DW for great Zionist pro-British gesture and material aid. Suggest you urge immediate financial action for acquiring material suggested your original message."[2]

The explanation of this is as follows: DW is Daniel Wolf, whom you will remember advising the Ministry of Supply to send out to the United States and South America in order to obtain certain "material". He arrived there some time ago, and has since been hard at work; the above is the message I have just received reporting on it. I shall certainly urge my friends to do their utmost to help.

With kind regards, I am,

Very sincerely yours,

Ch. W.

49. To Meyer Weisgal and Nahum Goldmann, New York.
London, 1 October 1940

English: T.: W.A.

Would consider it important step if you could negotiate action for acquisition material[1] as suggested my telegram September fifth.[2] Know I can rely on your understanding situation and doing best. Heartiest wishes for New Year which believe will bring relief and new hope.[3] Love.

Weizmann

---

48. [1] The letter, relating to acquisition of drugs, is noted in No. 31, n.2.
   [2] See No. 36, n. 2.

49. [1] I.e., arms from South America—see Nos. 36, 48. Wolf wrote to W., 6 Jan. 1941 (W.A.), that his work of the previous three months had met with 'more success than ever expected'.
   [2] See No. 36.
   [3] The Jewish New Year fell 3–4 Oct. 1940.

50. To Leopold Amery, London.   *London, 8 October 1940*
English: Or. Copy. T.W.: W.A.

My dear Amery,

Some time ago you were kind enough to mention that in India there is a large quantity of cane-sugar molasses available, and that the problem of its disposal is unsolved. If I remember right, you said that at that time much of it was being poured into the sea.[1]

I would now submit that there are two possible ways of converting this molasses into useful commodities:

   (i) By growing yeast on it; yeast in its turn can be converted into a valuable food-stuff;

  (ii) By submitting it to fermentation, and thus obtaining materials like acetone and butyl-alcohol, which are at present required in large quantities for war purposes, and will always be required, even in times of peace.

I would like to add that the fermentation of cane-sugar molasses has always been a matter of some difficulty—as witness the numerous patents taken out on this subject. But I believe I can now ferment molasses and cane-sugar molasses quite straightforwardly and without any difficulty whatsoever; the yields obtained are as good as those from cereals and other starchy materials, which are practically theoretical. The process is simple, and can be easily applied in a country like India. I remember that in the great War, we were fermenting rice into butyl alcohol in India, so I believe there must be a distillery or distilleries suitable for this purpose. Any plant which can ferment rice can be used, without any alteration whatsoever, for the fermentation of molasses. In other words, I believe work could be started almost immediately.

I should be most grateful for any guidance from you in this matter, and if you or the Indian Government should think it useful, I would be pleased to place the process at your or their disposal free of charge. I could also provide a chemist who could introduce the process for war purposes in India. In time of peace, should a private firm take up the process, we would naturally have to make some arrangement with them.

I believe we are at present buying large quantities of acetone in the United States, and I see no reason why we should continue to do so.[2]

Ever yours,
Ch. W.

50. [1] See Amery to W., 5 Sept. (W.A.).

   [2] Amery forwarded W.'s ideas to the Government of India, which requested information from W. on the suitability of existing plants used in acetone production. He indicated that

51. To Sir John Dill, London.   *London, 16 October 1940*
English: Or. Copy. T.W.: W.A.

Dear General Dill,

Yesterday I was officially informed by the Secretary of State for the Colonies of the decision just taken by the Cabinet with regard to the Jewish Units.[1] Lord Lloyd advised me to approach your office with a view to settling the practical steps which could be taken now in this connection.

I appreciate, of course, that no public utterance on the whole matter is to be made until after the Presidential Elections in America, but I think it would probably save time if we could meet as soon as you can manage in order to discuss in outline the various practical steps which would be required. You were kind enough to say when we last met that, when the time came, you would introduce me to an officer who would deal with these matters on your behalf. If you could do this, I would then not need to trouble you again; as it is, I feel very hesitant about taking up your time.[2]

With very cordial regards and many thanks, I am,

Yours very sincerely,

52. To Sir Archibald Sinclair, London.   *London, 16 October 1940*
English: Or. Copy. T.W.: W.A.

My dear Archie,

We were both very happy to see you for a minute yesterday. The three points which I then mentioned—in haste—to you were:

1) A Polish engineer by the name of Dobrovolsky at present stationed here (his telephone number is Mill Hill 2205) is in pos-

---

plant used for production of acetone and butyl alcohol from rice could be used for molasses without alteration, and he added full details of his chemical fermentation process. See Amery to W., 15 Oct., and their exchange, 27 Dec. 1940, 3 Jan. 1941 (W.A.).

51. [1] The Cabinet decided in principle in favour of a Jewish Army scheme 10 Oct. (Minutes in P.R.O., Cab 65/9). W. was in fact informed orally of the decision by Lloyd 14 Oct., confirmed in writing 17 Oct. (letter in P.R.O., F.O. 371/27126, E60/60/31, and in W.A.). Authorisation was given for mobilization of 10,000 Jews for incorporation in Jewish units within the British Army, a maximum of 3,000 to be Palestinians, the remainder to come from wherever the J.A. chose to recruit. Each recruit would require a guarantee of re-entry from his country of origin following demobilization. The units would be trained in Britain, and no commitment would be made about their theatre of employment. To avoid controversy in U.S., the decision was to remain secret until after the Presidential Elections of 5 Nov. 1940.

[2] Dill replied 22 Oct. (W.A.) that he would introduce W. to an appropriate officer after the American elections.

session of a very interesting project for an anti-aircraft gun. Sikorski[1] knows all about it. It would permit of the adaptation of all our present A.A. guns to perform what he thinks is a very important function, both from the point of view of accuracy and of range, which can be adjusted to cover almost any distance, high or low, which may be desired. Dobrovolsky is apparently a very serious person, and I understand from him that one of his suggestions has already been adopted by the Air Ministry. You can easily verify this.

2) My son Michael, stationed now at Aldegrove, is apparently engaged on research of some importance about which he is extremely excited. I thought I would just mention it to you, as he thinks that it is a subject in which you are personally interested. If and when you are at Aldegrove, you might perhaps summon him. I shall tell him that you may see him if you come. I believe he is a good engineer and a good pilot as well, and apparently the combination is a very valuable one for the piece of work he has in hand.

3) Do you think there is any chance of a flight to the U.S.A. apart from the Clipper? That is apparently booked up till February. It is becoming urgently necessary for me to go over, and I fear the Prime Minister would be very angry if he knew I was still here. I am doing all I can to get a Clipper passage, but so far without success. Is it troubling you too much to ask whether you can suggest some other way of getting across? I shall be very grateful for any advice you may feel able to give.[2]

I remain, with all regards,

Affectionately yours,

53. To Vera Weizmann, Southampton. *London, 21 October 1940*
English: H.W.: W.A.

Oct. 21, 40.

Verochka dearest,

We arrived safely here and so far the Dorchester, Lab, Office are standing up. I have sent you on the letters, amongst them one from Mike.[1] He seems to be a bit bored; I shall write to him tomorrow.

52. [1] General Wladyslaw Sikorski (1881–1943). Prime Minister of Poland 1922–23; Polish Military Commander and Prime Minister of Polish Government-in-Exile during W.W. II. Died in air crash off Gibraltar.

[2] Sinclair replied 21 Oct. (W.A.) that he had forwarded W.'s information about Dobrovolsky's project to the Air Staff, but was as yet without reply. No further correspondence on this subject has been traced. Regarding W.'s passage, Sinclair advised that the quickest route might be by an American boat from Lisbon. He could arrange W.'s flight to Lisbon, but the British Government was no longer running transatlantic flights from there.

53. [1] Untraced.

Have not seen Haining yet, probably tomorrow. Lorna[2] has telephoned, but it was in my absence, so did Mrs. Irwell.[3] Otherwise nothing new. Last night was quieter, but today there were warnings all day. Have definitely decided not to leave for the U.S.A. before end of November and have telegraphed accordingly to Weisgal. There is so much to do both politically and chemically that it would be wrong to leave it all at the height of its development. Work in the Lab is proceeding well and we have some gas. Otherwise things are difficult; the telephone is much disorganized.

I hope all is well with Maidie and yourself and that Benji is behaving.

Have just returned from the Lab and am waiting for Jerry[4] to come. I think Nurse will be coming here for the night.

Do look after yourself and don't catch colds. Let me know how you are getting on. Much love to you and to the children.

Your loving
Ch.

54. To Sir Robert Haining, London.   *London, 23 October 1940*
English: Or. Copy. T.W.: W.A.

My dear General,

I beg to enclose copy of the letter from Lord Lloyd.[1] At my last interview with him, he suggested to me that I should get into touch with you and your Department so that we might privately discuss the various technical details which arise out of his letter. I am naturally mindful that no step in public may be taken until the Presidential Elections are over, but I thought it would save a very considerable amount of time if you could appoint an officer to discuss these problems with me. I would, however, first like to have an opportunity of placing my views before you personally.

For your confidential information, I would like to add that some time ago I received an intimation from the Prime Minister that he thought I should go to America. In fact I booked a passage on the Clipper on October 21st, as he wished me to be in the States as early as possible. But after my conversation with Mr. Eden, I felt it nec-

---

[2] Mrs. Orde Wingate.

[3] Henrietta A. Irwell (1869–1941). A founder and first Vice-President of W.I.Z.O.

[4] British colloquialism for Germans.

54. [1] I.e., confirmation of the Jewish Army scheme. Continued W.O. reluctance to sanction a public statement incensed W., particularly as the Press had long discussed the desirability of a Jewish force, and he wrote to Lloyd accordingly (30 Oct., P.R.O. CO 323 1801/13117/15c). In passing W.'s letter to Shuckburgh, Lloyd added a note: *'On n'est jamais content.'*

essary to postpone my departure pending a definite decision on the question of a Jewish Force. This explains my presence here now—though I am at the same time aware that it would be desirable from every point of view for me to get to America as soon as I can. This is why I am anxious to gain time by getting through as much of the preliminary discussions as may be possible without waiting for the public announcement.[2]

Yours very sincerely,

55. To Brendan Bracken, London.   *London, 28 October 1940*
English: Or. Copy. T.W.: W.A.

My dear B. B.,

I am writing to let you know that I have got no further with the War Office; they seem to think they have to wait until the Presidential Elections are over. I see no reason why preliminary discussions should not take place now; it would save a great deal of time. I greatly fear that the new complications in Greece and the Balkans[1] may make it again impossible for the War Office to find time to discuss matters with me, which means that I shall have to wait indefinitely until they make up their minds to give some thought to the details of organizing a Jewish Force. I do not wish to press them unduly; my patience is almost unlimited. But as you know, I am anxious to get to the United States as soon as possible, and they are really making me waste valuable time when I might be doing useful work over there.

I wonder whether you could see me within the next day or two, so that we might consult as to what had best be done?[2]

Affectionately yours,

56. To Meyer W. Weisgal, New York.   *London, 29 October 1940*
English: T.W.: W.A.

Personal

My dear Meyer,

I can scarcely find words to apologise for all the trouble I am so constantly giving you, or to thank you for all you are doing to get

---

[2] The two met to discuss the proposals 31 Dec. 1940 (see No. 86).

55. [1] Germany seized Rumania's oilfields 7 Oct. Italy demanded cession of strategic points in Greece 28 Oct., bringing British military intervention in Greece.

[2] No record has been traced of any meeting between the two, and the army scheme remained without progress—see No. 62 and W. to Martin, 4 Nov., P.R.O. Premier 4/51/9.

me to America.[1] From your latest telegram I judge that you appreciate my difficulties. The project in which we are all interested has gone through all the stages, and we now have to deal with the technical and practical questions involved. As the gentlemen concerned are greatly occupied with current affairs, I simply have to possess my soul in patience until I can get a few hours with them in order to discuss and lay down the general lines of organization. Then we shall have to start work on those lines in the various communities concerned. You will understand that I cannot leave this matter half-way after having worked on it for over a year: this is my dilemma. But I have every hope that I shall be able to let you know my definite plans within the next week or so.

I know that you and our friends will bear with me, and will realise that I am not my own master just now.

With heartiest greetings to you all, I remain,

Affectionately yours,

Ch. Weizmann

57. To Nicolai Kirschner,[1] Johannesburg.   *London, 31 October 1940*
English: T.: W.A.

[In reply to] Yours twenty fifth, for your information only, concluding negotiations progressing favourably during which am bound make no statement whatsoever. Will inform you full particulars when agreement reached. Thanks suggestion [regarding] friend; will cable him appropriate moment.[2] Regards.

Weizmann

58. To Eliezer Kaplan,[1] Jerusalem.   *London, 1 November 1940*
English: T.: C.Z.A. S53/274.

Surprised your Treasury contemplates reducing London budget.[2] We cannot agree to any reduction view increasing costs here and

---

56. [1] For the frequent changes in W.'s travel plans, see cables in W.A.

57. [1] Biog. Index, Vol. XIX. Chairman South African Zionist Federation 1934–47.

  [2] Kirschner requested fullest particulars of the Jewish Army scheme, and urged that a public announcement be made (W.A.). The 'friend' whose intercession Kirschner wished to invoke was Smuts.

58. [1] Biog. Index, Vol. XVI. Member J.A. Executive, and its Treasurer from 1933.

  [2] On 25 Oct., David Baharal (director of J.A. Finance Department) had informed London of a proposed cut of £5,000 in its annual budget.

impossibility introducing cuts [in] staff, which already reduced [to] minimum requirements. Expected developments likely increase our financial needs here. Hope raise funds for special purposes in United States but London budget must be covered as hitherto.[3] Regards.

Weizmann

59. To S. F. Newcombe,[1] London.   *London, 5 November 1940*
English: Or. Copy. T.W.: W.A.

Personal

Dear Colonel Newcombe,
Thank you for your letter and its enclosed memorandum, which I am studying carefully.[2] I hope to write to you about it in some detail in a few days' time, but there is just one point which I should like to make at once—it is with regard to the attitude of American Jews, which I am afraid is not quite so simple as you have assumed.
No American Jew—Zionist or not, but especially Zionist—will

---

[3] Estimated K.H. income for the coming year being £400,000 rather than the £700,000 estimated by the last Zionist Congress (in Aug. 1939), Kaplan had to curtail the budgets of all departments—Kaplan to W., 4 Nov. (C.Z.A. S53/274). See also No. 100.

59. [1] 1878–1956. During W.W. I involved in Arab revolt in Hejaz; helped found Palestine Information Bureau in London; later, accredited representative in London of Palestine Arab Higher Committee.

[2] Newcombe had discussions in Baghdad, July 1940, with the ex-Mufti of Jerusalem and Nuri es Said, then Foreign Minister of Iraq. According to one report, they reached agreement whereby the Husseinis (the Mufti's family, traditionally the extreme party in Palestine) would support the British war effort and Iraq would supply two divisions for service in Libya, provided London immediately declared Palestine an independent state. Newcombe met W. in London 28 Oct., and sought help in pressing for implementation of the White Paper of 17 May 1939 (Cmd. 6019) to restore Arab confidence in Britain. W. replied that, on the contrary, the Zionists were fighting the White Paper. Newcombe put his proposals in a memorandum to W. (2 Nov., W.A.), specifying that Arab cooperation in the war depended on faith in immediate implementation of the 'constitutional clauses', 10 (4) of the White Paper—i.e., election of Palestinians as Heads of Departments on the High Commissioner's Executive Council, in the proportion of two Arabs to one Jew, and the creation of an independent Palestine State not later than 1949. Newcombe's memorandum contended that the terms of the Mandate had largely been drawn up by W. personally, without consulting the local population, and that over the years W. had been allowed by the Government to place his own interpretation on the Balfour Declaration and on the Mandate. Posing the alternatives of opposition to the White Paper or winning the war, Newcombe claimed further that Zionists dwelling in Palestine, as contrasted with those outside, were not opposed to the White Paper. He sent a copy of this memorandum to C.O. See J. C. Hurewitz, *The Struggle for Palestine* (New York 1950), pp. 148–50; W.'s report to J.A. Executive, 29 Oct. (W.A.).

ever be against Great Britain in this struggle.[3] But the attitude of Great Britain to the National Home in Palestine, and in particular the enforcement there by the Mandatory Government of laws in contravention of the Mandate, are things which might well damp their ardour for the British cause. I had opportunities of seeing for myself when I was in the States last March (at the time when the Land Laws were promulgated) how deeply American Jews felt in matters of this kind—and not only American Jews: a great many American non-Jews also felt that these laws had about them a flavour of Nuremberg which shocked them profoundly. You may perhaps have read Miss Dorothy Thompson's[4] article in the *Herald-Tribune*—and Miss Thompson is certainly one of the truest friends England has in the States.

As I have said, this is no more than an interim comment on one point of your memorandum; I shall try to write to you again about it very soon, and meanwhile remain, with kind regards,[5]

Very sincerely yours,

Ch. W.

60. To Richard T. Latham,[1] London.   *London, 7 November 1940*
English: Or. Copy. T.W.: W.A.

Dear Mr. Latham,

A cable has been received from Rabbi Stephen Wise of New York, who, as you probably know, is one of the most influential of the American Jewish leaders, proposing that arrangements should be made to collect about 250 members of the Palestine Pioneer Organization and *Youth Aliyah* (who have been sent from this country to various internment camps in Canada) into one or two special camps where they could continue their agricultural training in preparation for their immigration to Palestine when opportunity again offers.

I understand that Rabbi Wise has also cabled to Lord Lothian[2] asking for his good offices in furthering this scheme.

---

[3] Newcombe's memorandum claimed that the British believed that W. could at will influence all Jews, in America and elsewhere. W. was apparently incensed at the implication that Zionist policy, and he personally, were damaging British war interests.

[4] Biog. Index.

[5] See Nos. 65, 70.

60. [1] 1909–43. Lawyer, Fellow of All Souls, Oxford; lecturer at Kings' College, London. Joined F.O. 1939; member of F.O. Committee on Aliens.

[2] Philip Henry Kerr (Biog. Index, Vol. XIX). British Ambassador in Washington 1939–40.

I would like warmly to support the proposal made by Rabbi Wise for two reasons: first in the interests of the internees themselves—it would I feel be very valuable if they could do some useful agricultural work during their internment, and at the same time receive cultural instruction to fit them for a new life in Palestine. Secondly, such a gesture on the part of the British Government would be bound to have an excellent effect on Jewish opinion in the United States.[3]

I am, dear Sir,

Ch. W.

61. To Benjamin Bloch, Rehovot.   *London, 12 November 1940*
English: Or. Copy. T.W.: W.A.

My dear Bloch,

I have to thank you for your letter with regard to the account for the *pardess*.[1] I must confess to being not a little surprised by the behaviour of these people. The first I had heard about the *pardess* having resulted in my owing money was when I received your telegram, and I naturally wanted to know what it was all about. Whereupon these gentlemen immediately threatened me with legal proceedings. I am surprised, too, that my brother did not take the trouble to explain to them that I knew nothing about the whole matter; you might perhaps mention to him that I think he might have devoted a little more care to the business in your and my absence.

In view of the way these people are behaving, I think I had, perhaps, better give up the *pardess* altogether, and get rid of these few dunams of oranges, which seem to be merely a liability. Would you please advise me as to what I had better do about this?[2]

I hope you will by now have received the £2,175 Income Tax Refund, as well as the money due from the Family, and a substantial remittance from America. By the end of this year I hope to find myself in the States, and shall see that you are kept supplied with funds.

---

[3] Replying 9 Nov. (W.A.), Latham proposed that W. apply directly to the Canadian Government (see No. 64).

61. [1] Hebr.: citrus grove. Bloch had informed W. (7 Oct., W.A.) of an outstanding debt of £83 on the grove in the grounds of his house at Rehovot. Legal action was threatened, whereupon Bloch had settled the debt without prior reference to W. The Cooperative to whom the money was owed was virtually in liquidation, the war-time market for oranges having collapsed owing to lack of shipping.

[2] See No. 320.

We have asked Miss Hellinger[3] to let us have some data about the pink butyric, but so far have had no reply.

With kind regards to you and everybody,

Very sincerely yours

62. To Anthony Eden,[1] London.   *London, 13 November 1940*
English: Or. Copy. T.W.: W.A.

Dear Mr. Eden,

I am happy to know of your safe return.[2] You must no doubt be very busy, but I hope that you may be able to give me an appointment in the near future.[3] I am sorry to have to tell you that no progress has been made in the matter of the Jewish Fighting Force. To-day it is exactly two months since the conversation which I had with you, Lord Lloyd and the representative of the Foreign Office[4] — a conversation which gave me hope of immediate progress in the direction which we envisaged together.

I hope you have brought back favourable impressions of our preparations and prospects in the vitally important regions where you have been travelling.[5]

Ch. W.

[On 11 Nov. 1940 two dilapidated ships, the *Pacific* and *Milos,* with 1,771 Jews aboard, were towed into Haifa. The Palestine Government announced that the refugees would be interned in Mauritius for the duration of the war, and not allowed into Palestine afterwards—see No. 65, n. 2. A ship of the Messagerie Maritime line, *La Patria,* then in Haifa, was requisitioned for the voyage, and the refugees were transferred. On 24 Nov. a third ship, the *Atlantic,* was brought into Haifa with some 1,700 refugees aboard, survivors of the Jewish community of Danzig, as well as refugees from Austria and Czechoslovakia. The British immediately began the transfer of these refugees into the already crowded *La Patria.* By the next

[3] Esther Hellinger, b. 1899. Microbiologist; worked at Sieff Institute 1933–55.

62. [1] Later Lord Avon (Biog. Index, Vol. XVIII). Secretary of State for War 1940; Foreign Secretary 1940–45.

[2] Following developments in the Balkans, and Italian movement in the Western Desert, Eden had visited Egypt to reassure the Egyptians and a visiting Turkish military mission that the British were capable of defending Egypt and the Middle East.

[3] Receiving W. 15 Nov., Eden sanctioned technical discussions on the Jewish Army scheme with the General Staff, with timing, content, and manner of any announcement reserved for Cabinet decision. On 18 Nov. Eden forwarded a draft announcement of the scheme, incorporating F.O. and W.O. amendments, in line with the Cabinet decision of 10 Oct. (P.R.O., Premier 4/51/9).

[4] See No. 41, n. 1.

[5] W. informed J.A. Executive that Eden had been in optimistic mood—Minutes, 15 Nov. (W.A.).

day, 130 of them had been transferred, the rest having been taken to the Athlit refugee camp. An explosion then rocked the boat, and it sank within 15 minutes. Some 240 refugees and a dozen British police were killed by the explosion or by drowning. It was later revealed that the explosion resulted from a badly-executed *Haganah* operation to disable the engines of *La Patria,* but at the time the J.A. covered up the disaster with a mass suicide story which directed indignation on the Administration and particularly the High Commissioner. The survivors of the *Patria* tragedy were allowed by the Government to remain in Palestine, a decision due probably to W.'s personal appeal to Halifax. See *T. and E.,* pp. 495–96; W.'s report to J.A. Executive, 4 Dec. 1940 (W.A.). For Cabinet decision of 27 Nov. 1940, see P.R.O., Cab 65/10.]

63. To David Ben-Gurion, New York.   *London, 18 November 1940*
English: T.: W.A.

Lord Lloyd informs me ships now at Haifa are being followed by another contingent about 1,800 now at sea which may be followed by yet others. Government opinion is that this action may be prelude to wider and more systematic efforts by Nazis now in control of Roumanian ports. This aims first at getting rid of Jews, second at embarrassing Britain by creating conflict between Government and ourselves by introduction of German *agents provocateurs* and using this for propaganda among Arabs. Doing my best obtain alleviation of situation.[1] You must try prevent rise of feeling which may complicate situation. Cable your suggestions.[2]

Weizmann

64. To Vincent Massey, London.   *London, 21 November 1940*
English: Or. Copy. T.W.: W.A.

Dear Mr. Massey,

Lady Reading[1] will have spoken to you about a cable which she has received from Rabbi Stephen Wise of New York with regard to

63. [1] According to Blanche Dugdale, W. was prepared to acquiesce on Mauritius under certain conditions, but would try to have the people then at Haifa allowed into Palestine—see Rose, *op. cit,* p. 178.
   [2] Ben-Gurion replied 19 Nov. (Ben-Gurion Archives). He recognised the need not to embarrass H.M.G., and suggested that if Lloyd's information was correct the dangers indicated in W.'s cable could be averted by interception of the ships in the Straits (i.e., before their entry into the Mediterranean), rather than the Royal Navy escorting them to Haifa as hitherto. As to the 1,771 already at Haifa, he had reliable information as to their *bona fides,* which could be checked in cooperation with J.A. To avoid undesirable consequences they should be allowed to land and given immediate release. Doubtful cases should be interned for the duration. See No. 81.

64. [1] Biog. Index, Vol. XIV. She was Eva Violet, wife of 2nd Marquess of Reading, and daughter of Alfred Mond, 1st Lord Melchett. Active Zionist, President of British section of World Jewish Congress.

a proposal that arrangements should be made to collect about 250 members of the Palestine Pioneer Organization and *Youth Aliyah*, together with other intending immigrants to Palestine (who have been sent from this country to various internment camps in Canada), into one or two special camps where they could continue their agricultural training in preparation for their immigration to Palestine when opportunity again offers.

I communicated on this matter with Mr. R.T.E. Latham of the Foreign Office Committee on Aliens,[2] who told me in reply that he had sent a copy of my letter to the officer dealing with these matters in Canada on behalf of His Majesty's Government, but that since the conditions under which internees in Canada are interned are a matter within the province of the Canadian Government, it might be better if we were to approach that Government direct.

I would like to support the proposal made by Rabbi Wise because I feel that it would be very valuable to have these young people kept together and enabled to do useful agricultural work in an atmosphere calculated to fit them for their new life in Palestine. I should be most grateful for any help you can give.[3]

Yours sincerely,
Ch. W.

65. To Lord Lloyd, London.   *London, 22 November 1940*
English: Or. Copy. T.W.: W.A.

My dear Lord Lloyd,

You will remember that you asked me to see Colonel Newcombe, which I accordingly did on October 24th. Following on our conversation, Colonel Newcombe sent me a copy of a memorandum dated November 2nd.[1] I immediately sent him a reply about a misrepresentation which I could not leave unanswered even for a day; and I enclose a copy. But as I take it that his memorandum was addressed to you, and as I know that he has given it at least to one other Minister, I direct to you my considered comments on the whole memorandum.

2. The memorandum is a plea for the immediate implementation of the third part of the White Paper. The argument is that "the

---

[2] See No. 60.

[3] Massey replied 10 Feb. 1941 (W.A.) that he had been informed that it had not been found practicable to adopt the Wise proposal to set up special training camps, because of cost; refugee internees were being given considerate treatment and were being provided with as useful occupations as circumstances permitted (see No. 112).

65. [1] See No. 59, n. 2.

Arabs are either disunited or passive in our support, and some are attracted by various means to favour Germany and Italy," and that "the Palestine question is the test of British good faith to all Arabs and Moslems."

3. The White Paper remains a highly controversial subject. It has been condemned by leading members of the present Government, beginning with the Prime Minister himself, and by the Labour and Liberal Parties; and the Permanent Mandates Commission has shown it to be inadmissible under the Mandate. I cannot subscribe to Colonel Newcombe's version of the origins of the Mandate, or to the low valuation which he puts on the intelligence of all British statesmen concerned with Palestinian affairs before Mr. Malcolm MacDonald. Nor can I accept Colonel Newcombe as a more competent interpreter of League documents than the constituted League authorities. But I would be very loth to re-open the White Paper controversy, which would not help our war effort in any sphere or country.

4. The immigration clauses of the White Paper have been put into force, and even exceeded in practice, in a manner most painful to us;[2] the Land Regulations have practically closed 95 per cent of Palestine to Jewish land purchase—but, as Colonel Newcombe points out, the Arabs remain unimpressed and unhelpful. He therefore urges the implementation of the third part, though I search his memorandum in vain for any positive assurance that these constitutional developments would work a fundamental change in the "passivity" of Arab support. The attitude in this war of the Arab States, which owe their well-being and their very existence to British victories and power, can hardly be described as satisfactory; and it would indeed be straining anyone's credulity to suggest that their outlook and attitude would be transformed by a measure which Colonel Newcombe and his friends have, for almost two years, done their best to belittle, as setting up mere "bogus Ministers."

5. Unsatisfying as such a further concession would be to the Arab totalitarians, it would have a disastrous effect on Jewish opinion and feeling in Palestine and elsewhere. For while the Arabs of Iraq, Saudi Arabia, Egypt, etc., pursue a hundred different aims and ambitions, Palestine is our all, and the greater the disasters which daily strike European Jewry, the more we turn towards it.

[2] During the period Oct. 1939 to Mar. 1940, and Oct. 1940 to June 1941, no immigration certificates at all were issued, on grounds of the high rate of Jewish illegal immigration. During the second period, the Government further claimed that the stoppage of immigration was due to wartime travel difficulties and widespread unemployment in the *Yishuv* (Hurewitz, *op. cit.*, p. 139).

The implementing of a new part of the White Paper under a Government mostly composed of men who have publicly condemned it would tell world Jewry that Great Britain has definitely abandoned them to the Arabs, to be a hopeless minority in a Palestinian Arab State. While this measure would not sensibly change the attitude and calculations of the Arabs, it would deal a most severe blow to Jewish cooperation with Great Britain. Perhaps indeed the Arab politicians who, in their refuge at Baghdad, suggested this step to Colonel Newcombe, had this result in view. Unable to obtain immediately the independent Arab State in Palestine which they really want, and far from clear which side in the war they would prefer to see victorious, they wish at least to make certain that the Jews should not acquire merit with Great Britain.

6.　The Jewish programme for an Arab-Jewish settlement after the war is definite, and not subject to fluctuation. We ask for sufficient room in Palestine to settle a considerable number of immigrants, to develop a well-rooted community, and to build up our State (not a "Jewish autonomous area" of Colonel Newcombe's invention). We are prepared for this State to enter into a Federation with the neighbouring Arab States, provided that this Federation remains in close connection with the British Commonwealth. This programme lays foundations on which the national aspirations of both races can be worthily fulfilled, and, I submit, is much more on the line of British Imperial statesmanship than the niggling, restrictive provisions of the White Paper. If any Arabs wish to talk with us on this basis, under the aegis of His Majesty's Government, we shall be very willing to meet them, and to try to devise means whereby all parties concerned could give tokens of their sincere goodwill in this matter.

Yours v. sincerely,
Ch. W.

66. To John M. Martin,[1] London.　　　　*London, 22 November 1940*
English: Or. Copy. T.W.: W.A.

Personal

My dear Martin,

You may be interested to hear that, in the matter of the Jewish Force, I have got a step further forward with the War Office. I had on Wednesday a long talk with General Haining, who has appointed a Staff Officer, General Leigh, to discuss with us the details of or-

---

66. [1] Biog. Index, Vol. XVIII. Private Secretary to Churchill.

ganization, etc. We also reached a satisfactory understanding on our main problems.

Now arises the question of the announcement—which may take all sorts of forms. Mr. Eden said something about mentioning the matter to the Prime Minister, but I am not quite sure what he meant. The best form would seem to be a letter from the Prime Minister, if this could be arranged, and I am taking the liberty of sending you herewith, quite informally and unofficially of course, a short list of the points which such a letter should cover. If you think there is any chance of the Prime Minister acceding to this request it would mean a very great deal for the Jews—and especially for those of us now in captivity.

You might let me know what you think; I will, if I may, ring you up sometime early next week.[2]

With kind regards, I am,

Very sincerely yours,

Ch. W.

Draft of Guiding Principles for Establishment of Jewish Division.

Formation of Jewish Fighting Force is reply to offer made by Jewish Agency for Palestine. There has been more than an offer. Some 5,000 Palestinian Jews have already enlisted in every unit of the British Forces in Palestine which was open to them, and the Palestinian Jews are still asking for larger opportunities.

It is matter of justice that the Jewish people, the earliest and foremost victims of Nazi aggression, should be given place as a nation among the nations in arms against those destroyers of human values.

Jewish Fighting Force will be part of the British Army, but the War Office will organize it in full collaboration with Jewish Agency for Palestine.

It will be open to any Jew who is acknowledged to be worthy of it.

It will be formed and trained in England, but present intention is to use it in active fighting which is now proceeding in Mediterranean theatre of war.

Jews and Arabs should fight beside Britain against the totalitarian menace. Victory will give scope for realising the national aspirations of both races in harmony with each other.

---

[2] Martin replied 23 Nov. (W.A.) that as he was unable to raise the matter with the P.M. on a 'personal level', W. should put the proposal directly to Eden, requesting that the P.M. receive a copy.

67. To Meyer W. Weisgal, New York.   *London, 22 November 1940*
English: T.W.: W.A.

Personal

My dear Meyer,

I have telegraphed to you to-day[1] that at last I am able to fix a date for my departure—the earliest possible day in January. The project[2] which has been occupying our attention for so many months past, has at last come to some sort of fruition, and entered on the stage of practical realization; I feel that between now and the beginning of January we should have established the framework of the scheme so that the work both in Palestine and in America can go forward on proper lines. It is, as you will realise, now a question of personnel and organization.

I may be able to write you a few more details later on. Having reached this stage here, I am now anxious to push on with the work in America as soon as possible, and my departure thus becomes a matter of urgency. I am afraid I have given you a great deal of trouble, but it is difficult to convey any impression of the uncertainties of one's work and life here at present, and it is always hazardous to make any arrangements far ahead. But so far as it is humanly possible to see at present, the beginning of January should be perfectly all right. I would naturally like best to have two seats on the Clipper, as Mrs. Weizmann will be with me, and shipping is likely to be very uncertain.

Well, there is a great deal that I shall have to tell you when we meet, and a fair amount of hard work lies ahead of us. Although I am tired and over-worked, I feel confident that there is a better future for us all, provided we live up to the heavy responsibilities which will be placed upon us by the events of the past few months. I can scarcely tell you how much I am looking forward to meeting you and all our friends, and to the beginning of our work together.

I have lately had an opportunity of seeing *The New Palestine*[3] in its new form, and must confess to have found it rather depressing that, at a time like this, the American Zionist Organization can produce nothing more impressive than what is to be seen there. However, this is also a matter which will need attention when we meet.

Meanwhile, I send you and all our friends my affectionate regards and best love, and remain, as ever,

Yours,
Chaim

67. [1] W.A.
  [2] For a Jewish Army.
  [3] Weekly organ of Z.O.A.

68. To Walter Baer,[1] New York.   *London, 25 November 1940*
English: H.W.: W.A.

25 Nov. 1940.

My very dear Friend,

Ever so many thanks for yours of Nov. 4th which has reached us today.[2] We were delighted to have news from you. It seems such a very long time since I have spent those agreeable hours under your hospitable roof; much water and much blood has flown [*sic*] under the bridges.

I was happy to receive the news about Therese's marriage and we sent you a telegram which I hope has reached you. We also have an event to record; we have become grandparents: a boy by the name of David was born to Benji.

We are all well. Benji was in the Army and is now on sick leave; he is getting on well. Michael is in the Air Force and is also. quite well, I am happy to say. Vera is working, I'm trying to help as much as I can. One is very busy these days and that makes life much easier. We are confident of a better future, although the road to it may be hard and long, but I have no doubt that this country will face it with courage and fortitude.

It is possible that we shall go to the States in January and if you are still there we shall meet, I hope.

Give my love to Therese and Claude[3] and all the best to both of you, and let us hope for happier days to come.

In friendship,
Yours ever,
Ch. Weizmann

69. To Sami Gunzberg,[1] Istanbul.   *London, 2 December 1940*
English: T.: W.A.

Deeply grateful your assistance obtaining transit visas. Are advised local Turkish Consuls not yet granting visas. Assume authority not yet reached them and would be grateful if Consuls Scandinavia,

---

68. [1] Biog. Index, Vol. XVI. Swiss banker, friend of the Weizmanns.
  [2] Untraced.
  [3] Both unidentified.

69. [1] 1876–1966. Turkish Jew of Hungarian origin who had been Ataturk's dentist. Intermediary between W. and high Government circles in Constantinople, when Turkey had sought a Jewish loan, and W. saw in this a means to strengthen the Zionist position in the Arab-Jewish conflict, and to help Britain to resist Axis pressure in the Eastern Mediterranean—see Vols. XVIII, XIX. Gunzberg was now helping to secure Turkish transit visas for Jews in possession

Lithuania, Yugoslavia, Russia, Bulgaria, Roumania, Hungary could be telegraphically instructed [to] issue these.[2]

Weizmann

70. To S. F. Newcombe, London.   *London, 2 December 1940*
English: Or. Copy. T.W.: W.A.

Personal

Dear Colonel Newcombe,

The memorandum which you sent me under your covering letter of November 3rd was clearly addressed to Lord Lloyd, and I have directed my reply to him. I enclose a copy.[1] I have omitted to deal with the diatribe against myself,[2] as it seems to me to be completely irrelevant to the important questions at issue, and I feel that no useful purpose can be served by personal attacks on Zionist leaders such as seem to be a favourite subject with the friends of the Arabs.

In your memorandum all the British statesmen concerned with Palestine affairs up to 1939—Mr. Lloyd George, Lord Balfour, Lord Curzon,[3] Mr. Churchill, Mr. Amery, etc.,—appear as nitwits, and myself as the villain of the piece. It is only Mr. Malcolm MacDonald at the Palestine Conference[4] (so aptly re-named by you the "Arab Conference") who sees the light. This reminds me of the fond Scottish mother who, seeing her son's regiment march past, observed, "they are all out of step, except our Jock."

To please the Arabs, you invite us to accept the White Paper, a denial of all our rights—may I ask you on this point to re-read the

of Palestine immigration certificates and fleeing from Soviet-occupied territories—see W. to Gunzberg, 20 Aug., 7 Sept. 1940 (W.A.).

  [2] Turkey authorised the transit visas—see Gunzberg to Capt. Whithall, British Passport officer in Istanbul, 23 Jan. 1941 (C.Z.A. A169/2). Haim Barlas (J.A. Immigration Director of Istanbul) subsequently informed W. (20 Feb., W.A.) that the Turkish Government had published regulations giving transit rights through Turkey to all Jews guaranteed entry into country of final destination. The issue assumed some urgency because the immigration certificates held by the refugees were of specified validity only, and due to expire. Some of the *Patria* refugees interned by the British in fact held expired certificates. W. later secured C.O. agreement to extend their validity until 31 Mar. 1941.

70. [1] See No. 65.

  [2] See No. 59, n. 2.

  [3] David Lloyd George, P.M. 1916–22; Balfour and Curzon had been in his Cabinet. For their views, see Vols. VII–IX.

  [4] The Round Table Conference between Arab, Jewish and British delegations at St. James's Palace in Feb.–March 1939. Following the failure of the parties to reach agreement, the British Government issued the White Paper on Palestine in May 1939, severely restricting the future development of the Jewish National Home. MacDonald had been Colonial Secretary. See Vol. XIX.

present Prime Minister's speech in the Hansard of May 23rd, 1939 (columns 2177–2186)? In this he has given his opinion also about the constitutional proposals of the White Paper.

Our foremost desire is to help Great Britain to win the war, but we do not consider that we can best accomplish this by committing suicide. Even if the Zionist leaders, against whom you inveigh in memoranda and speeches, were to do so, the nation could not be expected to follow their example.

But fortunately there are more constructive ways in which both we and the Arabs can play a part in this war. We are doing, and shall continue to do, all in our power to assist Britain. Encourage your Arab friends, for whom Great Britain has done so much, to do likewise. As for the ultimate settlement, the scheme of a Jewish State (not of some ridiculous "autonomous area") federated with Arab States seems to us the most sensible solution.

Yours very sincerely,
Ch. W.

71. To Lord Lloyd, London.   *London, 5 December 1940*
English: Or. Copy. T.W.: W.A.

I see from Mr. Hall's statement in the House of Commons yesterday that it has been decided not to deport the passengers of the *Patria* from Palestine.[1] I hardly need tell you how thankful we are to you for this decision. I further note that at least the unfortunate passage in the statement broadcast from Jerusalem on November 20th, putting a ban on these immigrants even after the war, has been omitted.

But there is one important point to which I feel I must immediately draw your attention. Mr. Hall said that the position remains unchanged as regards *all other illegal immigrants who have arrived recently off the coasts of Palestine* or may arrive hereafter. This suggests to me that the ship which you mentioned as lying off the coast of Cyprus has now arrived in Palestine.[2] I understood you to say about this ship that it was utterly unseaworthy, and from Mr. Hall's remarks I must conclude that it is the intention to deport its passengers "as soon as the necessary shipping arrangements can be made." If this is so, it seems most regrettable that the ship should

---

71. [1] George H. Hall (Biog. Index, Vol. XXII). Colonial Under-Secretary 1940–42; Colonial Secretary 1945–46.

[2] This was the *Atlantic*. See Bridgenote preceding No. 63.

have been brought to Palestine at this juncture when feelings have been aroused by the *Patria* incident among Jews both in Palestine and elsewhere. I very much fear that any attempt to re-embark passengers landed in Palestine, or to transfer them from one ship in Haifa Bay to another, might lead to unfortunate incidents, and unhappy consequences.

I beg you to re-consider this matter and, whatever the Government decide regarding subsequent shiploads which may be intercepted, I submit that the people on board this third ship should be treated in the same way as the *Patria* passengers. We are anxious not to embarrass the Government, and not to allow a state of tension to arise between Britain and the Jews over a matter on which, I am sure, you will readily understand their human feelings. We are prepared to cooperate with the Government in seeking a solution should your fears regarding continued refugee immigration prove justified, even though such action is certain to create for us serious difficulties with regard to our own people. But please do not make such a course impossible for us by uncompromising action in the meantime.

Yours sincerely,

72. To W. P. Crozier,[1] Manchester.   *London, 6 December 1940*
English: T.W.: Photostat W.A.

My dear Crozier,

I felt I must send you a word to thank you for your inspired and inspiring article. In these terrible days friendship such as yours means more—if that is possible—than ever in the past.

It has been an agonising experience trying to save these people—and now we have succeeded, at least so far as the first ship is concerned.[2]

The best of good luck to you always, and God bless you.

Yours ever,
Ch. Weizmann

P.S. I am just writing a note to the P.M. about the situation in the States, which you may be interested to see. It will be ready sometime early next week.[3]

---

72. [1] Biog. Index, Vol. XIX. Editor of *Manchester Guardian* from 1932.

[2] See Bridgenote preceding No. 63.

[3] See No. 74.

73. To Lord Lloyd, London.   *London, 9 December 1940*
English: Or. Copy. T.W.: W.A.

Dear Lord Lloyd,

I would like to thank you for your letter of November 25th with regard to the sentences passed in October 1939 on forty-three Jews who were found training with illegal arms.[1] I am glad to hear that their case will come up for review in January.

As to the undertaking by the Military Authorities that the sentences in this case would be reviewed at the end of six months, I can hardly be labouring under any misapprehension. General Ironside[2] repeatedly told both myself and Mr. Shertok (e.g., when Mr. Shertok went to take leave of him in March this year) that these sentences would automatically come up for review at the end of six months, and that instructions to that effect were in the hands of the Military Authorities. General Ironside has since left the office of the C.I.G.S., but it may be that a record of the conversation referred to above is in his office. His A.D.C., Colonel MacLeod, was present, and I believe took notes.

Yours very sincerely,

Ch. W.

74. To John M. Martin, London.   *London, 9 December 1940*
English: Copy. T.W.: W.A.

My dear Martin,

In accordance with our arrangement, I would like to put down on paper what I have recently learned about the position in the United States.[1] As I have told you, my information comes from an unimpeachable source,[2] and curiously enough, the very day I met

---

73. [1] Members of *Haganah,* they were apprehended 5 Oct. 1939. One received life imprisonment, the others ten years. Lloyd's letter concerned a review of all cases tried by the military courts, and that of the '43' was due for review in Jan. 1941. The High Commissioner had claimed that no undertaking had been given to review the sentences after six months (i.e., in Apr. 1940). In fact they were released Feb. 1941, when many of them (including Moshe Dayan) were employed by British Intelligence on missions in Vichy-occupied Syria (see Shuckburgh to W., 5 Feb. 1941, W.A.).
[2] Sir William Edmund Ironside (1880–1959). C.I.G.S. March 1939–May 1940; C.-in-C. Home Forces 1940. Later Field-Marshal Lord Ironside.

74. [1] The letter was of course intended primarily for Churchill, who read it—see No. 88.
[2] Unknown.

you at lunch, I had in the evening an opportunity of meeting Mr. Purvis, the head of the Purchasing Commission,[3] and of hearing his talk on the present state of affairs in America to a small group of people, among whom was Lord Halifax. His views were almost identical with those which had reached me. After he had finished his talk, we went into a corner together to compare notes. We found only one or two differences, to which I shall draw attention as I come to them, and Mr. Purvis and I agreed that those points of difference should be emphasised, as they are of some importance.

There is no doubt in my mind that at present America is passing through the trough of a depression in regard to her attitude towards the war—a depression which naturally affects adversely her efforts to help us. The reasons for this change, which I believe to be only temporary, are complex:

First, there is the natural reaction which has set in after the excitement of the Election,[4] with which may be coupled the approach of the Christmas Holidays, when everyone is anxious to get away to Florida or California, and public life and interest in public affairs are bound to flag. You may have seen that the President himself is taking a fortnight's cruise to the South.

Secondly, there is developing a mass propaganda by the Germans, who are pouring in their agents by hundreds. Ostensibly these agents are far from being ordinary Nazis: many of them pass as anti-Nazis, deeply opposed to the horrible régime in Germany. They insinuate that the continuance of the war is engendering an ever-increasing bitterness in Germany which strengthens Hitler's grip on the people. America's help, and anticipated participation in the war, are presented as something which will galvanise the present régime into still more ruthless action. These people also pose as pacifists, saying that no doubt, with American cooperation, some equitable arrangement could be reached which would safeguard the interests of Great Britain, the British Empire, and America, and possibly lead to a gradual change of affairs in Germany, and thus, eventually, in Europe.

I am only sketching the sort of arguments that are being used; they assume different forms according to the circumstances and according to the class of people to whom they are addressed. But the above gives an idea of the general drift. The people responsible are usually cultured people, with an assured entry into any class

---

[3] Arthur Purvis (1890–1941). Employed with Nobel Explosives Co. (later I.C.I.) 1910–24; Director General, British Purchasing Commission in U.S., 1939–40; Chairman, British Supply Council in U.S., 1941.

[4] Franklin Delano Roosevelt was re-elected President by an overwhelming majority.

of society. For instance, there is hardly a single meeting of the various and numerous luncheon clubs at which one or two of these agents are not present. They are looked upon as distinguished strangers; usually well-introduced by some prominent American; regarded as authorities on European questions, and listened to with deference and interest.

I would like to emphasise that this danger is most serious in provincial towns, where the public is less well-informed, and infinitely more gullible, than in the great cities of the Eastern seaboard; where access to leading people and groups of leading people is much easier, and where the industrial war effort is mostly concentrated: e.g., Detroit, Pittsburgh, Cleveland, St. Louis, Indianapolis, Columbus (Ohio), and Chicago itself, and then on the Pacific coast, with their surrounding industrial districts.

(Mr. Purvis, in his review, did not emphasise this particular point; but when I drew his attention to it said it was most important that a special warning should be given on this account.)

I am informed that Detroit is particularly active in this respect, and that from there German activities radiate out into the surrounding country.

Thirdly, there are the Vichy French. Their propaganda, which is also carried out by men and women of distinction with excellent connections in the United States, assumes less blatant forms than the German. But they parade the French tragedy before the eyes of the Americans, inveigh against the blockade, insinuate lightly that, after all, the British are to a large extent responsible for the collapse of France, and, while praising to the skies Britain's gallant stand, manage to suggest that it is already a lost battle: it may last another few months, but in the spring the odds will be heavily against a Britain left without Allies or friends; it would be in everybody's interest to come to an "honourable" settlement now, before it is too late. Even people of the standing of André Maurois[5] and Louise Weiss[6] (the friend of Briand[7] and Blum) are not entirely guiltless in this respect. As for the others, they are much more outspoken, and perhaps less dangerous on that account.

Fourthly, because of our enormous expenditure of money in the United States, there is at present a wave of prosperity there. People are buying a great many things—cars, wireless sets, gramophones, and other luxury commodities. These have to be made, and therefore industrial production is deflected to the manufacture of luxury

---

[5] 1885–1967. Born Emil Herzog; French novelist and biographer.
[6] B. 1893. Prominent French journalist—see Vol. XV and *T. and E.*, pp. 453–54.
[7] Aristide Briand (1862–1932). French Premier 1909, 1913, 1921.

products which have nothing to do with aeroplanes or war weapons. (Mr. Purvis, while agreeing that there is some waste, believes that it will not play any important part in the future.)

Lastly, there is the position of the Jews. The Jews are the natural allies of Great Britain against Hitler. They understand only too well that no compromise is possible for Great Britain—and certainly not for them—whatever other people may think. They realise that if Great Britain either loses the war or makes a premature peace, their position even in America must go down. They would be ready to do their utmost for victory; they would be ready to fight as volunteers in the ranks (and I reckon on being able to enlist tens of thousands of volunteers in America when I go out there), and they are also ready to do a great many other things by way of speeding up production and deliveries on a scale much larger than at present. But I understand that representatives in the States of the Ministry of Information and the Foreign Office, and various consular authorities on the American continent, are spreading the view that one does not want to be under any obligation to the Jews. I would like to make clear at once that this does not apply to the higher authorities, and especially not to a man like Lord Lothian himself, who holds exactly the contrary view. But Lord Lothian does not come into contact with the vast expanse of the middle and lower strata of the American population. For them, much more may depend on the attitude of some vice-consul in a provincial town—in Texas, or California or the Middle West. And his attitude is very likely to be as indicated above. Of course, this idea, too, is propagated in various oblique ways: for instance, one is anxious, for the Jews' own sake, not to involve them in any accusation of trying to "drag America into the war." This is really rather too obvious a subterfuge, for the Jews are quite capable of looking after themselves; they know exactly how far they can go, and are far too sensitive to American public opinion to plunge headlong into a movement which might have such consequences.

Be that as it may, the fact is that the Jews feel that they are not wanted; moreover, they feel that they are not wanted because the British feel they have got them anyhow, so that there is no need to give them any encouragement. This attitude is bitterly resented. In the opinion of the American Jews, while Britain is playing up to Egypt and the Arab States, who have betrayed her already and will betray her again and again (particularly if the position of Egypt should become more precarious), the Jews are being cold-shouldered. Any action they might take is therefore paralysed from the start. On the other hand, if they could be "activated," they are closely connected with industry, trade, and political life in America. Many of them play a prominent part in various walks of life. They are by nature dynamic, and would certainly be a great accession of strength to our position in America. As I have told you, I am being asked every week, sometimes twice a week, when I am coming over. I expect to go very early in January, and something tells me that this will be a critical moment, when Britain will need to mobilise all her forces in order to counteract the various adverse currents referred to above when the new political season opens in the New Year.

Many are the dangers which we are facing and which we shall have to face in the first 6 or 7 months of 1941 —the night bomber, the submarine, the ocean raider, but I am quite sure that these difficulties can and will be countered. There is, however, another danger which seems to me more formidable than those to which I have alluded, namely the ever increasing German industrial potential. The Germans have enslaved millions of European workmen, skilled and unskilled, great numbers of experts, specialists, scientists, who all must live, and can only do so if they give their services to the Germans. They may do so with bitterness in their hearts, but the Nazis see to it that the performance of these chain gangs comes up to the standard. And thus we witness the great Renault works in France turning out tanks, the Creusot works turning out guns and ammunition of all sorts. The same is applicable to Czechoslovakia (Skoda), Holland, and Belgium.

The American output could easily cancel out this increase in German production and outstrip it, but this will only happen if American production is really effectively developed. The Jews of U.S.A. could play an invaluable part in this respect, if the matter is properly handled. In India, in the West Indies, in other British dependencies, infinitely more could be done to speed up the war effort. India has raw materials, even factories. They need skilled men. I have been approached repeatedly by Indians with a request to give them Jewish specialists whom they (curiously enough) prefer. I have given in lists of people to the India Office.

The C.O. administers countries abounding in riches which all could be turned to account, but colonial development is occasionally talked about and nothing much happens. We are far behind the Belgians in Congo or the Dutch in the East Indies. Our resources in Africa or in West Indies and in the Dominions are immense, but they are not used adequately for the purposes of this war, which to a great extent is one of skill and of applied science.

The Germans and Italians have lost a very high proportion of their scientists, but we have failed to make proper use of these forces, have wasted them through a muddled policy of indiscriminate internments, and through allowing some very distinguished representatives to go off to America where better prospects of employment were offered to them. The leaders of our industries have not availed themselves fully of a golden opportunity.

All this can, or must, still be remedied, and the Jews could do more than anybody else in this direction!

I do hope you will understand that in what I have said about the Jews, I am not introducing this subject in order to exercise pressure on your mind or on the mind of the Prime Minister, who I know understands our position very well, and has consistently shown himself to be one of the best friends we have ever had in this country.

I am only trying to place the facts before you, as objectively as is possible for me, and drawing your attention to the existence of a people who form a part of the American scene, who exercise an influence perhaps incommensurate with their numbers, and who at present are not only being neglected, but are being driven into a mood of sullen resentment. But I am convinced that the Jews of America could never be made to turn against Britain, however hard the Palestine administration and the Colonial Office may try.

I touched on many of the points mentioned above in the rather lengthy conversation which I had with Lord Lothian during his visit here, but at that time things were not so clear as they are now. Like Mr. Purvis, Lord Lothian urged me to come over as soon as possible, and I promised him that I would do so.

I do not want to make this letter unduly long. There are one or two points which I could have added, but I have tried to limit myself to the most important features of the situation, as I see it.

With kind regards,
Very sincerely yours,
Ch. Weizmann

75. To Viscount Halifax, London.　　　*London, 16 December 1940*
English: Or. Copy. T.W.: W.A.

Dear Lord Halifax,

It is now two months since I was officially advised by Lord Lloyd of the Cabinet decision to form a Jewish Fighting Force; he added, however, that no announcement on the subject should be made until after the Presidential Election in the United States. Six weeks have elapsed since the Election. I have had in the meantime some conversations with the War Office, but I was informed there last Saturday that further progress must await the public announcement, the terms of which have to be settled with the Foreign Office.

May I therefore ask for an appointment to discuss this matter?[1]

Yours very sincerely,

76. To Viscount Halifax, London.   *London, [20][1] December 1940*
English: Draft: T.W.: W.A.

Dear Lord Halifax,

I have to thank you for your letter of December 18th, concerning the proposed announcement of His Majesty's Government's intention to accept the offer put forward by the Jewish Agency for Palestine to raise 10,000 Jews for service in the British Army.

I fully understand the desirability—indeed the necessity—of obtaining the views of the British Embassy in Washington on the terms of this announcement. I hoped for an opportunity of putting before you the Agency's own suggestions with regard to the draft. The communiqué is to provide the basis on which our men are to volunteer for the Jewish Fighting Force and offer their lives for the common cause. When we see the draft it may be that we shall have suggestions to offer, or alterations to ask for. If these meet with your approval, will it be necessary to refer the matter once more to the Embassy in Washington?[2]

77. To Henrietta Szold,[1] Jerusalem.   *London, 21 December 1940*
English: T.: C.Z.A. A125/187.

Your eightieth birthday is a day of festival for the whole House of Israel. A people blessed with such daughters cannot perish. I pray that you live to see the fruits of your work ripen and the children whom you brought from lands of oppression established and flourishing in the Land of Israel.

Weizmann

75. [1] Halifax at first temporized, claiming that he had to await the reactions of the Washington Embassy to the draft announcement (Halifax to W., 18 Dec. 1940; W.A.). He received W. 1 Jan. 1941, when W. repeated his criticisms of the draft announcement as amended by F.O. and C.O. (report in W.A.). See also No. 76.

76. [1] No copy of the actual letter, if sent, has been traced.

[2] Halifax had stated that the draft announcement had been referred to the Washington Embassy at the express wish of Lothian.

77. [1] Biog. Index, Vol. XIII. Founding President of Hadassah, leader of *Youth Aliyah*.

78. To Joseph Herman Hertz,[1] London.   *London, 24 December 1940*
English: Or. Copy. T.W.: W.A.

Personal

My dear Chief Rabbi,

Thank you for your letter of the 18th December, enclosing Mr. Mirelman's telegram from Buenos Aires.[2]

As you know, negotiations have been proceeding with the Government here for months past with regard to the raising of a Jewish Fighting Force as part of the British Army. There is reason to hope that a definite decision will be reached very soon, and it will then become necessary to raise large sums of money from Jewries in all countries which remain free. Deeply as I appreciate the action of Argentine Jewry, you will, I know, understand that in these circumstances any world-wide action should await a definite decision on the main issue and its official announcement. As soon as I have any information on this point I will write to you again.

May I perhaps suggest that in the meantime it might be useful if Mr. Mirelman would get into touch with Mr. D. Ben-Gurion (c/o Palestine Emergency Committee, 41, East 42nd Street, New York City), who will be able to give him fuller information?

With kind regards, and warm greetings for *Chanukah,*[3] I am,

Very sincerely yours,

Ch. W.

79. To Anthony Eden, London.   *London, 24 December 1940*
English: Or. Copy. T.W.: W.A.

Confidential

May I offer you my heartiest congratulations and good wishes on your new appointment?[1] I trust that a return to your old Department may bring you real satisfaction and the same success that has been yours at the War Office.

---

78. [1] Biog. Index, Vol. VII. Chief Rabbi, United Hebrew Congregations of British Commonwealth 1913–46.

[2] This, 14 Dec. (W.A.), had stated that the Argentine Jewish community was raising funds for a Jewish Air Squadron for the defence of Palestine, and proposed that the Chief Rabbi initiate such drives in all free countries. The Mirelmans were a family of industrialists and Jewish community leaders. Probably the telegram was from Leon, who was U.J.A. President in the Argentine.

[3] Festival commemorating victory of the Maccabees.

79. [1] Eden replaced Halifax as Foreign Secretary 22 Dec., the latter being appointed Ambassador to U.S. following the death of Lothian.

I am sorry to trouble you in the first days of your new work, but there is a matter pending in our negotiations of which you will be aware. When I had the pleasure of seeing you last at the War Office, you suggested that I should discuss with the Foreign Office the question of the terms of the announcement shortly to be made concerning the Jewish Force. On December 16th I wrote in that sense to Lord Halifax, who replied on December 18th saying that a preliminary draft of the announcement had already been sent to Washington for their observations, and he thought it would be better if he were to discuss the matter with me after those observations had been received.

I do not know whether the reply from Washington has come in yet or not. I would only like to ask you to give me an early opportunity of talking the terms of the announcement over with you before they are definitely settled, since —as you will readily understand—a great deal turns on the form which the announcement may take.[2]

With many thanks in advance, and the Season's greetings and good wishes, I am,

Very sincerely yours,

80. To Lord Lloyd, London.   *London, 26 December 1940*
English: Or. Copy. T.W.: W.A.

My dear Lord Lloyd,
Allow me to thank you most warmly for your very kind message and for your good wishes, which I sincerely reciprocate.[1] I can assure you that I don't feel that *you* prevent me from having a happy New Year! You have to administer a law which was passed because it was believed to be a necessity—even if a tragic necessity. It is being carried into effect in Palestine with singular harshness and energy, which latter contrasts markedly with the sluggishness shown in carrying out the Mandate. But I believe that one day all this will be straightened out, and meanwhile my one fear is lest anything should happen to prejudice the future. Whatever the temporary difficulties, I have not lost faith in the justice of the English people, or of our cause. It is in adversity that we are tried. May it be given to you to carry your work to success, and to enjoy the fruits of your labours in peace and happiness during the better days to come.

---

[2] An appointment was not granted. See No. 86.

80. [1] See Lloyd to W., 24 Dec. (W.A.), stating how much he had been impressed by the latter's remarks during an interview the previous day about the possibility of producing octane fuel from sugar.

Thank you again for your note of the 24th, which reached me yesterday. I shall of course be delighted to meet Dr. Whitby.[2] I have no holiday plans, and am here all the time. Next Monday, the 30th, would suit me very well, and if it is convenient to Dr. Whitby, I would suggest the Laboratory at 25, Grosvenor Crescent Mews, S.W. 1, which is very centrally located—within two minutes of St. George's Hospital—say at three o'clock. Without wishing to anticipate in any way the results of Dr. Whitby's enquiry, I would like to say how much I was impressed by your remarks last Monday, and by your note.

I am naturally not in a position to obtain a general picture of the resources and possibilities within the British Empire, but from common knowledge one is forced to the conclusion that they are immense, *if developed*. The British Empire could, and I believe should, be made completely self-contained and independent. Especially in regard to the oil position, I feel that what you said on Monday afternoon went to the root of a vital problem which may face the British Empire at some not very distant date. The danger to which you alluded became clear to me during the years of "the troubles" in Palestine, when the vulnerability of the pipelines was daily demonstrated. To think that the source of one of the most vital commodities required for our fleet and for other Imperial purposes, is *outside* the Empire, and under the control of forces and factors which may turn against British interests, and which at best will try to extort from the Empire more than their pound of flesh for the use of that commodity, seems to me to be utterly abnormal and dangerous.

I can only repeat here what I said on Monday last: we can make fuel *in* the Empire, out of products *in* the Empire, and I would be more than happy to collaborate with you, or with whomever you may designate, for the achievement of this great purpose.

There are some other problems in the same category about which I would like to talk to you when you have a quiet half-hour to spare. This letter is, I fear, already too long, and I will end it here, with the sincerest good wishes for a happy New Year.

Yours v. sincerely,

Ch. W.

81. To Moshe Shertok, Jerusalem.   *London, 26 December 1940*
English: T.: W.A.

Cable full report regarding refugees *Atlantic* giving particularly following information: One, numbers landed and transported. Two,

---

[2] George Stafford Whitby, b. 1887. Director of Government Research Laboratories at Teddington, Surrey, 1939–42; professor at Akron, Ohio, from 1942.

composition, provenance, age groups. Three, when departed whither. Four, whether embarkation passed quietly without untoward incidents. Five, whether sick and children exempted from deportation. Six, reactions refugees and *Yishuv*.[1]

Weizmann

82. To Lord Lloyd, London.
English: Or. Copy. T.W.: W.A.

London, 30 December 1940

We have drawn the attention of the War Office to the presence in Palestine of a number of Jewish medical men available for service with the British Forces; some of them are men of international repute, while many others have had considerable experience of Army and hospital practice. I understand that so far only about sixteen of them have been engaged by the British Military Authorities. No doubt many more will be required for the British Forces in the Middle East, and if in some cases the services of Jewish doctors from Palestine were employed, this might save the need of sending doctors from here all the way to the Middle East, when perhaps in the near future they will be needed nearer home. The Jewish Medical Association in Palestine will be glad to cooperate with the Army Authorities in this matter.

I would very much appreciate it if you could see your way to support this suggestion.[1]

Yours very sincerely,
Ch. W.

83. To Lord Lloyd, London.
English: Or. Copy. T.W.: W.A.

London, 30 December 1940

Dear Lord Lloyd,

I enclose a memorandum about the difficulty which has arisen in regard to the granting of Palestine visas to Jews in the Baltic

81. [1] Shertok telegraphed his reply 15 Jan. 1941 (W.A.). Exact number on the *Atlantic* was unobtainable. Approximately 1,800 had arrived at Haifa. Some 155 had been transferred to the *Patria*; of these some 50 had perished; the remainder of those transferred to the *Patria* together with their relatives still on the *Atlantic* (17 men, 24 women, nine children) were allowed to remain in Palestine. The *Atlantic* refugees were from Czechoslovakia, Austria, and Danzig. The removal of the immigrants from Athlit camp, and their embarkation on a ship for Mauritius 9 Dec. 1940, had been accompanied by unprecedented scenes of violence. A few of the sick had been spared deportation, but not the children. The *Yishuv* organized a general strike in protest.

82. [1] Lloyd passed this note to W.O.—see his reply, 7 Jan. 1941 (W.A.).

States and other territories occupied by Russia who have received Immigration Certificates from the last Schedule. Professor Namier has been in communication with Mr. R. A. Butler on the subject, and the enclosed memorandum contains the proposals which we have made to meet the administrative difficulties mentioned by Mr. Butler in arranging for the identification of the candidates for visas. I assume that the matter will be referred to the Colonial Office, and I should be grateful for a favourable and speedy decision. The position of the people concerned is causing us much anxiety; many of them are in danger, and though the Soviet authorities have been allowing recipients of Immigration Certificates to leave for Palestine, there is no certainty that this policy will remain unchanged.[1]

Ch. W.

MEMORANDUM
Palestine Visas for Jews in the Baltic States and
Other Russian-Occupied Territories Who Have
Received Immigration Certificates

Out of the Palestine Immigration Schedule for the six months April–September 1940, authorisations were sent to the British Passport Control Officers in Lithuania, Latvia and Estonia to issue the following approximate numbers of Palestine visas:

Lithuania	about 1,000
Latvia	,, 200
Estonia	,, 10

Before, however, the Passport Officers could issue more than a small proportion of the visas, Russia occupied the Baltic States, and the British Consulates in those countries were closed. It was learnt that H. M. Consul in Kaunas, who had the bulk of the visas to issue, had taken to Moscow the covering documents, and hoped to issue the visas from the British Embassy there, and it was assumed that the officials from the Consulates in Estonia and Latvia had also taken their files to Moscow. The Jewish Agency, therefore, made representations to the Foreign Office, the Colonial Office, and

---

83. [1] On 21 Dec. 1940 Butler had informed Namier of Government agreement to the immediate emigration of Jews from unoccupied France to Palestine. The emigration of Jews from Soviet-occupied territories was being held up due to technical difficulties, and the issue had been referred to the British Ambassador in Moscow, Sir Stafford Cripps (P.R.O., W 11773/3520/48). Butler informed Namier 8 Feb. 1941 (W.A.) that Cripps had established that the Soviet authorities would in principle consider departure from Lithuania of Jewish refugees rendered stateless from former Polish territory, each case to be considered individually. Cripps believed that the Soviets would release Jews only from Lithuania, and then only those who fell within the restricted category of Polish-Jewish refugees; and that Jews who were nationals of the Baltic States would be treated as Soviet citizens and would not be eligible for emigration from the Soviet Union (W.A.).

the Palestine Government that visas should be granted by the British Embassy in Moscow.

Included among the recipients of the Immigration Certificates are Zionist veterans, persons with capital in Palestine, a few hundred children and youths, dependents of Palestine residents, and trained workers *(Chaluzim)*.

2. We understand that administrative difficulties have now arisen owing to the distance from Moscow of the immigrants and the difficulty of identifying them, and fears have been expressed of possible impersonation of people to whom such certificates have been granted. There are three places in which the identification of certificate-holders might be undertaken: Moscow, Istanbul, and on arrival in Palestine.

3. Of these three places, Palestine seems to us the most appropriate and the most feasible:

(a) *Moscow:* Apart from the difficulty of transit, which you mention, it is doubtful whether the Soviet authorities, who are hostile to Zionism, would admit into Russia a representative of the Jewish Agency to co-operate in the work of identification. Moreover, it would not be easy to arrange for responsible Polish and Baltic Jews to help in examining the candidates for visas, as by admitting their Zionist connections they might compromise themselves politically.

(b) *Istanbul:* The Turkish authorities will probably refuse transit visas to persons not in possession of Palestine visas. Otherwise Istanbul would have offered certain advantages because of the presence there of Mr. Barlas, the Director of our Immigration Department in Jerusalem

(c) *Palestine:* It seems, therefore, that it would be best for an official of the Palestine Government to proceed to Moscow and to grant the visas after preliminary examinations on the basis of the material available there. On arrival in Palestine, the immigrants could be subjected to a more thorough investigation in which the Jewish Agency would be glad to co-operate. Our Jerusalem Office could arrange that, besides representatives of our Immigration Department, responsible Jews recently arrived from Poland and the Baltic States should attend and help to establish the identity of the immigrants.

4. The danger of impersonation does not seem serious to us, nor have any such cases been found in all our previous experience. But should any such cases arise, the Palestine authorities would no doubt deal with them in the way they deserve. Naturally, the Jewish Agency would entirely disinterest itself in any persons trying to perpetrate such a fraud, whatever their motive might be.

5. The Immigration Certificates expire on March 31st, 1941, and

in view of the highly precarious position of Zionists under the Soviets, which look upon Jewish nationalists as "counter-revolutionaries", we are anxious that these people should be able to leave Russian territory for Palestine as soon as possible.

6. We understand that Sir Stafford Cripps has been asked to ascertain from the Soviet Government whether they would be willing to grant exit permits. On Saturday we received a cable from Istanbul reporting that 238 Polish refugees, including 20 repatriated Palestinians, had arrived from Kaunas via Odessa—these are presumably people who had received their visas before the British Consulates had left the Baltic States. Still, their arrival proves that the Soviet Government is willing to grant exit permits.

84. To Moshe Shertok, Jerusalem.   *London, 1 January 1941*
English: T.: W.A.

All our thoughts are with you. May God give us all strength to endure our bitter grief for loved friend and colleague. Please convey my deepest sympathy to family and friends. Always affectionately[1]

                                      Weizmann

85. To Abba Hillel Silver,[1] Cleveland.   *London, 1 January 1941*
English: T.: W.A.

My heartiest congratulations upon your election as Co-Chairman with Dr. Wise of the American Emergency Committee for Zionist Affairs[2] and as Chairman of its Executive Committee. It is an event fraught with significance for our cause at this critical moment when the Zionist world looks to America and American Zionism for political support. I am confident that you will place unreservedly at the disposal of the cause your great gifts and the qualities of vision, courage and statesmanship which you possess and which the movement requires. Warmest good wishes for success of your work and cordial regards.

                               Chaim Weizmann

84. [1] Dov Hos (Biog. Index, Vol. XVIII). Palestine Labour leader and Deputy Mayor of Tel Aviv, was killed with most of his immediate family in a motor-car accident 29 Dec. 1940. Only his 14-year old daughter survived. His wife was Shertok's sister.

85. [1] Biog. Index, Vol. X. Reform Rabbi, founding co-chairman U.J.A., 1938–44; headed American Emergency Council 1943.
   [2] I.e., the American Zionist Emergency Council, which embraced all major Zionist

86. To Alec W. Lee, London.   *London, 3 January 1941*
English: Or. Copy. T.W.: W.A.

Dear General Lee,
   Very many thanks for so kindly sending me the note of our talk with the V.C.I.G.S. on Tuesday last.[1]
                           Yours sincerely,
                               Ch. W.

87. To Benjamin Middleton, Chichester.   *London, 3 January 1941*
English: Or. Copy. T.W.: W.A.

Dear Major Middleton,
   Very many thanks for your letter of December 30th which I received only to-day.[1] The "difference of opinion" to which you refer was certainly quite "unilateral" and I regret it as much as you do. Apparently Sigmund[2] thinks I am the War Office, and has been suffering all the time under this delusion.
   I believe you may take it that neither Evetts nor Templer will be appointed, and we shall then have somebody else. I think the appointment will be made very soon now, and the communiqué will also be issued shortly.[3] The two things hang together, and the

bodies in U.S. Formed on the outbreak of war, it conducted all those activities which in London and Jerusalem were performed by the Jewish Agency, which had no apparatus of its own in America—see Vol. XIX. In Apr. 1941, the Council formed an American Palestine Committee, which carried the Zionist struggle to Washington through the affiliation of some 260 Congressmen, from both the Senate and House of Representatives.

86. [1] W. and Namier, at a meeting with Haining, Vice-Chief of Imperial General Staff, and Brig.-Gen. Lee of the W.O. staff, were informed 31 Dec. 1940 that Brig. Leonard A. Hawes was selected to command the Jewish Force. Hawes was described as a first-class organizer who had won a reputation in the trans-shipment of the British Expeditionary Force to France in 1939. The issue of a communiqué now awaited settlement of certain technical details and the problem of American enlistment without forfeiture of citizenship, matters that were the concern of F.O. and C.O. The troops would be billeted in Cheshire, and retraining should begin March or April 1941. The issue of kosher food was to be dealt with by the Army and the Chief Rabbi (report in W.A.).

87. [1] Middleton was presumably a friend of W.'s son Benjamin, from whom the Major passed on regards in his letter (W.A.). Middleton was enquiring about the Jewish Force, and whether he should tell Gen. Gerald Templer that his candidature for command of the Force had lapsed. With the departure of Wingate, the Zionists had recommended two candidates, Templer and Brig. John Evetts, both of whom had served in Palestine and been sympathetic to Zionism. It seems that Middleton was acting as liaison between the Zionists and Templer.
  [2] Sigmund Gestetner (Biog. Index). He had a country house at Bosham, near Chichester. Nothing is known of 'difference of opinion', but see Rose, *op. cit.*, p. 179.
  [3] W. knew the identity of the Commander, which was still secret—see No. 86, n. 1.

changes at the War Office and Foreign Office[4] of which you know
have complicated matters for me at the last moment when I thought
everything was already settled.

I hope to be in Bosham for a few hours on Sunday, and think I
may then be able to tell you something more definite.

Meanwhile I remain, with best regards,

Yours ever,
Ch. W.

88. To Moshe Shertok, Jerusalem.   *London, 3 January 1941*
English: Or. Copy. T.W.: W.A.

My dear Moshe,

I don't want you to feel that I am simply sending you a business
letter—it is extremely difficult for me to write you one at all, knowing
how you must be feeling—and I hope the attached note[1] will give
you some, even if a very inadequate, idea of what both Mrs. Weizmann and myself (and for that matter every one of your friends and
colleagues here) are feeling in these terrible days. But I know you
well enough to be sure that you will wish me to deal, no matter in
what personal sorrow, with the problems in which we are all interested and which we have to face.

1) I have met the gentleman who brought your letter and had a very
long talk with him. The impression I have of him fully confirms the
characteristics you mention in your letter.[2] He and his friends were
much exercised in mind about the ship at Istanbul, and it is their
wish, in the interests of their work and of our cooperation with them,
that nothing should be done to harm the usefulness of the ship—as
they put it: "Not a single illegal immigrant should be transported
on it," as this would immediately be seized upon by hostile forces
as an excuse for ordering a complete break-off of our relations with

---

[4] See No. 79.

88. [1] Presumably a note of condolence following the death of the Hos family (see No. 84).

[2] Shertok's letter, 17 Dec. 1940 (Hebr., W.A.), described in detail the episode of the
'illegal' boats (*Pacific, Milos* and *Atlantic*), the J.A.'s efforts on behalf of the refugees,
and the Administration's concern for Arab reactions (see bridgenote preceding No. 63).
Shertok indicated that W.'s intervention had been instrumental in securing permission for
the survivors of the *Patria* to remain in Palestine, and described the brutality with which
the *Atlantic* passengers had been transferred, laying personal responsibility on the High
Commissioner. The identity of 'the gentleman' delivering Shertok's letter is not exactly known.
He was evidently in British Military Intelligence in Cairo—Shertok described him as very
close to Wavell and the head of a special organization which cast its net over the whole East,
with which the J.A. worked in close cooperation. Two officers meeting such a description were
Lt. Col. Simon and Capt. Hammond.

them, and they would have to obey any such order from higher quarters.[3] These higher quarters[4] are, I gather, somewhat suspicious of this cooperation in Cairo, and definitely hostile to it in Jerusalem. I would like to say at once that in Cairo these suspicions are not based on any personal grounds; there is great personal respect for you and the others, but they feel—I believe wrongly—that there may arise a conflict between Zionist allegiance and British interests as they interpret them, and that in that case Zionism would come first. It is no use arguing with the gentlemen here; they understand; but I am merely putting down the view taken in higher quarters at your end. I think it is a completely wrong view, but we have to reckon with it. They obviously expect from Jewry in Palestine something quite different from what they expect from the Free Frenchmen or the Dutch or the Poles, who have certainly their own national interests, and are still the Allies of Britain. But this is merely another aspect of the abnormal relationship between Jews and non-Jews with which we are only too familiar, and we find ourselves again in a vicious circle: the anomaly will only disappear when we have a Jewish State, and in order to get a Jewish State we may have to cooperate with these people.

2) This reflection brings me to the other point about which you ask, namely the Jewish Force. It is a long chapter of disappointment and frustration, and I cannot possibly describe it to you in detail— it would take too long. If we survive this crisis and meet again, as

---

[3] The ship at Istanbul referred to was the *Darien 2*, later to become the subject of a clash between *Mosad* (organization for illegal immigration into Palestine) and *Haganah*. Fearing the imminent invasion of the Balkans by Germany, *Mosad* planned to use the ship to transport Rumanian and Bulgarian Jews to Palestine. *Haganah*, in close cooperation with a 'special department' in the British General Staff at Cairo, 'Department X', planned to aid the British war effort by acts of sabotage in the Balkans, particularly Rumania. Unaware of the *Mosad* plan, *Haganah* in July 1940 sold the *Darien 2* to the British, and it was fitted with torpedoes at Alexandria for use in the Black Sea for the *Haganah* operation. The *Haganah* group was also to organize Rumanian Jewry in the anti-Nazi resistance, and ultimately to penetrate into Poland to organize a similar movement there. Although the British rejected the *Haganah* plan, the *Haganah* group acting in liaison with British Intelligence feared that, were the ship used for illegal immigration, this would precipitate a breakdown in their military cooperation. W. in London was likewise concerned lest the British lose faith in cooperation with *Haganah*. Accordingly, in Aug. 1940 *Haganah* sent a representative to Istanbul to persuade the *Mosad* to return the vessel to the British, but the plight of refugees already on the ship convinced him of the more urgent need to use the ship for illegal immigration. The ship finally left Istanbul in Feb. 1941, loaded with Polish, Rumanian and Bulgarian refugees, arriving at Haifa 18 Mar. 1941. It was intercepted by British authorities, and the passengers interned at Athlit camp for some 18 months. (See Moshe Basuk, Ed., *The Illegal Immigrants* (Hebr., Jerusalem 1947), pp. 305–06; Y. Slutsky, Ed., *History of Haganah* (Hebr., Tel Aviv 1971) Vol. III, Pt. I; Uri Milstein in *Haaretz,* 13 Sept. 1974, quoting an interview with David Hacohen, the *Haganah* liaison with Department X.) See also No. 256.

[4] Presumably the C.O. and F.O.

I hope we shall meet, you may have an opportunity of reading the minutes of our numerous meetings here, from which you will get some faint impression of the painful road which I have had to travel, and of the humiliations and sufferings which have brought us at long last to a stage where there is a real hope of success. The draft of the communiqué lies before me now. We shall try to alter it so far as we can where it needs it. A commander of the Force has been appointed, and the minutes which the War Office has sent me to-day tell their own story, and give you the essential details.[5]

3) America: I have been postponing my trip to America from week to week for two reasons: first I wanted to bring the work on the Jewish Force to a conclusion, and so we all felt that my leaving London might jeopardise the position in this respect. At present it looks as if this particular hindrance to my departure is removed. The other point which has delayed me has been my own work at the Laboratory—but about this a little later on. You may be interested to see a copy of a letter[6] which I sent a few weeks ago to Mr. J.M. Martin (now, happily, the Prime Minister's favourite secretary) with regard to the situation in the States. I have had a message from the P.M. through Martin to the effect that he had read the letter with great interest, has shown it to many other people, and has brought it to the attention of the Ministry of Information.

4) I am seeing Sir Walter Monckton[7] of the Ministry of Information next Tuesday, and propose to deal with this problem, and also with the general attitude of certain subordinate officials of the Ministry towards our problem—an unsatisfactory attitude in spite of the fact that the Ministry has at its head men like Duff-Cooper,[8] Harold Nicolson and Monckton himself—all genuine friends—and in spite of the many friends we have in the Cabinet. This is a fundamental difficulty which is new neither to us nor to you; I am always reminded of the old Russian proverb: "God is very high and the Czar is far away."

5) This brings me to the information which we have received from Palestine, and the attitude of the Administration there. We have taken due note of all this, but we feel we would like to get the question of the Jewish Force settled before taking whatever steps may

---

[5] See No. 86.

[6] See No. 74.

[7] Later Viscount Monckton (1891–1965). Director-General, Ministry of Information 1940–41; Director-General, British Propaganda and Information Service in Cairo 1941–42.

[8] Alfred Duff Cooper (later Viscount Norwich, 1890–1954). Cons. M.P., Secretary of State for War, 1935–37; First Lord of Admiralty 1937–38, resigned in protest against Munich Agreement. Returned to Cabinet as Minister of Information May 1940–July 1941; Chancellor of Duchy of Lancaster 1941–43; Ambassador to France 1944–47.

be necessary in order to remedy an almost intolerable position.
6) I would like to record briefly for you a conversation which I had
with Lord Lloyd on December 23rd, and which has a bearing on my
own work mentioned above. After we had discussed some current
matters, Lord Lloyd suddenly opened up a new subject, in approximately
the following words: "When our Prime Minister thinks of
the Middle East, he thinks only in terms of Arabs and Jews—the
Jews being you (pointing to me) and the Arabs myself. This, of
course, is not so, and does not correspond to the realities of the
situation, which is much more complex. For example, if one surveys
the occurrence of oil on the earth's surface, one sees, as the greatest
oil-producing country, America, whose resources are gradually
dwindling, so that in twenty-five years' time there may be no oil in
North America, and long before that there may be a very considerable
shortage. Of course, America has reserves in the South—e.g.,
Venezuela and Colombia, but the British Empire would get only
a very small proportion of them. What are the other sources of oil?
The Caucasus is, so to say, blockaded by Russia; the Dutch East
Indies are far away, and their supplies are small, while Japan is already
casting covetous glances at them; the European oil wells, e.g.
Roumanian and Galician, are much too poor to be reckoned with
to meet the ever-increasing demands of the British Fleet and Air
Force, and the other mechanised appliances of war. The only substantial
sources accessible to the British Empire are those situated
in Mohammedan countries like Iraq, Persia, and the newly exploited
oil wells in the Arabian Peninsula. In other words, this is the reason
why one has to keep the Mohammedan world sweet."

My reply to this may be seen, in succinct summary, from the attached
copy of my letter dated December 26th.[9] I did add, however,
in speaking to him, that I thought a really great Colonial Secretary
would bend all his energies towards making the British Empire
self-sufficient and independent in this respect, as in many others. It
is humiliating to see that, with all the immense resources at its disposal,
the British Empire has yet to wait upon American manufacturers
to supply it with the wherewithal to carry on the war, because
the British have completely neglected the scientific exploitation of the
wealth at their own doors. I added, too, that I could make the British
Empire flow with oil, but he would have to give me Palestine for it—
and this time without any ambiguity. He replied: "If you can solve
this problem, you can get anything you wish." He also said he would
like to send me an expert with whom I could discuss the matter. I saw
this expert to-day, and talked to him for something like three hours.

[9] No. 80.

I think he carried away a favourable impression. On the heels of Lord Lloyd's letter making this suggestion there followed another note asking whether I would not care to see Lord Hankey, who is the head of the Imperial Research Committee. I of course agreed, and have arranged to see him on Tuesday next. I thought you might be interested in this intermezzo. If there are further developments, you will know them in time.

7)   I realise that my trip to America has now become an urgent necessity. Our people there are still very far from realising the terrible plight in which Jewry finds itself, and which they themselves will have to face, even after victory. The position of the Jews in Europe has, in my opinion, been irretrievably destroyed, and when the pall is lifted, we shall find only remnants of misery and wretchedness. I dread to think of the problems which will then face those to whom it may be given to survive this catastrophe. There may be two communities left intact: America and Palestine, and more than ever it is essential that the community in America should now be made aware of the duties and obligations imposed upon it by the accidental privilege of its present security. Whether at this time of my life I shall be able to do this as I have tried to do it in years gone by I cannot tell, but I need hardly say that I am ready to throw into this work the last ounce of strength and energy that I possess. More than ever one feels the loss of men like Dov Hos, Arlosoroff[10] and Bialik[11] at this stage of our tragic history.

I shall therefore try to get away from here as soon as ever possible—presumably some time this month. How long I shall have to stay in the States will depend on the scale of the activity there and the prospects of achievement—which I cannot gauge from here. It is a commonplace to say that we live here as in a beleaguered fortress; but this will be merely a sally into a freer world, and I would wish to return to the fortress as soon as I feel I have done whatever is possible in the circumstances. I have no clear picture of what the new forces in the American Organization are doing, or are capable of doing. The *New Palestine* makes painful reading, and I hope it does not reflect the sentiments and moral outlook of Jews in America.[12] Kaplan's letter,[13] which reached me rather late, probably

---

[10] Chaim Arlosoroff (Biog. Index, Vol. XIII). Labour Zionist leader and disciple of W. Assassinated by unknown assailants on Tel Aviv seashore 1933.

[11] Chaim Nachman Bialik (Biog. Index, Vol. X). National poet of modern Hebrew literature.

[12] American Zionists were evidently resentful of the attitude of some Zionists who regarded them solely as a source of money. See, e.g., editorial in *New Palestine*, 1 Nov. 1940.

[13] Untraced.

gave a fair picture of the situation, and I fear that since his visit[14] things may not have improved too much. I do not know what Ben-Gurion has been able to do there.

Well, I hope these few notes, with the enclosures, will give you some idea of our thoughts, our hopes, our disappointments, and our troubles here, where working conditions are, as you may imagine, somewhat difficult. The days are painfully short; the nights are long. Physical amenities do not improve as time goes on. We in the office are only a handful, and somewhat in the nature of a polar expedition. Great care is needed in order to avoid getting on one another's nerves, while having to battle constantly against the same difficulties in an atmosphere of hideous destruction. Although we all face life with quite a good deal of courage, sub-consciously one suffers from the raids, and from feeling and seeing the tears and misery of others. At the same time, I would be unfair if I omitted to tell you that it is an elevating, a grandiose, spectacle to see this small country facing a ruthless enemy single-handed under the leadership of a man who is growing in stature day by day—and who, I am happy to say, is consistently friendly to us. Lloyd always calls him "the Arch-Zionist!" Perhaps his friendship has not yet found expression in as much action as we would have liked to see. He is too over-burdened with the problems of the day. But it is a comfort to know that he is there, and that we are in his thoughts. Without the Prime Minister, many things would not have been done, and it is through the knowledge that he would arbitrate in our favour that we have avoided on occasion what might have been very painful happenings.

I will end by expressing my ardent wish that it may be given to us to meet again in better days to come.

Ch. W.

89. To Mikhail Weizmann, Haifa.   *London, 6 January 1941*
English: H.W.: W.A.

Jan. 6th. 41.

My dear Chilik,

This is just a note to let you know that we are well: ‎ברוך ד׳ יום יום‎.[1] Benji, Maidie and their little son David, who is now 2 months old, are all well—so is Michael. Mike has been with us for 12 days leave and has gone now back to his station.

---

[14] To U.S.

89. [1] 'Blessed be the Lord day by day' (Psalms 68:20).

We, the old people, are preparing to go out on our mission to the U.S.A. and we shall probably leave some time this month.

I do hope that the success of British Arms in Libya makes the position in Palestine much safer and let us pray that it will now be definitely spared.[2]

If the Mediterranean becomes clear, as it may do, I shall try to get to Palestine. The organization of a Jewish Force, which is still under consideration, but I think with prospects of success, may bring Michael to Palestine.

I hope you are all well. When our departure to the U.S.A. becomes definite and the dates are fixed I shall telegraph to you and also give you an address.

Love to all from your brother,
Chaim

90. To Lord Lloyd, London.   *London, 6 January 1941*
English: Copy. T.W.: W.A.

My dear Lord Lloyd,

I have now carefully considered the terms of the "Draft Announcement with Amendments suggested by F.O. and W.O." which you gave me on Thursday.[1] I do not propose to ask for changes of substance, though the announcement contains provisions which seem harsh. All I ask is that, if their substance must be secured, the necessary steps should be taken, but that our people should be spared the proclaiming of these provisions to the world; further, on a few other points, I ask that the actual arrangements should be stated as they stand, and not in terms which are bound to cause uneasiness and to produce difficulties in the future. I want the man who enlists in the British Army in response to this announcement, to do so with love and devotion for Gt. Britain and her cause, and I should therefore deplore it if things were to appear in it which are bound to hurt his feelings.

2.   The first two amendments are of a purely verbal character:

(a) "...there are numerous Jews in foreign countries". I suggest that for "foreign" the word "various" should be substituted; we may expect many excellent recruits from British Dominions and Colonies which have not introduced conscription,

---

[2] Wavell began his offensive 9 Dec. 1940, and by mid-December had driven the Italians from Egypt.

90. [1] This, headed 'Enlistment of Jewish Units', read as follows:

in the first place from South Africa; nor can Palestine be described as a "foreign country".

(b) Instead of "oppressors" I suggest the word "persecutors"—the Nazi onslaught against the Jews transcends the geographic limits of Axis power and occupation.

3. "Jewish offers of military assistance", "an offer made in responsible Jewish quarters", "selected on Jewish nomination subject to the approval of the War Office". The offer was made by me as President of the Jewish Agency to the Prime Minister, and was accepted as such. In your letter of October 17th,[2] you wrote to me, surely as to the President of the Jewish Agency and not as to a private individual: "the officers being selected by yourself or your representative, with the approval of the War Office." All the arrangements are being made by the War Office with the Jewish Agency. If we do the work, I submit that we are entitled to be gazetted for it, and not to have our name and identity obliterated as if it was embarrassing to admit cooperation with us. Moreover, such vague phrases will in practice land the War Office and ourselves in endless trouble with people and organizations claiming to be comprehended in them.

I must therefore most earnestly and respectfully urge that these three passages should read as follows: "the offer of military assistance made by the Jewish Agency"; "an offer has been made by the Jewish

His Majesty's Government recognise that, in addition to the Jews who as British subjects are already making their due contribution to our war effort, there are numerous Jews in foreign countries who would welcome the opportunity of active service in His Majesty's Forces against the oppressors of their race. His Majesty's Government have had under consideration for some time the possibility of taking advantage of Jewish offers of military assistance within the limits of our manpower requirements and of available supplies of equipment. Opportunities of enlistment for combatant service have already been provided for Jews in Palestine in connection with the formation of Palestinian (Jewish and Arab) infantry companies attached to British Units in the Middle East. Apart from this, an offer has been made in responsible Jewish quarters to raise 10,000 Jews for service in the British Army, and this offer has been accepted in the following form:

(i) Authority will be given to recruit 10,000 Jews for incorporation in Jewish units in the British Army.

(ii) Not more than 3,000 of these recruits will be drawn from Palestine. The remainder will be drawn from various parts of the world, where recruitment is possible. Each Jewish volunteer will have to satisfy the recruiting officer that he will be readmitted on demobilisation to the country from which he was recruited.

(iii) The Jewish units, including their officers, will be trained in the United Kingdom, the officers being selected on Jewish nomination subject to the approval of the War Office.

(iv) The Jewish units will be liable for service in any theatre of war.

(v) Equipment will be provided by His Majesty's Government as and when their resources allow. The cost of the equipment and maintenance of the Jewish units and of their pay and allowances, will be borne by His Majesty's Government.

[2] See No. 51, n. 1.

Agency"; "selected on the nomination of the Jewish Agency, subject to the approval of the War Office."

4. Besides the Palestinian Jews who have enlisted in the Infantry Companies, there are far greater numbers who have joined the R.A.F., the Pioneers and other Auxiliary Forces, and I submit that they too deserve to be mentioned. I therefore suggest that after the words "attached to British units in the Middle East" the words should be added: "in the R.A.F., and in various Auxiliary Services. So far some 6,500 Palestinian Jews have been accepted for service with the British Forces."

5. Our offer, ever since December 1st, 1939, was of a Division, and it is a Division which is planned by the War Office. The scheme communicated to me by the War Office on November 22nd under the heading "Proposed Organization of a Jewish Division" speaks of "an approximate strength of 10,000", but the Appendix names the exact figure of 10,160: moreover, on December 3rd, I was told by the War Office that another 2,000 must be recruited as a reserve to replace possible wastage. Further, it has been arranged that the Jewish Force should be one unit, of which the commander has already been designated by the War Office and accepted by us; and that it should be trained as a unit and act as such. I therefore suggest that the first time when the words "10,000 Jews" are used, consistently with recorded facts, the words "a Jewish Division" should be substituted for them; that paragraph (i) should read: "Authority will be given to recruit 12,000 Jews for incorporation as a Jewish Division in the British Army"; that in paragraph (iii) and (iv) the words "Jewish Division" should be substituted for "Jewish units", or if a variant on them is desired, that it should be called "the Jewish Fighting Force", which is the expression used by Mr. Eden in our talks.

6. The conditions laid down in paragraph (ii) sound harsh.[3] But their substance can be secured without hurting the feelings of those whom we shall call upon to offer their lives in the British service.

   (a) "Not more than 3,000 of these recruits will be drawn from Palestine." We can settle that this should be so, and this agreement can be communicated to the General organizing the Division, and to all responsible Recruiting Officers. Without their cooperation the figure cannot be exceeded.

   (b) "Each Jewish volunteer will have to satisfy the Recruiting Officer that he be readmitted on demobilisation to the country

[3] This relates to the re-admission of volunteers on demobilization. At their interview, 2 Jan. (report in W.A.), Lloyd had claimed that the Revisionists had been saying that the Jews were going to use the Force to 'gate-crash' into Palestine.

from which he was recruited". The question does not arise in the case of Palestinians or British subjects, or any Jews resident in the United Kingdom or countries under its control. Nor does any difficulty seem to arise with regard to the United States, the chief country we have in view. Should citizens or residents of other countries apply for admission to the Jewish Fighting Forces, to satisfy this stipulation the necessary arrangements will have to be made with the respective Governments. Meantime, the Recruiting Officers can be instructed not to accept recruits from any country but such as will be specifically named to them.

7. It stands to reason that any man enlisting in the British Army is "liable for service in any theatre of war". Nonetheless, it was repeatedly stated to us during the preceding talks that it was the intention of His Majesty's Government to employ the Jewish Fighting Force, after it has been formed, in the Middle East, though no guarantee could be given. It would be pleasing to the Jews if this intention was stated in public, and it would greatly encourage recruiting.

Yours very sincerely,
Ch. Weizmann

P.S. I enclose a draft of the Announcement with our amendments inserted in it, as to show how it would read.[4]

[4] The proposed amended text read as follows:

His Majesty's Government recognises that, in addition to the Jews who as British subjects are already making their contribution to our war effort, there are numerous Jews in various countries who would welcome the opportunity of active service in His Majesty's Forces against the persecutors of their race. H. M. G. have had under consideration for some time the possibility of taking advantage, within the limits of our manpower requirements and of available supplies of equipment, of the offer of military assistance made by the Jewish Agency. Opportunities of enlistment for combatant service have already been provided for Jews in Palestine in connection with the formation of Palestinian (Jewish and Arab) infantry companies attached to British units in the Middle East, in the R. A. F., and in various Auxiliary Services. So far some 6,500 Palestinian Jews have been accepted for service with the British Forces. Apart from this, an offer has been made by the Jewish Agency to raise a Jewish Division for service with the British Army, and this offer has been accepted in the following form:

(i) Authority will be given to recruit 12,000 Jews for incorporation as a Jewish Division in the British Army.

(ii) The Jewish Division, including its officers, will be trained in the United Kingdom, the officers being selected on the nomination of the Jewish Agency, subject to the approval of the War Office.

(iii) The Jewish Division will be liable for service in any theatre of war, but the present intention of H. M. G. is to employ it, after it has been trained, in the Middle East.

(iv) Equipment will be provided by H.M.G. as and when their resources allow. The cost of the equipment and maintenance of the Jewish Division and of their pay and allowances, will be borne by His Majesty's Government.

The amendments were proposed mainly at the suggestion of Namier—meeting of London Executive, 4 Jan. 1941 (W.A.). Apparently Lloyd did not reply to this letter. He soon succumbed to a fatal illness—see No. 94.

91. To Sir John G. Dill, London.   *London, 8 January 1941*
English: Or. Copy. T.W.: W.A.

My dear General Dill,

May I begin by thanking you most warmly for your hospitality last Saturday, and for your kindness and understanding in these difficult days? I appreciated it more than I can say.

It seems to me that I shall be leaving for America about the end of the third week of January. As regards the situation which I expect to find there, you may perhaps be interested to see the enclosed copy of a letter which I sent a few weeks ago to Mr. Martin, one of the Prime Minister's secretaries.[1] Since then, a message has reached me from the Prime Minister to the effect that he had read the letter with interest, and has shown it to several other people. Only to-day I heard from Lord Halifax that he had read it, and so have Sir Walter Monckton and Mr. Duff-Cooper.

This brings me to the importance of the announcement about the Jewish Force which is shortly to be made—and especially to its importance in view of the American situation.

I am enclosing herewith, for your information:

(a) The draft announcement as it reached us from the Colonial Office.

(b) Our criticisms of it, as set out in my letter to Lord Lloyd of the 6th January.

(c) The draft announcement modified in accordance with our suggestions.[2]

Since you were kind enough to say that in case I should find myself in difficulties in this matter, I might turn to you, I am venturing to send you this material in the hope that you may find time to look through it, and, if you feel that you can support any of the amendments which we have suggested, lend us your help in order to get the matter settled as soon as may be possible.

I had yesterday a short talk with General Hawes—unfortunately he is not very well at present, so that we could do little more than make contact. But I found him a man of deep understanding, with a keen desire to do his best for the Force. He struck me as being really interested in the work. And so once more I owe you my heartiest thanks for having selected such a Commanding Officer for us, and for enabling me to meet him.

With kindest regards, I am
Very sincerely yours,
Ch. W.

91. [1] See No. 74.
   [2] See No. 90.

92. To Anthony Eden, London. *London, 9 January 1941*
English: Or. Copy. T.W.: W.A.

Dear Mr. Eden,

Lord Halifax mentioned to me yesterday what you felt about the announcement now under discussion between the Colonial Office and ourselves. I appreciate the fact that you do not wish to take any part in the discussion unless and until it becomes necessary, and I still hope that we shall come to a satisfactory arrangement with the Colonial Office. If, however, the contrary is the case I shall be reluctantly obliged to trouble you, and to ask you to make your views known. But believe me, I shall not do that if I can possibly help it. Meanwhile, for your information, I am venturing to send you herewith:

(a) the draft announcement as received from the Colonial Office;
(b) our criticisms of it as set out in my letter of January 6th to Lord Lloyd;
(c) the amended draft embodying our suggestions.[1]

I should be very grateful if at some time you could spare a few minutes to look through these documents.

Yours sincerely,
Ch. W.

93. To Vincent Massey, London. *London, 9 January 1941*
English: Or. Copy. T.W.: W.A.

Dear Mr. Massey,

With reference to our talk yesterday I am sending you a note of the main points about the shale deposits at New Brunswick.

I understand from Dr. Kind[1] (who is a Director of the Merlin Trust Limited) that he and some friends of his have for the past two years been engaged on investigating the possibilities of exploiting these deposits. The results of their investigations seem to indicate a possibility of producing motor-spirit, fuel oil, ammonia, and electric power in substantial quantities from these deposits. (Apparently electric power is scarce in this part of Canada.)

According to reports received by Dr. Kind, it seems that the New Brunswick and Dominion Governments are interested in this important industrial project, and a letter confirming this was received by one of the Directors of the Merlin Trust from your Private Secretary.

---

92. [1] See No. 90.

93. [1] Franz Kind (1902–55). Czech chemist; founding-director Manchester Oil Refinery Ltd. (now Shell).

Dr. Kind and his friends propose to send an Experts Commission to Canada to study the matter on the spot, and draw up a detailed programme of work. Dr. Kind believes that Mr. C.D. Howe[2] is informed about the matter, and his presence in England would offer a good opportunity for him to meet Dr. Kind's experts, with a view to their explaining their plans to him, and incorporating any suggestions or modifications which he may think desirable.

I need only add that I believe the Merlin Trust to be a serious and responsible body. They are doing good work in Manchester, where they have built up an important oil refinery now engaged on the manufacture of fuel oil for the Ministry of Supply. Their experts are, besides Dr. Kind himself:

Dr. Paul Rosin—one of the most distinguished European authorities on fuel oil; he is a refugee, at present working here as consultant to a number of important British firms;

Mr. Moore—a consulting engineer, who is also an expert on fuel.

Should this group come to a satisfactory arrangement with the Canadian Government, it would in my opinion be possible to establish a series of ancillary industries of considerable importance from the point of view of raw materials.[3]

Yours sincerely,
Ch. W.

94. To Lord Lloyd, London.   *London, 13 January 1941*
English: Or. Copy. T.W.: W.A.

My dear Lord Lloyd,

I would like to send you a word of hearty congratulations and good wishes on the occasion of your assumption of the leadership of the House of Lords—I heard of the appointment with real pleasure, and trust that it may not impose too heavy an additional burden on your time and energies.

I was sorry to hear this morning that you are unwell; I do hope that it is nothing serious, and that it will not be long before you are fully recovered.[1]

With kind regards and all good wishes,

I am
Ch. W.

[2] Clarence Decatur Howe. Canadian engineer and statesman. From 1940 Minister of Munitions and Supply; from 1944 Minister of Reconstruction; and 1948 Minister of Trade and Commerce.

[3] No further correspondence on this subject traced.

94. [1] Lloyd had contracted miloma, a rare disease of which little was known to medical science, except that it was generally fatal. He died 5 Feb. 1941. See C. A. Adams, *Life of Lord Lloyd,* London 1948.

Orde Wingate

Dorothy Thompson

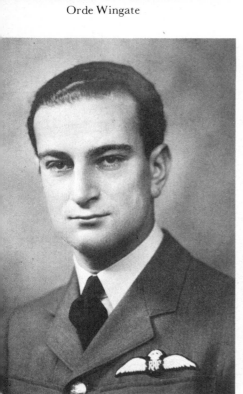

Michael Weizmann

Benjamin Weizmann

10, Downing Street,
Whitehall

18 February, 1942.

My dear Weizmann,

Many thanks for your letter of February 9. I understand your feelings and the feelings of your people in this matter and I assure you that they are not overlooked.

I am grieved to learn today of the news that has delayed your departure.

May I send you my heartfelt sympathy?

Yours v'ry,

Winston Churchill

Dr. C. Weizmann.

A letter from Winston Churchill.

In reply, quote: C.P.90

COMBINED OPERATIONS HEADQUARTERS,
WAR CABINET ANNEXE,
1A, RICHMOND TERRACE,
WHITEHALL. S.W.1.

Telephone:
WHitehall 5422.

9th February, 1942.

Dear Dr. Weizmann,

I enclose the letters which you so kindly said that you would take out for us. As you will see, they have been pre-censored, so you should have no difficulty with them.

The letter to Captain James Roosevelt is a letter of introduction to ensure your meeting the President, which should at all events facilitate things for you in America.

With Rollins's help I intend to continue the fight here, and if you will give me some really good "trinitrotoluol" to put under the vested interests, it may result in the unusual chemical reaction of producing toluene!

Best of luck in America!

Yours sincerely,

Louis Mountbatten

Dr. C. Weizmann,
Dorchester Hotel.

A letter from Louis Mountbatten

95. To Viscount Halifax, London.   *London, 14 January 1941*
English: Or. Copy. T.W.: W.A.

Dear Lord Halifax,

I am afraid that I may be intruding by sending you this letter, but I feel that it is only fair to you that you should be informed of the contents of its enclosures, since I fear that you may have to deal with the matters there raised very soon after your arrival in the States.[1] If that should be so, you might then have thought it strange that I should have kept such information back, and not warned you.

I need hardly tell you that I have thought the matter over very carefully, and have discussed it with our mutual friend Victor Cazalet.[2] I was very reluctant to trouble you during your last few days in England, which must, I know, be very crowded, but on the whole I felt that I had to pass the material on to you. Perhaps you may have an opportunity of reading it on board ship. It makes, I fear, unpleasant reading; and I would have given much to be able to change its character. But that was impossible.

With renewed apologies, and with my warmest good wishes for your journey, and for the success of your great work in the States,

I am

Very sincerely yours,

Ch. W.

96. To the Histadrut Committee, London.   *London, 16 January 1941*
English: Or. Copy. T.W.: W.A.

I am deeply sorry that a prior engagement prevents me from joining you today to celebrate the Twentieth Anniversary of the foundation of the *Histadrut*[1] and to meet my friends of the British and Palestinian Labour Movements. I should, however, like to associate myself closely with the tributes which will be paid to the magnificent contribution made to Palestine's upbuilding by the Labour Movement since the beginning of Zionist work there. The *Histadrut* is

---

95. [1] Unspecified, but probably extracts from Shertok's report of the deportation of the *Atlantic* passengers—see No. 88, n. 2.

[2] Biog. Index, Vol. XVIII. He was chairman of Parliamentary Pro-Palestine Committee, Parliamentary Committee on Refugees, and Committee for a Jewish Military Force.

96. [1] General Federation of Jewish Labour in Palestine, founded 1920. The *Histadrut* also sponsored a large number of co-operatives and subsidiaries, making it, apart from the Palestine Government, the largest single employer in the country.

so much a part and parcel of the life of the *Yishuv* that there is hardly any Jewish activity in Palestine in which it does not take a prominent share. One of its most important contributions to Palestine's development has been the education of Jewish youth for pioneer work, and its adaptation to the new and difficult conditions of Palestinian agriculture, and industry. Without the *Histadrut* the great colonising effort of the Zionist Movement would have been unthinkable. Its whole endeavour is based on a synthesis of two great ideals— national regeneration and social justice.

In offering my hearty congratulations to the *Histadrut* on the completion of its first twenty years' work, I would like to add my sincerest good wishes for the continuance and expansion of that work in the future for the general advancement of the Jewish National Home and of Palestine as a whole.

Chaim Weizmann

97. To Moshe Shertok, Jerusalem.   *London, 17 January 1941*
English: Copy. T.W.: W.A.

Strictly Private.

Moshe dearest,

Our friends[1] are leaving only tomorrow—I understand. Hence this note. The office is adding some of the latest material which might be of interest. I am most anxious to put before you the following problem. My departure is becoming a reality. The only thing outstanding is (a) the announcement which I hope will be settled within the next few days, and (b) some further discussions with Brigadier Hawes, the Commander who has been ill and is now on the road to recovery. The announcement is in Eden's hands at present and I am in touch with the F.O. All being well, I shall probably leave with Mrs. W. at the end of this month or early next month. I cannot postpone it much longer for reasons which you will appreciate.

I am not at all easy about leaving London in this depleted state. Although there is nothing particularly urgent or important on the agenda just now, except the matter about which Berl[2] is writing to you today;[3] but anything can happen at any moment. Of course,

---

97. [1] Unidentified.

[2] Berl Locker (Biog. Index, Vol. XV). Palestinian Labour Leader attached to J.A. Bureau, London 1938–45.

[3] Probably related to action to be taken regarding the deportation of the *Atlantic* passengers to Mauritius, deliberated at that day's Executive meeting (W.A.). Two courses were discussed: despatch of Wyndham Deedes, under cover of his work for German refugees, to

we had hoped that poor Dov [Hos] would have been with us, but fate has ordained it differently. Somebody must come here and come quickly! As Ben-Gurion is returning to Palestine, *you* should come here and stay while I am absent in the U.S.A. It is, believe me, most important and I would not have pressed it unless I was convinced of the urgent necessity. The office cannot be left in this state with only three people in attendance and without somebody important from Palestine. There is a great deal to do, particularly by way of laying plans for the future. It is not too early to begin now. I have spoken a great deal with various people about it and have gained the conviction that it is time for us to begin.

I shall see—I hope—the P.M. before leaving and shall put our hopes and wishes before him. He is friendly and has been consistently so. But *you must* be here. I cannot urge you strongly enough to follow my suggestion and please send me a telegram on receipt of this note.[4]

With fondest love,
Chaim

98. To Anthony Eden, London.   *London, 20 January 1941*
English: Or. Copy. T.W.: W.A.

Dear Mr. Eden,

In my letter of January 9th,[1] which I wrote on receipt of your message through Lord Halifax, I said that I would not trouble you about His Majesty's Government's announcement regarding the Jewish Division unless it became absolutely necessary. Lord Lloyd's continued illness has produced this necessity. The draft is not yet settled, and I am sure you will agree with me that this is not a document that can be drawn up without regard to Jewish reactions, for it is the basis on which Jews are to offer their lives for the British cause. I am sure that in a quarter-of-an-hour's talk we could settle the matter, and I therefore ask you to be so good as to spare me that length of time. I have to press this matter, because the delays have been so prolonged (the question of the Jewish Force was settled at

Mauritius to check the condition of the refugees and to collect evidence; and to forward to C.O. Shertok's indictment of the High Commissioner, a step which could damage still further the Agency's relations with the Palestine Administration. See also No. 101.

[4] Replying 4 Feb. (W.A.), Shertok doubted the feasibility of his coming to London. He did not leave Palestine that year, as he was in charge of recruitment, and liaison with the British Army in the Middle East.

98. [1] No. 92.

our Conference of September 13th!) and my departure for America has been correspondingly delayed. Now I *must* start in the first week of February. And as in my absence Mr. L. B. Namier will be charged with this business, may I bring him with me when you are good enough to give me an appointment?[2]

Yours sincerely,

Ch. W.

99. To Sir Archibald Sinclair, London.   *London, 23 January 1941*
English: Or. Copy. T.W.: W.A.

Personal

I quite understand about the message—I daresay I ought not to have asked you, but I was anxious to do what I could to support a campaign which is going to be vital for us. Please forget the whole thing.[1]

About the Army Co-operation Squadron, it seems to me that I ought, perhaps, as a matter of courtesy, to have a word with Brigadier Hawes about it before writing to you. But unfortunately he is laid up for a week or so. As soon as he is able to deal with business again, I shall see him, and shall then send you a letter at once.[2]

With many thanks for all your help,

I am
Yours ever,
Ch. W.

[2] The meeting took place 24 Jan. (W.'s record in W.A.). Eden said that the Government had been taken aback by the numerous amendments proposed, and no commitment could be given that the Jewish Force would be used in the Middle East. W. and Namier said that they would not insist on this point. As to the paragraph relating to return of recruits to country of origin, W. stated that the clause revealed the Government's suspicion that the Army would be used as a back-door into Palestine; but the Jews had no intention of using back-doors after the war, for it was not the 10,000 Jews in the army who would clamour for Palestine, but 16 millions—at least two millions would have to immigrate there after the war. Eden 'made a gesture of despair', saying he would call a meeting of the departments concerned the following week to settle the issue finally. According to W., Eden gave the impression of one who was carrying out a policy he had inherited reluctantly but faithfully.

99. [1] W. had asked Sinclair for a message of encouragement to the forthcoming U.P.A. National Conference in Washington. Sinclair felt that as a member of the Government he was unable to send such a personal message—see their exchange, 17, 21 Jan. (W.A.). Contrastingly, Amery, Secretary of State for India, felt no such compunction, and agreed to send a message (W.A.).

[2] In fact Air Co-operation Squadron—see No. 106.

100. To Eliezer Kaplan, Jerusalem.   *London, 24 January 1941*
English: T.: C.Z.A. S53/274.

Deeply resent your treasury's treatment London office by continual reductions budget without consultation Executive here. Impossible reduce our expenditure further without stoppage essential work which unthinkable present time. You reduced firstly from fifteen thousand to ten thousand then further reduction January instalment. Now hear that Zionist Executive arbitrarily refuse pay its quota one thousand. [*Keren*] *Kayemet* unpaid January instalment. Under these circumstances work here will cease. Though [we] may need more, insist you provide time being minimum eleven thousand taking over one thousand of Zionist Executive if they really [are] unable contribute, though unappreciate why London cut entirely [while] other Zionist services continue. Please urge Ussishkin instruct Anglo-Bank continue monthly payments five hundred seventy five.[1]

                                                          Weizmann

101. To Lord Lloyd, London.   *London, 24 January 1941*
English: Or. Copy. T.W.: W.A.

My dear Lord Lloyd,
    I feel it my duty to communicate to you the enclosed papers on incidents reported to have occurred at *Athlit* in connection with the deportation of the *Atlantic* passengers; as supplying a background, I add extracts from a covering letter from Mr. Shertok, and minutes of an interview of his with the High Commissioner.[1] Two years ago, I should have considered the alleged occurrences utterly inconceivable under British rule. Now, unfortunately, I have reason to believe the story to be substantially correct, though undoubtedly there will be divergencies in the evidence concerning detail.
    Obviously now the first thing is to ascertain the facts beyond any possibility of doubt; but the men against whom this most serious indictment is brought cannot conduct an enquiry into their own doings, nor pronounce judgement on them. If such outrages have in fact been perpetrated, it is essential that the responsibility for

---

100. [1] The London J.A. office submitted its annual budget to Jerusalem 14 Jan. 1941, anticipating £17,100. This was made up from contributions by K.H., J.N.F. and Agency Executive. Kaplan had earlier warned of cuts, but protests from London continued (see budget, and related correspondence including Kaplan to Baharal 13 Mar., Linton to Kaplan Apr. 1941, in C.Z.A. S53/274). See also Nos. 58, 240.

101. [1] See No. 88, n. 2.

them should be fixed. For if they become known, as they must, justice done in the face of the world can alone prevent injury to the good name of Britain and prevent the recurrence of such events in Palestine.

Yours very sincerely,
Ch. Weizmann

P.S. I also enclose a copy of a cable from Mr. Shertok dated January 15th and received by us on the 16th.[2]

102. To Herbert G. Wells, London.   *London, 25 January 1941*
English: Or. Copy. T.W.: W.A.

Dear Mr. Wells,

Ever so many thanks for so kindly sending me your book.[1] Inspired by the inscription, I have got into touch with "the firm" to see about the exchange of oranges and furs; I hope to see Mr. Maisky[2] in the course of next week.[3]

With kind regards, and again many thanks,

Ch. W.

---

[2] See No. 81, n. 1. Lloyd replied 29 Jan. 1941 (W.A.) that he awaited a full report from the High Commissioner, and until then would suspend judgement on the allegations made by Shertok's 'anonymous' eye-witness. MacMichael forwarded his own report to Moyne late Feb. 1941. He claimed that allegations of police brutality or drunken behaviour were entirely untrue, and that the operation had been carried out in a disciplined manner, with great forbearance and good temper. The screams from the huts had been part of a campaign of obstruction, and stories of blood and hurling bodies into lorries were fictitious. Reports that victims had died of typhus on the way to Mauritius were false, there had been some fatalities from typhoid, but this had been contracted on the ships proceeding to Palestine, due to the indescribable overcrowding for which the organizer of the transport must take responsibility. In the light of this information, Moyne decided not to institute the independent inquiry proposed by J.A. (see Moyne to Namier, 31 Mar. 1941, W.A.).

102. [1] Presumably this was *Guide to the New World: A Handbook of Constructive World Revolution,* advocating a fundamental world law of freedom and security, embodied in a Declaration of Human Rights. It was published in London Jan. 1941.

[2] Ivan Maisky (1884–1975). Russian Ambassador to Gt. Britain 1932–43.

[3] Wells had raised with Maisky the possible purchase by Russia of oranges from Palestine. W. discussed with Maisky payment in New York, with furs—W.'s report to J.A. Executive, 30 Jan. 1941 (W.A.). This came to nought, as Russia did not import any kind of fruit—Maisky to W., 10 Feb. 1941 (W.A.).

103. To Josef Cohn, New York.   *London, 27 January 1941*
English: T.W.: W.A.

My dear Josef,
It is quite possible that this letter will reach you only after my arrival in America, but as I am not yet absolutely certain about the date of my departure, I thought I had better send you a few lines, which kindly show to Meyer [Weisgal].

I have before me your letter of December 24th, and also your letter of the 1st of January.[1] Frankly they fill me with sadness. This is no reflection on your efforts; I am sure that you and Ruskin are doing your best, and that Meyer is giving you his best advice and support. But it seems that our friends in the States have not yet learnt the lesson which the last years have taught us, and you are compelled to run after people in order to extract from them small contributions for Palestine in the midst of this most critical emergency. I could say a good deal about this, but I will leave it till we meet.

You ask me about certain matters—e.g., changing the name of the fund in order to make it more attractive to the Canadians, or negotiating with Kramarsky's and Sonneborn's[2] representatives here. It is difficult to convey to you how utterly incongruous all these things look when seen from our angle here. If people want to support Palestine, they should do it without strings, and without imposing additional burdens on me. I would rather have the budget at Rehovot curtailed, (and let them go through some of the same difficulties as confront us here) than adapt myself to the point of view of those who live in false security, and believe we can deal with Palestine now in the same way as we could three years ago. These people simply cannot read the writing on the wall, and continue to live in a fool's paradise until the hour of their doom strikes. Then, in despair, they will search for a solution—and will find none.

This is also the reason why I have refused to write to Heinemann,[3] but I do not mind your reading this letter to him. I am sure you understand, and that Meyer also appreciates the position. I would

---

103. [1] Cohn had reported delays in payment of contributions to the Weizmann Research Foundation, requiring W.'s personal attention on his arrival. American contributions were short of estimate by some £4,000 (Cohn to W., 1 Jan. 1941, W.A.).

[2] Rudolf G. Sonneborn, b. 1898. Industrialist, in oil and chemical field; on Board of Trustees of National Petroleum Association. As a young man of 21 he had worked with the Zionist Commission in Palestine, later was active in work for Hebrew University, as well as Sieff Institute. In 1945 organized the secret 'Sonneborn Institute', which raised funds for *Haganah*.

[3] Dannie H. Heineman (1873–1962). Electrical engineer; director of a great engineering concern in Belgium. Active supporter of Sieff Institute and Weizmann Institute.

also like you to send copies of this letter to Ruskin and Nate Shapero.

All I can add at present is that the Institute is engaged on important work; to the testimony of the High Commissioner I could add a great many similar letters of encouragement. If that is not enough for our American subscribers I am afraid I have nothing more to offer them, except—if I may adapt the words of the Prime Minister—work, sweat, blood and tears. It seems to me that American Jewry is a long way from realizing that yet.

I can now see the end of my work here at least for the time being. The matters which have engaged my attention for the past year seem to have come to maturity, so that I hope to be able to leave very soon now. I would like to stay in America as little as possible and return here, for my place is here. But all this we can discuss when we meet. I send you and Meyer my best love, and all good wishes for the successful progress of your work.

Yours ever,
Ch. Weizmann

104. To Anthony Eden, London.   *London, 28 January 1941*
English: Or. Copy. T.W.: W.A.

Dear Mr. Eden,

May I revert to Article (ii) of the proposed announcement?[1]

In my letter to Lord Lloyd, on January 6th, I asked that, if the substance "must be secured, the necessary steps should be taken, but our people should be spared the proclaiming of these provisions to the world"; and further on I made certain suggestions to that purpose. If these are considered insufficient, would it be possible for your Conference[2] to settle other ways of securing the substance of Article (ii) without proclaiming it to the world? Surely there must be some way of doing this. But to us it is of the utmost importance that it should not be done in a way which is bound to hurt the feelings of our people throughout the world.

Yours very sincerely,
Ch. W.

---

104. [1] See No. 90, n. 1.

[2] Lloyd had in fact requested that the meeting be deferred until he was himself well enough to attend (Eden to W., 27 Jan., W.A.).

105. To F. Hoenigsberger, London.   *London, 30 January 1941*
English: Or. Copy. T.W.: W.A.

Dear Dr. Hoenigsberger,
    Thank you for your letter of the 28th. I enclose a letter for M. Masaryk,[1] which I hope you will find of service.
    With all good wishes and kind regards,
                                            Very sincerely yours,
                                                        Ch. W.

106. To Sir Archibald Sinclair, London.   *London, 3 February 1941*
English: Or. Copy. T.W.: W.A.

My dear Archie,
    You may remember that in our last talk you asked me for suggestions concerning the Air Co-operation Unit for the Jewish Division. I did not submit any to you so far, as I felt that we, who are not experts on such matters, could not venture on it without professional advice.
    Brigadier L. A. Hawes has now been appointed to the command of our future Division, and although this must remain secret until the official announcement is made, I understand that he takes up his duties at the War Office tomorrow.
    Would you feel inclined to appoint someone on your behalf to discuss the problem with Brigadier Hawes and Lewis Namier?[1]
                                            Yours ever,
                                                        Ch. W.

107. To Lady Lloyd, Offley (Hertfordshire).
                                            London, 5 February 1941
English: T.: W.A.

Both personally and behalf Jewish Agency for Palestine desire offer you our sincerest sympathy in your great sorrow and irreparable loss.[1]

                                            Weizmann

105. [1] Jan Masaryk (Biog. Index). Foreign Minister of Czechoslovakia, 1941–48. Hoenigsberger had requested a letter of introduction to the Czech statesman, hoping for a post in the newly-established Czechoslovak Labour Office in London. W. described Hoenigsberger to Masaryk as 'a chemist of distinction who worked for many years at the Aussig Chemical works in Czechoslovakia' (W.A.).

106. [1] The issue was deferred pending final decision on the Jewish Force.

107. [1] Lloyd died that day.

108. To Under-Secretary of State, Colonial Office,[1] London.
London, 5 February 1941
English: T.: W.A.

Behalf Jewish Agency desire offer you and H. M. Government deepest sympathy heavy loss sustained in untimely death great Colonial Secretary, most devoted servant Empire.

Weizmann

109. To S. Salman Schocken,[1] New York.   *London, 6 February 1941*
English: T.: W.A.

Sorry hear Mendelsohn may be leaving Palestine for another appointment. Suggest try utmost create Chair for him at Jerusalem so as secure his services for country.[2] Regards.

Weizmann

110. To Sir John Shuckburgh, London.   *London, 6 February 1941*
English: Or. Copy. T.W.: W.A.

My dear Shuckburgh,

I was very happy to get your letter of yesterday, with the good news of the remission of sentences on "the forty-three",[1] as well as on the four people remaining in prison in connection with the Ben Shemen case, and on six of the young men from *Mishmar Ha-Yarden*. I need hardly tell you how much we appreciate the action now taken by the General Officer Commanding,[2] the High Commissioner, and the Colonial Office.

Yours very sincerely,
Ch. W.

108. [1] George Hall.

109. [1] Biog. Index, Vol. XII. Publisher, philanthropist; Chairman Executive Council, Hebrew University. W.'s information came from David Werner Senator (Biog. Index, Vol. XIV), Administrator of the University.
[2] The Hebrew University was apparently unable to offer the architect a post and he took up a practice in New York.

110. [1] See No. 73.
[2] (Sir) Philip Neame, V.C., b. 1881. G.O.C. Palestine Aug. 1940–Feb. 1941.

111. To Winston S. Churchill, London.   *London, 7 February 1941*
English: Or. Copy. T.W.: W.A.

Dear Mr. Prime Minister,

I must begin this letter by offering you my most sincere condolences on the death of Lord Lloyd. He is a grievous loss to his country, and in particular to you to whom he was so loyal a friend and collaborator.

It distresses me to have to add to your burdens at this moment, but it is this very fact of Lord Lloyd's death which compels me to do so. The appeal of men in imminent peril cannot wait, and since the Colonial Office is today without a head, I have no choice but to lay their case before you. We have received a telegram from Jerusalem asking for our help with His Majesty's Government on behalf of Rumanian Jews who are now in danger of being massacred.[1] The cable asks us to urge a substantial allocation of immigration certificates for Palestine to be used for certain members of the Rumanian Jewish community, and for numbers of young Jews who urgently await assistance. Even if the policy of the White Paper, 1939, is to be strictly adhered to, there are still almost 40,000 certificates available. Many of the young Rumanian Jews coming to Palestine at present may be expected to enlist in the Jewish Fighting Force within the British Army.

As you know, mass massacres of Jews have already taken place in Rumania, with every circumstance of brutality exceptional even in these days. The number of victims tortured to death or shot out of hand already rises to thousands. What is happening exceeds even the worst scenes witnessed in Germany.

Thousands of Jews in Rumania are in a state of despair and panic. The question which is as vital to His Majesty's Government as to the Jewish Agency is whether this stream of refugees, in so far as it turns to Palestine, should be canalised and controlled, or whether every ship-load should become a problem giving rise to painful incidents which we all would wish to avoid.

Were Lord Lloyd alive I should appeal to him. Now I must turn to you direct.[2]

Ch. W.

111. [1] Following Rumania's identification with the Axis Powers, 23 Nov. 1940, a struggle developed in that country with the revolt of the Iron Guard against the government of Ion Antonescu. Violence ensued, and the Iron Guard in Bucharest engaged in a pogrom, 21 Jan. 1941, that claimed 120 lives, among them the Zionist director in the city. (Far more savage occurrences were to follow.) W.'s intervention was implored from Jerusalem to obtain immigration certificates for their colleagues in Rumania—his report to Executive meeting, 5 Feb. 1941, W.A.

[2] Martin replied for the P.M. 12 Feb. 1941 (W.A.), stating that while the P.M. had every

112. To Vincent Massey, London.   *London, 19 February 1941*
English: Or. Copy. T.W.: W.A.

Dear Mr. Massey,

Thank you for your letter of the 10th February with regard to the suggestion that members of the Palestine Pioneer Organizations and *Youth Aliyah,* interned in Canada, should be placed in separate agricultural camps.[1] I note that the Canadian authorities, though they have been able to provide a certain amount of agricultural work for individual camps, do not find it practicable to adopt the proposal made by Rabbi Wise, in view of the heavy overhead expenditure which it would involve.

I am shortly proceeding to the United States, and I hope also to visit Canada. I shall then discuss with Rabbi Wise, and other leading members of the Jewish community, whether something could not be done to overcome this difficulty.[2]

In the meantime, I should like to express my sincerest thanks to you for all the trouble you have so kindly taken in this matter.

Yours sincerely,
Ch. W.

113. To Osbert Peake, London.   *London, 19 February 1941*
English: Or. Copy. T.W.: W.A.

Dear Captain Peake,

I should be very grateful if you could possibly help me in the following matter.

We are just launching this year's appeal for funds for the Palestine Foundation Fund in this country, and aim at raising £75,000. We have invited a delegation of Palestinians to assist in this campaign, and three of its members—Mr. Leib Jaffe,[1] Managing Director of the Palestine Foundation Fund, and Mr. and Mrs. Theodore Kollek[2]—arrived here from Palestine a few days ago. The main

sympathy for the plight of Rumanian Jews, the High Commissioner in Palestine had to be consulted. Even were it possible to reconsider suspension of the immigration quota for Oct. 1940–Mar. 1941, there were practical difficulties to overcome. See also No. 118.

112. [1] W.A.
[2] No further discussion of this subject traced.

113. [1] Biog. Index, Vol. 1.
[2] 'Teddy' Kollek (Biog. Index). Then an official of J.A. Political Dept.

task of this delegation is to visit the various Jewish communities in the provinces. For this purpose they will require (as they are technically "aliens") to be exempted from the Aliens (Movement Restrictions) Order.

Mr. Jaffe and Mr. and Mrs. Kollek were accordingly sent by us to the local Police Station where they have registered, but they were informed that applications for exemptions should be addressed to the Home Office. I am, however, aware, from another case, that the Home Office leaves the question of such exemptions to the discretion of the local Police. As the campaign has already started, I am naturally anxious to avoid any delay, and I wonder whether it would be possible for the Home Office to authorise the Marylebone Lane Police Station to grant exemptions to the three persons concerned? I need scarcely say that I can freely vouch for their reliability.

Yours very sincerely,
Ch. W.

114. To Messrs. Fitzpatrick Graham & Co., London.

London, 21 February 1941

English: Or. Copy. T.W.: W.A.

Dear Sirs,

In reply to your letter of February 19th regarding investments, this is to inform you that, apart from the £4,000 which I mentioned to you as ready for investment, I would also like to invest a further £3,500—a total of £7,500 in all. I would like this to be invested in the following manner:

About £3,000 in Government stocks;

About £4,500 in Imperial Tobacco, Distillers, Tate and Lyle, and General Electric, as you may think best—or perhaps in all four.

The shares should be equally divided between Mrs. Weizmann and myself.

I enclose herewith two cheques, each for £1,819.13.3, making a sum of about £3,640. Whenever you require the balance, please let me know, and I shall send you a cheque.

I enclose the papers about Mrs. Weizmann's Indian stock; would you please let me know what to do about this? Would you also advise me about an investment for Miss Usher, so that she shall suffer no loss of income?

With many thanks in advance, I am,

Yours faithfully.

115. To Michael Weizmann, Limavady, Co. Derry.

London, 21 February 1941

English: Or. Copy. T.: W.A.

We leave presumably between fourth sixth March.[1] Would love see you. Cable whether possible. Best love.

Father

116. To Brendan Bracken, London.

London, 24 February 1941

English: Or. Copy. T.W.: W.A.

Strictly Personal and Confidential

My dear B.B.,

I hear from Martin that the P.M. is reluctant to see me—possibly for the reasons which you always gave.[1] I am still relying on your good offices to arrange a short interview for me: it is difficult for me to leave on a mission of such a character without really seeing him. (He is trying to refer me to Morton—but that is not at all the same thing!)[2]

I take it that you are reserving the last evening for us. Do let us know how things are developing.

Affectionately yours,
Ch. W.

117. To Richard Lichtheim,[1] Geneva.

London, 24 February 1941

English: Or. Copy. T.W.: W.A.

Dear Lichtheim,

I have received a copy of your letter to Montor[2] of January 13th dealing with the position of the Jewish people in Europe.[3] Knowing how careful you always are in selecting your material and verifying

---

115. [1] The W.s were due to leave London for Bournemouth, near Poole whence they were to take the flying-boat to Lisbon, and proceed to U.S. A note in W.'s Diary for 13 Mar. 1941 mentions Michael, but it is unclear whether they actually met.

116. [1] Perhaps out of embarrassment at being unable to hasten the Jewish Army venture.
[2] (Sir) Desmond J. Morton, b. 1891. Churchill's Personal Assistant 1940–46. A meeting did in fact take place—see No. 129.

117. [1] Biog. Index, Vol. X. Represented Z.O. at Geneva during W.W.II.
[2] Henry Montor (Biog. Index, Vol. XVI). U.J.A. Executive Vice-President 1939–50.
[3] Untraced.

your facts, I was a little surprised by your statement regarding the interned Jewish refugees here, and the attitude of the Jewish community. First of all, you are mistaken in saying that "nearly all" the Jewish refugees were interned. As a matter of fact, numbers of Jewish refugees, classified as "C", were not interned at all, and many of them were so classified precisely because they *were* Jews who had had to leave their countries owing to Nazi persecution.

Your second point suggests that there was no reaction on the part of the Jewish community here or of enlightened non-Jewish opinion. Both these assumptions are erroneous. The Jewish Board of Deputies, the Refugee Committees, and other Jewish bodies, made every effort on behalf of the interned refugees, and so did many leading non-Jews in Parliament and elsewhere. We did not let the Government or public opinion lose sight of the fact that the Jews were the first victims of the Nazi regime, and that, therefore, although they hold German or Austrian passports, they were not "enemy aliens", but were in fact allies anxious to help in the war effort.

I am sending a copy of this letter to Montor, so as to correct an impression which I am sure you would not have wished to create, and which more careful drafting would have avoided. With kind regards, I am

Yours very sincerely,

118. To Lord Moyne,[1] London.　　　　*London, 24 February 1941*
English: Or. Copy. T.W.: W.A.

Dear Lord Moyne,

Thank you for your letter of the 19th February, and for your sympathetic interest in the plight of the Rumanian Jewish community.[2] I am much afraid that, terrible as is their present situation, they have not yet seen the worst of their sufferings.

The difficulties of transport from Rumania to Palestine, and of identifying the emigrants selected, should not, I think, prove insuperable. The Turkish Government is granting transit visas to holders

---

118. [1] Biog. Index. He had succeeded Lloyd as Colonial Secretary.

[2] See No. 111. Moyne had written that W.'s proposal was not now practicable as Britain had broken off diplomatic relations and its diplomatic and consular staff had already left Rumania, which was regarded as enemy-occupied territory. Machinery for verification of *bona fides* of applicants for immigration had disappeared. Further, on security grounds, it was impossible to facilitate immigration from enemy or enemy-occupied territory (W.A.).

of immigration certificates, so that Jews from Rumania who hold such certificates would be able to travel to Palestine via Turkey. As regards the machinery for identification, may I suggest that the American Consulate-General in Bucharest should be asked to grant them visas? (Similar arrangements have been made for twenty-five children now in unoccupied France.) I feel sure that the American authorities would agree to do this if it were put to them that the granting of a Palestinian visa to a Jew in Rumania is, in present circumstances, tantamount to saving a life. Our Palestine Office in Bucharest would vouch for the identity and *bona fides* of each applicant. A second examination could be held in Istanbul, by His Majesty's Consul there, and in this Mr. Barlas, the Director of our Immigration Department, who is at present in Turkey, would gladly cooperate. The Palestine Government might also care to send an official to Istanbul for this purpose. Alternatively, the second examination could take place on the arrival of the immigrants at the Palestine frontier, and here, too, the Jewish Agency would be glad to help. I should like to add that the danger of substitution is very small.

I understand that about 2,500 certificates issued under the last schedule have not been used, and are available for re-issue. My colleagues in Jerusalem have applied to the High Commissioner for some hundreds of these certificates to be allotted to persons in Rumania who have already transferred their capital to Palestine in advance of their emigration. They have also asked for some 300 certificates for selected Zionist veterans, trained agriculturists, skilled industrial workers, and relatives of Palestinian residents. I should like warmly to support these requests, which may already have been transmitted to London for a ruling.

The tragedy of Rumania is so great that a few hundred certificates will serve to save only a tiny fraction of the people in danger, but the fact that even a few hundred people have been snatched from the jaws of death will keep the spark of hope alive in those who must continue to live in agony and suspense.[3]

Yours very sincerely,

Ch. W.

---

[3] Moyne replied 25 Feb. 1941 (W.A.) that he was consulting MacMichael. Further, W.'s suggestion of issuing new certificates to Rumanian Jews presented difficulty; but he was hopeful about those who already held immigration certificates. See also No. 121.

119. To Messrs. Fitzpatrick Graham & Co., London.
London, 26 February 1941
English: Or. Copy. T.W.: W.A.

Dear Sirs,
Property in Palestine, and 16 Addison Crescent, W.14.
With regard to the Will, I have received the enclosed letter from
Bristows.[1] The whole thing seems to be so complicated that I really
do not feel that it is worth proceeding with it. It will take endless time
and cost a lot of money. I should be glad to know what you think.

There is just one question, however, which I should like to ask
you. As you know, the house in Haifa is left in my will to my brother
Chilik. In case of Mrs. Weizmann's death, who would pay the death
duties on this house?

The whole question seems so complicated that it is almost impossible to deal with it by correspondence. If you think these questions should still be pursued, perhaps I could meet Mr. Crickett
again some time on Friday, or perhaps Monday of next week?[2]

I am, dear Sirs,
Yours faithfully,
Ch. W.

120. To Desmond J. Morton, London.   *London, 27 February 1941*
English: Or. Copy. T.W.: W.A.

Dear Major Morton,
I would like to thank you most warmly for your kind reception when
I saw you a few days ago, and also for the prompt action you were
good enough to take to help me get accommodation on the Clipper.

I am quite ready to leave as soon as the travelling arrangements
are definitely settled, though there is still one point which is causing
considerable anxiety. It is the continuing delay with regard to the
publication of the communiqué about the Force. Briefly, the story
is as follows:

About six months ago the Prime Minister gave his consent to the
formation of a Jewish Force. There were numerous discussions
both with the Colonial Office and the Military Authorities, and Lord

---

119. [1] This letter, from W.'s solicitors, had set out a scheme for establishing trustees for his
London and Palestine properties to obviate death duties (W.A.).
[2] The matter was left in abeyance (W.–Fitzpatrick exchange, 27 Feb., 1 Mar. 1941, in
W.A.).

Lloyd wrote to me confirming the Government's decision on October 17th last year. A little later on a Commander, Brigadier L. A. Hawes, was appointed. The War Office, the Foreign Office and the Colonial Office all informed me that the communiqué would shortly be issued. A draft of it was shown to me, and my colleagues and myself suggested certain amendments. These were fully discussed with Mr. Eden and Captain Margesson[1]—Lord Lloyd being at the time unwell. I was definitely under the impression that the whole thing was settled. I was also told, though tentatively, that I should probably hear about it before my departure for America, which was then set for February 26th.

I now hear that, for some reason unknown to me—perhaps the absence of Mr. Eden—the matter is again being postponed, and it seems quite possible that I may have to leave England without even knowing what form the communiqué will take. As it will be the principal instrument I shall have for securing the goodwill of our people in America, it would clearly be unreasonable if a formula should be imposed upon us which will not serve the purpose for which it is intended.

I hope to see Lord Moyne in the course of this week, and possibly he may be able to shed some further light on the situation. But I would ask of you most earnestly to do anything you can to see that the communiqué is settled as soon as possible, and to secure for me an opportunity of seeing and discussing it in its final form before I leave here.

Forgive me for troubling you in this matter; it is, I believe, not without its importance. The formation of a Jewish Force is a new and significant departure, and once the first division has been formed, there is no reason why other units should not be organized, provided that the British Government gives its encouragement. I understand that the question of man-power is now assuming great importance. We have still some seven or eight million people in America and in the British Dominions, also in certain Oriental countries. We might even succeed in getting people out from some of the occupied parts of Europe. A substantial reservoir of man-power thus remains to be tapped—and a reservoir of high quality. It all turns on the first step, i.e., the formation of the first contingent. I do not know precisely what has held up our progress, but I do sincerely trust that we may count upon your help to secure the satisfactory settlement of the last stage of the preliminary negotiations

120. [1] Henry D. (later Viscount) Margesson (1890–1965). Secretary of State for War Dec. 1940–Feb. 1942.

on this problem, which I am deeply anxious to see concluded before I have to leave England.[2]

Yours very sincerely,
Ch. W.

121. To Lord Moyne, London.   *London, 27 February 1941*
English: Draft.[1] T.W.: W.A.

Dear Lord Moyne,

Many thanks for your letter of the 25th February, and for your kind efforts in regard to Jewish emigration from Rumania.

I see that you have also raised with the High Commissioner the question of those Jews in Rumania who already hold immigration certificates. I did not mention this question in my letter to the Prime Minister[2] or in my letter to you,[3] as I had assumed that no problem would arise about those who were already in possession of certificates. This view is supported by the reply which I received from Mr. J. H. Peck of the Prime Minister's Secretariat, to my letter of February 7th:

> "So far as concerns the Jews in Rumania who already hold valid immigration certificates for Palestine (and who would, of course, be admitted into the Territory), Mr. Churchill understands that the Foreign Office have already been in correspondence with Professor Namier about the possibility of finding a ship."

After the outbreak of war, permission was given for the emigration from Germany and German-occupied territory of some 3,000 Jews who had received immigration certificates prior to the declaration of war. Verification of identity was in this case carried out in Trieste, and I am glad to say that no untoward incident resulted from this decision on the Government's part.

I do sincerely trust that, subject to proper identification—the proposals in my letter of the 24th February could apply equally to the holders of certificates and to new immigrants—the people to whom certificates have already been allotted will be enabled to leave Rumania, via Turkey, for Palestine.

---

[2] Morton replied 28 Feb. (W.A.) that he had already been in touch with Moyne, who would be informing W. of the position. Morton volunteered his own good offices towards a speedy solution.

121. [1] This letter was not sent. W. and Moyne met that day.
   [2] See No. 111.
   [3] See No. 118.

The request which I originally made was that, in view of the tragic situation of the Jews in Rumania and the terrible danger to which they are exposed, some hundreds of certificates should be made available for those who have already transferred their capital to Palestine (I understand that the applications are in possession of the Palestine Government), and also for some veteran Zionists, skilled agriculturists and industrial workers, etc., and that these certificates should be issued in place of an equivalent number of certificates issued under the last schedule, but not used, of which I believe there are about 2,500.

I should like to repeat this request, and sincerely hope that it may receive favourable consideration.[4]

122. To Lord Moyne, London.   *London, 28 February 1941*
English: Or. Copy. T.W.: W.A.

My dear Lord Moyne,

I would like first of all to thank you for giving me so much of your time yesterday;[1] I deeply appreciate it.

As regards the announcement about the Jewish Force, the lapse of time, and the many changes which have intervened, may justify me in trying to set out the facts in writing for your convenience.

Discussions on the formation of a Jewish Force have now lasted half a year. On September 3rd, 1940 I put the problem to the Prime Minister, who gave his approval to the idea of a Jewish Force as set forth in the attached note (a copy of which I left with him).[2] He suggested that I should get into touch with the Military Authorities and, the same day, I sent a copy of the note to General Dill. On September 13th, I met Lord Lloyd, Mr. Eden, and a representative

---

[4] The High Commissioner agreed to admit Rumanian Jews in possession of certificates issued before 15 Feb. 1941, the date on which Britain broke off diplomatic relations with Rumania, subject to authentication of identity and documents. W.'s proposal that immigrants travel via Turkey, and be examined by British Passport Control at Istanbul, was accepted. No exceptions would be made to the rule not to issue certificates to immigrants from enemy or enemy-held territory—Moyne to W., 4 Mar. 1941 (W.A.).

122. [1] No note of interview traced.
[2] See No. 33.

of the Foreign Office, and the outlines of the present scheme were then agreed upon. After this the matter came before the Cabinet, and on October 17th Lord Lloyd wrote me a letter of which I enclose a copy for easy reference. Everything seemed ready, but action was to be suspended until after the United States Presidential Election. November 5th came and went, but the delay continued. It was not until January 2nd, 1941 that we received a draft of the proposed announcement from Lord Lloyd, and on January 6th I submitted to him our comments on it.[3] On January 24th I saw Mr. Eden, and received the impression that everything was settled, barring Clause (ii) of the announcement. Even this I had thought was finally settled after my interviews with Captain Margesson on February 3rd and with the C.I.G.S. on February 5th.[4]

Meantime, the War Office had started work on the scheme. In November a Liaison Officer was appointed, Brigadier Lee, to conduct more detailed conversations with us, and the first plan for the Jewish Division was officially communicated to us on November 22nd. On December 31st, General Haining suggested to us the name of Brigadier Hawes as the Commander of the Jewish Force; we accepted his nomination with pleasure and immediately set to work with him to draw up detailed schemes. But the one thing which still holds up progress is the absence of the announcement.

I was therefore taken aback to gather from you yesterday that all the arguments for and against the formation of a Jewish Force—which had been fully thrashed out between the various Departments, and at interviews which I had had with Lord Lloyd, Lord Halifax, Mr. Eden as Foreign Secretary, Mr. Eden as War Secretary, and Captain Margesson—seemed to have come once more under consideration.

As regards certain points which arose in our talk yesterday, may I re-state some of my arguments:

(a) The Arabs: Lord Lloyd was extremely sensitive to possible Arab reactions. He was therefore opposed to raising a Jewish Force in *Palestine,* but as appears from his letter of October 17th, even he had no objection, even before General Wavell's victories, to some 3,000 Palestinian Jews being taken out for training in England.[5]

---

[3] No. 90.
[4] Haining informed W. 7 Feb. 1941 (W.A.) that his questions regarding amendments to the proposed announcement of the Jewish Force were concern of F.O. and C.O., not W.O.
[5] See No. 51, n. 1.

Without them a Jewish Force would be unthinkable, and as almost 8,000 Palestinian Jews are actively serving with the British Forces in the Middle East, it is hard to see what reasonable objection can be raised to the inclusion of 3,000 more in a Jewish Force trained in England.

(b) The Jewish Agency: It was suggested that the naming of the Jewish Agency in the announcement might arouse suspicions in the minds of our opponents. Suspicions cannot be exorcised, but must not be allowed to inhibit action. Unlike other peoples who have national governments, the Jews have no normal governmental channels. There is only one world-wide body representing the Jewish National Movement. It is, therefore, the obvious and appropriate body to organize the Jewish Force. It has its constituent organizations all over the world, and especially in America, and is in close contact with the younger generation from whom volunteers will be drawn. It has the machinery for selecting suitable applicants in various countries. The Agency will naturally cooperate with local organizations, but none of these has either the experience or the machinery to handle work of the scope entailed in the creation of a Jewish Force. Moreover, the absence of any explicit reference to the Jewish Agency would open the door to numerous claims, and would render practical work extremely difficult, if not impossible. Lord Lloyd, in writing to me on October 17th, was obviously not addressing me as an individual, but as the elected President of the Jewish Agency; it was as such that I was designated to cooperate with the War Office in the selection of officers, etc. Finally, I should make it clear that the Jewish Agency represents not only the Zionist Movement, but also a number of influential Jewish bodies in England, and important non-Zionist organizations in America and other countries.

One more practical point: General Wavell's Army includes at present roughly 8,000 Jews in both fighting and auxiliary services. They appear to have given a good account of themselves. The overwhelming majority of them were selected by the Jewish Agency, which is closely cooperating with the Military authorities.

You were good enough to suggest that I might see Captain Margesson again, and that you would say a word to him to facilitate my doing so. I feel sure you will understand my anxiety to see this matter of the announcement satisfactorily settled before my departure, so that the work in America and elsewhere may go forward without delay.

My journey to the United States has already been postponed several times by reason of the delays in issuing the communiqué, but I must go soon if I am to go at all. The Cabinet Office has telegraphed to Lord Halifax asking him to help in securing a Clipper passage for me on March 8th. As soon as we hear from Washington, I ought to leave.[6]

Yours very sincerely,

ChW.

123. To Alfred Duff Cooper, London.   *London, 4 March 1941*
English: Or. Copy. T.W.: W.A.

Dear Mr. Duff Cooper,

Thank you for your letter of the 20th February, regarding the Hebrew broadcasts from Jerusalem.[1] I am glad to learn that the local authorities have asked the *Vaad Halashon* to cooperate in improving the broadcasts both as regards quality and language.

What I had in mind when I spoke to you, however, was the scheme of propaganda in Hebrew which I understand has recently been worked out in London. An excellent poster has been issued, by the Ministry of Information, of the Prime Minister, but the Hebrew inscription is not correctly translated, and even contains some spelling mistakes. Hebrew broadcasts are also regularly given from London, but apparently they are not heard in this country. It seems to me that it would have been very useful had publicity been given to these broadcasts, so that Jews in this country, as well as in Europe and America, who understand Hebrew might listen to them. The Jewish Agency, which has had long experience of propaganda among Jews, could, I feel sure, have offered useful suggestions, both as regards the material and the language of these broadcasts, had it been given an opportunity of doing so.

---

[6] The departments concerned in fact held a meeting on the subject that day, attended by Moyne, Margesson, and Butler on behalf of Eden. Moyne wanted either drastic modification of the scheme, or a six-month postponement. His modifications were: to cut out all recruiting from Palestine; to make it clear that while the proposal had come from J.A., the Government would accept recruits independently of J.A.; and thirdly, to make it clear that the Force would *not* be used in the Middle Eastern theatre (see Minutes, 28 Feb. 1941, in P.R.O., F.O. 371/27126, E739/60/31).

123. [1] Following a previous complaint by W. at the quality of Hebrew broadcasts, Duff Cooper had replied 20 Feb. 1941 (W.A.) that the quality and language of the broadcasts was constantly under review; the staff of the Palestine Broadcasting Station worked closely with *Va'ad Halashon* (the Hebrew language academy). Further, criticism had greatly decreased during past weeks; the authorities in Palestine were alive to the 'importance of evolving, by way of the microphone, a real Palestine Hebrew which shall be a worthy vehicle of thought and expression.'

I hope you will not mind my drawing attention to this matter; I only do so because I believe it to be one in which we might be able to help.[2]

Yours very sincerely,
ChW.

124. To James A. Malcolm,[1] London.   *London, 5 March 1941*
English: T.W.: C.Z.A. Z4/20030B.

My dear Malcolm,

In reply to your enquiry[2] you will be interested to hear that some time ago I had occasion to write to Mr. Lloyd George about your useful and timely initiative in 1916 to bring about the negotiations between myself and my Zionist colleagues and Sir Mark Sykes and others about Palestine and Zionist support of the Allied cause in America and elsewhere. But naturally I could not very well refer to the fact that in 1922 it had been the intention of Mr. Lloyd George to recognise your valuable services in the War in this regard (and others). Unfortunately the whole matter has been lost sight of, but possibly it can be revived again. I do hope that it will, as appropriate recognition of your services would be well deserved.[3]

Yours ever,
Ch. Weizmann

[2] Duff Cooper replied 15 Mar. 1941 (W.A.) that the poster concerned had been prepared by Dr. Birnbaum, recommended to the Ministry as one of the best Hebrew scholars available. He would remember J.A. as a useful source of information. Further, W. was mistaken in thinking that broadcasts issued from London. (In fact, the broadcasts were recorded in London by a Palestinian Jew, Mr. Abrahami, of the London-Palestine Investment Company. The broadcasts were not heard in London, due to C.O. opposition, but flown direct to Palestine and transmitted from there, having first been censored by the military in London, and then by the Palestine Administration—see Linton note, 27 Feb. 1941, in W.A.).

124. [1] Biog. Index, Vol. VII. Armenian Merchant. London Representative International Armenian Committee in London. Worked for Arab-Armenian-Jewish cooperation.

[2] Malcolm to W., 27 Feb. (W.A.), requesting a letter testifying to his role in negotiations leading to Balfour Declaration. See also W. to A. J. Sylvester, Vol. XVIII, No. 427.

[3] A copy of this letter was forwarded by Malcolm to Brodetsky in 1949, on publication of W.'s autobiography, *T. and E.* Malcolm protested that W.'s book made no mention of his services, whereas a biography of Lloyd George had.

125. To Lord Moyne, London.   *London, 6 March 1941*
English: Or. Copy. T.W.: W.A.

Dear Lord Moyne,
I have to thank you for your letter of March 4th.[1] The decision
to postpone the formation of the Jewish Division for four or six
months is, as you rightly expected, deeply disappointing to us, the
more so because the difficulty of equipment has been present in our
minds from the beginning, and—as I said to Mr. Eden a few months
ago—we would naturally have awaited our turn.[2]
Indeed, the decision is a sore blow. For a whole year the Jewish
Agency have waited for their offer of cooperation to be accepted,
and now for six months we have been working on the scheme, and
the course of the negotiations had led us all to believe that the matter was practically settled.
As the postponement raises a number of serious practical questions for us, without wishing to argue about the decision itself, I
should be grateful for an opportunity of seeing you at your early
convenience.[3]

Yours very sincerely,
ChW.

126. To Moshe Shertok, Jerusalem.   *London, 7 March 1941*
English: T.: W.A.

Colonial Secretary's letter [to] Weizmann fourth March states
"Prime Minister decided owing lack equipment project must for
present be put off for six months but may be reconsidered again in
four months. Matters have of course changed very much in last few
weeks owing shipping and other difficulties[1] and I can assure you
this postponement in no sense reversal of previous decision in favour
your proposal".
As we are assured postponement not reversal we wish consider practical measures which would hasten formation Jewish force when plan

---

125. [1] W.A. For text, see No. 220.
[2] Churchill's decision was due largely to further objections from Wavell (see No. 122, n. 6;
No. 126, n. 2; No. 143; also Churchill to Moyne, 1 Mar. 1941, in P.R.O. F.O. 371/27126,
E739/60/31).
[3] There is a note in W.'s Diary for lunch with Moyne 11 Mar. 1941, but there is no note
of what transpired, if indeed the meeting took place.

126. [1] Preparation was then taking place for the campaign to aid Greece.

resumed primarily by training officers, NCO's cadres for Jewish division, which could best be done [in] connection with and if necessary under cover of Jewish formations already serving Middle East. Propose. making this suggestion to Moyne within next few days. Suggest you go Cairo see Smuts, Eden, Dill, Wavell.[2]

Weizmann

127. To Christopher Eastwood, London.   *London, 10 March 1941*
English: Or. Copy. T.W.: W.A.

My dear Eastwood,
   The enclosed copy of the American "Jewish Frontier" has just reached us. I have marked an article of Hayim Greenberg's, which I think it might be useful if Lord Moyne could find a moment to read before our lunch tomorrow.[1] Greenberg is a responsible person, and has considerable influence in American Labour circles.

Very sincerely yours,

Enclosure.

[2] Shertok spent two weeks in Cairo, reporting back 6 Apr. 1941 to J.A. Executive in Jerusalem. He was not received by Eden or Dill, but had meetings with Wavell and the General Staff. Wavell repeated the argument that delay was due to shortage of equipment, but Shertok claimed that it was not logical that this should only now be realised, after a commander had been appointed and a draft announcement prepared. He felt that efforts to persuade the Cairo authorities were pointless, for it was from there that opposition had ultimately come. Shertok had therefore confined his efforts to seeking to persuade the General Staff to concentrate the Jews scattered among various units, and to form a specifically Jewish unit from the Palestine Buffs. Wavell replied that he would consider this, but while he fully understood the Jews' position, they had to understand that of the British. Shertok also sought the appointment of more Jewish officers (J.A. Executive Minutes, C.Z.A. Vol. 33, 11). Shertok's letter to W. of 17 Dec. 1940 (see No. 88, n. 2) stated that so far 20 Jewish officers had been gazetted.

127. [1] Feb. 1941 issue of this New York monthly, founded by the Labour League for Palestine, with article by the Editor. Basing itself on a letter smuggled out of Palestine, the article censured the Palestine Government as the worst kind of colonial administration, specifying limits on freedom of expression, distrust of the Jews as material for the army, restriction on land purchases, and brutal treatment of 'illegal' immigrants. It condemned the 'systematic and brutally executed liquidation of Zionism', that ensured that the White Paper remained inviolate.

128. To Moshe Shertok, Jerusalem.   London, 12 March 1941
English: T.: W.A.

Secret saw Prime Minister who very cordial confirmed that only postponed and said that he would see it through[1]

Weizmann

129. To Sigmund Gestetner,[1] London.   Bournemouth, 15 March 1941
English: H.W.: W.A.

March 15th. 41.

My dear Sig,

I enclose an envelope containing a brief but accurate record of what the P.M. has told me when I saw him at 10 Downing Street on Wednesday March 12th.[2] This envelope is to be opened in case something happens to us on our trip to U.S.A. and back.

I would like to thank you most heartily for all your kindness to us and to our children and for your thoughtfulness in coming here to see us off. It made the departure ever so much easier. We both send our love and *au revoir*.

Affectionately,
Chaim

ENCLOSURE
Bournemouth, 13 March 1941

The meeting with the P.M. which took place on the 12th about 3.30 p.m. at 10 Downing Street came as a surprise. I was talking to Mr. Brendan Bracken and then Martin appeared and announced to me that the P.M. would see me for a few minutes. The gist of the conversation is recorded in the Minutes of the Executive, but the most important part was not revealed by me to the whole of the Executive. I did tell it to Victor Cazalet, to Berl Locker, to Linton and to yourself recently: at the end of our conversation the P.M. said that he was thinking of a settlement between us and the Arabs after the war. The man with whom we should come to an agreement is Ibn Saoud.[3] He, the P.M., would see to it and would use his good offices. I.S. would be made the Lord of the Arab countries, the "Boss

128. [1] See No. 129.

129. [1] Biog. Index. Industrialist, close friend of W.
[2] According to the Minutes in W.A., the Prime Minister told W. that they had no need of a long conversation, as their thoughts were 99 per cent the same. Churchill added that whenever he saw W. it gave him 'a twist in his heart'. He concluded that he had had to postpone the Force as he had to postpone many other things, but that he would not let W. down.
[3] Ibn Saud, Abdul Aziz, king of Saudi Arabia (Biog. Index, Vol. XVIII).

of the Bosses" as he put it. But "he would have to agree with Weizmann" (he put it that way) with regard to Palestine. "I will see you
through", the P.M. said. I swear to the truth of this statement.

Ch. Weizmann

[W. left England on 15 Mar. 1941 for Lisbon, and after some days there he and
V.W. flew to New York, arriving on 22 Mar. They spent four months in America, including three days (8–11 May) in Canada. Many letters, not reproduced, were
notes of thanks to his hosts. For full reports of his impressions, see Nos. 152, 153.]

130. To Henry Morgenthau, Jr.,[1] [? Washington.]

New York, 5 April 1941

English: Copy. T.W.: W.A.

Please accept my heartfelt thanks for having given me the great
opportunity of discussing our difficult problem with you.[2] Your
encouragement and your advice are so valuable and so important at
this critical juncture in the life of the Jewish people, that I can
scarcely find words to give expression to the deep emotion which I
experienced yesterday.

I do sincerely trust that my somewhat cautious approach to the
problem which you have adumbrated will not be misunderstood by
you, as I am sure you realise the delicate position in which I find myself, in the dual capacity of a British citizen and of leader of a world
movement. We all are animated by one urgent desire: to win the
war; and I have to be extremely careful not to do anything which
may possibly be interpreted as embarrassing to my Government,
and particularly as irritating to Mr. Churchill, who is a friend of our
people and who will, I am sure, as I had mentioned to you, do his
utmost to bring about a satisfactory settlement of the Palestine problem. By "satisfactory settlement" I understand the same thing as
you do, namely, the possibility of absorbing, in a reasonably short
time, something like three million people. Nevertheless, you may
rest assured that I shall do my best to impress upon Lord Halifax,
and of course, upon the President, when I have the honour of seeing
him, the urgent necessity of doing something now to relieve the
pressure on our people in the countries of distress.

It is, in my humble opinion, providential that you should be called
at this time to a post of such magnitude and importance; and, ani-

130. [1] Biog. Index. U.S. Secretary of Treasury 1934–45.
[2] No record of the interview traced, but it may be presumed that the 'difficult problem'
discussed was that of gaining British agreement to raise a Jewish Army.

mated as you are by a sincere desire of helping our people, you will, I am sure, with God's help, succeed in this great task ahead.

At some future time, when I have found my bearings in this country, and after I have had an opportunity of making closer contacts with events and of listening to opinions in the Jewish Community, you will, I hope, be able to spare a little more of your time for another conversation at your convenience.

I remain, with many thanks and kind regards,

131. To Arthur Lourie, New York. *New York, 6 April 1941*
English: Or. Copy. T.W.: Photostat W.A.

My dear Arthur,

You remember my having reported to the Emergency Committee[1] with regard to a letter which had to be written to Mr. Henry Monsky[2] of the *Bnai Brith*[3] on the question of the enlargement of the Jewish Agency. I think it would be best if your committee[4] would draft a letter as soon as possible and perhaps send on the draft to me here, as I would not like to write anything which would not be entirely in accordance with the wishes of the committee. Please do not postpone the matter as I would like to send off the letter to Monsky at the very earliest opportunity.[5]

I had an excellent talk with Morgenthau Friday night. You have already received the copy of my letter of acknowledgement to him.[6]

Affectionately yours,

132. To Henry Monsky, Omaha. *New York, 8 April 1941*
English: T.W.: Photostat W.A.

Let me first thank you once more for your very kind hospitality, and for the generous support extended to me by you and your organization during my recent visit to Chicago. It was a source of great

---

131. [1] The American Zionist Emergency Committee (Council after 1943).

[2] 1890–1947. Lawyer, American communal leader; National President of *Bnai Brith* 1938–47.

[3] Oldest and largest Jewish service organization, established in U.S. 1843.

[4] Lourie had come from the J.A. London office to act as Secretary of the committee in New York.

[5] See No. 134.

[6] No. 130.

satisfaction to me to be able to spend those two days with you and to have the opportunity of seeing you in action.

You will remember that I promised to write you two letters, one regarding the Jewish Agency, and the other concerning the Daniel Sieff Research Institute. I have had a full discussion of the problem of the Jewish Agency with our Emergency Committee in New York, and the promised letter will follow in a few days.[1]

At this time, I would like to give you some data regarding the Institute, its possibilities and its future. You will have gathered, from the pamphlet which I left with you, that the Institute was founded by the Marks and Sieff families, which have contributed almost the entire amount of money required for the building and equipment, as well as for the cost of building a clubhouse, which serves as a meeting and recreation center for the staff. Up to date I should estimate, roughly, that about $300,000 were expended for the building and equipment. The budget of the Institute has expanded gradually, and amounts to about £20,000.0.0 at this time; and it will continue to rise due to the new requirements inherent in the development of the institution and also owing to the emergency situation arising out of the war.

It is believed, therefore, that about $100,000 will be required to meet the budgetary needs. Up to 1940, the budget was covered by contributions primarily from Europe, so there was no need to appeal to our American friends. Messrs. Marks and Sieff have always carried, and are still carrying, a considerable part of the budget. The balance comes from various institutions and individuals in Europe. Since the outbreak of the war, the European income, with the exception of that portion derived from England, has practically disappeared.

It is not likely that the European contributions, or that even the English remittances, will be repeated in 1941, with the exception of those made by the Sieff and Marks family, so that I fear that almost 75% of the budget will have to be raised in America.

I have always striven, in order to place the future of the Institute on a solid foundation, to obtain contributions from institutions rather than from individuals, and this emboldens me to ask your very kind cooperation. Should you agree—as I hope you do—to place before your Executive the suggestion that the *Bnai Brith* contribute towards the budget of the Institute something in the nature of $15,000 for the next five years, your organization will be instrumental in helping to maintain one of the most important institutions in Palestine.

132. [1] No. 134.

Supplementing the statement embodied in the pamphlet, I would like to say that the rapid development of the Institute is in direct response to the increasing and urgent needs of the country. Its researches cover the fields of general chemistry, biological chemistry, technical chemistry, chemical botany—all problems which are closely allied with the developments of war. Owing to the requirements created by the war situation, the Institute is engaged at present in the elaboration of three major problems of technical importance, which have already yielded practical results and will, I am sure, constitute a contribution to the war effort, namely:

1) Fermentation of starches and sugar in various parts of the British Empire.

2) Conversion of oil residues as obtainable in the refinery of Haifa and elsewhere into essential material required for the war, and

3) The manufacture of drugs and pharmaceuticals for the requirements of the army and civil population in the Middle East.

Apart from these problems the Institute is engaged in purely scientific research which is published in the scientific journals in England and America.

Since the war there has been a great scarcity of drugs in the entire Middle East and even in India, as this trade has been wholly in the hands of the Germans, and has therefore at present practically disappeared. We have been concentrating our energies on replacing, to some degree, the deficiency thus created, and have actually built a small factory attached to the Institute, so that in connection with a very important English pharmaceutical firm, we are beginning to place on the market drugs otherwise unobtainable. These drugs have been tested by the authorities in London and found satisfactory, and were we provided with sufficient funds, and were we not handicapped by difficulties of shipping and transport, we could manufacture and sell four or five times more than the supplies which we are now producing, and we would cover a market extending from Egypt to India, India included. A representative of the Institute participated in the Eastern Conference held in New Delhi, and my statement is based on his report. The small factory which we have built, and which is already operating, although not as yet at its full capacity, has been created by means of a fund of £20,000.0.0 placed at the disposal of the Institute by Mr. Daniel Wolf of Amsterdam.[2] I enclose a photograph of the new factory, and as it is the only copy which I possess I would be grateful if you would kindly return it to me after you have viewed it. I believe that I make no overstatement

[2] See No. 21, n. 6.

when I say that the scientific and technical attainments of the Institute, young as it is, can be safely classified with the performance of similar important institutions in Europe and America; and I am looking forward to a time when the Daniel Sieff Institute, supported and strengthened as it will be by the generosity of the Jewish Community in America, will not only occupy a position of prominence in the scientific world, but will play a leading part in the up-building of Palestine.

In conclusion I would like to remark that we have located the institution in Rehovoth because it is the home of the Agricultural Research Station, which is primarily responsible for the colonizing activity of the Jewish Agency in the last 20 years; and both institutions, working in close collaboration, are rapidly becoming the guide and instructor of our population in matters of agricultural and technical development.

I hope that these few remarks will be sufficient to present to you and to your colleagues the nature of the work in the Daniel Sieff Institute, which I trust will commend itself to the generosity of your organization.

I remain, my dear Mr. Monsky, with kind regards,

Ch. W.

133. To Louis E. Levinthal,[1] Philadelphia.   *New York, 10 April 1941*
English: T.W.: Photostat W.A.

My dear Judge,

This is just a line of thanks for your telegram, and also to send you and your father, and the rest of the family my heartiest good wishes for Pesach.[2] I would like to see you in the near future, when you happen to be in New York, where I expect to remain for the rest of Pesach.

I am somewhat worried and disappointed in our Philadelphia friends that they did not live up to the promise which they gave me in the course of my visit last year with regard to the Rehovot Institute. I did very much rely on your support, and the fact that it was not fully forthcoming has become a source of difficulty. I do appreciate that in your position it may not be easy to press for the payment of money, but our friends in Philadelphia must have fallen

---

133. [1] Biog. Index. Elected Z.O.A. President in 1941.

[2] His father, Rabbi Bernard Louis Levinthal (1865–1952), was a founder of the Union of Orthodox Rabbis of America in 1902, and of American *Mizrachi*.

down on the job (to use an American expression). I should feel extremely grateful and gratified if an effort could be made to send some money to the Rehovot Institute for and during Passover. Please let me know at your earliest convenience what could be done in this respect, as I have always held Philadelphia in such high regard that I would not wish to associate its name with a disappointment.

With cordial regards and all good wishes I am

Yours sincerely,

134. To Henry Monsky, Omaha.   *New York, 11 April 1941*
English: T.W.: Photostat W.A.

My dear Monsky,

I have been thinking a good deal about the problems which we discussed[1] and I have naturally consulted my American colleagues with respect to them.

We all agreed on the desirability of strengthening and perhaps widening the framework of the Jewish Agency, and I am going into the matter further with a view to determining how best to set about it. Before reaching a decision it is important that I should speak to the leading non-Zionist members of the Agency in this country, and I propose to do this in the very near future.[2]

I hope to see you again before long. With cordial greetings, I am

Yours sincerely,
Chaim Weizmann

135. To Israel Goldstein,[1] New York.   *New York, 14 April 1941*
English: T.W.: Photostat W.A.

Dear Dr. Goldstein,

It was a source of deep satisfaction to me to have had the opportunity to attend the Triennial Convention of *Bnai Brith* in Chicago and to meet the leaders and delegates of the great Jewish fraternal organization.

I was naturally particularly happy that they should have chosen

134. [1] See No. 132.
     [2] See No. 138.

135. [1] Biog. Index, Vol. XVII. Conservative Rabbi; President J.N.F. of America 1933–43.

to mark the occasion by voting to contribute the sum of $100,000 to the Jewish National Fund to make possible the establishment of a colony in Palestine, in honour of Henry Monsky, President of *Bnai Brith*, thus duplicating a similar contribution made by them five years before in behalf of Palestine.

Today, more than one hundred families, among them the sons and daughters of former members of the *Bnai Brith* Lodge in Germany, are settled in the colony of Moledet, established through the generosity of *Bnai Brith*. I feel confident that with the new grant *Bnai Brith* will make possible the construction of a colony of equal significance and value to the future development of the Jewish National Home. That the *Bnai Brith* has seen fit first in honouring Senator Alfred M. Cohen[2] and now in paying tribute to Henry Monsky, his successor and president, to make such generous contributions to the Jewish National Fund is a heartening manifestation of the deep interest of its membership in the reconstruction of *Eretz Israel*.

In this critical hour for our people, of whom so many are today condemned in the lands of their birth to a fate of suffering and despair, the reclamation of the soil of Palestine not only provides the basis for increased colonization but constitutes a symbol of hope for Jews everywhere.

There can be no more enduring and meaningful tribute to the statesmanlike leadership of Henry Monsky than the settlement that is to be established on the soil in his name.[3] May it endure and flourish as a living testimonial to the constructive values in Jewish life to which Mr. Monsky is so ardently devoted.

With Zionist greetings, I am

Sincerely yours,
Chaim Weizmann

136. To William L. Schloss,[1] Indianapolis.　　*New York, 16 April 1941*
English: Or. Copy. T.W.: W.A.

Dear Mr. Schloss,

I am writing to thank you for your wire of the 14th, the terms of which make it doubly difficult for me to tell you how sorry I am that,

---

[2] 1859–1949. Lawyer, Ohio State Senator 1897–1900; President *Bnai Brith* 1925–38. For the settlement Moledet founded in his honour, see Vol. XVII, No. 221.

[3] The village Ramat Zvi, in honour of ('Zvi') Monsky, was established near Ein Harod.

136. [1] B. 1909. Industrialist, banker; Jewish communal leader in Indianapolis and chairman of its U.J.A. campaign.

although I had originally undertaken to visit Indianapolis later this month, events have made it inevitable that I should have to cancel that arrangement.[2]

I had very much looked forward to being with you, but a new factor has intervened and it has become essential that I should be in Washington at that time. A function has been arranged for the end of the month—a dinner of the newly formed American Palestine Committee[3]—to which I attach considerable importance and which I am bound to attend. Prior to that there are a number of political matters which will require urgent attention on my part and for which I shall have to be in Washington before the dinner. All this makes it necessary for me to alter my original plan.

I deeply regret any disappointment this may cause my friends in Indianapolis, but I am sure that so far as the campaign is concerned, they will all realise that my own presence is of little importance in relation to the urgency of the call from our fellow Jews, and that in these days of crisis everyone of us will do his duty to the best of his ability.

I would, if I may, add one further personal word. It is not a request for indulgence on your part, but a statement of facts which have to be recognized, and of which I ask your understanding. Twenty years ago, as a younger man, I might perhaps have been physically able to spend a day visiting each of a series of cities and have been none the worse for it. Today, at 67, these journeys involve considerable physical strain, and in view of the arrangements made, even though conceivably it might have been possible for me to squeeze in a day prior to my departure for Washington, I am sure you will agree that it should not be expected of me.

Please convey to all your colleagues every good wish for the success of your efforts. I am sure that the Jewish community of Indianapolis will rise to the sense of the grave responsibilities which face us.

Yours sincerely,
Dr. Chaim Weizmann

137. To John M. Martin, London.   *New York, 17 April 1941*
English: T.: W.A.

Propose [to] write full report situation after return from second trip [to] Middle West and Washington end month, but submit urgently

---

[2] This (W.A.) expressed disappointment at cancellation of the engagement which, according to Schloss, could ruin the campaign.

[3] See No. 85, n. 2.

that some Labour representatives like Wilkinson, Wedgwood [or] Tom Williams[1] should come here for quiet [and] not much publicized tour to contact workmen in industrial areas. Secondly, respectfully submit [to] chief urgency [in] hastening consummation project Jewish Force, also further enlistment in Palestine. This would be most helpful here. Would not wire these matters if were not convinced of it after careful study situation.[2] Regards

Weizmann

138. To Herbert H. Lehman,[1] New York.   *Washington, 2 May 1941*
English: T.: W.A.

Have today sent following telegram to about thirty friends throughout country for conference we discussed the other day: "I am inviting a small number of friends to meet me for luncheon at one o'clock and during the afternoon on Sunday May 25 at the St. Regis Hotel Fiftyfifth Street and Fifth Avenue New York for an informal consultation on questions arising out of the present emergency. I want to make it clear that the meeting has no financial implications whatsoever. I am extremely anxious to obtain your views on the present situation and the immediate future. Will appreciate deeply if you will write or wire me at the St. Regis Hotel that I may have the pleasure of meeting with you." Look forward to seeing you. Sincerely,[2]

Chaim Weizmann

137. [1] Ellen Wilkinson (1891–1947): Lab. M.P. 1924–47, Parliamentary Secretary to Ministry of Home Security 1940–45, Minister of Education 1945–47. Josiah Wedgwood (Biog. Index, Vol. XI): Lab. M.P., strongly pro-Zionist, author of *Seventh Dominion,* 1928. Williams (Biog. Index, Vol. XIX): Lab. M.P., Parliamentary Secretary to Ministry of Agriculture.
[2] Rommel's successful counter-offensive into Egypt began 31 Mar. 1941. This telegram was in response to a J.A. wire to W., urging a direct approach to the Prime Minister on the Jewish Force. The J.A. had sent Moyne a memorandum emphasising the urgency of forming Jewish units in Palestine for military service and self-defence—J.A. London office to W., 14 Apr. 1941 (W.A.). On 22 Apr. Isaiah Berlin (attached to the Embassy at Washington) passed on to W. a message from Eden, to the effect that there was no hope that recent events might lead to any modification of the decision to postpone the Jewish Force (W.A.). On 1 May 1941 the Ministry of Information informed Martin that Wedgwood would go to U.S., but Miss Wilkinson could not be spared (P.R.O., W.O. 32/9502).

138. [1] Biog. Index, Vol. XI. Banker, Governor of New York State 1932–42. While opposing the idea of a Jewish State, he favoured free Jewish immigration into Palestine.
[2] The conference was an attempt by W. to unite American Jewry on a single pro-Palestine platform. Among those who attended were: Israel Goldstein, Edmund I. Kaufman,

139. To Eliezer Kaplan, Jerusalem.   *New York, 8 May 1941*
English: T.: C.Z.A. S53/196.

[In reply to] yours May 5,[1] apart from Moshe [Shertok] who useful if sparable Palestine, also Ruppin[2] [on] economic aspects. Doubtful [of] desirability [or] effectiveness [of] sending delegates, [for] purposes proposed.

                                                                Weizmann

140. To Nathan Straus, Jr.,[1] Washington.   *New York, 15 May 1941*
English: T.W.: Photostat W.A.

I am most grateful to you for your charming note which I appreciate deeply.[2] The one outstanding quality of my speech was certainly its brevity. I was allotted five minutes, of which I used four, and it seemed to me that I said all there was to be said on this occasion.

I have been through a number of American, and some Canadian cities—twelve in all. It was a biggish strain, but it gave me a fairly clear idea of the situation, as far as general problems are concerned, and our movement in particular. You will remember that when I had the pleasure of seeing you and Mr. Morgenthau, and when we discussed the advisability of my seeing the President, it was my suggestion that such a meeting, if it could be arranged, should take place after I had completed the main part of my program. This is

Herbert Lehman, Louis Lipsky, Henry Monsky, Emanuel Neumann, Bernard Rosenblatt, Paul Uhlmann, Edward Warburg, Meyer Weisgal and Stephen Wise. W. discussed the rehabilitation problems which would be the responsibility of the Palestinian and American Jewish communities after the war, and intimated that the conference had been called to ascertain the minimum platform on which those assembled could unite with regard to Palestine. W. accepted the consensus of the meeting that an exploratory committee should be appointed (by himself) to seek a common denominator between Zionists and non-Zionists (record in W.A.). See Introduction; No. 149, n. 2; No. 169.

139. [1] Kaplan had proposed, on behalf of the Jerusalem Executive, despatch of delegates to various countries to encourage Jewish communities, enlighten public opinion and to raise funds, the first delegation to visit South Africa. He had requested W.'s views regarding such a delegation to U.S. and Canada, and suitable candidates (C.Z.A. S53/196).
   [2] Arthur Ruppin (Biog. Index, Vol. IV). Economist, sociologist, head of J.A. Department for Settlement of German immigrants.

140. [1] 1889–1961. Of the family of merchants distinguished in public life; newspaper reporter, editor; New York State Senator 1920–26; Head of U.S. Housing Authority 1937–42; President of Radio Station WMCA.
   [2] Untraced.

now the case, and it is my intention to leave for the West Coast at the end of this month. I am wondering whether it would not be proper to [words missing] if his time and health permit, or to wait until I return. I would be greatly obliged if you would care to give me your opinion on a matter of such importance.

Both Mrs. Weizmann and myself are very much looking forward to seeing you and Mrs. Straus soon, when an appointment can be conveniently arranged. But in the meantime I am wondering whether you could possibly come to the luncheon on Sunday, May 25th. I don't know whether I mentioned that it is a strictly private affair and that Governor Lehman will be present.[3]

With warm greetings to you and Mrs. Straus, in which Mrs. Weizmann joins me, and with thanks for your very kind help and counsel, I am

141. To André Meyer,[1] New York.　　　　　　*New York, 16 May 1941*
English: T.W.: W.A.

My dear Friend,

I beg to enclose some letters relating to the food preparations about which we spoke yesterday. In looking through the papers, I find that I have only two English patent specifications, and I shall have to ask Washington to send me copies of my three American patents which have been granted to me. But perhaps the English specifications will give you or your experts an idea of what the process is.

I also include copy of an American application granted to Professor Willstaetter[2] who has collaborated with me in this matter, and I have the rights of each of those patents transferred to me. You may have heard the name of Willstaetter; he is the leading organic chemist in the world, a Nobel prize man of great distinction, and for the last 9 years we have worked together on this subject. I also enclose copy of a report by Mr. John Heron and Sons, who is the chief chemist of the Society of Brewers in England and who has tested my material from the point of view of addition of the same to beer. The determination of the vitamin content of the product has been carried out in the College of the Pharmaceutical Society, University of Lon-

---

[3] See No. 138, n. 2. Straus did not in fact attend.

141. [1] Biog. Index, Vol. XXII. French banker; joined Lazard Frères & Co. in 1926, and from 1940 director of its New York branch.

[2] Richard Willstaetter (Biog. Index, Vol. XVI). German chemist resident in Switzerland. Nobel Prize 1915.

don, and the reports are included herewith. I also enclose a short report by Messrs. B. Rigdon, Ltd., who are practical brewers.

All these reports speak for themselves. I would like to add that I have only single copies of all these documents, and would be greatly obliged if you would return them to me at your earliest convenience; or, better still, if somebody in your office could make copies of them and so return to me the originals. I shall need these documents for my friends in Seattle in case I have to negotiate with them.

I would like to re-state briefly what I have mentioned to you in passing in the course of our conversation yesterday. The process which is laid down in three patents granted to me both in England and in this country and in other countries aims at the production of a foodstuff rich in vitamins, chiefly of the group B, based on yeast, preferably brewer's yeast, which is a by-product obtainable in considerable quantities in all breweries; but baker's yeast can be used the same way, although the latter has the disadvantage of containing less vitamins. It is quite possible that if production on a large scale is contemplated, one would have to make one's own yeast, and in that case one could produce a yeast rich in vitamins, independently both of brewer's and of baker's yeast. The foodstuffs can be made out of yeast alone or out of yeast in combination with other materials like

 a. skimmed milk
 b. soya meal
 c. peanut meal or ground nut meal
 d. cotton seed cake, etc.

In short, any vegetable or animal protein. I don't insist on animal proteins because

 1. They are more expensive
 2. A product containing animal proteins would not be saleable in the East both for religious and economic reasons. But we did prepare quantities of our foodstuffs out of meat residues and out of blood from slaughter houses. The main interest of this process, however, is the use of vegetable proteins which are found in great abundance all over the world. I would like to add that this process has been taken up in England by Messrs. Bovril, Ltd., who have established a small factory in Devonshire and are producing a product out of yeast and skimmed milk, and we are now about to conclude a contract with them for the extension of the license for a product out of yeast and peanuts, of which I have shown you a sample yesterday. The British Government, which is faced with a serious food problem, is contemplating the manufacture of the peanut products in India where millions of tons of peanuts are available, and in the last telegram from Mr. Amery, Secretary of State for India, they

spoke of something like a hundred thousand tons of this product, which in a concentrated form would cover a great deal of the required food supply for the next winter. As these developments took place in my absence, I am unfortunately not in a position to give you more precise information about it, except what I know myself from telegrams. As soon as I hear more regarding the developments, I shall place the available information before you.

In brief, the process has been tested on an industrial scale by Bovril, Ltd., who have taken out two licenses for England and Argentine. It is being seriously considered by His Majesty's Government, which proposes to operate through an important firm in India, known under the name of Sir William Wright and Company. Any expert reading the patents (or if he wishes to discuss this matter with me) will soon learn that the process is extremely simple and that the plant required is easily set up, attainable, and equally simple. No high temperatures or pressures are required. The only piece of apparatus of any importance required is the evaporator, a kind of apparatus which need not be constructed especially and probably would be the same as used in factories making condensed milk or similar products. The temperature throughout the whole process never exceeds 55 to 60 degrees Centigrade, and the consumption of fuel is therefore negligible. The yield of the product is almost quantitive. The only loss throughout the operation is the husk or the cellulose of the material used. Otherwise, everything is converted into an edible palatable foodstuff which can be used either in a form of liquid like Bovril or Oxo or in form of a paste or tablets. It entirely depends upon the degree of concentration.

I think I have given you the main features of the problem, and no doubt if an expert is consulted on this matter, he will probably be able to confirm these views.

I also enclose an exchange of correspondence between the India Office and myself, the content of which is self-explanatory. These documents are rather precious, and I should like to have them returned.

With kind regards I remain,

Yours always,
Ch. Weizmann

P.S. Jacques Errera[3] has just been here and I have shown him this letter, of which I believe he fully approves.

---

[3] B. 1896. Head of Department of Physical Chemistry at Brussels University from 1930.

142. To S. Salman Schocken, New York.   *New York, 21 May 1941*
English: T.W.: Schocken Papers.

Dear Mr. Schocken,

I have received your telegram[1] pressing me to give a date for Los Angeles. I would like to inform you that so far we have made no arrangements whatsoever for Los Angeles, and I am therefore not in a position to give a date. It is impossible for me, in view of the pressure under which I am working and the seriousness of the position, to make definite plans as yet.

Upon thinking the matter over, I believe that matters relating to Rehovoth and the University had better be kept distinct and apart from each other, as mixing both institutions together would only create confusion and will give the impression of my competing with the University by talking of Rehovoth, or vice versa. As matters stand at present, I have already heard from various quarters criticisms charging that I do not take sufficient interest in University matters. You have been in this country now for a considerable length of time, and as far as I can understand, you are able to devote most of your time to University problems. You have an organization, a secretariat and a circle of powerful friends—established since many years. During my previous visits, I have always done what I could for the University and would have done it now, if not for the extraordinary pressure and anxiety under which I have to live and work, which could tax the powers of a man much stronger than I am. The reproaches, therefore, which come to my ears, are not only unjustified but unkind. May I add that my duties as chairman of the Board of Governors are limited and do not include any obligation on my part to raise money for the budget of the University, this being definitely the duty of the University administration. It must be remembered that the Institute of Rehovoth has nobody at all to rely upon, excepting Mr. Sieff and myself. Mr. Sieff is a stranger in this country, and it is not easy for him, under the special circumstances, to do effective work, although he is trying his very best. Again, in ordinary times, Rehovoth has never addressed itself to the American public, and received its comparatively small budget from a very limited circle, primarily in England, and from other European countries. This situation has radically changed in the course of the last year, and in order that Rehovoth exist in these critical days, I was very reluctantly compelled to seek assistance for it amongst some of my friends in this country. I have studiously avoided interfering in any way with the financial effort which the University is making:

142. [1] Untraced.

on the contrary, whenever I had an opportunity to speak about the University during my talks on Rehovoth, I did so. Moreover, the contributions which Rehovoth was asking for are comparatively small, and have come from persons who are acquainted with Rehovoth and were willing to show their appreciation in helping it along in these difficult days.

The University has a good name, a tradition of long standing, and with a certain amount of work on the part of the organization which you are creating and for which you have ample time and opportunity, it should not be difficult to raise the quota which you have set yourself, and it would be a kindness on the part of the University committees if they would save me from having to make any further effort in view of the hard strain to which I have been subjected in these two months.

With kind regards I beg to remain, dear Mr. Schocken,

Yours very sincerely,

Ch. Weizmann

143. To Samuel I. Rosenman,[1] New York.   *New York, 22 May 1941*
English: T.W.: W.A.

Dear Judge Rosenman,

I was both glad and grateful for having had the opportunity the other evening of talking to you about some aspects of the situation in Palestine and in particular about the vexed question of arming the Jews. I would like to place this subject in writing before you and I shall do so as briefly as I can.

I do not have all the documents here with me and I therefore have to rely on my memory; but I think that the salient facts of the situation are sufficiently vivid on my mind for me to rely on them as being in complete conformity with the truth.

You may remember that soon after the outbreak of the war I wrote a letter to Mr. Chamberlain, then Prime Minister, offering on behalf of the Jews in Palestine every possible cooperation. This letter was gratefully acknowledged by the Prime Minister. The correspondence was published in the press, and here the matter rested for a long time.

By cooperation we meant primarily two things: first, manpower in Palestine which could be supplemented by recruiting of volun-

---

143. [1] Biog. Index, Vol. XXIII. Jurist, Counsel to Presidents Roosevelt and Truman; appointed to New York State Supreme Court 1932; facilitated W.'s approaches to Government circles in Washington.

teers in the various Jewish communities which were then still more or less intact, inasmuch as they were not subjected to military service in their respective countries. There was quite a number of this category available, and together with the Palestinians, they might have formed a force of at least three or four divisions. In Palestine itself all the available youth has placed itself at the disposal of the military powers, and in the expectation of some action to be taken by them. I suppose the matter was discussed by the High Commissioner of Palestine and the Colonial Office in London, and at the end we were informed that the military authorities in Palestine would be prepared to enlist Jews *pari passu* with Arabs. As the Arabs came forward in very small numbers and had to be coaxed into enlisting, the whole thing moved very slowly, and after six or seven months passed, about two companies each were formed, which means 600 Arabs and 600 Jews were enlisted in total as fighting units. This number has been increased to about 1,000 each by now.

I don't know whether the Arabs are maintaining their numerical strength, but the Jews certainly are. Apart from this fighting unit the military authorities agreed to enlist Jews into auxiliary services, such as lorry drivers, mechanics, ground workers for the R.A.F., stevedores in the ports, as well as doctors and specialists of all kinds. The number of this force amounts today to about 9,000 (nine thousand) and all of the above-mentioned, lorry drivers, mechanics, etc., are practically counted as a fighting force.

We were not satisfied with this position. When the Chamberlain Cabinet went out of office, we appealed to Mr. Churchill and the whole subject of Jewish enlistment was reopened. We met with more sympathy on his part, but our efforts were to a great extent opposed by the late Lord Lloyd, then Colonial Secretary, who although a very fair-minded gentleman, was rather pro-Arab in his sympathies and inclined towards appeasing the Arab extreme nationalists, and such appeasement is always carried out on the back of the Jews. A classical example of this policy is the White Paper, which as you know has been condemned by Mr. Churchill himself in the severest possible terms.

We submitted to Mr. Churchill the following suggestion: As the military authorities are reluctant to form a force in Palestine, a compromise might be arrived at by forming an extra-Palestinian division in which some Palestinians might participate. Mr. Churchill agreed to this procedure, referring me to the military authorities and at long last a discussion took place between Mr. Eden, who was then in the War Office, Lord Lloyd in the Colonial Office, and a representative of the Foreign Office and myself. It was agreed to form such a force, to be organized and trained in England, and that it should consist of 3,000 Palestinians and 9,000 volunteers from other countries. This proposal was submitted to the Cabinet and passed; and a letter to that effect was addressed to me on October 17th, 1940. (As you see it took a long time to get a Cabinet decision, in spite of the unqualified support of the Prime Minister.) Even after the receipt of this letter it was quite a while before the next practical step was taken, which consisted in the appointment of a general who would organize and eventually command this force. I cannot exactly recall the date on which this appointment took place, but it was about two months before I left England. The general set to work almost immediately. He proved to be a highly efficient man who understood the problem and was in sympathy with it. An organization in its skeleton form was about to be set up; all that was needed in order to go ahead was a public announcement. A formula or text of such announcement was given to us by the Government, and we asked for some modifications of it. Again discussions took place between the three officers [*sic*] and myself. (I must have covered many miles between the various offices in Whitehall.) Matters, however, became more complicated because of the general re-shuffling of the Cabinet: Lord Lloyd died suddenly; Lord Moyne, quite fresh to the problem, became his successor. Halifax, who was on the whole a supporter of this scheme, left the Foreign Office to come here; his place was taken by Eden, who when he became Foreign Secretary almost forgot what he did when he was War Secretary. The new War Secretary, Captain Margesson, had to be put in possession of all the facts and all that had passed, which was a great effort—particularly with the conditions under which one had to work in London. But as Lord Moyne has proved to be very friendly and sympathetic and accessible, the matter began to look as though we were coming to a definite favourable conclusion of a long series of frustrations and efforts.

Meanwhile the situation in the Middle East has changed, and apparently on the instance of General Wavell, the Prime Minister was compelled to inform me personally that, sorry as he is, the implementing of the whole project has to be postponed for 4 or 6 months. This happened about ten days before my departure, and that is how the matter stands today. The reason given to me in the official letter announcing the postponement was lack of equipment; but I am quite certain that the main reason is political. Wavell's attitude and probably the attitude of the local administration in Palestine is no doubt dictated by the desire to appease the Arabs, and it was quite clear to me from conversations I have had with Lord Moyne and others that, although the lack of equipment may have played some part in this decision, the political aspect of the problem was the second decisive cause.

The other direction in which we have offered help repeatedly was the organization of industries and supplies in Palestine for war purposes and the cooperation of Palestine with India, which is gradually becoming the Eastern arsenal of the British Empire, but which seriously lacked trained and skilled specialist manpower. Although the India office under Mr. Amery is quite aware of the great usefulness of such cooperation and he is doing everything to further it, we have not come to any really organized effort in this direction, although the industrial and intellectual community in Palestine is cooperating with the army and we have supplied it with a fair amount of technical help. We have done a great deal of building (airdromes, barracks, concrete reinforcements, pillboxes) and our workshops are carrying out the repairing and replacing of parts in vehicles, tanks, etc. But for the baleful influence of the Palestine administration this effort could have been much greater and might have proceeded much more smoothly and effectively. The army is willing to utilize the possibilities of Palestine, but it is handicapped by the unimaginative and reactionary attitude of the Administration. I have not seen Colonel Donovan[2] myself, but from what I hear on good authority he had a good insight into the situation in Palestine and I believe that he would probably corroborate all that I am saying.

Lastly, the burning problem of arming the Jews at present is naturally a matter of grave concern to all of us. I think something has been done in Palestine in a half-hearted way, and something in the nature of a home guard is being organized; but again I fear that the argument might be advanced that the lack of equipment is preventing the authorities on the spot from doing the thing properly. I do not believe that this argument is so weighty and I think that equipment could be found with just a little good will. Young men in Palestine are mostly trained men. About 22,000 of them are those who have been in the supernumerary police in the time of the disturbances before the war and have therefore received almost a complete military training. The others have trained and organized themselves for years for purposes of self-defence and have always shown a great sense of discipline and are on the whole an intelligent group of people who know how to carry and handle arms. With a little

---

[2] William J. Donovan (1883–1959). Lawyer; unofficial representative of American Secretary for Navy 1940–41; Co-ordinator of Information from July 1941; Director of Office of Strategic Services from June 1942.

encouragement and the necessary equipment they could quickly be made into an effective force.

I wonder whether the authorities in Palestine are conscious of the terrible responsibility which they are taking upon themselves by dealing half-heartedly with so grave a matter and thus exposing the Jewish community to mortal danger from two sides—the Nazis and the Arabs.

Please forgive the length of this letter. I have tried to shorten the statement as much as possible but I think that I should place you in possession of all the facts and some of the history. I know that I need not say any more on this matter as you are fully aware of the gravity of the situation.

With kind regards,
Yours v. sincerely,
Ch. Weizmann

144. To Winston S. Churchill, London.   *New York, 25 May 1941*
English: T.: W.A.

Deeply distressed and mourn with you loss so many valiant sailors and great British battleship.[1] But with magnificent spirit of British nation under your great leadership the fight against evil will be won with God's help. Deepest sympathy and affection.

Chaim Weizmann

145. To Pierre van Paassen,[1] New York.   *New York, 30 May 1941*
English: T.W.: Photostat W.A.

I was delighted to receive your book,[2] of which I have heard so much but which, unhappily, due to the pressure under which I have been working since my arrival in this country, I have not yet had the opportunity of reading. So that I am looking forward, in the course of my journeyings along the West Coast, to the great pleasure of a few hours with your book.

---

144. [1] H.M.S. *Hood,* sunk by the *Bismarck* the previous day. The *Bismarck* itself was sunk by the British 27 May 1941.

145. [1] 1895–1968. Dutch-born Unitarian minister and writer. A passionate Zionist, he headed the Committee for a Jewish Army in U.S. from 1942.
[2] This may have been *That Day Alone* or *The Time is Now,* both having appeared 1941.

It is a source of deep regret to me that my very heavy program prevented our meeting, and that now another month must elapse before we can get together as I leave for the West tonight. I shall be returning to this hotel the first part of July. Do give me a ring here at the hotel early next month, so that we can arrange an appointment.[3]

146. To Dorothy Thompson,[1] New York.   *New York, 30 May 1941*
English: T.W.: Photostat W.A.

Dear Dorothy,

I am off tonight for a month's grind on the West Coast on my usual peregrinations. I am leaving with a heavy heart. It was my hope that out of the crucible of this war a better world would emerge. The first inkling of the "shape of things to come" we had this morning out of the mouth of the Secretary for Foreign Affairs.[2]

Apart from its other shortcomings, about which I need not dilate, there was one grave and significant omission—the Jews and Palestine. It is inconceivable to me how any statesman fighting against the common enemy can for even a brief moment forget the first victims of these dark forces. You understand my feelings; I have expressed them in a cablegram to the Prime Minister and also to some other friends in 10 Downing Street.[3]

Should you have an opportunity to give expression to what I know must be your feelings, you will be serving not only my people but the whole of humanity.

May I offer you my congratulations on the honour which has been bestowed on you by McGill University.[4]

I hope to see you when I return to New York the first week in July. Perhaps we may even meet in Vermont.

Affectionately yours,

Am endeavouring to make it possible for our friend Meyer to give

---

[3] It is not known whether they met.

146. [1] Biog. Index. She was then syndicated columnist for *New York Herald Tribune*.
[2] At the Mansion House, London, Eden stated 29 May 1941: '. . . It seems to me both natural and right that the cultural and economic ties between the Arab countries, and the political ties too, should be strengthened. His Majesty's Government for their part will give their full support to any scheme that commands general approval'. The speech was universally regarded as a British invitation to the Arabs to establish some form of Middle East Federation.
[3] See No. 148.   [4] She had been awarded an Hon. Ll.D.

his time to your movement for at least the next six months.[5] All the luck in the world!

Ch. W.

147. To John M. Martin, London. *Grand Canyon, Arizona, 2 June 1941*
English: Radio Message: Photostat W.A.

A. Information reaching me indicates many leading Britishers in Palestine convinced effective German occupation Syria would serve as death blow to British position[1] in Middle East.

B. Vital to forestall Germans by British entry into Syria.

C. Am informed further, one reason why British hesitating to move is lest American public opinion react unfavourably.

D. If this report correct I venture with great respect offer my opinion on basis fairly extensive tour and careful observation [of] American scene.

E. Believe above view American reaction wholly mistaken and on contrary am sure British initiative [. . . .][2] indicated would be welcomed.

Weizmann

148. To John M. Martin, London. *En route to Los Angeles, 3 June 1941*
English: Radio Message: Photostat W.A.

A. Absence of any reference to Jews in Eden's speech on post war reconstruction made most painful impression not only on Jewish community but also on very many other well wishers of British cause.

B. That they who have suffered most should be forgotten is a

---

[5] Her movement, the 'Ring of Freedom,' was 'to forge masses of people into a big democratic movement upon which the new world would be founded.' Weisgal worked for it from his J.A. office—see Weisgal, *op. cit.* W. contributed $5,000, advanced by K.H. to his special political fund (correspondence in W.A.).

147. [1] Rashid Ali, Iraqi Premier, had come into open conflict with the British in Iraq early in May 1941. On 12 May 1941, in response to an appeal by Rashid Ali, some 120 German aircraft began to arrive in Iraq, using landing-grounds in Syria *en route*, by arrangement with Vichy Government. British and Free French Forces invaded Syria 8 June 1941.

[2] Words unclearly transmitted over radio telegram.

grievous disappointment to those who look to a better world after victory.

C. Would urge speediest opportunity be found correct this omission before adverse opinion crystallises.[1]

149. To Meyer W. Weisgal, New York.   *Los Angeles, 4 June 1941*
English: T.: W.A.

Anxious [to] avoid friction with Stroock's group.[1] Therefore suggest call committee[2] together only in informal and exploratory way. Fully agree [to] invitation [of] members World Executive including Hexter but composition [of] committee may possibly be altered after meeting Stroock. Seen your telegram [to] Josef.[3] Would gladly agree your suggestion but believe situation here quite primitive and effort may be useless. Love to you and everybody.

Weizmann

148. [1] See No. 146, n. 2.

149. [1] Solomon Stroock (1874–1945). Lawyer; among non-Zionist founders of J.A. Chairman of Executive, American Jewish Committee from 1934, its President 1945. The Committee was formed 1906, in order to 'prevent the infraction of civil and religious rights of Jews in every part of the world.' While joining the Zionists in protesting against British curtailment of immigration into Palestine, it denounced the concept of 'diaspora nationalism' inherent in the programme of American Jewish Congress and World Jewish Congress.

[2] Relates to proposed action following the conference of 25 May 1941 (see No. 138). On 10 July 1941 Stroock proposed a meeting between evenly-balanced delegations of Zionists and non-Zionists, whose conclusions should then be accepted as the view of the American Jewish community. At a preliminary meeting of the Zionists alone, it was agreed that emphasis be laid on the reorganization of American Jewry, rather than to seek immediate non-Zionist agreement to the full Zionist programme. (Present at this meeting were Israel Goldstein, Nahum Goldmann, Edward Jacobs, Louis Lipsky, Emanuel Neumann, David de Sola Pool, Morris Rothenberg, Silver, Wise, Weisgal and W. (W.A.). No record of the joint meeting is available, but it evidently agreed to further discussion, which continued during the following autumn, W. having returned to England. See Introduction.

[3] Weisgal to Cohn, 4 June 1941 (W.A.). This concerned the prospect of W.'s raising contributions for the Zionist Political Fund among the film colony. W. met, *inter alia,* Harry Warner (of Warner Brothers), Louis B. Mayer (of M.G.M.), Edward G. Robinson, Spencer Tracy, Walter Wanger and David Selznick (W.A.).

150. To Benjamin V. Cohen,[1] Washington.

San Francisco, 14 June 1941

English: T.W.: Photostat W.A.

Dear Ben,

I am glad to know that you returned to this part of the world, and I am looking forward to an opportunity of a meeting and a chat with you. It is our plan to be back in New York near the 4th of July, and perhaps we can arrange to get together around that time.

In the meanwhile Mrs. Weizmann and I need your good offices in behalf of her sister and brother-in-law, Rachel and Joseph Blumenfeld. Joseph Blumenfeld is an eminent chemist, and has done outstanding work at the Sorbonne with Urbain, and lately has worked with Joliot. The latter is a son-in-law of the late Curie. He has also been connected with important chemical industries in France. With two sons, Serge and Michel (both of military age), the Blumenfelds have been stranded in unoccupied France, from where we have been trying to bring them to America for many months. I am asking Arthur Lourie to give you a record as to the efforts made in their behalf, and Mrs. Weizmann and I would be extremely grateful for your assistance in rescuing the family from its present plight.

The difficulty seems to be chiefly in obtaining an exit permit from the French authorities and I am informed by very reliable people that a word from the American Consul or diplomatic representative to the Vichy authorities might easily have the effect of releasing these people from their bondage. A permit for them to come to the U.S.A. does not represent any insuperable difficulty, as they have already been granted a visa some months ago and this would have to be renewed now.

Should you wish to write me, Arthur will be able to forward your letter on to me.

Mrs. Weizmann joins me in sending you thanks for whatever you can do to help the Blumenfelds, whose position is causing us sleepless nights. We both hope that we shall meet upon our return to the East.[2]

---

150. [1] Biog. Index, Vol. IX. Lawyer, of the inner circle of advisers to Roosevelt from 1933; appointed adviser to U.S. Ambassador in Great Britain 1941.

[2] No further relevant correspondence with Cohen traced. Blumenfeld telegraphed W. 1 Nov. 1941 (W.A.) that he had received permits for his family to travel to U.S.

151. To Philip Lilienthal,[1] San Mateo, Calif.
Yosemite Valley, Calif., 15 June 1941
English: T.W.: Photostat W.A.

Dear Mr. Lilienthal,

Both Mrs. Weizmann and I wish to thank you most sincerely for the very kind hospitality extended to us by Mrs. Lilienthal and yourself for a most delightful evening in your charming home. As you see we are now enjoying a few days' rest in this lovely spot.

I do hope that I am not imposing too heavy a burden on you in asking you to undertake the sponsorship of the [Daniel Sieff] Research Institute. Now is the time to further the industrial development of Palestine through scientific research, and it would be most gratifying and encouraging to add the name of your city to the growing roster of supporting communities throughout the United States. I had a word with Mr. Louis Lurie[2] yesterday, and he promised to do his share. Perhaps you would wish to get in touch with him.

Mrs. Weizmann joins me in sending you and Mrs. Lilienthal warm greetings and best wishes.

152. To Felix Frankfurter,[1] Washington.
Arrowhead Springs, Calif., 21 June 1941
English: Copy. T.W.: W.A.

Now that my tour is completed, I am taking a few days' rest here, before returning to the East where there is still a great deal to be done. I have still to pay a visit to Boston. It may interest you to hear some of the impressions which I have gathered on this extensive tour, which included a visit to practically all the important communities of this country, with a lengthy stay in New York and two visits to Washington. (I also visited several Canadian cities, but I am not including them in this report.)

THE POSITION OF THE ZIONIST MOVEMENT: There is definitely a very sound sentiment for Palestine which has developed a great deal in the last years, and is much more real than it was say ten years ago. The progress made in Palestine, the personal acquaintance of many Jews with such progress on the spot, and I suppose the general position of Jewry in the world has brought our work

---

151. [1] B. 1889. Cattle rancher. Vice-President, Mount Zion Hospital, Calif. 1935–42.

[2] B. 1888. Real-estate dealer and builder in San Francisco.

152. [1] Biog. Index, Vol. VII. Supreme Court Justice 1939–62; previously active in Zionism.

much nearer to the consciousness of the Jews than it was ever the case before. I do not mean to imply, however, that the communities are doing all they could for Palestine, but relatively speaking, very marked progress can be registered. This could be enhanced manifold if the Zionist Organization were in a position to utilise the sentiment and guide these potential energies into constructive and effective channels. I am afraid that this is not always the case. There are in each community devoted, hardworking and conscientious Zionists, and there is even a young generation of American Jews grown up in the movement, who would be capable of doing more than their actual performance; but somehow Zionists still remain outside the mainstream of Jewish life and have not reached out beyond a narrow compass. The reason is, I think, primarily social. Zionists are re-cruited mainly from the lower middle class and to a smaller extent from the middle classes. The upper middle classes are still either aloof or a minority of them is hostile and ignorant. Another reason is, in my opinion, a lack of good educational literature. The Jewish press, with a few exceptions, is not on a very high level. The central organ of the Zionist movement is utterly inadequate for such times as these and for the demands which are being placed on the Zionists.[2] It is not in consonance with the dignity and importance of an organ-ization like the Zionist Organization of America. The labour Zion-ist organizations have a much better literature, but they are also even more sectarian than the general Zionists and their papers are read only by a small number.[3] There is not a single book in America on Zionism which is up to date and which could be placed in the hands of intelligent Jewish or non-Jewish readers, and to which one could refer all those who wish to be better informed about the movement. The speakers again, with some very notable and dis-tinguished exceptions, indulge most in commonplaces and sentimen-tal phraseology and are not familiar either with the facts or with the great problems and great possibilities of Palestine and the Middle East. I believe that the sort of talks which one used to hear 5 or 6 or 10 years ago do not draw any longer, as the public is more educated and more exacting and I further believe that by giving them the true picture, even emphasizing the difficulties and dangers, one is more likely to gain their confidence and their support than by merely indulging in spread-eagle emotional outpourings which are, in my opinion, obsolete and valueless. There is a vast field still to be laboured, and there are not enough highly qualified workers

[2] Relates to *New Palestine*. See Nos. 67, 88.
[3] See ref. to *Jewish Frontier*, No. 127, n. 1.

to do the ploughing and the sowing. The officers of the movement in their majority are men of the highest qualities but somewhat tired and oppressed with the heavy burdens which they have been carrying with so much courage in the last 20 years. This melancholy reflection is applicable to myself in the first instance. Not enough new blood has come to our relief. (Incidentally, it is a phenomenon not only characteristic of our movement alone, but of a great many others, particularly in Europe. That the burden of war should rest primarily on Churchill, and that Lloyd George should still be discussed as a possible candidate for the Cabinet post, is something which is very analogous to the state of affairs in our own movement.) In our case Palestine has absorbed a great many of our young forces and in normal times it could have become a reservoir to be used for enlightenment and strengthening of the various centers of the *Galuth*.[4] At present it is unfortunately impossible, and so the old leaders have to carry on and make the best of a situation which takes up their energies to the utmost.

I shall not stop to discuss in this letter the various currents and cross-currents prevailing in the central organization. I have seen and felt something of it. One could not help noticing the waste of a certain amount of energy which is expended on undue friction inside the machine, but I have tried not to interfere in any way with all that—although in the present state of our affairs it is not merely a local problem but it affects vitally our whole present and our future. America is the only great Zionist organization left and the smooth working of the machine and its manning with the proper people is a matter of first-class importance not merely locally.

THE NON-ZIONIST JEWS represent on a whole an amorphous mass both organizationally, intellectually and politically. There are, however, groups which begin to assume a more precise shape, like the *Bnai Brith*, the Union of American Rabbis[5] and certainly the labour people, the first-named built up in a large degree of Zionists who prefer, for some reason best known to themselves, the easier life of being connected with an Order than the more vigorous demands being placed on them by a movement like ours. Outside of these few organized bodies, which do not exercise as yet too much influence because of lack of program, there is the vast mass of Jewry ready to be guided, but on a whole, leaderless. Of course, the labour people are again an exception, having a definite purpose, a definite program and a definite outlook, and will probably play an increasingly greater part in the shaping of things to come. The one common fac-

---

4 Hebr.: 'diaspora'.
5 Union of Orthodox Rabbis of America, founded 1902.

tor uniting all is a sort of malaise oppressing the minds of Jews, a fear, an uneasiness which is running through the smuggest amongst them. They feel an overhanging threat, without knowing how to meet it, and I believe there is every reason for such an attitude of mind. The structure of the American Jewish community as a whole, their stratification and place amongst the general population, are painfully reminiscent of the situation in Germany at the end of the 20s and the beginning of the 30s. In some respects the situation here is easier, the Jews are integrated into an Anglo-Saxon civilization and not a Germanic one, but on the other hand their number is three times as great as it was in Germany, and their contribution, particularly in the fields of intellect, has not yet attained the height which it did in Germany in the first quarter of this century. If the Jews of America will be given a chance their performance will, I believe, be a greater and better one than that of the German Jews; but they have not yet had time to develop fully their potentialities. I was struck by a great number of young Jewish citizens of only first generation in America, modest intelligent workers, who are beginning to make their mark in science and the arts despite ever-increasing restrictions in opportunity. If things go normally here, and I ardently hope that will be the case, this will grow very much to the benefit of this country and probably to the honour of the Jewish community. But will it be allowed to grow and develop? This is the burning question which sub-consciously torments a great many Jews and is certainly a terrible problem facing us Zionists. Along with a new young generation of modest and honest workers, there is a certain part of Jewish bourgeoisie—rich, quasi-powerful, loud, vulgar, pulling a weight far in excess of their numbers, ostentatious—who, in the eyes of the Gentiles, they and almost they alone represent Jewry, and this is a grave danger. I shall not trouble you with examples, but I have met too many along my route and I am sure that you are more conscious of this state of affairs than I am. I believe that something can be done to mitigate some of the evils. There are no radical measures, but the few things which are being done lack courage, imagination and rational thinking. A typical example of it is the so-called anti-defamation work, or the extraordinary statements which one meets too often, that Zionist propaganda or the discussion of a Jewish State is responsible for the increase of anti-Semitism in this country. One could lay hands on one or two phenomena right here infinitely more dangerous than the above-mentioned problems, and they alone could account for a great deal of animosity towards the Jews on the part of the Gentile population. Two great organs shape public opinion, like the moving picture industry and the broadcasting systems, and both are controlled by Jews. As for the first, this control is in hands, into which one would not like to entrust such a delicate and important mechanism, which could accomplish a great deal in the direction of a proper education of the American people. It is not surprising that well-educated Americans, free from prejudice, resent bitterly such a phenomenon like Hollywood, of which I caught a glimpse during my tour. I am certain that the others would on a whole produce an equally unpleasant Hollywood, but they are the majority—are always right; and we, the minority, are always wrong. It does not enter within the purview of this letter, nor is it my business to suggest measures for the amelioration of this state of affairs, but I believe only Zionists could offer constructive proposals even in this direction, and if I have an opportunity to discuss it with you I shall try and develop this theme a little more fully. It is an urgent problem and I am afraid American Zionists cannot be absolved from the duty of taking a hand in its solution.

THE OPPOSITION: It came to my notice that some Jewish diehards are organizing themselves[6] with a view of combatting the Zionist aspirations and demands, which may be formulated as our peace aims. I do not know how serious it is, and I am not aware whether the number of such people is great and whether their influence is far-reaching, but it is something which cannot and must not be ignored by us because our non-Jewish opponents will always utilize any schism in order to thwart our endeavours. Even the most generously disposed Gentile statesman always becomes confused and weakened if he notices a divergence amongst the Jews. The Gentiles somehow expect the Jews always to be united; Jewish problems must be decided unanimously and the democratic majority principle is not applicable to us; they do not concede to us differences of opinion which are so common and natural in political lives of other peoples. And the moment a group of Jews, however small, proclaims an opinion which happens to differ from ours, it somehow affects the minds of the statesmen more deeply than both the nature of the views and the character of the exponents would justify. The British Government, and particularly that of Palestine, have always made good use of such an opposition, and are likely to do so in the future in an increased measure. Our embassy in Washington is listening carefully to non- or anti-Zionist Jews, is not capable or willing to assess the value and specific gravity of this opposition, is generally out of touch with any real democratic movement, looks to the Jewish notables for guidance and instruction in Jewish affairs, and transmits their opinion carefully to London, as it suits them. The non- or anti-Zionist Jews are easier to deal with, are perfectly

---

[6] See, e.g., No. 365, n. 8.

ready to accept the White Paper, and in fact are in fear of any expansion of our political rights in Palestine. They are, therefore, natural allies of our Gentile opponents. This danger extends a little further: in the State Department the gentlemen responsible for the Middle East are, in my opinion, in their conceptions, not one iota different from the Colonial Office officials; in fact, they are interchangeable. You could replace Murray[7] with Sir John Shuckburgh and it would not be noticeable either in Washington or in Downing Street. Murray and his assistants are quite well informed about matters Palestinian, but their information is tainted with an anti-Zionist bias. At the end of a very long conversation Murray remarked naively that when he was in Palestine the British officials had told him that a Jewish State would necessarily have Bolshevik tendencies. His office naturally imparts its information to men like Sumner Welles[8] or Hull,[9] and in its turn the information reaches the President,[10] who in spite of great sympathy for our cause cannot help being influenced by these opinions. Unless the President can form an independent opinion after having heard both sides of the story, it is likely that the attitude of his own officials, coupled with the British point of view, may affect his views to our disadvantage. You have no doubt seen the correspondence which has passed recently between Dr. Wise and the President concerning the re-arming of the Jews.[11] He has seriously adopted the British point of view which advanced the lack of equipment as the only obstacle in the way of our re-arming. We know that that is not quite correct. There may be a certain lack of equipment, but the main reason for not arming the Jews is political and bound up with the appeasement of the Arabs. The President, of course, cannot know that the Arabs

[7] Wallace Murray (Biog. Index). Chief of Division of Near Eastern Affairs at State Department.

[8] Biog. Index. Under-Secretary of State.

[9] Cordell Hull (Biog. Index). Secretary of State.

[10] Franklin Delano Roosevelt (Biog. Index, Vol. XIX).

[11] Wise had notified Roosevelt that, due to the latter's expressed interest, improved measures for the defence of Palestine had been taken. The President's immediate intervention was required, Wise continued, to warn Britain of the reaction should the Jews of Palestine be slaughtered owing to failure to arm them adequately. Roosevelt stated in reply that he believed Palestine's first line of defence lay in Egypt, Iraq and the Balkans, where British arms were severely extended. Further, in the N. Eastern campaign the British required the support not only of the Jews but of the far more numerous Arabs throughout the region. Therefore Roosevelt could only 'call to the attention of the British our deep interest in the defense of Palestine and our concern for the defense of the Jewish population there.' (This exchange, 13 May, 9 June 1941, in Wise Papers, Brandeis University.) See also Wise to Silver, 15 May 1941, ascribing to Presidential intervention Britain's abandonment of the 'parity rule' in recruitment.

are armed to the teeth and that they have been getting large quantities of arms from Syria, from the Germans and Italians and have probably appropriated a great deal of the British equipment, as was the case in the last war. Eden's speech is another case in point.[12] I am sure that he deliberately omitted to mention the Jews who have suffered so much in all these years. The President's attention must be called to this situation particularly now, when the United States is going to have such an increasingly important voice in the future settlement of affairs. All this political work has to be done expeditiously and methodically. You remember how much effort was expended on both sides of the Atlantic during the period preceding the issuance of the Balfour Declaration: you will feel with me that at present the situation is more complicated and requires a much greater expenditure of talent and energy in order to prepare the ground for a future favourable settlement. Neumann is doing very well, but he will be the first to admit that that is not enough and I do not know whether our office in Washington realizes how much should be done and what should be done. I confess I feel very uneasy about it all.

My letter has become very lengthy and I hope you will forgive its wordiness but that is a summary of a great many impressions gathered by one who is trying to observe closely the state of things here which must vitally affect our future. My time is up and I intend to return to London some time next month. I have left a great many things undone—some attempts like the re-organization of the Jewish Agency have been initiated—but this will need following up and very careful handling. I wish I could stay longer, but it is not possible for moral and other reasons. Whether I shall be returning within a measurable time to my work here is difficult to foretell at present, but I feel that some tightening up of our organization here will be urgently required. It will have to concentrate on the main political problem confronting us. The financial question can, I believe, take a second place, although money to maintain the structure in Palestine is naturally required, but this sort of money ought to come in more easily now than it did in years gone by. As for the finances required when the great opportunity will come, they will not be obtained by drives, however successful, but only by a loan supported by the Democracies, but this is again primarily a political problem.

You remember that we decided that I would attempt to see the President toward the end of my stay. I think the time has come now. Would you advise me to write directly to Sumner Welles, who was willing to arrange such an interview, or should I ask Mr. Morgenthau

[12] See No. 146, n. 2.

to fix it up for me? Please read this letter carefully and I would be grateful for a short reply[13] and for your advice regarding the last question. We intend to leave here after the 1st of July and hope to reach New York (the St. Regis) on the 2nd.

We both send our love to you and Mrs. Frankfurter.

Ch. W.

153. To Lord Moyne, London.

Arrowhead Springs, Calif., 21 June 1941

English: Or. Copy. T.W.: W.A.

I am afraid that you will think me remiss in my duty and failing to keep my promise to write to you. But my excuse should be that the work here has been very hard, entailing a great deal of travelling. I did not wish to write before my impressions had crystallized and this required the completion of the program first. I am now at the end of my tour, which was somewhat extensive. Apart from a lengthy stay in New York and two visits to Washington, the latter covering about ten days in all, I have been to Chicago, Cleveland, St. Louis, Kansas City, Detroit, Pittsburgh, Baltimore, Montreal, Ottawa, Toronto, and finally Los Angeles and San Francisco.

I have had an opportunity of seeing things at fairly close range and of meeting numbers of people, both Jews and non-Jews, in various stations of life. I am now taking about ten days' rest here and intend to return to New York on July 2nd in order to finish one or two things which still require attention, then to visit Boston, and to leave for home about the middle of July. I hope to get accommodation promptly so that, all being well, it is my intention to be in London about the 20th or 25th of next month, which is slightly more than a month from now.

THE WAR POSITION: Things are moving very rapidly here, and it is always somewhat hazardous to try and give a clear description of a dynamic state of affairs. In the three months spent in this country, one has seen great changes, both in the state of public opinion and in the actions of the administration, which is closely watching public opinion and adapts its steps to its moods. There is no slightest doubt that the President and his colleagues are determined to do all in their power in helping England to the limit of their possibility. This desire is sincere and genuine and the notion that England is the first line of defense for the United States is not merely a catch-

---

[13] Among those receiving copies of this letter were Wise, Silver, Lipsky and Jacob Blaustein (W.A.). No reply from Frankfurter traced.

phrase for propaganda purposes, but forms a fundamental conception determining the attitude of the Government. I doubt whether
the President would like to engage American man-power into this
struggle; he would naturally be happy if he could avoid doing it,
but I am sure—and this is confirmed by some of his utterances made
confidentially to his close advisers—that he sees clearly where the
logic of events is driving this country, which can no longer escape
the cruel necessity of taking its stand as a belligerent. The task before the President is neither easy nor simple. It is a vast and heterogeneous country. The Irish and the Germans are, in the majority,
hostile to England and some of them probably friendly to the dictators. They form important groups, influential in local politics if
perhaps not very powerful nationally. There are the Italians, a great
many fascist in outlook, but of course there are the friendly Poles,
Greeks, Czechs and Norwegians. There is also the usual group of
appeasers with which we are so familiar from our own history, led
primarily by Lindbergh and Wheeler,[1] and they have gathered
some momentum in these three months. They are constantly being
reinforced by German propaganda and make abundant capital
out of our difficulties and misfortunes. Talking to the common people—taxi-drivers, or on trains or in small places—one notices that
even in remote districts away from the Atlantic seaboard—there
exists a remarkable unanimity amongst the small people who condemn the attitude of the minority very strongly. In the eyes of the
common folk they are identified with Fascism or Nazism. But the
country is vast, and in spite of excellent communications by rail
or plane, in spite of the radio, the movies and the press, it is not
easy to weld and mold opinion into a harmonious whole, and this
accounts for the apparent slowness with which the administration
moves. It does seem slow to us, but I believe it to be very rapid,
under the circumstances prevailing here. After all, there is some
logic in the attitude of the non-interventionists, that the danger to
America is still remote and that, given a few quiet years in which to
prepare, this Colossus can ward off almost any onslaught: Why
rush? etc. etc. Remembering what we ourselves preached and prac-
tised before the collapse of Czecho-Slovakia and even during the
first year of the war, is it to be wondered that this American minority
can produce a plausible argument? And I think that we should be
the last to judge them severely.

153. [1] Charles A. Lindbergh (1902–74): Aviator, accomplished first solo flight across
Atlantic 1927; his decoration by German Government, 1938, attracted considerable criticism
in U.S., as did his 'neutrality' speeches there 1940–41. Burton Kendall Wheeler (1882–1975):
Senator, strongly isolationist, 1923–47.

There is another set of arguments which one hears from the young intelligent public—college graduates, professors and intellectuals generally. "What kind of war is it? Is it the old imperialism under a new guise, and if we are to fight, we ought to know what is going to be the future better world. Is it really going to be a genuine democracy?" And here again these young doubters are able to point to a great many weaknesses in our structure and to portents which do not inspire them with too much confidence—like some of the vague statements uttered by our statesmen. I am not referring to Jews, about whom I shall write later, but I am speaking of the young American intellectual who is occasionally tainted with a sort of mild parlour Bolshevism but to whom democracy has a real meaning, not merely as a formal political or parliamentary way of conducting business but as a mode of life. He somehow misses it in England, which he does not know and which he judges merely by the representatives who come over here and who are not his ideal of democrats. I was anxious about this—and I don't know whether you have noticed a cablegram of mine sent some time ago to 10 Downing Street recommending that people like Wedgwood, Tom Williams, Ellen Wilkinson should come here, unostentatiously.[2] They should go into the workshops, into the colleges and talk to the people and enlighten them. There are young people only too anxious to learn—they are not hardened in their opinions—but they hate being bamboozled by propaganda. I was happy to read that Wedgwood is already in this country, and am looking forward to seeing him on my return to New York. I hope that others may be spared to come over. They have a real task to perform. This category of young men and women may appear somewhat leftist to you, but upon them and the workingmen a great deal will depend here, as the war goes on.

PRODUCTION: One can obtain some idea of the potentialities of this country by visiting the middlewestern industrial centers. Some of them I have enumerated. It is no exaggeration to say that when this district alone gets into full swing it can produce more than the whole of Europe. But apart from this nucleus there are enormous possibilities both in the East and in the West, and one sees everywhere new plants being laid down and production getting under way. Experts and trained observers, university men in close cooperation with industry, have assured me that it would take another 4 or 5 months until the so-called "tooling" is completed

[2] See No. 137.

and then the amount of material produceable in 1942 is almost incalculable. I believe that at present the production is no more than 30% of the possible potential, but it is being stepped up quite rapidly, although not uniformly in all branches. Aircraft production moves quickly, tanks are slower, and I fear that the chemical industry is somewhat lagging behind. However, it is not easy for a stranger to assess these things properly, although I had access to people who seemed to know what they were talking about. I would like to add at the conclusion that things in Washington are at present in a state similar to ours two years ago. The gigantic problems are towering before the people and Government offices have increased in size enormously. I think the population of Washington has grown to a great number in a comparatively short time, and the heads of the administration have to grapple with unprecedented problems under severe pressure and as most of them have already two terms in office behind them they create the impression of tired men incapable of bringing a fresh mind to the complex questions facing them. I have no doubt, however, that the administration will have recourse to the ample reserves of intelligent human material available in this country. A short period of empiricism is bound to precede the creation of an adequate administrative machinery adapted to the new situation.

It is difficult to say what the origin of the labour troubles is. It may be due partly to sabotage, partly to propaganda, but I should imagine on a whole to a genuine fear on the part of the working classes of losing the privileges which they have gained under the New Deal after so much heart-searching and struggle (and frankly, I cannot blame the workingmen, whose position is only now becoming normalized). There is still a great deal of greed and profiteering here and the workman is suspicious of the employer whom he suspects as being out on a war-racket. I am informed on good authority that so far these strikes, although rather spectacular, have not seriously interfered with production, but as a symptom they are disconcerting. One can imagine that the President was very reluctant to call out the armed forces in order to break a strike, and he does so only *in extremis*, wisely relying on his mediation board and not on physical force. This situation of course may also be very much simplified if the country is placed on a war footing, which is of course very different from a state of national emergency which exists now. It will certainly come, although it may take time. The events in Russia and the blackmailing on the part of Japan may hasten this process and by the time this letter reaches you all that I am saying may prove to be obsolete. (Since dictating these words yesterday the war between Russia and Germany became a fact.

What effect it will have on this country is impossible to say at present.)[3]

THE JEWISH PROBLEM: I think I am right in saying that of all the ethnic groups comprising this country there are two which have taken a very definite stand in the problem of American entry into the war; they are the Anglo-Saxons and the Jews. For the latter the conquest of the Nazis constitutes a question of life and death and they are imbued with the conviction that only through America's joining up immediately with England in this struggle the world can become free again, and in union they see the salvation of humanity as a whole and perhaps of themselves in particular. I am using the word "perhaps" advisedly. Whereas it is axiomatic that the primordial requirement consists in the wiping out of the Nazi-Fascist evil, they have many reasons to doubt whether a military victory will bring them the relief and satisfaction to which they are entitled. They view the future with grave concern and they are appalled by the problem which will face Jewry after this war is over and they genuinely doubt whether the statesmen who will be reshaping the future world will show any generosity and foresight in their approach to the Jewish problem and its settlement, and that they will not merely dispose of it by improvising some form of a makeshift or compromise. (The Russian complication draws into the vortex another four million potential victims.) For the Jews here—like everywhere else I believe—the acid test of democracy is determined by the way their own grievous problem will be dealt with. A rising tide of anti-Semitism is evident in this country and the Jewish situation here contains many elements of grave danger. This, of course, makes the Jewish population here much more wide-awake to the realities as compared with the others, much keener to get on with the war, although on the other hand they are thwarted in this endeavour by a creeping fear that the non-interventionists may choose the Jews as a target for their accusation that they are dragging America into the war. This fear which was conspicuous about a year ago has greatly diminished now but it is still lingering on and dampens to some extent the fervour of the Jews.

In this state of mind Palestine plays no small part. You hear from time to time, no doubt, that there is opposition to Zionism and Palestine amongst the so-called influential Jews. This is not to be denied, but the term "influential" as far as the Jewish community is concerned cannot be applied to the very small number of so-called prominent Jews who may be trying to speak to British and American

---

[3] Germany invaded Russia 21 June 1941.

statesmen on behalf of Jewry but who would never dare to do so publicly as they know only too well that they would be violently disavowed by the overwhelming majority of the Jews. If ten years ago these rich and powerful people may have had some claim to leadership, they have lost it almost completely by now. They can only work subterraneously, utilize their social connections in order to press forward their point of view, but their value is almost nil in the eyes of the Jews, although I confess that some non-Jews, ill-informed about the real state of things, mistake them easily and sometimes too willingly for Jewish leaders. They are, of course, easier to deal with than the representatives of Jewish democracy. Palestine means nothing to some of these notables because they have been divorced from Judaism and therefore they will be ready to make concessions, for instance, to adopt the White Paper. In the eyes of some representatives of the British and Palestine admin-istrations such self-appointed Jewish leaders are always welcome and the others are conveniently dubbed "extremists." My visit here has made me acutely aware of this state of affairs. I may say without exaggeration that 95% or more of the Jews in this country are anxious to see the Palestinian problem settled fairly. Being at the same time animated by a keen desire not to embarrass His Majesty's Government at present, they are waiting patiently until the tide has turned, but then they rightly expect fair treatment for the Jews with regard to the Palestinian problem. They genuinely believe (and this belief is shared by a great many representatives of the administration including the President) that a decent settle-ment can be arrived at between the Jews and the Arabs, if the prob-lem is approached not merely from the point of view of expediency and appeasement but if inspired by a genuine desire to do justice. The Jews and a great many non-Jews believe that whatever the Arabs have now and are likely to have in the future, is and will be due entirely to the efforts of England and America and therefore it will depend upon the sense of justice of these two countries to bring about a satisfactory solution which they are entitled to enforce if necessary. England has, at present, its best friends in the Jews who are exposing themselves to a great many risks in view of the state of affairs in this country now. I could quote a whole galaxy of dis-tinguished men in every walk of life both in the capitals like Washing-ton and New York and in the provincial towns who are making every effort to speed things up and to help England in every con-ceivable way. I do not think that England has a better friend than Secretary Morgenthau. You know how much a treasury can ob-struct things, but he has done everything in order to smooth the way even at the risk of being reproached that he is doing these things as a Jew and not merely as a patriotic American. As a matter of fact he is both in a very high degree. He feels keenly that it is his duty as an American to render every possible assistance to England but he is also deeply concerned about the position of the Jews and the attitude of Great Britain towards Palestine. His is not an enviable position and I am afraid that many of us share the same fate. You will understand, therefore, that we were much exercised by the problem of re-arming the Jews in Palestine and even more by Mr. Eden's speech.[4] I know all the arguments concerning the first problem and you were good enough to discuss it very fully and frankly with me before I left for this country. But things have been moving so rapidly in these three months that it is difficult to understand the static attitude of the British Government with regard to the arming of the Jews in Palestine and to a Jewish army, particularly in view of the picture which the Arab world presents today. We feel deeply that appeasement, which may have disappeared from the English mind as far as world politics is concerned, has found its last strong-hold in the attitude of our British statesmen towards the Jews. The Arabs have betrayed and are betraying, and in the term "Arab" I include Egypt; therefore they must be appeased. The Jews are doing the impossible under difficult circumstances to render every assistance; therefore they can be ignored. All this seems so utterly absurd, short-sighted and un-English that I sometimes wonder whether this fear of the Arabs is not merely a feint which covers—subconsciously perhaps—something much deeper, namely, fear and suspicion of the Jew. This is an ancient experience to us dating from Pharaonic times. I am conscious that perhaps I am generalizing a little too severely, but I am giving you the general impression created in the Jewish mind and also on a great many Americans whom you can count amongst the best friends of England, foremost amongst them a person like Dorothy Thompson. Eden's speech, to return to it for a second, was vague and indefinite, and sinned by the deliberate omission to mention the Jews who have suffered so much at the hands of Nazism and to whom a word of comfort should have gone out at this time of trial and tribulation. I felt deeply shocked by this omission and have telegraphed to the Prime Minister to that effect.[5] I had reason to do so because the Prime Minister was particularly kind and encouraging to me before I left England.[6] I believe implicitly in what he said to me although it was a private statement. I believe in a future just settlement; I am

---

[4] See No. 146, n. 2.
[5] No. 148.
[6] See No. 129.

certain that the White Paper will eventually become a war casualty; that perhaps His Majesty's Government will be-think itself and take out from the pigeon-hole the Royal Commission's report[7] which it has adopted once and was ready to carry out, and find that with certain important readjustments the report and its ideas may become the basis of an imaginative constructive conception of a better Palestine reshaped after the war. I confess to you that I have been trying to adumbrate these ideas in many circles and have found deep understanding and sympathy in spite of some counter-propaganda which occasionally emanated from the Press Department of the Washington Embassy. I can assure you that this has served the British cause much more than some official statements, and it is likely to serve it in the future in an increased measure.

I am afraid that my letter has become lengthy and I hope that you will forgive both its size and its frankness. It would have been useless for me to write unless I might put before you the things as I see them and by doing so I hope to serve the cause of England and of my own people. I believe that the stars in their courses have decreed that these two causes are inter-twined. The binding link is the reverence which the two peoples have for the precepts of the Bible, which will survive this age of confusion. Those who tamper with them commit a grave sin against the two peoples, which in the end must be expiated.

I am looking forward to seeing you soon and to report personally and in greater detail on the impressions which I have gained during my stay in this great and most interesting country where I have learned a great deal and where I have tried in some small measure to help our common cause.

P.S.   I hope that you will find it possible to show this letter to the Prime Minister as I do not wish to trouble him with a lengthy document.

154. To Jacob Blaustein,[1] Baltimore.
Arrowhead Springs, Calif., 23 June 1941

English: Or. Copy. T.W.: W.A.

My dear Mr. Blaustein,

I am writing to you from here where I find myself after the work has been completed in our last two cities of Los Angeles and San

---

[7] Peel Commission, which recommended partition of Palestine (see Vol. XVIII).

154. [1] 1892–1970. Industrialist and philanthropist; a founder of American Oil Company,

Francisco. We both needed a rest badly and we are taking it here where the main hotel is closed, so that the place is very quiet indeed and we are enjoying the privacy of a small bungalow. We intend to return to New York on the 2nd of July, and will probably leave for England soon after the 15th.

For your private and confidential information, you will receive copy of a letter which I have just sent to Justice Frankfurter, and I am asking Meyer Weisgal to forward it on to you.[2] This letter sums up very inadequately my impressions gained on this tour, and it is for your information only.

I am hoping to see you before I leave this country, and it may be that I shall still have to go to Washington, and in that event we might meet there.[3] I have not dealt with the matter of the JTA because it would be useless now to communicate with Palestine, as they are at present living under very high pressure and in great danger. We have drawn Dr. Landau's[4] attention to the situation, which I believe he would easily understand. But as soon as things become easier, I propose to deal with the matter and come to some positive conclusion.

I would feel greatly obliged to you if you could activate the collection of money for Rehovoth where it is needed now very very badly, and I shall be grateful to hear from you at your earliest convenience.

With kind regards to you and Mrs. Blaustein, in which Mrs. Weizmann joins me, I am

Ch. Weizmann

155. To Benjamin Bloch, Rehovot.

English: T.W.: W.A.   *Arrowhead Springs, Calif., 23 June 1941*

My dear Dr. Bloch,

I was really delighted to receive your letters of May 23rd here.[1] They have reached me comparatively quickly and brought me explanations which I have urgently required.

of which President 1933–37; Vice-Chairman of American Petroleum Administration's Marketing Committee during W.W.II. President of American Jewish Committee 1949–53.

[2] See No. 152.

[3] Apparently they did not meet in Washington.

[4] Jacob Landau (1892–1952). Journalist, founded and directed Jewish Telegraphic Agency in London. Established his headquarters in New York 1940; there, with an American group, he founded the Overseas News Agency, specializing in news of minority peoples of all races and religions. See also No. 165.

155. [1] Only one letter traced (W.A.) concerning a possible decrease in the Sieff Institute

I have now concluded my tour here and am taking a few days' rest before returning to New York, where I intend to stay from the 2nd to the middle of July, and then return to London. We have been able to interest a great many circles in the work of the Institute, and I think that this interest has found practical expression in strengthening the Foundation. I am not in a position to determine exactly how much money will come into the treasury within the next two or three months, but I believe that we have promises amounting to about $90,000 over and above what we have already sent to you. By this time you will have received £4,000 from the American side, and you will probably get another £2,000 soon from Canada. There is always a certain amount of loss, as there are usually a few people who do not live up to their promises and so it is safer to reckon on $75,000. As far as I can see from here, the state of your finances is as follows: By the end of this month (which means for the 1st six months of this year) you will have received

£ 3,000	from	M[arks] and S[ieff]
4,000	"	the Foundation here
2,000	"	Canada
750	"	Eng. Zionist Fed'n
250	"	Walter Baer
1,700		with your cash surplus carried over from 1940
£11,700		Total

Now your budget is £12,000. You have spent £4,000 on account of Wolf's money. I fear from reading between the lines of your letter that £12,000 will not suffice as a budget, and therefore it is just as well to add another £1,500 so that your total requirements to the end of 1941 are £17,500, against which you have received £11,700, so that we have to send you another £5,800 at the end of this year. You are still to receive from the [Marks and Sieff] family £3,000 and from South Africa £500 at least, so that the remaining £2,300 will have to be supplied by the Foundation here, and I shall give instructions to that effect before leaving. I have mentioned to you before that we can reckon on an income of $75,000 in 1941, after deducting another $10,000 roughly, which will still have to be sent to you; and the Foundation will be left with a cash surplus in dollars of something like $60,000. This money I would like to keep as a reserve for the year 1942 as we do not know

budget for the coming year. Bloch pointed out that even according to the existing budget, £12,000, he would need either to dismiss staff or reduce salaries. He also wrote of beginning production at their new pharmaceuticals factory.

whether England will still be able to continue its contribution and you will have to rely almost entirely on America. Neither can I assume that in 1942 the income from the Foundation will be the same as this year, if I am not in America again. If I should come over there would be no difficulty in raising another hundred thousand, but all that is uncertain. I thought I should let you know what the exact financial position is. All that one can do now is to look ahead 18 months, and that is a great deal in these critical times. I hope that this statement is satisfactory to you and will help you in some way to get over your difficulties.

With reference to your second letter of May 23rd, giving me a brief statement on the work of the chemists, I can only say that apart from a short statement by Dr. Simon and Dr. Hirschberg,[2] I have received no report at all from Miss Goldschmidt or from Miss Hellinger, and I am therefore not in a position to judge. Possibly these things have gone to London, which I left more than 3 months ago. They certainly have not been sent on to me by Bergmann amongst the various reports which have reached me. I am not in a position, naturally, to suggest subjects for work or to express an opinion about their current operations. I would like, however, to draw to Miss Hellinger's attention that the culture of the pink butyric which I have received from her proved to be impure and we have isolated two definite and different organisms, one colorless, which is a weak fermenter, and the other, pink, which is strong. I think I have mentioned the matter to her before and she should bear it in mind for the future. As soon as I return to London I shall consider with Dr. Bergmann and the government authorities whether it is wise for Miss Hellinger to come over. There may be something in that suggestion, but it can only be done if the Minister of Supplies [sic] considers her presence here useful from a war point of view. I am sending your letter on to Lewis Ruskin and Nate Shapero in Detroit, as I believe it will serve as an incentive for them to go forward psychologically in placing the Foundation on a secure basis.

Give my love to my family in Haifa and everywhere else. I have not been writing to them because there is really very little to say. All that one wants to know is that one is alive, and that they surely know from our correspondence. My love to my sister Anna and all good wishes.

---

[2] Ernst Eytan Simon (1902–73): biochemist. B. Germany, emigrated to Palestine 1935; employed at Sieff Institute, later at Weizmann Institute. Yehuda Hirschberg (1903–60): Physical chemist. Joined Sieff Institute 1933; later head of Laboratory of Photochemistry and Spectroscopy at Weizmann Institute.

Letter 156   *Aet. 66*

I hope that you may be spared the horrors of war. We all here feel with you and pray for your safety.

> With affectionate regards to you I am,
> Yours ever,
> Ch. Weizmann

156. To Albert K. Epstein, Chicago.

Arrowhead Springs, Calif., 23–24 June 1941

English: Or. Copy. T.W.: W.A.

I was glad to receive your letters.[1] You must never hesitate to write to me as your letters are always welcome.

I am afraid that it is too late in the season to think of a collection amounting to such a sum as you mention, although the Zionists should feel it a duty and an honour to do it. There was an idea that on my return now collection for a large fund should be initiated, but I am informed from New York that it is risky at this time of the year as most of the people are dispersed. When I was in Canada I spoke to our Zionist friends there and they definitely promised me $100,000 if America goes forward with a correspondingly large sum. I shall, however, take this matter up with the leaders to see whether some attempt could not be initiated in the late summer after the hot season is over.

With the exception of one visit to Boston and of tying up some loose ends in New York I have completed my program, although the term "completed" is merely a metaphor. Sometimes it appears to me that I have only just begun, but my time is up and I have to return to London in July—probably the second half of the month. We shall be passing through Chicago on the morning of the second, and I understand from the schedule that we shall have half of an hour stop there. We shall inform you in good time so that I am still looking forward to seeing you, even for a short while, and perhaps arrange for a meeting in New York where we could discuss some Zionist matters and also some of the chemical problems which I have raised with you, and which have now matured a little further— and you will be interested to hear about it.

Will you please give my kindest regards to Professor Ipatieff[2] and recover from him the papers which I gave him as I am afraid I shall not be able to see him personally. I may telephone him from

156. [1] Untraced.

[2] Vladimir Nikolaevich Ipatieff (1867–1952). Russian-born Professor of Chemistry at Northwestern University 1931–35, then Professor Emeritus. Director of Research, Universal Oil Products Co.

New York after I have seen him[*sic*]. Do you think that Pines[3] might be invited to work on some of my processes if and when a serious organization is created which will take up the manufacturing? You need not trouble to write to me here, but you can answer these questions personally, and you can also bring me the papers. Also, if you have more copies of the picture taken by your son of Ipatieff and myself, I would be very glad to have a few of them.

My love to you and Harris[4] and to your family from both of us.

Affectionately yours,

24 June 1941

Many thanks for your note which arrived this morning.[5] I believe that I already informed you that there is a group of serious financial people in New York ready to take up the cracking process and I have also invited Prof. Berl of the Carnegie Institute in Pittsburgh,[6] who as you know is a very distinguished technologist, to act as technical adviser to this group, which he has accepted. These people are prepared to proceed with the setting up of a pilot plant, if necessary, or, alternatively, to obtain information from London which may possibly entail bringing Dr. Bergmann over. The latter would depend upon the outcome of the negotiations with the ICI in England, who have apparently, judging by repeated telegrams, advanced very considerably. From information received, which is not absolutely clear as the telegrams arrived in a mutilated form, it seems that the ICI is prepared to support the processing of about 25,000 tons of oil residue per annum and to pay a royalty of a pound or 30 shillings per ton of raw material. I was waiting to hear the final result before communicating definitely with you on this matter, but as you know such things always take longer than anticipated. Perhaps by the time we meet next week there may be something definite to report and we can lay plans accordingly.

We are having a very good rest here which is an ideal place. This respite will be over soon but it is doing us a great deal of good. We were both feeling extremely tired after the exertions of these months. I cannot help feeling that this work has to be continued in an ever-increasing degree but I fail to see who will do it after I return to London. However, I cannot help it any further.

Much love to you and Harris.

[3] Herman Pines, b. 1902, Poland. Emigrated to U.S. 1928; research chemist Universal Oil Products Co. 1930–52.

[4] Benjamin R. Harris, b. 1896. Chemical engineer, head of Epstein, Reynolds and Harris, Consulting Chemists and Engineers in Chicago; brother-in-law of Albert K. Epstein.

[5] Untraced.

[6] Ernst Berl (1877–1946). B. Austria, emigrated to U.S. 1933; Research Professor Carnegie Institute of Technology.

157. To Stanley A. Weigel,[1] San Francisco.

Arrowhead Springs, Calif., 23 June 1941

English: T.W.: Photostat W.A.

My dear Mr. Weigel,

I have to begin with an apology for giving your letter of the 13th[2] my attention at this late date, but I really had no free moment until we reached here where I am trying to get a few days' rest, at the end of a difficult tour, before returning to my work in New York and subsequently proceeding to London. I am sure you will understand and forgive the delay.

You are asking me a somewhat difficult question. It is not easy to suggest or to assign a piece of work for Palestine for one who is, as you say, rather dissociated from Jewish life, and who lives in San Francisco—far removed from the mainstream of Jewish endeavour and activities. But I have been thinking your inquiry over, and the best thing that I can do—and I am certain that that is right—is to suggest to you a preliminary study of the problem before you really make up your mind to associate yourself with a piece of practical work. The Jewish problem and Palestine are complex questions of many facets, and one cannot just step into it without understanding and agreeing to the trends. If one wishes to associate himself with it intelligently, a preliminary inquiry is indicated. It is again not easy for me to suggest to you what you should read, to begin with, and I don't know whether you can put your hands on books easily in San Francisco on the subjects under consideration. There is a vast literature both on the Zionist movement and Palestine, as well as on the Jewish question in general, but for your guidance I might suggest the following:

1) *The Jews of Today*, by Arthur Ruppin.
2) *A Selection of Essays on Jewish Nationalism*, by Achad Ha'am[3] (translated into English by Leon Simon).
3) *The History of the Zionist Movement*, by Gelber.[4] (It is written in German and I do not know whether there is a translation of it available—neither do I know whether there is an English translation of my speeches, of which a selection has been published in German a few years ago.)[5]

---

157. [1] B. 1905. In legal practice, San Francisco 1928–62; then district court judge.

[2] Untraced.

[3] Pseudonym of Asher Zvi Ginzberg (Biog. Index, Vol. I). Philosopher, writer; father of cultural Zionism, and W.'s mentor.

[4] Nathan Mikhael Gelber (1891–1966). Austrian historian; emigrated to Palestine 1934, employed until 1954 at K. H. Office. Prolific author.

[5] As *Reden und Aufsaetze*, ed. G. Krojanker, Tel Aviv 1937.

4)   *The Report of the Royal Commission on Palestine,* and my opening statement made before the Commission.

5)   *A Series of Reports by the Executives of the Jewish Agency,* presented annually to begin with, and you should ascertain from either Judge Golden or Mr. Leo Rabinowitz[6] of your city how to obtain these books—or they may be in possession of some.

I would generally recommend to you to have a good talk with either or both of these gentlemen who are well acquainted with the movement.

I am afraid that you may consider me rather formal, but I do believe that the only way of serving the Zionist cause effectively is to become acquainted with it fully. You will then not require my advice, but you will be able to decide things for yourself much more freely.

With best wishes, I am,

Sincerely yours,
Chaim Weizmann

158. To Dorothy Backer,[1] New York.
Arrowhead Springs, Calif., 25 June 1941

English: Or. Copy. T.W.: W.A.

Dear Mrs. Backer,

I was delighted to hear from Meyer that George[2] is back. He also mentioned to me that you expected a confidential memorandum on the political situation. I think that instead of doing that I had better enclose copies of two somewhat lengthy letters which I have sent out from here to Felix Frankfurter, giving a summary of the impressions I gained about the position of our movement during my tour these three months, and the other letter to Lord Moyne, Colonial Secretary. You will easily see from these two documents how much work there is to do in order to make reasonably sure that our cause will not go by default. There is nothing said in these two documents about the work which will be required to be done in Pales-

---

[6] Isidore Michael Golden (1878–1941): Asst. District Attorney, San Francisco 1918–32; superior court judge 1934–41. Further information on Rabinowitz untraced. W. wrote to them both that day mentioning Weigel (W.A.).

158. [1] B. 1903. Wife of George Backer, daughter of Jacob Schiff. Associated with *New York Post* from 1939, when it was purchased by her husband. Following divorce in 1942, she became its owner, and eventually editor-in-chief. She later married Rudolph Sonneborn.

[2] George Backer (1902–74). Publisher, politician and communal leader; served on New York City Council; publisher and editor, *New York Post*.

tine and the Middle East, primarily the various Arab groups with which we can maintain contact. It involves the production of good literature in English, French and Arabic, creation of a distinguished group of writers and journalists who would try and place our case before the public opinion through the medium of the great journals and newspapers in this country and in England. It requires sending people to the Middle East like Egypt, Iraq, Syria and India to get in touch with prominent Moslem and Hindu leaders in their respective countries. I have indicated sufficiently to you so that you could form an idea as to what sort of program has to be fulfilled in a comparatively short time. This will require a heavy fund, which as far as I can see can only be raised in this country, in Canada, and perhaps to a smaller degree in England. Canada has promised me $100,000. If America would raise anything like it commensurate with its population to that of the Canadian community, then I feel that we might have enough for our purpose.

Please give my love to George.

Ch. Weizmann

159. To Arde (André) Bulova,[1] New York.

Arrowhead Springs, Calif., 25 June 1941
English: Or. Copy. T.W.: W.A.

I have been waiting for an opportunity to write to you for many weeks, but the pressure of work and this trip to the coast have prevented me from discharging this pleasant duty up to this writing. I have now completed the tour and am taking a short rest here with the intention of returning to New York on July 2nd.

I am very happy to have had the occasion of meeting with you in the course of my visit to the States this year, and to have found such clear-thinking realization and understanding on your part of the various problems which we discussed. You may perhaps recall that we were prevented from meeting during my visit to this country last year due to your absence from America, to which you returned after I had already left these shores.

It is most heartening to me that as a result of our recent conversation something may be created in Palestine which is a prerequisite for the development of a fine-mechanical industry. We do have there some highly qualified experts, like Professor Goldberg[2] and others

---

159. [1] D. 1958. Chairman, Bulova Watch Company.

[2] Emmanuel Goldberg, b. 1891. Physicist; head of Instrument Department at Carl Zeiss Company in Germany until 1933; in France 1933–37, when settled in Tel Aviv.

previously connected with the firm of Zeiss, and I believe that we could train quite a number of young Jews in this important branch of industry. We both seemed to be in agreement in feeling that this industry will find an easy market in countries of the Near and Middle East, India included. I would like to add that the establishment of a workshop, such as we discussed, in the very near future by an American industrialist of your reputation during an international emergency is bound to have an important moral effect not only on the Jewish community in Palestine but also here. It is now being realized that the Middle East is strategically a direct concern of the U.S.A.

I am looking forward to seeing you again soon.[3] It is my intention to leave for London about the middle of July.

With kind regards, I am

Ch. Weizmann

160. To Shalom Horowitz,[1] Jerusalem.

Arrowhead Springs, Calif., 25 June 1941

English: Or. Copy. T.W.: W.A.

Ever so many thanks for your letter.[2] I was delighted to hear from you and to find that you were able to throw off for the time being your ordinary routine work and devote yourself to matters of social importance.

What you write to me about B. Levin is a very terrible example of handling a problem by the authorities concerned, which should be dealt with sympathetically and understandingly. Levin is not a genius, but the little I know about his work and the opinions I heard expressed about it in Paris seem to entitle him to much more favourable consideration than the University authorities have shown. In his particular case more delicacy of understanding was expected. I do not know whether I shall have an opportunity of taking it up with Mr. Schocken who is here trying to gain friends for the Uni-

---

[3] W. and Bulova did not in fact meet again during 1941. They next corresponded in 1946 on the possible training of Palestinians at Bulova's factory (W.A.).

160. [1] Biog. Index, Vol. XIV. Attorney; Trustee of Daniel Sieff Institute; on Executive Committee Hebrew University, Jerusalem.

[2] 13 May 1941 (W.A.). Horowitz was administrator of the estate of the Zionist leader and writer Shmarya Levin (Biog. Index, Vol. III), whose son Baruch held a research post in bacteriology at Hebrew University, a post now in jeopardy due to insufficient funds. Horowitz wrote that while the University recognised that the research was valuable, the Senate had decided that it discontinue due to lack of funds. He sought W.'s help in raising £P300 for the coming three to four years, to enable Levin to be retained.

versity, but I am prepared to promise now that I shall secure the sum of money mentioned by you for the next 3 years so that B. Levin may be enabled to continue his work without let or hindrance. I am here for only a few days, taking a rest after a grinding tour which is now completed, and as soon as I get to New York I shall carry my promise into effect, and you may receive the money probably before this letter comes into your hands.[3]

I am grateful to you for having drawn my attention to this problem.

With all good wishes to you and all the other friends in Jerusalem, I am

Ch. Weizmann

161. To Abe Cahan,[1] New York.   *New York, 8 July 1941*
English: T.W.: Photostat W.A.

On my return from a coast to coast tour of this country, I see in the papers that you are celebrating your 81st birthday. I hasten to extend to you my sincerest and most heartfelt wishes for the fulfilment of your own desire so well expressed by you. May it be given to you to see the end of this dark period and the beginning of happier days for mankind and for our own people.

I shall now be staying here for a day or two, spending the weekend in Boston, and I shall try to come and see you before leaving for Europe.

With renewed good wishes and affection, I am

162. To Robert Szold, New York.   *New York, 10 July 1941*
English: T.W.: Photostat W.A.

Dear Mr. Szold,

I have read your letter of the 8th[1] with the utmost astonishment. I am at a loss to understand its purpose, or to account for the extraordinary tone of rancor and misinterpretation which runs through it.

---

[3] W. cabled Horowitz 8 July (W.A.) that he had secured half the sum required, and had left the matter with Weisgal, who notified W. 25 Aug. 1941 (W.A.) that $1,200 had been raised. Levin later established the Rafa Pharmaceutical Company in Israel.

161. [1] 1860–1951. Russian-born editor, author, Socialist leader; emigrated to U.S. 1897. Founded Yiddish daily *Forward* 1897, and was its editor for almost half a century. Wrote in Yiddish and English; a Zionist from 1925.

162. [1] Copy in W.A. This charged W. with disloyalty to the current Z.O.A. chairman, and with canvassing for the return of Lipsky and Weisgal, whose 'regime of 1920–30' proved, according to Szold, disastrous to American Zionism.

Let me begin with your observations on my purported remarks regarding Mr. E. I. Kaufman. I am perfectly clear in my memory as to what I said; and I permit myself to think that I have had some practice in conveying my meaning. Not only would it have been in the poorest taste for me to have "mercilessly attacked" Mr. Kaufman; it would have been doing violence to my own feelings about a sincere personal friend and an honourable gentleman. In any case, had I indulged in such tactlessness and unprovoked hostility, it seems to me that some reaction on the spot would have been called for by those who pretend to have a higher regard for Mr. Kaufman. It is needless for me to say that I have no intention of entering into a defence. My purpose is to make the matter clear and to anticipate and prevent the harm which your inexplicable expression of opinion may cause.

I made, as I thought it my duty to do, certain constructive suggestions for the harnessing of all our available forces. To construe this as a proposal to displace Mr. Kaufman indicates, I venture to say, a spirit of obstruction. It is quite clear from certain passages in the letter that this spirit derives from old animosities which the urgency of the moment, as well as the passage of time, should have eliminated from the Zionist scene. May I point out the rather extraordinary fact that not a single expression of opinion remotely resembling yours has reached me, orally or in writing, from any one else who attended the meeting?

I was meticulously careful throughout my stay in America not to interfere in any internal affairs of the Z.O.A., and I don't propose to be dragged into them now. I resent, therefore, any imputation to that effect.

It is not my place to comment on your amazing description of the period of 1920–30 in American Zionism. But I would consider myself derelict in my duty both as President of the Zionist Organization and as a friend and colleague of Mr. Lipsky, if I did not protest with the utmost sharpness against your contemptuous references to his personality and his services to the movement.

I am particularly grieved to note that in the case of Mr. Weisgal you do not content yourself with what is, I venture to say, an irrelevant expression of personal distaste, but permit yourself imputations as to his honesty which really calls for an explanation.[2] I have from time to time entrusted Mr. Weisgal with Zionist work of considerable importance. I am, I believe, thoroughly familiar with his abilities and his character; and I must emphatically reject your

---

[2] For the meeting of Zionist leaders convened by W. and referred to here, and for Szold's appraisal of Weisgal, see the latter's memoirs, *op. cit.*, pp. 167–68.

slanderous references to him. I have felt it my duty to show your letter to Mr. Weisgal.

Do let me say this in conclusion. The times are too grave and too terrible to permit personal bitterness, on any side, and however deeply felt, to play a part. The real burden of my remarks on Tuesday was that there is a tremendous piece of work to be done and little time in which to do it, and that we need all the available forces including, naturally, the President of the Zionist Organization of America. No other possible construction by any *tour de force*, could be placed on my remarks.[3]

Sincerely yours,

163. To Viscount Halifax, Washington. *Boston, 13 July 1941*
English: Copy. T.W.: W.A.

With this visit to Boston, I shall have finished my tour through this country. It was rather extensive and most interesting, and I was able to gather a great deal of information.

It is my intention to return to England as soon as possible. Wedgwood, with whom we met yesterday, tells me that he is leaving here on the 20th from Baltimore, directly for England. If it were possible for Mrs. Weizmann and myself to go by the same line I would be most grateful if the Embassy could extend this facility to us. The prospect of going through Lisbon is not particularly attractive, firstly because it is longer both as to route and time, and secondly because Lisbon is full of Nazi spies. Wedgwood is leaving on the 20th. I have still some matters to finish in New York, and there is a possibility of my having to go to Washington in connection with some chemical problems; so that any opportunity for returning between the 20th and the 25th would suit me very well.

If I am in Washington, may I call upon you to tell you of the impressions which I have gained in the course of my tour. Should my trip to Washington not take place, I shall be hoping to see you in London, as I understand from the press that you intend to be there

---

[3] No reply traced. W. sent copies of Szold's letter to Wise, 9 July, and to Kaufman, 11 July. Wise wrote to Szold 10 July 1941, stating that he did W. a 'great injustice' by his 'woeful misinterpretation of the spirit of W.'s statement,' and that far from being unduly critical of Kaufman, W. was 'sharply and perhaps unjustly critical of the entire Zionist leadership in America.' Wise himself so resented the criticism as to consider whether they should not hand in their resignations, leaving W. to find 'younger and stronger successors.' However, Wise believed that W. had handled Kaufman with great reserve, carefully avoiding wounding him or his friends. He also believed that it had been W.'s policy not to intervene in Z.O.A. internal conflicts (Wise Papers, Brandeis University, U.S.A.).

in the middle of August. Meanwhile, I beg to apologize for troubling you with this note, and to thank you in advance for any help you can give me in this matter.[1]

With kind regards to Lady Halifax and yourself, and with very best wishes for your trip I remain

Ch. Weizmann

P.S. I shall be returning tomorrow, Monday, to my permanent address in New York, the St. Regis Hotel.

164. To Israel Goldstein, New York.   *New York, 18 July 1941*
English: T.W.: Photostat W.A.

I have just received a letter from my old friend Mr. Naiditch[1] in which he outlines to me the story of Mr. Fisher's behaviour towards him in the case of the 600,000 francs which he had handed over to Mr. Fisher on behalf of the J.N.F.[2] I suppose that the facts are known to you and that their repetition, therefore, is unnecessary, but the story seems to me to be rather appalling.

Firstly, an exchange was offered to Mr. Naiditch which deprives him of about 50% of the amount originally agreed upon, and instead of paying him the equivalent in American currency in cash, he is being offered three year bonds. I find that a great injustice is being inflicted upon Mr. Naiditch: here is a man who has been serving the Zionist cause faithfully for something like 50 years and has always been a generous contributor to everything Zionistic. When he lived in France he was the central figure to whom everybody turned in case of need. It is hard to become a refugee at his advanced age and have to build up a new position in a strange country. But he is doing it with great energy and dignity. Under the difficult circumstances in which he finds himself at present every sum in cash which he can command is of the utmost importance to him and I fail to understand why the National Fund, or rather, Mr. Fisher, has thought it necessary (a) to make a profit on this transaction to the detriment of Mr. Naiditch, and (b) to withhold a cash payment and spread it over three years, which in Mr. Naiditch's cir-

---

163. [1] Replying 14 July (W.A.), Halifax stated that places had been reserved as W. requested, the plane being due to leave 23 July. Halifax would not himself be in Washington for some days, and therefore hoped to meet W. in London. The Weizmanns arrived back at the Dorchester Hotel, London, 25 July 1941.

164. [1] Isaac Naiditch (Biog. Index, Vol. VI). A founding-director of K.H.; a founder of Dead Sea Potash Company and Palestine Electric Corporation.
[2] Mendel N. Fisher (d. 1975). J.N.F. Executive Director in U.S. 1936–64.

cumstances and at his age is harsh, unfair and really unworthy of an institution like the Jewish National Fund.

I am sure that you will see that justice is done to Mr. Naiditch and I trust to your sense of fairness to deal with this matter promptly and in a manner worthy of the tradition of the J.N.F. I understand from Mr. Naiditch that Mr. Ussishkin[3] does not know anything about this matter, and under the present difficulties of communication it is not possible for him to apprise him of this matter; otherwise I would have done it at once. I propose, however, to write him at the earliest opportunity. But once more I would like to express the hope that you will settle this question so that there should be no need for me to appeal to the Executive or to the President of the J.N.F.[4]

With many thanks and kind personal regards I am,

165. To Louis Lipsky, New York.   *New York, 18 July 1941*
English: T.W.: Photostat W.A.

My dear Lipsky,

As you know, during my stay here I have had several conferences with Messrs. Blaustein, Backer and Landau with reference to Palcor and the J.T.A. There seems to be a desire on the part of the J.T.A. to come to an understanding with Palcor, with a view to eliminating competition and unnecessary expenses, and with the intention, at the same time, of creating a more cordial relationship between the J.T.A. and the Zionist group here.[1]

I am fully aware of the circumstances which gave rise to Palcor. I am equally conscious of the need for a great body like the Zionist Organization to have its own organs for public relations. But I also feel that there is a genuine desire on the part of the men with whom I have discussed the matter to arrive at an equitable arrangement whereby our interests will be fully served and protected.

It has been my policy not to interfere with Zionist administrative affairs. My life would not be worth much if I became involved in these thousand and one details which must, of necessity, be taken off my shoulders. In this case, however, I would be grateful if you

---

[3] Menahem Ussishkin (Biog. Index, Vol. I). J.N.F. President 1923–41.
[4] No reply to this letter, nor a letter to Ussishkin on this matter, traced.

165. [1] J.A. had in 1933 established its own news agency Palcor to counterbalance what it then considered the one-sided reporting of J.T.A., which showed Revisionist leanings. Landau had been subsidised from official Zionist funds. The agencies worked parallel until 1948 when, with the establishment of the State, Palcor was dissolved. See also No. 154.

and your associates, together with Mr. Montor, would get into conference with Messrs. Blaustein, Backer and Landau, in order to explore the possibility of a mutually advantageous arrangement. I on my part am prepared to recommend to our friends in Palestine the acceptance of an adjustment of the situation if and when it is finally consummated on this side. Weisgal knows my views on the situation, and, if desired, he can be helpful in the effort to arrive at an understanding.

You know how deeply interested I am in the creation of a united Jewish front. We need every available force. The removal of friction in this matter may be a contributing factor. I know that I shall have your cooperation.[2]

With best wishes, I am

Sincerely yours,
Chaim Weizmann

166. To André Benoît Meyer, New York.   *New York, 20 July 1941*
English: Or. Copy. T.W.: W.A.

I would like to refer to the conversation which took place between yourself, Prof. Errera and myself last evening. It was agreed that you will be good enough to undertake the necessary soundings and steps in connection with the placing before interested parties of my patents (concerning foodstuffs) which have already been granted, and the cracking of oil residues (which have been applied for) and possibly the patents concerning fermentation which have also been applied for. These interested parties may either acquire them themselves for purposes of manufacturing or of entering into negotiations with existing chemical firms which would undertake the exploitation of these processes.

It was agreed that Prof. Jacques Errera would act as your consultant and adviser in this matter, and that he would use the good offices of the Grosvenor Laboratories in New York for the above-mentioned purposes. In case of need you would call upon the advice and services of Prof. Ernst Berl of the Carnegie Institute (home address Schenley Apartments), whose acquaintance you have made recently. Should you desire to deal with the fermentation problem, I suggest that you invite Dr. H. J. Prebluda (whose home address is 3916 Maine Avenue, Baltimore), with whom I have spoken repeatedly and who would answer your call when he receives it, as I have informed him only yesterday of such an eventuality. The preliminary investiga-

---

[2] No reply traced.

tions which would be carried out by Prof. Errera should not take too much time, and should not involve you in any too great expenditure. The sum of something like $5,000 for the next three months was mentioned. If at the end of this period it is found that there is a reasonable probability of a successful outcome of these negotiations, then it is proposed that a holding company should be formed and the distribution of interests in this holding company and the protection of my interests should be left open for the moment, as it is hoped that I will be back in November when you would have a plan ready on which I am sure we shall all agree easily.

Prof. Errera called to see me this afternoon and I showed him the papers which are all collected and classified, and I now hand them over to you herewith. I have also left there a letter of introduction to my patent agent in Washington requesting him to give you both all information which you may require in connection with the applications.

This renders substantially in brief the results of our conversation and I would only like to express my profound gratitude to you for the very kind interest you have taken in this matter. I feel that I have left it in very safe hands and that the way we have marked out is likely to lead to success. As you know, I intend to leave on Wednesday hoping to reach London about the 25th. In London we have been carrying out negotiations with the I.C.I. and other parties, which have, judging from the telegrams, advanced considerably. I shall, as soon as I get home, in view of the results of these negotiations, send you a full report of all the technical results obtained, both in the laboratory in London and in the pilot plant in Manchester.

167. To Westminster Food Officer, London. *London, 11 August 1941*
English: Or. Copy. T.W.: W.A.

Dear Sir,

Dr. Ch. Weizmann—AYOV/1/172
Mrs. Vera Weizmann—AYOV/1/170

The Hotel Manager has shown me your letter to him of August 8 (L.90/RFM/ME), from which I note that the Board of Trade has decided that "persons entering the country after July 28th should not be issued with pages of margarine coupons," from which I infer that persons who returned *before* that day are entitled to the issue of these coupons. Mrs. Weizmann and I returned to this country after four months' absence in America (during which, for obvious reasons, we had made no purchases of clothes) on the night of the

24th/25th July, and would therefore appear to be entitled to the pages of margarine coupons from our old Ration Books in the normal course. I should be grateful if you would let me know whether these coupons can be supplied from your office, or whether I have also to write to the Board of Trade at Bournemouth, even though we returned to this country within the time-limit laid down.

I am, dear Sir,

Yours faithfully,

Ch. W.

168. To Josef Cohn, New York.   *London, 12 August 1941*
English: T.W.: W.A.

Dear Josef,

I was somewhat surprised on receipt of your letter to read that the £1,000 for Rehovot will be sent "soon."[1] I fail to understand why this money was not sent immediately—as we agreed before my departure from New York. From telegrams received from Palestine it is evident that the money has still not been sent. What is the reason for this delay? You have the money; you know that Rehovot had funds only up to the 1st of August, and that failure to send this £1,000 promptly would cause me much worry. And yet you leave me uninformed on a matter of this importance. In future I would like to see instructions given carried out without delay; it would save trouble, and also telegrams, which are an unnecessary expense.

Please wire me at once on receipt of this letter when the £1,000 were actually sent off, and also whether Stone[2] has sent the money due from him, and whether that has been transmitted.

In future please try to see that such matters are attended to promptly; the delay is causing a great deal of difficulty for Dr. Bloch, who finds himself without the money for his budget, which he has every right to expect in due time.[3] It causes a great deal of hardship to other people, too, which can and should be avoided.

Yours very sincerely,

Ch. Weizmann

---

168. [1] Cohn to W., 24 July 1941 (W.A.).

[2] Dewey Stone (1900–1977). Boston merchant; U.J.A. chairman 1955–63; first chairman of Board of Governors of Weizmann Institute.

[3] See No. 155.

169. To Meyer W. Weisgal, New York.   *London, 12 August 1941*
English: T.: W.A.

Hear that our friends of National Labour Committee for Palestine[1] complain they have been overlooked in constitution [of] preparatory committee for reorganization Jewish Agency.[2] Must confess [I] had been unaware of this fact and feel something should be done in order secure immediate participation of friends who have worked loyally for twenty years. Please contact Wertheim, Hamlin[3]
Regards[4]
Weizmann

170. To Jan Christiaan Smuts,[1] Pretoria.   *London, 15 August 1941*
English: Or. Copy. T.W.: W.A.

Private

My dear Friend,

I returned from the United States just over a week ago, and feel that I must write to you at once with regard to the situation which I find on my return. I shall try to be as brief as I can, but even so I am afraid this may prove a rather lengthy letter, and I must ask your indulgence.

Political developments have recently been moving rapidly in the Middle East. On the eve of the Allied operations there, Syria and the Lebanon were promised independence by the British Government and the leader of the Free French Forces. Later, General Catroux[2] announced that this promise would be implemented immediately on the completion of the occupation of Syria. Mr. Eden, in his speech on May 29th (later published as a White Paper—Command

169. [1] Founded by American Jewish trade unionists 1923 as *Gewerkschaften* (Yidd., 'United Hebrew Trades') to raise funds for *Histadrut*, and promotion of trade unionism in Palestine. Assumed English name 1936.
[2] I.e., committee of Zionists and non-Zionists that was to unite the various streams of American Jewry.
[3] David Wertheim (1890–1953): General Secretary of *Poalei Zion* in U.S. 1930–45; on Zionist General Council 1935–53. Isaac Hamlin (1891–1967): among founders of K.H. in U.S.; Secretary of *Poalei Zion* fund-raising campaign; settled in Israel 1955.
[4] Weisgal, Wertheim and Hamlin jointly wired W. 28 Aug. 1941 (W.A.) that appropriate arrangements had been made.

170. [1] Biog. Index, Vol. IX. Prime Minister and Minister of Defence of South Africa 1939–48.
[2] Georges Catroux (1877–1969). Free French High Commissioner in Levant following conquest of Syria June 1941; Governor-General of Indo-China 1939–40; of Algeria 1943–44; Ambassador in Moscow 1945–48.

6289—and thus given the weight of a statement of policy) promised the Arabs a greater degree of independence and unity, and His Majesty's Government's "full support to any scheme [for such unity] which commands general approval." Mr. Lyttelton[3] has been sent to Cairo as a member of the War Cabinet, and will presumably, apart from co-ordinating and concentrating the economic side of the war effort in the Middle East, also deal with political and diplomatic problems. The press reports conferences in Cairo between the various Arab States, and the discussion of plans for an Arab Federation. It thus seems that the shaping of the political destinies of the Middle East is not to await the end of the war, but is already the subject of discussions which may later prove to be decisive.

Palestine lies in the very heart of the Middle East. It is the most vital interest of the Jewish people. Yet so far the Jewish people, and its internationally recognized representative, the Jewish Agency for Palestine, have neither been consulted nor mentioned. In Mr. Eden's speech there is not a word about the special position of Palestine or the rights and interests of the Jewish people in Palestine. It is true that we have been informed by the Colonial Secretary that the words "general approval" in the passage from the speech quoted above were intended to cover also the rights of the Jews with regard to Palestine. This assurance, welcome as it is, cannot be regarded as a satisfactory answer to our misgivings. The fact remains that it was not thought necessary to consult the Jewish Agency on the subject of Palestine before Mr. Eden's announcement, and that even afterwards, the assurance given orally was only elicited by an enquiry from the Jewish Agency. It would be important to know whether the Arabs have been informed of this connotation of the words "general approval." Remembering how the McMahon correspondence, and the Hogarth Declaration[4] (first brought to light in 1939) were exploited by the Arabs, and even by a British Government, in order to explain away the interpretation of the Balfour Declaration and the Mandate accepted by the League of

---

[3] Oliver Lyttelton (later Viscount Chandos, b. 1893). Minister of State Resident in Middle East June 1941–Mar. 1942; Minister of Production 1942–45; Colonial Secretary 1951–54.

[4] McMahon-Hussein Correspondence embodied negotiations between the High Commissioner of Egypt and the Sharif of Mecca 1915–16, wherein the British promised the Arabs a large measure of independence in exchange for Arab support against the Turks. After the war, controversy centred on whether or not Palestine had been excluded from the area then promised to the Arabs. Hogarth Declaration was a reassurance given by Cdr. David George Hogarth (Director of Arab Bureau at Cairo) to Sharif Hussein, Jan. 1918, that the recently issued Balfour Declaration would not affect the rights of the Arab nation, but that Jewish settlement and finance would benefit the Arab world.

Nations, and by His Majesty's Government itself, for nearly twenty years, we are naturally apprehensive of similar difficulties which may arise in future through the lack of clarity of Mr. Eden's speech.

This complete neglect of the Jewish people as an active factor in the Middle East fits into the policy followed in regard to our affairs since the outbreak of the war. The White Paper of 1939 and the Land Transfer Regulations of March, 1940,[5] were forced through Parliament against the better judgment of the opponents of appeasement. But even after appeasement has been dropped as a general policy, it survived in regard to Palestine. It would not, I feel, have been unreasonable to expect a lenient interpretation of existing laws: within the framework of the law, the Palestine Administration could have done much to alleviate the sufferings of the Jewish people, and to open to the Jews, in Palestine and elsewhere, every avenue to full cooperation in the war effort of the Allies. Unfortunately a very different policy was adopted.

The Jews in Palestine were systematically prevented from taking their full share in the common struggle against Nazism. The most restrictive interpretation was placed on the immigration clauses of the White Paper, in order to reduce legal immigration to a minimum; and for the first time, mass deportation, accompanied by ill-treatment, was applied to "illegal" immigrants. The half-yearly immigration quotas were withheld in October 1940 and May 1941, and even the issue of 100 immigration certificates for leading Zionist workers from Greece was refused on the ground that it was impossible to save all the 75,000 Jews from Greece. But for this rigid immigration policy, many thousands of Jews from countries under Nazi occupation would by now have been in Palestine. Many valuable lives would thus have been saved to work or fight on the Allied side, instead of rotting in concentration camps or slaving for the Nazi war effort.

Our endeavours to obtain the consent of the British Government to the creation of a Jewish Fighting Force have so far produced no concrete results. Some four months ago the plan seemed near to realisation, but was shelved for political reasons. We are trying to revive it now. In Palestine, under the spur of immediate danger, some steps have been taken to organize Jewish home defence, but only about 9,000 Jews have been admitted to service in the Army, though tens of thousands are eager to enlist. All they ask is to serve in Jewish units, so that the national identity of the people first singled out by Hitler for hatred and persecution should not be submerged.

---

[5] The Land Transfer Regulations in fact became law 28 Feb. 1940. They severely restricted the area within which Jews might purchase land in Palestine.

They want to serve under their national flag. It is the pride of Jews the world over that Jewish soldiers have won praise from their British commanders for their conduct in Libya, Greece, Abyssinia and Syria; it is their sorrow that the way to full participation in the historic struggle on which the fate of our people depends is not yet opened to all of them.

This atmosphere of organized silence and camouflage, even on the part of their friends, is too rarely broken. The sufferings of the Jews, like their deeds in the war, are seldom mentioned directly. They are made to feel that the very mention of the word "Jew" may compromise the Cause. The reasons for this silence are not far to seek. There is an unwillingness to be identified with the Jews, for fear of Goebbels' slogan: "This is a Jewish war." There is the desire not to incur obligations to the Jews by accepting, openly and unreservedly, their collective help in the war. There is the fear of doing anything which might be used by the Axis for propaganda among the Arabs. And this last fear is being exploited by those whose chief concern, even at this moment, seems still to be to safeguard at all costs the White Paper policy.

Developments in the Middle East have been utilized by the Arab leaders to achieve a very advantageous position: when loyal they have to be rewarded; when rebellious they have to be placated, and it would be tactless to mention the case or the rights of the Jews. This is a situation in which the Jewish people and their leaders cannot acquiesce.

When victory is won the Jewish problem will not have disappeared. Those then responsible for shaping the future will have to face that problem with courage and determination, and to find for it a definite and radical solution. At present there are about eight million Jews—one-half of the Jewish people—under Nazi domination, and their physical destruction is proceeding at a pace which it is difficult to estimate. How many of them will survive will depend on the length of the war, but it is clear that some millions of Jews, stripped of their all, and uprooted from their former habitations, will have to try to remake their lives in the new world which will emerge after the war. It is difficult to see a newly reconstructed Poland or Czechoslovakia prepared to absorb Jewish minorities to the same extent as before the war—indeed, indications to this effect are already apparent. I think it is a not unreasonable estimate to say that not more than half of the former Jewish communities of these, and other, countries will be able to re-establish themselves there after the war. There will thus be some three or four millions of homeless Jews, pauperised and tortured into desperation, to be cared for by someone. Primarily the responsibility will fall on the

Jewish community of America, and on those few smaller communities which may still survive intact. But it is obvious that a problem of such magnitude cannot be solved unless aid is given by England and America. I can see nothing practical emerging from all the neo-territorialist projects which have been discussed, and even from the purely refugee point of view, Palestine is the only country capable of absorbing masses of immigrants within a reasonable time, provided only that the necessary political conditions are established.

British statesmanship is right in thinking ahead, and trying to hammer out, in close consultation with those primarily concerned, definite plans for the future. But all concerned must be consulted and considered, and no gaps or obscurities left to create misunderstandings in the present and dangers in the future. The principle of holding out to the Arabs prospects of such higher degree of independence and unity—by way of Federation or otherwise—as they can achieve among themselves, appears to be reasonable. But it must be made clear from the outset that these advantages to be acquired by the Arabs in the vast territories at their exclusive disposal cannot be given them at the expense of the vital rights and interests of the Jewish people, whose claims, hallowed by uninterrupted ties of thousands of years, and internationally recognized in the Mandate, are limited to what Lord Balfour called " the small notch" of Palestine. Nor can these rights of the Jewish people be made dependent on the concrete advantages which the Arabs will receive from a victorious Britain, or on the constitutional settlement which the Arabs may be able to reach among themselves. Both are outside the sphere of Jewish influence, and we can hardly be asked to pay other people's bills.

The ultimate formulation of our detailed demands in regard to Palestine will obviously be the task of the entire Zionist movement and the Jewish Agency for Palestine. But without prejudicing that formulation, I can, I think, venture on some indication of the problem as I see it. After the war, the Jewish people will need a territory large enough to receive the bulk of the Jewish immigration to be expected, and to form the foundation of a sound and self-supporting Jewish commonwealth. This State or Commonwealth must have such degree of sovereignty as will secure its independence and freedom from outside interference. The Jewish people can never agree to being a permanent minority in one Arab State (as envisaged in the 1939 White Paper), nor yet to be subject to a combination of Arab States so far as its vital interests (immigration, internal administration, education, finance, security, etc.) are concerned. The last few years have brought the Jewish National Home to a stage in its development which makes almost impossible a continuance of the tutelage exercised under the mandatory regime, and some new form of government will have to be devised. In fact, even in 1937, the Royal Commission already adumbrated some such necessity. But apart from political considerations, the purely economic aspect makes it imperative that the National Home should become autonomous in its fiscal policy. Otherwise the financing of a considerable immigration of people stripped—as the Jews will be after the war—of everything, will be impossible.

I believe that on the basis of the foregoing principles, the British Empire, the Americans, the Jews and the Arabs, could work out, in friendly consultation, the basis of their mutual relations. The conception is not a new one. It was the basis of the agreement which I signed with the Emir Feisal (the spokesman of the Arabs at the Peace Conference) in 1919.[6] It should not prove impossible even now to recreate the atmosphere necessary for such an agreement, if Great Britain will lose no time in making it clear that no settlement of Middle Eastern problems is possible without securing to the Jewish people their right to return to full nationhood in Palestine.

Since my return to London I have had two long talks with Lord Moyne,[7] whom I believe to be anxious to do his best, and who has given the matter some thought. His idea—it is still very vague—is to make the Arab Federation conditional on an arrangement between ourselves and the Arabs with regard to the National Home. But he always comes back to the curious statement that "of course the Jews and the Arabs have to come to an agreement between themselves." And such an agreement is rendered almost impossible by the mere existence of the 1939 White Paper. Whenever we do talk to any of the Arabs with whom we are in contact, they simply reply: The White Paper has settled the problem: no more immigration is to take place, and there is therefore nothing to be discussed between us. We know that whatever the Arabs got out of the last war, and whatever they may get out of this one, will be due entirely to Great Britain and America. They are in an extraordinarily favourable position: not only have they done nothing to help the war effort (on the contrary!), but they are likely to get—as an American friend put it—ninety-eight cents to the dollar. One might, I think, expect the two great democracies to tell the Arabs frankly that it is their considered opinion that the Jewish National Home must grow by

[6] For the terms of the Feisal-Weizmann Declaration, 3 Jan. 1919, which provided for the closest collaboration between the newly-independent Arab State and the Jews, who were assured of their right to free immigration into Palestine, while assurances were given guaranteeing the rights of Arab tenant farmers, see Vol. IX. As to Feisal, see Biog. Index, Vol. VIII.

[7] On 28 July and 1 Aug. (notes of interviews in W.A.).

immigration; they would thus remove the barriers which prevent Arabs and Jews from coming together at present. But the whole policy hitherto pursued has tended in the opposite direction.

I have just returned from America, and I can see that I have said little here about what I found there. I enclose a copy of a letter which I wrote, towards the end of my stay, to Lord Moyne,[8] and hope that you may find time to read it. The American Jews have no wish to embarrass the British Government; but they do feel that, with the heavy responsibility devolving upon them, they simply cannot allow this drift of British policy to continue unchallenged. Sooner or later, either directly or through their Government, the American Jews will formulate their ideas, and a clear stand will have to be taken by the British Government. It will not be possible to gloss over the situation indefinitely, and I am anxious that you should be fully informed about it, and should give us the advantage of your advice, and—if you can—your support, in the critical days which lie ahead.

With kindest regards, I am
As ever yours,
Ch. W.

171. To Brendan Bracken, London. *London, 19 August 1941*
English: Or. Copy. T.W.: W.A.

The Palestine section of the Middle East Exhibition gives a greatly distorted picture of present-day Palestine. Palestine and Transjordan are lumped together under one heading;[1] and since in other sections the pictures of the rulers are shown, Emir Abdullah presides over both. The word "Jew" is mentioned once only—in the population statistics. The rest of the pictorial section consists of the following photographs:

Temple area, with the Mosque of Omar;

Arabs passing through the Damascus Gate, Jerusalem;

A group of girls grading oranges—the girls are obviously Jewish but this fact is not mentioned;

Two persons described as "Inhabitants of Palestine," one an Arab, the face of the other is not seen;

---

[8] See No. 153.

171. [1] The Palestine Mandate as ratified by the League of Nations in 1922 included Transjordan, which was severed from the cis-Jordan area at the Cairo Conference in March 1921, to provide an Emirate for Abdullah. The exhibition was organized by and displayed at Ministry of Information. It later toured the Provinces.

Irrigation work in the Valley of Esdraelon—probably Jewish but this is not mentioned;

Dead Sea chemical industry, with only Arab workers seen, although the majority of workers are Jews;

Tankers taking oil from the pipe-line, Haifa;

Desert patrol of the Arab Legion in armoured cars;

Arab Legion in Transjordan.

The work done by Jews for the upbuilding of Palestine is completely ignored. There is nothing about the University in Jerusalem, about Jewish settlements, the Jewish city of Tel Aviv, Jewish industries, etc. The nine thousand Jewish volunteers serving with the British Forces are not mentioned. Palestine is described as a mandated territory, but not a word is said about the aim of the Palestine Mandate or the Balfour Declaration. A table is covered with Arab pamphlets and cartoons, but there is not a single Hebrew one. The bookshelf contains a History of the Arabs, a Cook's Guide to Palestine, Mr. Morton's book on the Middle East,[2] the Chatham House pamphlet on Palestine,[3] and one or two other publications of a like nature. Not even Government reports are included. The impression conveyed is that Palestine is just another Arab country, like Iraq.

2. The B. B. C. is now broadcasting in about forty languages daily. I submit that it would be a great encouragement to the Jews if broadcasts in Hebrew could also be given. Apart from the half-million in Palestine—who speak Hebrew as the language of their daily intercourse—it is understood by millions of Jews in Central and Eastern Europe and the Americas, especially of the younger generation. But to all Jews the fact of Hebrew broadcasts from London would be of moral value.[4]

3. Since the outbreak of the war the Jewish Agency has repeatedly offered its cooperation to the Ministry of Information. For this purpose the Agency proposed a regular liaison with the Ministry, and I asked Mrs. Edgar Dugdale to act as our representative. Our

---

[2] *The Middle East*, by H. V. Morton (London 1941), describes the author's tour of Egypt, Palestine, Iraq, Turkey and Greece. The section on Palestine is devoted to the Christian Holy Places, and ignores the existence of Jews, Zionist colonies and industry.

[3] Chatham House was the home of the Royal Institute of International Affairs, a body working in close cooperation with F.O. It adopted a distinct pro-Arab slant. See Elie Kedourie, *The Chatham House Version* (London 1970).

[4] Bracken informed W. 9 Sept. 1941 (W.A.) that Jerusalem broadcast in Hebrew for some 50 minutes daily, to cover Hebrew speakers in Palestine and Middle East. Hebrew speakers being so scattered in Europe, it would have been difficult to reach them in any one service, especially with the B.B.C. broadcast schedule so crowded. The B.B.C. did not in fact begin Hebrew broadcasts until 1950.

offer was not accepted, and the attitude of members of the Ministry, especially of the Middle Eastern Department, did not, to say the least, encourage us to seek any further contacts with it.

In February 1941, Mrs. Dugdale met Dr. Rushbrook Williams[5] at Lady Reading's house, and the upshot of a long conversation was an agreement that it would be desirable to have a liaison between the Jewish Agency and the Middle Eastern Department of the Ministry of Information for exchange of views and information. Subsequently, the Middle Eastern Department informed us through Lady Reading that in their opinion any official connection between the two offices might prove embarrassing to both, and that the Ministry of Information would prefer unofficial personal contact between themselves and Mrs. Dugdale. Our answer was that either the Ministry of Information wants to work with the Jewish Agency or it does not: the idea of an "unofficial connection" did not seem to us desirable. On February 28th Mr. Harold Nicolson wrote to Mrs. Dugdale that he would talk to Dr. Rushbrook Williams again about it. A few weeks later, Lady Reading told Mrs. Dugdale that Dr. Rushbrook Williams expected to hear from her again on the subject of liaison between the Jewish Agency and the Middle Eastern Department of the Ministry of Information. She wrote to him personally on March 25, 1941, but he did not think it necessary to acknowledge receipt of the letter.

4. The war effort of the Jews, and especially of Palestine Jewry, has been regularly passed over in silence by the Middle Eastern Department of the Ministry of Information, and when this was impossible, it has been camouflaged or belittled. Here are two examples:

(a) At the end of July 1940, the Palestinian Auxiliary Military Pioneer Corps, which had done good work in France, came over to this country. After it had been inspected by Lord Lloyd, a notice appeared in practically the entire British Press containing the phrase that "the corps comprises 22 nationalities, including Arabs and Jews"; a common source was obvious. When I complained of this phrasing to Lord Lloyd and said that ninety per cent. of the corps were Jews, Lord Lloyd replied: "No, ninety-five per cent." The original "nationalities" to which these Jews did not want to belong (this was the sense of their migration to Palestine), were thus used to obliterate the real character of the Corps.

(b) On March 1st, 1941, a note was given out to the Press—obviously again by the Ministry of Information—on "recruiting progress in Palestine." It stated that since the outbreak of the war "many

[5] 1890–1978. Author and journalist; Director of Middle East Propaganda at Ministry of Information.

Jews and Arabs" had enlisted in various Army units, and then added: "many Palestinians have joined the R.A.F." The paragraph concluded with the sentence: "Approximately 6,000 Jews and 3,000 Arabs are now serving with the British Army in the Middle East." This statement, as far as the Army was concerned, was correct—yet it was misleading: for the "many Palestinians" of the R.A.F. were in reality 1,500 Jews who have thus been subtracted from the Jewish war effort.[6]

172. To Lord Moyne, London.   *London, 19 August 1941*
English: Or. Copy. T.W.: W.A.

Dear Lord Moyne,

Mr. Namier and I saw Brigadier Lee at the War Office on the 12th. He suggested that this time the political problems arising out of the Jewish Division should be settled before the War Office is asked to deal with the technical work of raising and training the Division. This seems to be a reasonable suggestion likely to facilitate the work.

Perhaps the best approach to the political problem will be by way of the public announcement to be made about the Division. I therefore enclose a copy of the "Draft Announcement with Amendments suggested by the F. O. and W. O."[1] sent to us by Lord Lloyd on January 2nd, 1941, and of our comment on them, with "Proposed Amended Text" sent to him on January 6th. From a talk which Mr. Namier and I had with Mr. Eden at the Foreign Office on January 24th, we gathered that certain of our amendments had been favourably considered, though no new draft incorporating them was shown to us. The most important questions still outstanding arose out of Article (ii) of the draft Announcement; but even these will, I believe, be easily settled in view of developments which have supervened in the course of the last six months.[2]

> Yours sincerely,
> Ch.W.

---

[6] Bracken agreed in reply (W.A.) that Jewish achievements should have featured more prominently, but pleaded lack of space. As to liaison between J.A. and the Ministry, 'democratic principles' prevented him from by-passing C.O., with whom the Agency would have to continue to have all its dealings. The extant copy of W.'s letter ends here and it is not known whether there was a continuation.

172. [1] See No. 90.

[2] Moyne replied 28 Aug. 1941 (W.A.) that the position regarding equipment was little easier than previously, particularly with the entry of Russia into the war. The Government would have to postpone consideration of the Jewish contingent a further three months.

173. To Meyer W. Weisgal, New York.   *London, 19 August 1941*
English: T.W.: W.A.

My dear Meyer,

Dorothy Thompson is returning to the U. S. in a few days' time, and will bring you greetings from us and tell you how we are and what the position is. I have not seen much of her here, but am spending the evening with her to-night, and hope to have the opportunity of a talk then.

At present I am nursing a plan to go to Palestine in October or early November, and from there to the States. But this is, of course, dependent on the general position.

B. G. arrived from Palestine a couple of days ago, and on the whole the new situation appears to be not too bad.[1] Do write and tell me how you are progressing with the two Agency Committees and whether Josef is doing anything substantial for Rehovot; I simply hear nothing from him—he has apparently dried up.

Love to you and Shirley[2] from us both; I look forward to an early letter from you.

Yours ever,
Chaim

174. To Reginald Coupland,[1] Oxford.   *London, 25 August 1941*
English: Or. Copy. T.W.: W.A.

My dear Coupland,

Ever so many thanks for so kindly sending me the memorandum, which I have read with great interest.[2] I am looking forward to seeing you soon, and to having rather more time with you. Meanwhile, I shall try to see some people here and find out exactly what they have in mind. In the light of this information we might usefully discuss your memorandum in a few weeks' time.[3]

---

173. [1] The 'new situation' evidently refers to the new Free French régime in Syria, following the defeat of Vichy Forces.
  [2] Mrs. Weisgal, formerly Hirshfeld.

174. [1] Biog. Index, Vol. XVIII. Member of Peel Commission and author of original Partition plan.
  [2] This elaborated on a scheme for a Federated Palestine, to remain under British Mandate until it could be included in a Pan-Syrian Federation. Provision would be made for outside arbitration in the event of disagreement over the status of the Jewish State (Coupland to W., 22 Aug. 1941, W.A.).
  [3] There is no record of any subsequent meeting.

I immensely enjoyed seeing you again, and so did Mrs. Weizmann. We both send you our affectionate regards.

Yours ever,

Ch. W.

175. To Meyer W. Weisgal, New York.   *London, 26 August 1941*
English: T.W.: W.A.

My dear Meyer,

I hope Dorothy [Thompson] has given you all my messages. You will realise that the position remains as before, and I believe it will be possible for me to go to Palestine first, before returning to the States. As at present advised and if no further changes occur, we would leave here about the middle of November for Palestine, and proceed from there to America.

B.[en] G.[urion] is here, and has brought us some news of recent developments in Palestine. He also thinks of coming to America in the winter if the question of the formation of a Jewish contingent has been revived by then.

I quite understand that you expect no developments in the matter of the enlarged Agency until the middle of September;[1] I hope you will utilize the interval to get some sort of holiday. Vera and I intend to make a break for a fortnight in the middle of September.

Kindest regards to everybody, and my love to you and yours,

Affectionately,

Chaim

176. To Anna Kallin,[1] London.   *London, 29 August 1941*
English: Or. Copy. T.W.: W.A.

Dear Miss Kallin,

I am very much obliged to you for your note of the 28th, and its most interesting enclosure.[2]

Baroness Budbey[3] mentioned to me that there are frequent ref-

---

175. [1] Weisgal had had meetings with representatives of the American Jewish Committee, but a joint meeting of Zionists and non-Zionists had to await September—his letter of 12 Aug. 1941 (W.A.).

176. [1] Of Bedford College, London; in Russian Intelligence.

[2] She had sent him *Soviet War News* for 26 Aug. 1941, issued by Soviet Embassy in London. It contained a report of a great Jewish rally in Moscow, 24 Aug., addressed *inter alia* by Solomon Mikhoels, Peretz Markish, David Bergelson, Ilya Ehrenburg, Sergei Eisenstein, Samuel Marshak and Peter Kapitza, with an appeal to the Jews of the world to join with U.S.S.R. in crushing Hitlerism. See No. 181.

[3] I.e., Baroness Budberg (d. 1974). A professional translator; monitored foreign broadcasts.

erences in the Soviet programmes and bulletins to the war-contribution which the Jews of Russia are making. I wonder whether it is asking too much of you to ask whether you could possibly send me any relevant extracts?

I am seeing M. Maisky[4] on Monday in connection with this appeal, and I will, if I may, communicate with you again afterwards to let you know the results of the conversation.

Very sincerely yours,

Ch. W.

177. To Dame Edith Lyttelton,[1] Esher.   *London, 29 August 1941*
English: Or. Copy. T.W.: W.A.

My dear Dame Edith,

I am most grateful to you for your kind letter of August 27th.[2] I believe that it would be most useful if you could forward to your son a copy of my letter to Field-Marshal Smuts.[3] In this letter I refer to a letter of mine written from California to Lord Moyne,[4] and I think it would be as well to include a copy of this also, so as to give Captain Lyttelton some idea of the American background. I enclose further copies of the two letters, as I believe that the copy previously sent to you was not very legible—for which I apologise.

With regard to the other material, I think it would perhaps be better for me to ask the Jewish Agency to supply it to Captain Lyttelton from Jerusalem. My opening address is not reprinted in the Report of the Royal Commission; it is, of course, included in the Evidence, so that it is perhaps not necessary to send the pamphlet at all.

Given proper political conditions in Palestine, and adequate territory—the "line" proposed by the Royal Commission would require considerable modification—I believe that the immigration problem can be dealt with within the confines of Palestine. We could probably come to some satisfactory arrangement with Transjordan as well, and there would be no need to look for other territories. I am sure that all the territorialist projects present, both politically and from the colonisation point of view, almost insuperable difficulties.

---

[4] See No. 181.

177. [1] D. 1948. Wife of Alfred Lyttelton, mother of Oliver, Minister of State in Cairo. An author, she had been a substitute British delegate to League of Nations Assembly, 1923–31. An old acquaintance of W. They had recently met—see W. to Dame Edith, 25 Aug. (photostat in W.A.).

[2] She had agreed to forward W.'s documents to her son in Cairo. Further, she advanced the idea that, although the Jews had established themselves in a portion of Palestine as their central home, they should also have a 'colony' in Africa to solve their refugee problem (W.A.).

[3] No. 170.   [4] No. 153.

I deeply appreciate what you are kind enough to say about my statement, and also about the necessity for my going out to Palestine as soon as possible. I shall try to hasten my departure so far as I can, but we have only just got back from America, and there is a great deal of work to be done here. Things move slowly, too, in times like these. I do hope that it will not be too late if we arrive there early in November.

With many thanks, and kind regards, I remain,

Yours very sincerely,

Ch. W.

178. To Menahem Ussishkin, Jerusalem.   *London, 29 August 1941*
English: T.: C.Z.A. A24/39.

Sincerest congratulations [and] heartiest greetings your birthday. I pray your vigour [and] energy, which [are] so essential these trying days, continue undiminished and you'll live to see complete realisation our old dream and hopes. With profound blessing you and family. *Chazak*.[1]

Yours,

Chaim Weizmann

179. To Harry Sacher, London.   *London, 4 September 1941*
English: Or. Copy. T.W.: W.A.

My dear Harry,

Brodetsky and I have discussed with Anthony de Rothschild[1] the possibility of our reaching some measure of agreement on our aims. I suggested to Anthony that we might have a meeting of a dozen or so people, representing the Zionists and his own group, and he has agreed to such a meeting at New Court on Tuesday next, the 9th, at 2.30 p.m.

On our side, I am inviting, in addition to yourself, Ben-Gurion, Brodetsky, Namier, Locker, Simon Marks, and Stein.[2] I have not yet heard from Anthony whom he is inviting, but I know he has

---

178. [1] Hebr.: 'Be strong'.

179. [1] Biog. Index, Vol. XVI. A leading non-Zionist communal figure in Britain. Though opposed to Jewish statehood, he recognised the significance of Palestine in absorbing some portion of European refugees.

[2] Leonard J. Stein (Biog. Index, Vol. VI). President, Anglo-Jewish Association; Editor, Vols. I, VII, *Weizmann Letters and Papers*.

spoken to Lionel Cohen and Jimmy Rothschild,[3] and I have suggested to him that he might invite Israel Feldman[4] in his capacity as Chairman of the Palestine Committee of the Board of Deputies.

I need not tell you how important this meeting may be, or how anxious I am that you should be present. I do hope you will be able to come.[5]

Yours ever,
Chaim

180. To Meyer W. Weisgal, New York.   *London, 6 September 1941*
English: T.: W.A.

Myself [and] colleagues cordially agree to view expressed yours third,[1] and would be extremely happy if Wise would head movement in America this historic hour. Still I hesitate send personal message lest may be interpreted as undue interference internal affairs and may create misunderstanding and harm. Intend leaving beginning November for Palestine proceeding thence to States. Vera asks [that] you sound Edward G. Robinson,[2] possibly through Behrman,[3] whether he would accept invitation from important Women's Appeal Committee come here short visit.[4]

Love.
Weizmann

---

[3] Lionel Cohen (Biog. Index, Vol. XVI): Jurist, President of Jewish Board of Guardians. James Armand de Rothschild (Biog. Index, Vol. VI): Zionist philanthropist; Lib. M.P. 1929–45.

[4] B. 1888. Physician; formerly Vice-President Board of Deputies; Chairman of British Section of *Youth Aliyah*.

[5] For Minutes of meeting, see No. 186, n. 1.

180. [1] Cable, 3 Sept. 1941 (W.A.), reporting that ill-health prevented Kaufman from standing for a second term as President of Z.O.A. Weisgal proposed that W. urge Wise to accept the office, to eliminate factional strife and provide the movement in America with an outstanding personality as leader—see No. 183.

[2] 1893–1973. Film actor.

[3] Samuel Nathaniel Behrman (1893–1973). Playwright.

[4] V.W. headed the 'Comforts Committee for a Jewish Army,' serving Jewish soldiers in the British Forces.

181. To Ivan Maisky, London.   *London, 8 September 1941*
English: Or. Copy. T.W.: W.A.

Dear Mr. Ambassador,
    I enclose herewith, on behalf of the Jewish Agency for Palestine,
our reply to the appeal made at a recent Pan-Jewish meeting in Moscow, and should be grateful if you could arrange to have it transmitted.[1]

Yours sincerely,
Ch. W.
President

TO MOSCOW ANTI-FASCIST COMMITTEE

Your appeal to World Jewry to unite against Hitler and all that he
stands for has reached us, and we whole-heartedly respond to it.
From the very outset Hitler has made the Jews his chosen victims.
In the countries which, one by one, have fallen under his sway he
has re-enacted his cruelties in an intensified degree. Fascists all over
the world have followed his lead. Now he has reached the Soviet
lands. With deep sorrow we hear of your sufferings. But we are proud
of the fight which you are putting up in the Soviet armies, whose
achievements have earned universal admiration and have strengthened faith in victory. That faith we did not and shall not lose, even
in the darkest hours. Where enslaved, the Jews bear their fate with
dignity; where free—they fight. In Palestine, the Jewish community,
numbering now half-a-million, plays its part in the struggle. Ten
thousand Jews have enlisted in Jewish military formations, or in the
British Navy and Air Force. They have fought with distinction in
Libya, Abyssinia, Greece, Crete and Syria. Many more thousands
eagerly await their turn to enlist, and should the enemy ever reach
Palestine, men and women of our people will fight as you do. Tens
of thousands in other countries ask for a chance to serve in a Jewish
Army, so that we might, as a people, take our place in the struggle
for the common cause.
    We send our fraternal greetings. You may assure all your fellow-
citizens that the Jews of the world will not fail the common cause.

---

181. [1] The 'Pan-Jewish' meeting in Moscow was organized by the Moscow Jewish Anti-
Fascist Committee. Maisky forwarded the message (Maisky to W., 10 Sept. 1941, W.A.).

182. To Winston S. Churchill, London.   *London, 10 September 1941*
English: Or. Copy. T.W.: W.A.

Dear Mr. Prime Minister,

I wish to thank you for the very kind message which you sent me through Mr. Martin.[1] I deeply appreciate it. Still, our position has become so serious (nay, critical), that I feel I must lay the facts before you by letter if I cannot do so personally.

Two years have passed since, on the outbreak of the war, I offered to His Majesty's Government, on behalf of the Jewish Agency for Palestine and the Jewish people, the fullest active support of Jews in Palestine and throughout the world. A whole year has elapsed since you gave your personal approval to our offer to recruit "the greatest possible number of Jews in Palestine for the fighting services" and to form "Jewish military units abroad for service in the Middle East or elsewhere." But during these two years our readiness to serve has earned us only rebuffs and humiliations. Even in Palestine, where the need for our services was acknowledged, our most zealous endeavours have not received a single word of public acknowledgement. Ten thousand Palestinian Jews have fought in Libya, Abyssinia, Greece, Crete and Syria. But our people are never mentioned; our name is shunned; all contact or cooperation with us is kept dark as if it were compromising.

In March last, before I left for the United States, I was given, in a letter from the Colonial Secretary,[2] the assurance that the formation of the Jewish fighting force was reluctantly postponed—but merely postponed, at the utmost for six months. I know with what enthusiasm the announcement that it is to be formed at last would be received by our people in Palestine and throughout the world. But this is not to be, even now. Even in Palestine, our people, for whom the defence of their country and of the British position in the Middle East may be literally a matter of life and death, are permitted to serve only under humiliating limitations and conditions.

Tortured by Hitler as no nation has ever been in modern times, and advertised by him as his foremost enemy, we are refused by those who fight him the chance of seeing our name and our flag appear among those arrayed against him.

I know that this exclusion is not in your own intentions or spirit. It is the work of people who were responsible for the Munich policy in Europe and for the White Paper in Palestine. We were sacrificed

---

182. [1] Untraced (possibly a telephone call). In an interview 1 Sept. 1941 (record in W.A.), W. had asked Moyne for a definite answer regarding the Army scheme.
[2] See No. 125, n. 1.

in order to win over the Mufti of Jerusalem and his friends who were serving Hitler in the Middle East; whereas the only thing which can secure the Arabs is British strength in the Middle East, as has been clearly shown in Iraq.

But are the Jews so utterly unimportant as the treatment meted out to them suggests? I have spent four months in America, travelling up and down the country, and closely watching the American scene. Forces over there are finely balanced; the position is uncertain. There is only one big ethnic group which is willing to stand, to a man, for Great Britain, and a policy of "all-out aid" for her; the five million American Jews. From Secretary Morgenthau, Governor Lehman, Justice Frankfurter, down to the simplest Jewish workman or trader, they are conscious of all that this struggle against Hitler implies.

It has been repeatedly acknowledged by British statesmen that it was the Jews who, in the last war, effectively helped to tip the scales in America in favour of Great Britain. They are keen to do it—and may do it—again. But you are dealing with human beings, with flesh and blood, and the most elementary feeling of self-respect sets limits to service, however willing, if the response is nothing but rebuffs and humiliations. American Jewry waits for a word—a call—from His Majesty's Government. The formation of a Jewish fighting force would be that signal. Equipment cannot be the determining factor: there will always be some alternative use for whatever equipment is available; and fresh recruits are all the time being called up in the British Commonwealth by their hundreds of thousands, while we are told to wait for one single Division because of lack of equipment. If the spirit of American Jewry is roused, the influence which this will exercise on America's rather sluggish production will return to you that equipment with manifold gains.

Let me feel, Mr. Prime Minister, that our friendship is not spurned on the British side, nor our name obliterated at a time when Hitler is endeavouring to obliterate our very existence.[3]

Yours very sincerely,

Ch. W.

183. To Louis E. Levinthal, Philadelphia. *London, 11 September 1941*
English: T.: C.Z.A. A182/79/43.

Heartiest congratulations and good wishes.[1] Sincere thanks for your greetings which cordially reciprocate. Am confident that under

[3] See No. 204.

183. [1] On his election as Z.O.A. President—see No. 180.

your leadership American Zionists will exert every endeavour, even more than hitherto, to rise to height of responsibilities now resting on their shoulders. Look forward with pleasure and high expectations to our cooperation in great cause.

Affectionate greetings to you and your father.

Ch. Weizmann

184. To Wladislaw Sikorski, London.   *London, 16 September 1941*
English: Or. Copy. T.W.: W.A.

My dear General Sikorski,

I have been discussing with Major Cazalet,[1] who has been good enough to take an interest in the matter, how best we can secure the continued services in the fund-raising work of the Jewish National Fund of Mr. Dov Biegun,[2] who is liable for military service with the Polish Army, and is called up for the end of September.* I shall not try to make out a case to the effect that Mr. Biegun's continued service with the Fund is vital to the military effort. But it *is* vital to the fund-raising work, and, as you know, the Jewish National Fund is the foundation of all our work in Palestine, and its maintenance, even in time of war, seems to us essential if the Jewish National Home is to be in a position, when peace comes again, to play its proper part in the solution of the Jewish problem. Mr. Biegun is one of the Fund's two first-class money-raisers in this country at present, and it is practically impossible to bring over anyone from Palestine to replace him. If he has to go, the work here will be gravely prejudiced, to the detriment of the funds—and hence of the land available for our settlement work at the end of the war.

This is why I have felt that I had to write to you personally, contrary to my normal rule (which is not to make any appeals for exemptions from military service), to ask whether it would be possible for you to look into the matter personally and, if you feel you can do so, arrange for Mr. Biegun to be exempted from call-up.[3]

With apologies for troubling you and sincere thanks in advance,

I am
Yours very sincerely,
Ch. W.

* Decision of the 31st July, L.dz. 1923–2005 (O.I.) Adm. Rez.-41.

---

184. [1] He was British Government's liaison officer with Sikorski from 1940.

[2] B. 1911. Czech journalist, co-editor of *Selbstwehr*, organ of Czech Zionist Movement, employed by J.N.F. Czechoslovakia. In Britain from 1940.

[3] Exemption was granted.

185. To The Zionist Record,[1] Johannesburg.

London, 17 September 1941

English: T.: W.A.

Please convey my cordial New Year greetings good wishes to all fellow Zionists South Africa. As in past you have, during past year of unprecedented sufferings for our people and imminent danger to Palestine, fulfilled your Zionist duty. It is great comfort to know that in all countries where Jews still free to act on behalf their people they are becoming more and more conscious of their evergrowing responsibilities for fate and future our nation, which [is] inescapably bound up with victory democracies in this world struggle. We are proud to know Jews all countries doing their duty along with their fellow citizens, and that our young people in all free countries are eager to give all possible additional service in cause of humanity. Though their services are still only hesitantly admitted and their national character still not recognized, thousands our young men from Palestine have joined colours and fought gallantly all Middle Eastern fronts. Tens of thousands have offered their services and are prepared meet enemy and sacrifice their lives in defence their national home should he ever reach its shores. But even while battle rages and we bear our share in it, we can never forget peculiar sufferings our people at present and problem survival we shall have to face after war. In this titanic struggle a powerless people may easily be forgotten. We must exert all our energies prevent this. Work for Zion can never cease and can in no circumstances be interrupted. Strengthening of *Yishuv* expansion our work is unconditional duty all Zionists; only thus shall we achieve right and strength to place justified demand of scattered people for their ancient home before those who will ultimately be responsible for shaping future of nations.

Weizmann

186. To Harry Sacher, London.

London, 25 September 1941

English: Or. Copy. T.W.: W.A.

Dear Mr. Sacher,
I attach hereto a copy of the minutes of the meeting at New Court of September 9th.[1] These minutes are only being circulated to our side.

185. [1] Weekly publication.

186. [1] See No. 179. According to the Minutes (W.A.), Anthony de Rothschild was against

I also enclose a copy of the memorandum which it is proposed to send to Mr. Anthony de Rothschild for distribution to his friends. Would you be good enough to let me have any observations you may care to make on it for the consideration of the Political Committee? We are anxious to send the memorandum off early next week, and should therefore be very grateful if you could manage to do this by Monday.

Yours sincerely,

CONFIDENTIAL

MEMORANDUM

At the meeting at New Court on Tuesday, September 9, 1941, there was general agreement on the following points:

(a) That we have to count, at the end of the war, with a vast Jewish emigration from European countries.
(b) That Palestine will have to play the major part in receiving these emigrants.
(c) That it is therefore necessary to secure in Palestine freedom of immigration and land-purchase, and an economic and fiscal system which will render possible the settlement of a maximum of Jewish immigrants.

2. In Palestine large-scale immigration requires planned development—we must, so to say, create economically the country which we colonise. The work initiated some sixty years ago by Baron Edmond de Rothschild, and developed along new lines and on a much bigger scale by the Zionist Organization, has proved the possibility of such colonisation and our capacity for achieving it: half a million Jews are already settled on one-fifteenth of the area of Western

establishment of a Jewish State that might lead to discrimination by other states against their own Jews. He favoured a spiritual home in Palestine. W. employed arguments he had used with non-Zionists in America, dwelling on the scope of the post-war Jewish problem; Palestine alone could now be envisaged for homeless Jews, and he saw the whole of the country west of the Jordan as a Jewish State, with perhaps a voluntary transfer of the Arab population. Sir Robert Waley Cohen regarded a Jewish State as 'peculiar and dangerous', and he feared they were 'starting with the same sort of aims with which Hitler had started'. Lord Rothschild stated that if non-Jews were treated as foreigners in a Jewish State, then Jews outside Palestine would receive like treatment. W. assured them that Arabs would enjoy full civil rights. Ben-Gurion stressed that maximum Jewish immigration was possible only under a Jewish Administration. He would not insist on a State in name, but the functions of a state in regard to land-purchase, immigration, labour and industrial legislation, and defence. It was agreed that W. draw up a memorandum summarizing the proposals put forward at the meeting.

Palestine. But much more will have to be done now, and in a much shorter time. This is possible only under an administration wholeheartedly devoted to the task, and under a political, economic and fiscal regime designed for the purpose. The work calls for a Jewish Administration, set up by the Jewish people and responsible to it, sharing the aims and hopes of the immigrants and settlers, conscious of their own future and the fate of their people depending on their work. It is our contention that large-scale Jewish immigration and settlement in Palestine, even for economic and administrative reasons, cannot be secured otherwise than through a Jewish Administration.

3. But it was political considerations, largely extraneous to Palestine and the Mandate, which caused the Mandatory Administration, throughout its twenty years, to refrain from actively promoting Jewish settlement, indeed to retard and restrain it, and finally to set a term to it in the White Paper of 1939. We are agreed in rejecting the White Paper, which has been publicly condemned by leading members of the present Government, foremost by the Prime Minister; it is unjust, and cannot be enforced. Immediate self-government would mean Arab Government, under which no large-scale Jewish immigration could possibly be expected, and probably none at all would be admitted. Even now Palestine Jewry is sufficiently strong to make it impossible to convert Palestine into an Arab State. But a mere cancelling of the White Paper, and reversion to the previous system is not practical policy either. It is clear that the British Government do not desire to be burdened with the task of implementing, over a number of years, a policy tending to establish a Jewish majority in Palestine; gradual infiltration, which leaves the future uncertain, undefined, and contested, is bound to breed anxiety, hatred and strife. If large-scale Jewish immigration and the Jewish future in Palestine is to be secured, it must be done through a single act of international statesmanship within the framework of the general peace settlement.

4. The Arabs after having played a more than doubtful part in this war—in Iraq, Egypt, Palestine, etc.—will greatly profit from a British victory by obtaining independence in Syria and Libya, and as large a measure of national unity as they themselves are capable of achieving. On the other hand, it is essential to obtain such a settlement in Palestine as will help to solve the Jewish question, one of the most disturbing problems in the world. The Arabs must, therefore, be clearly told that this small country shall form the Jewish Homeland, that the Jews will be encouraged to settle in it and will control their own immigration, and that here the Jews who desire it should be able to achieve their freedom and self-government by establishing

a State of their own, and ceasing to be a minority dependent on the will and pleasure of other nations. In that State there will be complete civil and political equality of rights for all citizens, without distinction of race or religion, and in addition the Arabs will enjoy full autonomy in their own internal affairs; but if any Arabs did not wish to remain in a Jewish State, every facility will be given to them for transfer to one of the many and vast Arab countries.

5. The question is asked how, during the transitory period a minority is to govern the country? This puts the matter on a wrong basis: the Administration to be set up will not emanate from the Yishuv alone, but from a joint total of Jews settled, and intending to settle, in Palestine. There is no need to argue how that total is to be defined: the conception of a special relationship between future Jewish immigrants and Palestine is inherent in the Balfour Declaration and the Mandate, and it is on this basis that the Jewish Agency for Palestine, representing world Jewry, was conceded a special and unique position in the affairs of the country.

6. Considering the strategic and economic importance of Palestine, the inclusion of the Jewish State in the British Commonwealth would be to the interest of both; but we should also be ready, if necessary, to consider joining, under proper safeguards, in a Federation with Arab States.

7. To us who consider ourselves members of a Jewish nation, like unto all nations, a Jewish State in Palestine is more than merely the necessary means for securing further Jewish immigration and development. It is a moral need and postulate, the decisive step towards normality and true emancipation. We believe that after the war Jews everywhere can only gain in status and security through the rise of a Jewish State, especially if it is a part of the British Commonwealth. Anti-Semites, determined to reduce the Jews to abject slavery or to drive them into exile, have not waited with doing so for a Jewish State to arise.

8. To sum up:

(a) further large-scale settlement in Palestine postulates a Jewish administration and a system envisaging a Jewish State in Palestine;

(b) 'while the setting up of the Jewish State in Palestine will have to be part of the general peace settlement, care must be taken in the meantime that nothing is done which might impede an ultimate favourable settlement;

(c) we ask you who are concerned about the future of the Jews as individuals and as a community, to join us on this common basis.

187. To David Lloyd George, Churt.   *London, 29 September 1941*
English: Or. Copy. T.W.: W.A.

My dear Mr. Lloyd George,

The American Zionists are arranging to celebrate the twenty-fourth anniversary of the Balfour Declaration throughout the Jewish communities of the United States, and a large public meeting will be held in New York on November 1st. Our American friends are very anxious to hear you on this occasion, and I understand that Dr. Wise has telegraphed to you asking whether you would agree to record a speech for radio transmission.

The Jews of America, more than any other ethnic group there, have come out solidly for all aid to Britain in this struggle against the evil of Nazism. They have hitherto had very little encouragement, though the Jews were Hitler's first victims, and might therefore be expected to be the first to desire his overthrow; nonetheless, in the peculiar circumstances obtaining in America, it has required a good deal of courage on their part to take the step they have taken. I feel sure that a few words from you would be a source of much-valued encouragement and inspiration to them all, and I do hope that you will feel able to accede to Dr. Wise's request.[1]

With kindest personal regards, and all good wishes,

I am,
Very sincerely yours,
Ch. W.

188. To Anthony de Rothschild, London.   *London, 30 September 1941*
English: Or. Copy. T.W.: W.A.

Dear Mr. de Rothschild,

At the meeting held at New Court on September 9th, it was decided that I should commit to paper some of the items which we had there developed. I am sorry that a number of circumstances —among them my own absence from London—have somewhat delayed the preparation of the enclosed memorandum. I am sending you twelve copies, and shall be glad if you will kindly arrange to have them distributed to those whom you invited to the meeting.

Mr. Lionel Cohen suggested that I should also deal with the question of procedure; it seems to me, however, that in the first instance an opportunity should be given to you and your colleagues to ex-

---

187. [1] Lloyd George declined to record a message (letter of 10 Oct. 1941, W.A.).

amine our proposals with a view to reaching an agreement which can be said to represent the views of all important sections of British Jewry. It will probably be advisable to call another meeting in the near future in order to discuss the proposals, and the question of procedure could then be most suitably examined.[1]

Yours very sincerely,

Ch. W.

189. To Sir Archibald Sinclair, London. *London, 5 October 1941*
English: Or. Copy. T.W.: W.A.

My dear Archie,

Ever so many thanks for your note of the 2nd,[1] which I have just found on my return here from Harrogate. I would have loved to dine quietly with you on Thursday, but unfortunately that happens to be the only night I am not free: Victor Cazalet has arranged a dinner with some M.P.'s, and it is a long-standing arrangement which concerns quite a few people. I would be very grateful, therefore, if you could give me another chance, either this week, if you have another evening free, or next at your convenience. I am free every evening both weeks—except, as it happens, this Thursday.[2]

Ever yours,

Ch. W.

190. To Jan Masaryk, London. *London, 10 October 1941*
English: Or. Copy. T.W.: W.A.

My dear Friend,

I was deeply touched by your kind message of sympathy[1] on Ussishkin's death.[2] We lose in him a pillar of strength which we can ill afford to lose in these dark days. And now the same week brings us the heavy tidings of Brandeis' passing.[3] You will know what I feel—and yet I know that the work must go on and will go on.

In deep gratitude for your friendship,

I am
Yours ever,

Ch. W.

188. [1] For memorandum, see No. 186. As to Rothschild's reaction to it, see No. 202.

189. [1] This (W.A.) invited W. to dine with Sinclair 'quietly in my attic.'
　　[2] Apparently they did not meet that month.

190. [1] Untraced.
　　[2] Ussishkin died 4 Oct. 1941.
　　[3] Louis Dembitz Brandeis (Biog. Index, Vol. VII). First Jew to be appointed to U.S. Supreme Court; the leading American Zionist during, and immediately after, W.W.I.

191. To Mikhail Weizmann, Haifa.   *London, 12 October 1941*
English: H.W.: W.A.

12 October, 1941.

My dear Chilik,
It is a very long time since I have written to you. Writing is very difficult. The knowledge that a letter takes such a long time to reach its destination makes writing almost useless. From telegrams which the Institute receives rather often from here you know that we are well and "carrying on." But a few days ago we received a letter from Moshe Weizmann[1] in which he informs me that Feivel is seriously ill. I have felt it all along that something must be wrong with him, as he usually writes. But the characteristic part of Moshe's letter was that he did not find it necessary to say a single word about himself or the other members of the family, neither did he enquire about us. He is a curious fellow and it makes the impression as if he enjoys to impart bad news. There is something definitely unpleasant about the whole tone of his letter.

I am terribly grieved to hear about Feivel and we only hope that he will recover and be spared for the years to come.

There is little I have to say about us. We intend, if it is at all possible, to arrange to come to Palestine about end of November. I am most anxious to get there for many reasons. As soon as the question of transport is fixed I shall let you know. Meanwhile I send you, your family, and everybody my heartiest good wishes. My love to Feivel and may he recover speedily.

Affectionately,
Chaim

192. To John Gilbert Winant,[1] London.   *London, 13 October 1941*
English: Or. Copy. T.W.: W.A.

Dear Mr. Ambassador,
This is just a word to thank you for your kind reception of me last Friday, and to confirm the time of the Memorial Meeting to Judge

---

191. [1] Their brother (Biog. Index, Vol. I). Head of Organic Chemistry Laboratory at Hebrew University, Jerusalem.

192. [1] 1889–1947. U.S. Ambassador in London 1941–46.

Brandeis (though you will of course be getting a formal invitation), which is fixed for Tuesday, October 21st, at 4 p.m. We deeply appreciate your and Mr. Johnson's[2] consent to be present.

May I also take this opportunity of reminding you of your kind promise to dine with Major Cazalet and myself on Thursday this week, at eight o'clock, at the Dorchester Hotel?

Yours very sincerely,
Ch. W.

193. To Benjamin Bloch, Rehovot.   *London, 13 October 1941*
English: Or. Copy. T.W.: W.A.

Private

My dear Bloch,

You will have received my telegram informing you that I have instructed Ruskin to transmit to you £1,500—a little more than you asked for. As to the other request, I have received information from Hadassah that they are willing to advance you $10,000, and have instructed Josef to negotiate this matter as quickly as possible, so that you may get the money without very much delay. I shall see again what I can do with Marks, and when all this has been completed, I hope your financial difficulties will be relieved, and that you will be able to proceed with the completion of the factory.[1]

I have now received the reports of the various scientists, and I am sorry to have to tell you that they have made me thoroughly unhappy. The results are very meagre, and I cannot for the life of me understand how so much time can have been spent on so little.

I have also received a copy of Horowitz's letter to Rosenfeld,[2] and this also has hardly contributed to my peace of mind.

The position as it presents itself to me, from a distance, is clearly this: In the past two years very little has been done, either scientifically or technically, by way of contributing to the war effort, and I am asking myself how I can justify the expenditure of a considerable budget in these critical times for so small an output. Of course I am ready to make all allowances for the difficulties now obtaining in Palestine, which are not conducive to fruitful scientific work, but having done so, I still feel that Hirschberg, Rosenfeld, Simon, and

---

[2] Herschel V. Johnson (1894–1966). First Secretary at American Embassy 1934–37, then Counsellor, with rank of Minister from 1941. Minister to Sweden 1941–46; delegate to U.N., 1946–47; Ambassador to Brazil 1948–53.

193. [1] For pharmaceuticals, at Rehovot.

[2] Bruno Rosenfeld, b. 1903. Biochemist Sieff and Weizmann Institutes. Awarded Weizmann Prize, Tel Aviv, 1949.

(of course) Herlinger, and perhaps some others, have not lived up to the traditions of the Institute, and have not justified the confidence which we placed in them as independent workers.

I hope soon to be in Palestine, and I definitely intend to give them notice then; unless they radically change their ways, they will have to leave the Institute fairly soon. When normal times return, we shall have to replace them by people worthy of the part which members of the Daniel Sieff have to play. I am sorry to have had to come to this conclusion, and I am really trying to be absolutely impartial in this matter. I know how hard it will be for them, but the interests of the Institute must come first.

I have a few candidates in view through whom we may be able to build up a new team which will be more effective than the group which is working with us at present, and which, though it began so well, is apparently not able to conduct independent research work. Rosenfeld might have done it, I believe, but he has apparently taken a different line, and has, I fear, rendered a disservice to the Institute.

Dr. Bergmann and myself have completed two pieces of work which we really believe will be of both technical and scientific interest and importance. Of course nothing can be published at present, but we have material which would form the basis for a series of scientific publications of very considerable interest. I shall tell you all about it when I have the pleasure of seeing you personally.

As soon as our plans are more or less fixed I shall let you know when to expect us. There will be the question of quarters. We hope to stay in Palestine about two months. I do not know whether it is worth while opening the house; it is a costly and troublesome business for so short a time. But if General Clark is prepared to share the house with us, we could all live there, and that might be a solution. But I must leave it to Dr. Goldschmidt to decide what is best. Incidentally, I think I have a lot of clothes and linen still at the house, so that I need not carry much luggage with me from here. Would you kindly enquire from Miss Goldschmidt, and send me a telegram about this?

Hoping to see you soon, I am,
Affectionately yours,
Ch. Weizmann

194. To Meyer W. Weisgal, New York.   *London, 13 October 1941*
English: Or. Copy. T.W.: W.A.

My dear Meyer,

It is a long time since I wrote to you; I have been waiting in the hope of being able to give you something definite about my plans.

But you know how difficult it is to be definite these days. I believe, however, that the time is approaching when I shall probably be able to leave here for Palestine.

1. Dr. Jacobs and Cancer Research.[1]
2. *New York Times* articles:[2] Since I received these articles— which we all like very much—I have had a request from Hamilton Fish Armstrong to do him an article of about 4,000 words for *Foreign Affairs*.[3] Miracle of miracles, I have actually been able to write it, and it is finished now. It will go off at the end of this week. It is on somewhat different lines from the N.Y.T. articles; I shall send you a confidential copy, and you can judge for yourself. It will probably appear in the December issue. I shall now settle down to the N.Y.T. articles, and hope to have them ready quite soon.[4]
3. Rehovot: I am somewhat worried about the Institute. Unless matters are followed up with great energy, we may find ourselves in difficulties in 1942. I would be extremely grateful to you if you would have a serious talk with Josef and work out a plan for gathering in the fruits of my efforts, so that we may secure the Institute's full requirements for the coming year.
4. I am looking forward to George Backer's arrival here; of course I do not believe for a moment that he will go with me to Palestine— he always says things like that but they practically never materialise. We shall be able to verify his statement when he is here.

I have had a telegram from Dorothy,[5] the contents of which you probably know. I have replied that I will only be in a position to accede to her request when I am again in America. I can see no way of helping her from here. I do hope she understands.

Josef has sent me the full account of her speech! I thought it a little too long, but on the whole very good.[6]
5. We have had very little news about the Cincinnati Conference, but I think the election of Levinthal is a very fortunate one for the

---

194. [1] Paragraph 1 omitted; deals with scientific matters.

[2] Three drafts produced by Maurice Samuel on Zionism, Palestine, and the Jews in the post-war world, as basis for articles by W. in *New York Times*.

[3] The article appeared in the issue of Jan. 1942 as 'Palestine's Role in the Solution of the Jewish Problem'.

[4] W. did not in fact write articles for *New York Times*.

[5] Dorothy Thompson to W., 2 Oct. 1941 (W.A.) describing activities of her 'Ring of Freedom'. She pleaded for another six months' help from Weisgal, after which the organization would run itself.

[6] Cohn to W., 27 Sept. 1941 (W.A.), with Press reports of a 'Ring of Freedom' rally. This unanimously adopted a resolution calling on the U.S. President to repeal immediately the Neutrality Act of 1937, which provided that, on the outbreak of war, the President had to issue a declaration naming the belligerents. Thereafter the supply of war material to the parties named would be illegal.

unity of the Organization.[7] I am writing to him,[8] and incidentally he may now perhaps be in a position to do something in Philadelphia for the Institute. (You know that they have let us down—and he also knows more than most people!) Perhaps he would use his influence to retrieve the position?

As soon as I know definitely what my movements are likely to be I shall telegraph to you. Meanwhile I send you my best love—also from Mrs. Weizmann. We both thank you very much indeed for the parcel you have been good enough to send us.

Affectionately yours,

Ch. W.

195. To Meyer W. Weisgal, New York.   *London, 13 October 1941*
English: T.W.: W.A.

My dear Meyer,

I have just dictated an "official" letter to you, and I feel the urge to add a few personal remarks on a subject which has been much in my mind these past few weeks.

Though I have read little about the Cincinnati Convention—indeed, the press reports here have been scanty—I feel, and this was already clear to me when I was in the States, that the Movement there is entering upon a new phase. The death of Ussishkin in the East, and of Brandeis in the West, marks the end of an era. The election of Levinthal to the Presidency of the Z.O.A., which I regard as a very fortunate sign, marks the entry into the new period. The Movement has become more American. The younger generation, not brought up in the old traditions, is coming to the fore, and this is a healthy and desirable development. (Not that Levinthal is entirely this type, and this is partly why I believe his election to be a happy choice.)

There is only one great danger in the new situation. It has developed at a time when there is practically no European Jewry and no European Zionist Movement. It has perhaps come partly because of the void created by the disappearance of European Jewry. Although the American community has matured greatly in the past twenty years, it has not yet sufficiently advanced to be wholly weaned from the influence of Europe; one of the proofs of this is the lack of outstanding leadership both in Zionist affairs and in the general affairs of the Jewish Community. Whereas it is entirely

---

[7] See No. 183. This was the Z.O.A. Convention which elected Levinthal as President.
[8] See No. 197.

natural and desirable that the younger people should assert themselves, and begin to take responsibility, it is to be feared that a too rapid emancipation from past tradition may lead to the creation of a gulf between European, and even Palestinian, Jewry and the important American Organization when the war is over. In some of the speeches at the Convention I could sense a sort of undertone to the effect that Zionism in America must be "American." I wonder what is the precise meaning of that slogan? Of course the organizational forms, like the methods of transacting Zionist business, will, in America, be American. But the kernel of Zionism—its core and substance—are universal, and cannot be compressed to fit the straitjacket of this, that or the other local Organization, however important it may be. Over-emphasis of this question of "Americanization" may at the moment be primarily due to the temporary obliteration of something like eight million Jews in Europe, who will arise again after the war. Their very tragedy will constitute a tremendous force. If, however,—God forbid!—they should not survive the present upheaval, that will mean that Hitler will have triumphed—and in that case I fear there is very little hope for American Jewry. As I do not for a moment believe that any such contingency can come to pass, I believe it would be a very serious mistake—a moral aberration even—for the American Zionists to take over their heritage in such haste, while the other fellow is down. I incline to think that it would even be "un-American"! Kaufman's election was itself a sort of danger-signal; it has happily been corrected now,[1] but the undercurrent which it indicated is still there, and remains as a threat to the fundamental values of the Movement.

Levinthal is one who has been brought up in the old tradition, but is at the same time capable of understanding the new trends. I only hope he may have enough leisure to study this delicate situation, and enough strength to direct the new forces into channels of cooperation with the future European Jewish community and with Palestine.

In the circumstances created by the war, the position of the Executive has become precarious. There has been no Congress; we keep our old mandate because of *force majeure*. I doubt very much whether we represent in any way the new forces which have arisen in the U.S.A., and I personally feel this anomaly deeply. But for the fortuitous circumstances of war, I would not have served any longer in my present office, and this for two reasons:

---

195. [1] Kaufman, the previous President, had had to stand down due to ill-health.

(a) the Americans might wish for somebody nearer to them; and
(b) I have served long enough, and it is for a younger man to take over the leadership.

The discomfort caused by this curious position is one of the reasons why I was anxious to have a meeting, in America, of all those Zionists who can still be reached. It would not have replaced a Congress—that is constitutionally impossible—but it would have strengthened morally the present Executive. Such an Assembly might possibly have considered the creation of some *ad hoc* body in the U.S.A.—perhaps a modification of the Emergency Committee, which has been the object of so much undeserved criticism. But I gather that Zionists are not very keen on a large-scale meeting, and would prefer to limit it to a rump A[ctions] C[ommittee], which—in my view—would not answer the purpose at all.

Well, I have told you how I feel. Let me know, when you have time, how the scene looks to you, and what you think about it all.

With much love from us both to you and Shirley, I am, as ever,

Affectionately yours,

Chaim

196. To Meyer W. Weisgal, New York.   *London, 14 October 1941*
English: H.W.: Photostat W.A.

October 14th, 1941

Meyer dear,

There is every chance that we shall get passage on the plane to Palestine some time towards the end of November. I saw the Air Ministry yesterday and they promised to do their best. There was an opportunity to go over the whole situation. There is no need for me here to go over the pros and cons of the Government's policy with regard to Palestine; they are too familiar to you to merit wasting too much time on it. But one set of arguments cropped up which I would like to bring to your attention and to that of our friends—namely America. Our opponents in the Cabinet maintain the following point of view: it is true that in the last war the Jews of U.S.A. played an important part and contributed greatly towards the entry of America into the war. But things have changed. The Jews are deeply divided with regard to Zionism. The American Government did nothing when the White Paper was issued and is therefore indifferent to the question of Palestine. We need not take America into consideration, and can pursue our policy of placating the Arabs.

It is, of course, quite true that the White Paper produced no reaction on the part of the American authorities, but of course it is a fallacy to generalise it. Apart from the attitude of the Government, Jewish and liberal public opinion dislikes the Palestine policy and that is important enough. I shall, of course, tell it to Winant, with whom I'm on good terms, but it is vital that something should be done to indicate that this quasi-indifference of the American Government is only in appearance and not in fact. Please act on it. Of course Wise, Lipsky, Neumann and the others ought to go to Washington and see Welles and explain the situation. A word from the White House and we could get the Army.

Love,
Ch.

197. To Louis E. Levinthal, Washington.   *London, 15 October 1941*
English: Copy. T.W.: W.A.

My dear Friend and President,

I should have written to you earlier, but I waited in the hope of learning a little more about the Convention in Cincinnati. Unfortunately, owing to abnormal circumstances, we have only very scanty and belated reports. I need hardly repeat what I have already said in my telegram to you—namely that I am genuinely delighted to see you at the head of our affairs at this critical period. This election testifies to a great sense of responsibility on the part of American Zionists. I trust that your arduous duties as a Judge will not prevent you from giving time and attention to the many urgent problems which are bound to confront you in these times of stress. May I once more offer you my sincerest good wishes: may your work be crowned with success, and may it be given to you to guide the destinies of the movement in America into constructive and cooperative channels. If I may say so with respect, you are eminently fitted to perform this important task at this moment. The tradition of your family, and particularly of your dear father, for whom I have, as you may know, a deep reverence and affection, coupled with a modern American outlook, should enable you to understand the new young forces which have arisen in the Movement, without impairing the continuity of Zionist thought, sentiment and action, which is so intimately bound up with the history and experience of the last fifty years.

There is no doubt that Zionism in America is entering upon a new phase, and this is a healthy and normal sign. The deaths of Ussishkin in Jerusalem and Brandeis in Washington are symbolic of the end of an era.

213

But I am a little disquieted by the tendencies and undercurrents which are noticeable in American Zionism today, and which seem to indicate a desire on the part of the young to emancipate themselves too rapidly from the influence of European trends. If such a development were to take place in normal times I would welcome it heartily as a sign of maturity and of natural evolution. I gladly admit that the consciousness of American Zionists has deepened and grown; I believe it would be a serious mistake on their part—and a deplorable moral aberration—to "write off" European Jewry just now, while they are down, and try to take over their heritage too hastily. An intimate connection between American Zionism and Palestine can be maintained through the link provided by the European Jews. The temporary obliteration of these communities is our greatest tragedy, but it is also a powerful moral force. The epic of the Warsaw Ghetto in these days; the dignity and fortitude with which its people face untold sufferings; the existence of a Zionist effort in such abject conditions—these are things which inspire both hope and awe. Some American Jewish intellectuals are, I believe, falling into grievous error when, in their flirtations with Palestine, they speak and think of it as a "museum piece," in a perverted Achad-Ha'amistic sense, and over-emphasise the role of America as "the" heir to Judaism, where great things—"really great things"—can and will be done. They like to compare themselves with Babylon as ראשי גלותא.[1] In some respects this comparison is only too true, but I fear not in the sense in which they wish it to be understood, namely that something tantamount to a modern תלמוד בבלי[2] will be produced in the U.S.A. I don't see on the horizon the תנאים and אמוראים[3] of Babylonian stature, and Kaplan's *Hagaddah* is a poor effort![4]

European Jewry is the first defence line of American Jewry, and if it—God Forbid!—should fall, there is mighty little hope for the Jews of America, just as there is no hope for the American people if England should go down.

I am sure that all these ideas must long have been present in your own mind, and that I am not telling you anything new. But the matter has a practical aspect to which I am anxious to draw your attention. You realise, no doubt, how precarious is the present posi-

---

197. [1] Hebr.: Exilarchs (lay heads of Jewish Community in ancient Babylonia between early 3rd and late 5th C., C.E.).

[2] Hebr.: Babylonian Talmud.

[3] Hebr.: *Tannaim* and *Amoraim,* rabbinical authorities of Talmudic period.

[4] Ritual performed at home on Passover eve. *The New Haggadah* by Rabbi Mordechai Kaplan (b. 1881) in collaboration with Eugene Kohn and Ira Eisenstein, reflected the ideas of Reconstructionism, a movement which saw Judaism as a self-contained civilisation.

tion of the Zionist Executive. There was no Congress, and consequently no renewal of the mandate. The whole of the European
movement is swallowed up in darkness. Apart from Palestine and
the communities of the British Empire, the only parts of it left intact
are the Zionist Organizations of the Western Hemisphere. If the
separatist tendencies gain the upper hand, we shall be faced with
the destruction of the universal character of Zionism, and thus lose
the only asset which we still possess. The danger exists, and I am
happy that you are there to watch it, so that it may not become a
real menace. You understand both sides, and stand, so to say, between the two generations.

I was most anxious that during my next visit to America we
should have a Pan-American Zionist Conference, which might be
attended by representatives from Palestine, South Africa, and other
countries still accessible. Such a meeting might be of incalculable
value both כלפי פנים and כלפי חוץ.[5] Don't let them reduce it to
something like a rump meeting of the A[ctions] C[ommittee]. I
have every reason to think that such a conference would be of importance politically. It could not, of course, replace a Congress, but
it would be the next best thing, and would strengthen the hands of
those who, like myself, have to carry on simply because of *force
majeure*. I saw the Air Ministry yesterday, and hope that they will
arrange for my passage to Palestine in November. From there I shall
find my way to the States. I shall let you know exactly what my
movements are as soon as I know them myself.

My affectionate regards to you, to your family, and in particular
to your Father.

Ever yours,
Ch. Weizmann

198. To Moshe Shertok, Jerusalem.   *London, 15 October 1941*
English: H.W.: W.A.

15 Oct. 1941

My dear Moshe,
These documents,[1] and Victor [Cazalet] will tell you all there
is to say.[2]

I have decided to reverse my programme and go to the U.S.A.

---

[5] Hebr.: internally and externally.

198. [1] Only one document has been traced, Moyne's letter as given in n. 2 below. W. wrote
this note on a typed copy for Shertok.

[2] Having discussed the Jewish Force with Lyttelton, then in London, Moyne reported to

first and then make my way to Palestine. To go to Palestine from here would take about 6 weeks, which I cannot afford much as I would love to visit Palestine before going to America. But there is almost no choice. We shall meet before long and I'm not losing courage.[3]

Affectionately and love to you and all friends,

Chaim

the Cabinet that W.O., being doubtful of the military value of 10,000 Jews, and apprehensive of Arab repercussions, now opposed the scheme. F.O. were not opposed, but wished the announcement to be so formulated as to reassure the Arabs that the Force would not be used in the Middle East. Moyne felt that such a qualification could cause W. to reject the whole project. The Cabinet duly decided to reject the scheme, again on grounds of lack of equipment. See Moyne memorandum of 30 Sept. 1941—P.R.O., M.S.C. (41)17, in Cab 95/8; Cabinet decision of 13 Oct. 1941, in Cab 65/19. On 15 Oct. Moyne wrote to W. as follows: 'I very much regret the delay in sending a definite reply to the request which you made during our discussion here on the 1st of September about the proposal for the formation of Jewish contingents for the British Army. When I reported our conversation and your desire that there should be a definite decision, and that you should not be left in further suspense, the Prime Minister referred the whole matter for further consideration to the Ministers concerned. The results of their examination of the problem have now been considered by the Cabinet, to whom copies of your letter to Mr. Churchill of the 10th September had already been communicated by the Prime Minister's direction. Viewed from the standpoint of military requirements and the supply situation, it at once became apparent that the present shipping and supply situation has grown much more complicated in consequence of the undertakings of assistance on a vast scale that have recently been given to the Soviet Government, and that it would indeed entirely preclude the idea of transporting to this country recruits in considerable numbers for a Jewish Force from the United States and from Palestine. I am very sorry that this decision must be profoundly disappointing to you, and would much like to see you some day next week to discuss various possibilities.'

[3] Moyne received W. and Ben-Gurion 23 Oct. 1941, when W. accused the Government of having broken its promise, and Moyne denied that it had ever promised a Jewish Army. W. then asked that the Jewish companies of the Palestine Buffs be at least allowed their own name, badge and a unified organization. Moyne replied that the Government's advisers thought this would raise difficult problems; he presumed the Jews wanted a Jewish Army for the Peace Conference, that they needed the publicity. C.O. had already stated in the Commons that some 10,000 Palestinian Jews were serving with the British Forces, and the Jews could use that. Moyne asked how many Jews would be likely to immigrate into Palestine after the war, W. having mentioned 2-3 millions. W. and Ben-Gurion stated that they wanted freedom of immigration. Moyne disputed the Zionist claim that Palestine alone could provide a solution to the Jewish problem—record of meeting in W.A.

199. To Lord Lugard,[1] **Dorking.**   *London, 20 October 1941*
English: Or. Copy. T.W.: W.A.

My dear Lord Lugard,
  Your letter of October 1st reached me only about five days ago;[2] I do not know whether it was delayed in the post, or whether there is some other explanation of its taking so long to arrive.
  I was delighted to hear from you; I have thought of you very often these last months, but somehow could not find the courage to trouble you with our affairs in such critical days for the world at large. I would have been very happy to come and see you—for there is much I should like to tell you and ask your advice about—had I not felt it would be burdening you too much. I have been away in America, and returned some two months ago; I am now trying to arrange a passage to Palestine, with the intention of proceeding from there to America again early next year.
  What you write about Eritrea is interesting, but I scarcely believe that the climate of the country would lend itself to any large-scale European settlement. Besides, I always feel that the achievements of the Jews in Palestine, which is their religious, national, and traditional centre, could not be duplicated in any other country. And all the energies we can muster after the war will be needed for the work in Palestine, where I am convinced that, given suitable political conditions and freedom of immigration, we can absorb sufficient numbers of Jews to relieve the pressure in the distressed areas of Europe.
  I have today finished an article for the New York *Foreign Affairs,* which may perhaps be of interest to you, since it deals with the very problems which you raise in your letter.[3]
  I hope you manage to keep well, and are not leading too strenuous a life, and remain, with kindest regards, and many thanks for your letter,

Very sincerely yours,
Ch. W.

---

199. [1] Biog. Index, Vol. XIV. British delegate to Permanent Mandates Commission of League of Nations 1922–36. Chairman of International Institute of African Languages and Cultures.
  [2] W.A. This proposed occupation of Eritrea by Jews unable to be accommodated in Palestine, provided Eritrea was not returned to Italy at the Peace Conference.
  [3] The article indicated the unsuitability of the various regions proposed for large-scale Jewish immigration: Madagascar, British Guiana, Alaska, San Domingo, and part of Southern California (*Foreign Affairs,* Jan. 1942, p. 326). See also No. 200.

200. To Lord Moyne, London.   *London, 20 October 1941*
English: Or. Copy. T.W.: W.A.

Dear Lord Moyne,

Major Victor Cazalet has mentioned to me that you have discussed with him the possibility of Madagascar as a country for Jewish colonisation (apart from Palestine). You are, no doubt, aware that the Polish Government sent a Commission to investigate conditions in Madagascar from this point of view. They have never published their Report, but the article at pages 381 ff. of the enclosed copy of the *Contemporary Jewish Record* (New York, August, 1941) may perhaps interest you in this connection.[1]

I should perhaps add that the Record is in no sense a Zionist publication. It is produced by the American Jewish Committee, which contains very few Zionists, a good many non-Zionists, and some anti-Zionists.

Yours very sincerely,
Ch. W.

201. To Lucien Harris,[1] Manchester.   *London, 23 October 1941*
English: Or. Copy. T.W.: W.A.

Dear Mr. Harris,

The Executive have been discussing with leading members of the different Zionist bodies in London, as well as with the British section of the Jewish Agency for Palestine, the present political situation and the steps which ought to be taken to mobilise all Zionists and Jewish forces in this country, under the direction of the Jewish Agency, for the advancement of our aims in Palestine. The Executive are convinced that every Jew in this country can greatly contribute, at this critical moment, to safeguarding the future of our people and our homeland, and can and must take an active part in

200. [1] The Polish Commission was sent to Madagascar 1937, with a view to the eventual forced settlement there of part of its Jewish population. This 'Madagascar Plan' was adopted by the Nazis, who envisaged the transfer of all European Jewry to the island. The article referred to pointed out the difficulties and dangers of settling a white population in an isolated, backward, disease-ridden tropical wilderness, contending that all studies had led to this conclusion, and that only a small plateau area of the island was fit for colonisation.

201. [1] B. 1912. On E.Z.F. Executive Council; employed at J.A. Information Dept., 1941 and 1946–48; in R.A.F. 1942–46; Public Relations Officer of Hadassah Medical Organization, Jerusalem, from 1952. This invitation was addressed to Zionist leaders throughout Britain.

our political work: in enlightening British public opinion on the general Jewish situation, and on our efforts and achievements in Palestine which provide the only lasting solution of the Jewish problem.

The Executive have, therefore, decided to establish a special Department, the task of which will be to bring before British public opinion, as well as before the Jews of this country, the urgency of the Jewish problem and the important part which Palestine can play in its solution through large-scale immigration and colonisation under suitable political conditions. Such a Department can only perform its functions adequately if it has behind it the full weight of Zionist and Jewish support.

The Executive have accordingly decided to convene a special Conference of selected keymen from London and the provinces, at which Dr. Weizmann and Mr. Ben-Gurion will report on the present political situation, the position in Palestine, and the problems facing us during and after the war; and where Dr. Brodetsky will outline a plan for our work in this country. A general discussion will follow.

The Conference will be held at the Anglo-Palestinian Club (43/44 Great Windmill Street, Piccadilly, London, W.1.) on Sunday, November 9th, under the Chairmanship of Dr. Brodetsky. The morning session will open at 11 a.m. with statements from Dr. Weizmann and Mr. Ben-Gurion; lunch will be provided (1.30 to 2.30 p.m.) in the Club's restaurant; and Dr. Brodetsky's statement will follow in the afternoon. The Conference will close at 5.30 p.m.

We should like to extend to you an urgent invitation to attend this meeting; we sincerely hope that you will be able to be present, and to take part in the important work which the new Department will have to undertake. Would you kindly let us know as early as possible whether we may expect you at the Conference.[2]

Yours sincerely,
Ch. Weizmann
S. Brodetsky

[2] At the conference, W. publicly revealed for the first time the course of negotiations with the Government for a Jewish Division, from his offer of Jewish cooperation to Chamberlain 29 Aug. 1939 until Moyne's letter, 15 Oct. 1941, announcing abandonment of the scheme (record in W.A.).

202. To Anthony de Rothschild, London. *London, 23 October 1941*
English: Or. Copy. T.W.: W.A.

Dear Mr. de Rothschild,

Thank you for your letter of October 17th.[1] I confess that we were very much surprised by the wholesale denial of everything which we had understood to be common ground between us. I expect to remain in this country for another four or five weeks, and should be very glad if the statement setting out the views and proposals of your group could reach me in time for me to consider them with my friends.[2]

Yours very sincerely,
Ch. W.

203. To Sir Archibald Sinclair,[1] London. *London, 23 October 1941*
English: Or. Copy. T.W.: W.A.

My dear Archie,

It is being pointed out by those who are against any public recognition of Jewish interests, or regard for Jewish feelings, concerning Palestine that the experience of the last three years shows that the British Government have nothing to fear from Jewish reactions in America: the Jews there are divided among themselves on the subject of Palestine; the American Government did not react in any way against the White Paper.

On this I would pass the following comments:

Jewry recognises that the first thing at present is to defeat Hitler, and that the foremost champion in that fight is Great Britain. Great Britain can therefore draw upon an enormous fund of Jewish goodwill, and even deliberate wastage does not exhaust it to the point

---

202. [1] Writing on behalf of the 'non-Zionists', de Rothschild denied that paragraphs a, b, and c of W.'s memorandum (see No. 186) correctly represented the measure of agreement reached at their meeting. He would later send W. a detailed argument (W.A.).

[2] See No. 244 and ns. there.

203. [1] Sinclair was an old and trusted friend of W. and Zionism, hence this *cri de coeur*. He had notified W. 10 Jan. 1941 (W.A.) that opposition to a Jewish Air Unit might be expected from R.A.F. G.H.Q. in Palestine, and that the Prime Minister had warned him against raising the issue before the Jewish Division scheme was settled, in deference to C.O. He had later written explicitly to Namier, 26 May 1941 (W.A.) that formation of the Jewish Division must precede that of the Air Unit. On 11 Mar. 1943 the Colonial Secretary, then Oliver Stanley, announced that no separate Air Unit recruited exclusively from the Jewish community in Palestine would be established, ample opportunities existing for all who wished to enlist in R.A.F. (Hansard, Commons, Vol. 387, col. 887).

where it would change into hostility. Nonetheless, treatment such as H. M. Government has meted out to the Jews during the past three years produces bitterness, which inhibits action. The loss is real, even if it cannot be exactly measured.

It would be much greater if my colleagues and I had not actively worked and spoken for the British cause, and withheld from the public knowledge (as far as we could) some of the measures of H. M. Government, and the performances of the Palestine Administration.

This deliberate policy on our part began even before the outbreak of war, because we, in common with the leaders of the present Government, saw war coming. At a Conference in this office in March 1939 (after the Palestine Conference, but also after Hitler's entry into Prague) we discussed with our American colleagues the line they should pursue after their return to the United States. Dr. Stephen Wise then said that whatever they did, they must bear in mind that soon Great Britain might be at war with Germany, and they would wish to throw in every ounce of their weight on the British side; were they to come out full blast against H. M. Government's White Paper policy now, and work up American opinion, it might be difficult to reverse. We all felt that he was right.[2]

I will not dwell at length upon a series of incidents (e.g., refusal to admit to Palestine Jewish children endangered in Poland, searches for arms and provocatively savage sentences on Jews concerned, etc.), but I pass to the next milestone, the Land Regulations.[3] You will remember that we asked to have their validity tested by the Judicial Committee of the Privy Council; we could not take them to the Palestine Courts, because H. M. Government had forestalled such action by a specific Order-in-Council. When I returned from America in March 1940, I prepared a letter to *The Times* challenging H. M. Government, who professed to fight for the rule of law and decency, to take their White Paper before the Judicial Committee; I refrained from sending it. Orderly Jewish demonstrations over the Land Regulations were followed in Jerusalem by the British police breaking into private houses, beating up harmless people, etc. A boy of 17, Menachem Prives, had his skull battered in, and died. We thought of having a Parliamentary Question on this case, and consulted Mr. Amery. This was at the time of Narvik.[4] He thought such publicity might injure British interests, and so we desisted.

[2] See Vol. XIX.
[3] Of Feb. 1940.
[4] Apr. 1940, during Britain's unsuccessful attempts to aid Norway against German invasion. For Prives incident, see No. 8, n. 1.

Could we have indicted British policy in America when France was falling? Moreover, we hoped that the coming of our friends into office would produce a change in London, which might even percolate to the Palestine Administration. There was a promise of a Jewish Division. It has not materialised. The negotiations were dragged on, there were postponements and delays. The Jewish Agency has been the target of bitter criticisms and attacks on the part of the Jewish people, suffering from hope deferred. But so far I have made no public statement about the treatment we have received. The anger of Jewry, including American Jewry, has been turned against what looks to them like inefficiency and laxity on the part of the Agency, rather than against the British Government.

In the meantime the *Patria* incident occurred in Palestine, and the atrocious scenes in Athlit camp when refugees were forcibly deported to Mauritius.[5] For the last ten months we have been asking that some evidence concerning the methods then applied by the police should be obtained from people other than those responsible for the outrages (e.g., that Sir Wyndham Deedes[6] be sent to Mauritius under cover of social welfare work, and that the ships' officers should be questioned as to the conditions in which the refugees were brought on board).

Again, though refused any satisfaction, we refrained from giving publicity to a cause which could have been exploited in America against Great Britain—the Lease-Lend Bill was under discussion. I have told you about my conversation with Morgenthau who wanted to bring 300,000 Jews into Palestine now, and urged me to see the President about it. The latter, whose word is law (as Morgenthau put it), would support such a claim before H.M. Government. Money for such an operation could, in Morgenthau's opinion, be made available. I refused to entertain the idea, and was subjected to a good deal of criticism from him for being too timid, etc. (He used stronger language.)

And so the story goes on. What do those who trade on our restraint want us to do? Must American Jews be goaded into a rampant anti-British attitude before any attention is paid to their feelings? Must we publish the record of the things done to us in the last three years?

The argument which turns against us our care for the Allied Cause strikes me as unjustified, unjust, and short-sighted.

As to disunity among the Jews of America, that is simply not true. The overwhelming majority would like to see free immigration

[5] Nos. 63, 81.
[6] Biog. Index, Vol. VIII. Chief Secretary of Palestine 1920–23.

into, and settlement in Palestine, and resent the discriminatory legislation contained in the White Paper. Of course, there is a small group of out-and-out opponents, and possibly they find their way to the British Embassy, but it would be a dangerous mistake to assume that these Quislings represent anybody but themselves.[7]

Ch. W.

204. To Lord Moyne, London.   *London, 28 October 1941*
English: Or. Copy. T.W.: W.A.

Dear Lord Moyne,

Last Thursday, October 23rd, you informed us of the final decision of His Majesty's Government cancelling their promise regarding a Jewish Fighting Force.[1]

Absolutely convinced that this promise, emphatically re-stated in your letter of March 4th, would be carried out, the Jewish Agency has kept silence when bitterly criticised for its apparent apathy in a matter which has been eagerly pressed by the Jewish people in all free countries. I now find myself compelled to give a public explanation of our otherwise inexplicable inaction.[2]

Yours very sincerely,

Ch. W.

205. To Victor Cazalet, London.   *London, 29 October 1941*
English: Or. Copy. T.W.: W.A.

My dear Victor,

I heard from you that Lord Moyne complained to the delegation of M.P.'s who went to see him about Palestinian matters that Palestinian Jewry is "vilifying" the Administration.[1] I wish he had specified.

---

[7] Sinclair replied 28 Oct. 1941 (W.A.) that 'timing is one of the vital factors of success in politics', and that whereas he could not guarantee what the result might have been otherwise, he regretted that W. had not been able to give the Government more time (i.e., regarding its final decision on the Jewish Division).

204. [1] See No. 198, n. 3.
    [2] See No. 201, n. 2.

205. [1] Cazalet had organized a delegation of M.P.'s to the Colonial Secretary to protest, in private rather than in the Commons, at the Government's policy in Palestine, particularly as regards the mobilization and recognition of the services of Jewish soldiers (see Cazalet to W., 3 Oct., and memorandum of 10 Oct. 1941, in W.A.).

Possibly he referred to the case of Menachem Prives, and of the *Atlantic* passengers in Athlit Camp. The first case is that of a boy of 17 done to death, with his skull broken in six places, not in a street brawl or a wild demonstration, but as a result of direct personal attentions from several British policemen. The Administration carried through its own "investigation," failed to ascertain the facts, and tried to close the matter with an insulting letter to the Jewish Agency (see enclosure).[2]

The second case is that of the deportations from Athlit Camp to Mauritius. Specific allegations have been made of the brutal ill-treatment by the British police of those victims of the Nazis. Suggestions of discreet methods of obtaining independent and reliable evidence were pressed by us on the Colonial Office (see enclosure)—again to no purpose.[3]

In short, when accusations are raised against the British Administration in Palestine, the Colonial Office thinks fit to accept the statements of those whose conduct is impugned as conclusive evidence; while those who demand an enquiry more consistent with normal British practice are described as "vilifiers." If the Palestine Administration has a good case, and a sound defence, why should methods be employed reminiscent of those of the French General Staff in the Dreyfus affair—when every demand for impartial enquiry was turned down as a "vilification" of the French Army?

Yours,

Ch. W.

206. To Sir Archibald Sinclair, London.　　*London, 31 October 1941*
English: Or. Copy. T.W.: W.A.

I am very grateful to you for your letter of October 28th, and for all the trouble you have taken.[1] I quite appreciate the difficulty in obtaining accommodation to the Middle East at the present time. Going by sea to South Africa would, however, mean the loss of six weeks or so in travelling, which I do not feel able to afford at this critical time. I have therefore decided to reverse my plans, and instead of going to Palestine first and then to America, I propose to leave here for the States about the end of November, or

---

[2] See No. 8, n. 1.
[3] See No. 101.

206. [1] W.A. Reply to W.'s request for priority seats for V.W. and himself to fly to Palestine. Sinclair stated his difficulty in justifying a priority for V.W. Hence he suggested alternative routes involving sea travel.

at latest the beginning of December, try to finish my work there by the spring, and then find my way to Palestine either by the American Line to Lagos, or by the Trans-Pacific route.

The problem thus reduces itself to finding passages for Mrs. Weizmann and myself to Lisbon at the end of November or beginning of December, and we should be deeply grateful to you for anything you may be good enough to do for us in that direction.[2] I have telegraphed to the States for Clipper seats round about that date.

Thanking you again most heartily for all you have done to help, I am,

> With kind regards,
> Very sincerely yours,
> Ch. W.

207. To Sir Charles Tegart,[1] London.　　　*London, 31 October 1941*
English: Or. Copy. T.W.: W.A.

Dear Sir Charles,

I was deeply touched by your kind note about Joshua Gordon.[2] His death is indeed a tragic loss for us, and leaves a void in our personal lives, as in the life of the movement in Palestine. He had a genius for friendship, and the hearts of all who knew him are heavy at his going.

I am glad to think that you had an interesting visit to Manchester, and that the pilot-plant lived up to its promise.[3] I really believe that we have got over the worst of our difficulties now. If I may, I will let you know how things develop.

With kindest regards from us both to you and Lady Tegart, I am,

> Very sincerely yours,
> Ch. W.

[2] See No. 209.

207. [1] Biog. Index, Vol. XIX. During the Arab rebellion in 1937 he organized security installations in Palestine.

[2] 1889–1941. Responsible for security and organization of Jewish Settlement Police from 1931. Tegart's letter of 29 Oct. 1941 (W.A.) paid tribute to Gordon's assistance in Palestine.

[3] Tegart had noted that the pilot plant working on W.'s process for producing aviation fuel ('ketones') seemed to have passed its teething troubles. On retirement from active police duty, Tegart was apparently engaged as a governmental adviser (Tegart to W., 29 Oct. 1941. W.A.).

208. To Jan Christiaan Smuts, Pretoria.   *London, 3 November 1941*
English: T.: W.A.

Thank you for your heartening Balfour Day message which will
be source of lasting encouragement [and] inspiration for us all in
these dark difficult days.[1]

                                     Weizmann

209. To Sir Archibald Sinclair, London.   *London, 10 November 1941*
English: Or. Copy. T.W.: W.A.

My dear Archie,
    I must apologise for troubling you again over my transport, but
I have just received the enclosed telegram from Palestine, which I
should like you to read.[1]
    Perhaps I may add a word of explanation. You know, I expect,
of the gap in our ranks in Palestine left by the death of Mr. Ussishkin, the President of the Jewish National Fund, and a real pillar
of the Movement. We now hear that Mr. Rutenberg[2] is seriously
ill, and out of action for some time to come. Mr. Ben-Gurion is
here in London, and about to leave for the United States. This will
explain the acute disappointment felt by the Executive in Palestine
at the postponement of my visit there. I feel it very deeply myself,
as you know. Dame Edith Lyttelton has recently strongly advised
me to go to Cairo as soon as possible, and have a talk with her son
there. But the prospect of travelling by ship, either to Lagos or the
Cape involves the loss of something like five or six weeks on travelling, which I can ill afford in these times of stress.
    I am therefore addressing myself to you again, as to an old friend
who will understand the seriousness of the position, to ask whether
there is any possibility of Mrs. Weizmann and myself getting to
Palestine by air. I realise the difficulties, and know, of course, that

---

208. [1] Smuts had broadcast to U.S. on 2 Nov. 1941, recalling the circumstances in which
the Balfour Declaration had been issued in 1917, and appealing to Christian world not to
forget 'The People of the Book'. He concluded: 'The Balfour Declaration is not dead...the
structure that will arise from it will be greater than the Declaration itself.' Text in W.A.

209. [1] See Shertok to W., 9 Nov. (W.A.), insisting that W.'s 'mission to America would
benefit enormously from fresh first hand impressions wartime Palestine'.
    [2] Pinhas Rutenberg (Biog. Index, Vol. VII). Founded Palestine Electric Corporation;
President of *Va'ad Leumi* (Jewish National Council) 1929–31, 1939–40.

At the Extraordinary Zionist Conference, Biltmore Hotel, New York, May 1942. Seen on the platform with Weizmann are, *from left*, Israel Goldstein, Judge Louis Levinthal, David Wertheim, Arthur Lourie, Louis Lipsky, Meyer W. Weisgal, Stephen Wise, David Ben-Gurion, Nahum Goldmann, Tamar de Sola Pool, Abba Hillel Silver.

Herbert H. Lehman   Henry Morgenthau, Jr.

Berl Locker with David Ben-Gurion

the journey may be none too pleasant; I would not trouble you again about it if I did not feel that I could really be of some use in Palestine, and that I should also be of much more use in America if I could come there direct from Palestine.[3]

With apologies for taking up so much of your time, I am, as ever,

Affectionately yours,

Ch. Weizmann

210. To R. Seligsohn, Stratford-on-Avon. *London, 12 November 1941*
English: Or. Copy. T.W.: W.A.

My dear Mr. Seligsohn,

Thank you for your letter of October 27th[1]—I am sorry not to have replied earlier.

You will, I expect, have seen from my recent public statement that the Jewish Army question is for the time being closed. Enlistment in the Palestine Forces of the British Army remains limited to people already in Palestine, and though there are many here who, like yourself, are anxious to be transferred, I am afraid I know no means of arranging this. I expect you will have had similar replies from Lord Reading[2] and Lord Samuel. I am sorry, but all I can advise is patience for the time being.

I remember your family very well,[3] and am happy to know that you are here in England, and serving the common cause so far as you can.

With kind regards, and best wishes,

I am
Yours very sincerely,
Ch. W.

---

[3] Sinclair was unable to help (his letter, 15 Nov., in W.A.). W. consequently travelled directly to U.S. He did not in fact visit Palestine until Nov. 1944.

210. [1] B. Berlin, 1910. A corporal in Pioneer Corps, Seligsohn requested W.'s help for a transfer to a Jewish or British unit in Palestine. He explained that he had been a communal rabbi in Bonn, arriving in England 1939, and wished, with others like him, to serve more usefully than in the Pioneers.

[2] Biog. Index, Vol. XIV. He was then Commanding Officer of Pioneer Corps.

[3] Seligsohn stated that his grandfather had owned a sawmill in Germany, and had business relations with W.'s father (who had been a timber merchant).

211. To Nicolai Kirschner, Benoni, South Africa.

London, 12 November 1941

English: T.: W.A.

Cannot understand your anxiety.[1] No commitment whatsoever. Serious readjustments mean exactly what has of late been adumbrated. No prejudice to greater possibilities. Regards.[2]

Weizmann

212. To Jan Masaryk, London.

London, 12 November 1941

English: Or. Copy. T.W.: W.A.

My dear Friend,

I would be very grateful indeed for your support in the matter raised in the enclosed letter with regard to Dr. Herbert Steiner.[1]

You know that I am normally very reluctant to make applications for deferments of calling-up for military service, but the work on which Dr. Herbert Steiner is engaged in Manchester is really work of national importance—in connection with explosives—and I do not see how he can be spared. I shall be most grateful for any help or advice which you can give.[2]

Yours ever,
Ch. W.

213. To Isaac Hamlin, New York.

London, 17 November 1941

English: T.: W.A.

To Convention National Labour Committee for Palestine I send most cordial greetings. Wish could be with you share your deliber-

211. [1] Kirschner had cabled 11 Nov. 1941 (W.A.) that W.'s letter to Moyne (No. 172—copy sent to Kirschner 26 Aug.) contained 'a new conception of the Jewish Force that was liable to jeopardise greater possibilities.' The letter to Moyne was accompanied by 'Draft Amendments', in which W. stated his doubts whether the Jewish Agency could now raise even 3,000 men from Palestine, as 9,000 had already enlisted for service with British regiments. He expressed willingness to withdraw the condition that the Force must serve in the Middle East. Kirschner wished the Agency to insist on W.'s publicly-declared formula (of 9 Nov. 1941), i.e., recruitment in Palestine of the maximum number of Jews in Jewish units.

[2] Kirschner replied that his anxieties were unallayed, but W. re-affirmed that they were not justified—exchange of 24, 25 Nov. 1941 (W.A.).

212. [1] D. 1969. Czech chemist, employed at Manchester Oil Refinery. 'Enclosed letter' untraced.

[2] Steiner received deferment—see W.'s letter of thanks to Dr. Frey (Masaryk's secretary), 1 Dec. 1941, W.A.

ations for strengthening effort American Jewish Labour in this combat with Jewry's most horrible foe and for securing safeguards our people's rights in new world to be constructed after war, especially right [to] create its independent home in land of its ancestors. European Jewry suffers now as never before. Our sacrifices in life and blood are unprecedented. Goebbels today honours us by proclaiming every Jew enemy of Nazism. Nearer Hitler feels himself to defeat, greater [the] danger [of] grand-scale annihilation Jewish life. Our hearts go out to our brethren in territories tortured by barbarian. It is our sacred duty to demand from those responsible for conduct present struggle and for shaping future a secure place for our people in both. American Jewish Labour can play honourable part this struggle by standing united behind our demands.

Weizmann

214. To S. Salman Schocken, New York.   *London, 26 November 1941*
English: T.: W.A.

Support your view.[1] Regards.

Weizmann

215. To Eduard Benes,[1] London.   *London, 27 November 1941*
English: Or. Copy. T.W.: W.A.

My dear President,

I was delighted to have news of the appointment to the National Committee of a leading Zionist from Czechoslovakia,[2] and deeply appreciate it.

If you have ever a little time to spare, I should very much like to have a talk with you one day before I leave again for America at the end of December. I will leave it to you to suggest a time, for I know how busy you must be.[3]

With very kind regards, I am,

Yours sincerely,

Ch. W.

214. [1] Relates to request for W.'s endorsement of Schocken's opposition to co-option of Max Soloveichik (Biog. Index, Vol. XI) to H.U. Executive Council. Schocken recalled that his own choice, David Horowitz, had declined—see his telegrams 25 Nov., 9 Dec. (W.A.). W. cabled his support of Schocken's view also to Senator 12 Dec. 1941 (W.A.). See also No. 242.

215. [1] Biog. Index. Premier, Czechoslovak Government-in-Exile, 1940–45.

[2] Arnost Frischer (1887–1954).

[3] Nothing is known of any subsequent meeting.

216. To Lord Davies,[1] **London.**   *London, 27 November 1941*
English: Or. Copy. T.W.: W.A.

Dear Lord Davies,

Thank you very much for your kind letter of the 23rd, and for the copy of *Hansard.*[2] I deeply appreciate your question and interest which you are taking in the future of my people and in regard to Palestine, as well as in our request for a Jewish Fighting Force.

The figures given by Lord Croft[3] do not, of course, include about 1,500 Palestinian Jews who are serving with the R.A.F. I confess to being greatly disturbed by the statement made immediately afterwards by Lord Moyne about the Jewish Force. It was incomplete, and Lord Moyne, no doubt inadvertently, conveyed an erroneous impression which is damaging to us. I am preparing a letter to him, and shall, if I may, send you a copy as soon as it is ready.[4]

I need not tell you how deeply I am touched by your generous offer of help; there was never a time when we needed it more.

I hope to leave for Palestine and the United States at the end of December; it would give me very great pleasure if you could spare the time to see me before I go.[5]

With kindest regards and renewed thanks,

I am
Very sincerely yours,
Ch. W.

---

216. [1] David Davies, 1st Lord Davies of Llandenam (1880–1944). In 1933 he founded the New Commonwealth Society, to work for a more effective League of Nations.

[2] Letter untraced.

[3] Formerly Brig.-Gen. Henry Page Croft (1881–1947). Parliamentary Under-Secretary of State for War 1940–45.

[4] See No. 220.

[5] Davies' reply, 4 Dec. 1941 (W.A.), voiced agreement that Moyne's statement had been unsatisfactory, and regretted that the Government had behaved 'so scurvily in its treatment of the patriotic offers which you had made on behalf of the Palestine Jews'. While welcoming a meeting (there is no record of one taking place), he feared that there was little a back-bencher in the Lords could do for W.'s 'noble enterprise.'

217. To Oliver Harvey,[1] London.   *London, 28 November 1941*
English: Or. Copy. T.W.: W.A.

Dear Mr. Harvey,
    May I trouble you in the following matter?
    We have been in touch with the Colonial Office about a recommendation from the Foreign Office to the British Embassy in Ankara for Mr. Eliahu Epstein,[2] an official of our Political Department in Jerusalem. Mr. Epstein, who is an authority on Middle Eastern questions, was in Turkey in May last, and was then asked by the British authorities there to visit Iran and Iraq with a view to enlisting the support of the Jewish communities of those countries for the British war effort. I gather that his trip was regarded as very successful. Mr. Epstein is now again in Turkey, and would like to discuss with the Russian Embassy there questions connected with the distribution in Russia of about a hundred Palestinian Immigration Certificates to Polish Zionists now in Russian territory. I understand that the British Embassy in Ankara is prepared to introduce him to the Russian Embassy if they receive a recommendation from London in that sense.
    The Colonial Office has taken up the matter officially with the Foreign Office, but I thought it might be useful if I mentioned it to you. We shall be very grateful for anything you may feel able to do to help.[3]
    With kindest regards, I am

218. To Walter Wreschner,[1] Zurich.   *London, 28 November 1941*
English: T.: W.A.

Heartiest congratulations good wishes celebration twentieth anniversary Swiss *Keryesod* in which for many years Zionists non-Zionists, leading personalities Swiss community have worked together under

---

217. [1] Later Lord Harvey (1893–1968). Principal Private Secretary to Eden 1941–43; Asst., then Deputy Under-Secretary of State, F.O., 1943–47; Ambassador to France 1948–54.
    [2] Later Elath (Biog. Index, Vol. XVIII). Then director, J.A.'s Middle East Dept.
    [3] Following W.'s intervention, the Embassy at Ankara gave the required introduction and the Soviet Ambassador, A. Vinogradov, received Epstein 6 Jan. 1942, and agreed to pass Epstein's request to Moscow (that J.A. representatives be allowed to visit Moscow to deal with the immigration of the Polish Zionists). Epstein was advised of a likely delay in Moscow's reply, and in fact returned to Palestine without it. His report to Shertok, 25 Jan. 1942 (W.A.), expressed doubts about the success of an approach via the Ambassador rather than directly to Moscow. He pointed out that Russia's alliance with the West had brought no change in Russian internal policies, and they should not hope for early legalisation of the Zionist movement in Russia.

218. [1] B. 1904. Attorney, K.H. President in Switzerland.

your leadership and that of Dr. Mayer for Palestine cause. Please convey my warm greetings good wishes Sunday's Conference, which meets in our people's darkest hour. But even in wartime we must prepare for problems which will face us after war. We must consolidate what already achieved Palestine and lay foundations for absorption large masses our people, rendered homeless and stripped of everything. Their thoughts turn to their ancient homeland and as soon as victory comes their feet will take that road. They unable contribute financially; therefore falls on Jewish communities still free to act to shoulder burden which they forced drop. I know that Swiss Jewry with its long tradition wholehearted support our cause will seize opportunity make maximum contribution *Keryesod* and thus to rebuilding our homeland.

Weizmann

219. To Chief Passport and Permit Officer, London.

London, 1 December 1941

English: Or. Copy. T.W.: W.A.

Dear Sir,

I understand that travellers to the United States who will be speaking in public have to sign an undertaking that they will leave the United States if requested to do so by H.M. Ambassador in Washington. As I shall no doubt be addressing some meetings in America, I give this undertaking herewith.

Yours faithfully,
Ch. W.

220. To Lord Moyne, London.   *London, 1 December 1941*

English: Or. Copy. T.W.: W.A.

Dear Lord Moyne,

I write to draw your attention to the unfortunate impression which, I am afraid, your statement in the House of Lords on November 25th about the Jewish Fighting Force must have, inadvertently, created. I am confident that, when you have looked again at the relevant documents you will find it only fair to the Jewish Agency and to myself to correct this wrong and damaging impression. If so, might it not be possible to arrive at some form of correction?

Your statement suggests that when you took over the Colonial Office, the negotiations were still some way from agreement on substance and that the final failure was caused by precipitate action on my part. May I remind you of the events and their sequence? You stated that the Government "decided at the end of 1940 to accept, in principle, the project submitted" by me on behalf of the Jewish Agency, and that Lord Lloyd conveyed to me "the Government's decision" at the beginning of January this year. Our offer had been accepted in principle by the Prime Minister on September 3rd, 1940; practical details had been discussed between Mr. Eden, Lord Lloyd, a representative of the Foreign Office, and myself on September 13th, when general agreement was reached. The detailed scheme approved by His Majesty's Government was communicated to me in writing by Lord Lloyd on October 17th. What I received from him on January 2nd was not "the Government's decision", which by then was many weeks old, but merely the draft for its public announcement; and the "various points" that now arose concerned the text of that declaration, and not its substance, which we had accepted, albeit, on certain points, against the grain. When on January 24th Mr. Namier and I saw Mr. Eden, we all felt that these differences in detail—about which, moreover, progress had been made in the meantime—could now easily be settled in one joint meeting with the War Office and the Colonial Office, which Mr. Eden hoped to convene within a few days (Lord Lloyd's grave illness prevented this). So certain was everybody that the scheme was complete, and would be proceeded with, that a liaison officer between the War Office and the Jewish Agency was appointed early in November; a plan for a Jewish Division was communicated by the War Office to the Agency on November 22nd, and the officer to command the Division was designated on December 31st— he started work, was given an establishment, and discussed with us all sorts of practical points; financial arrangements were the subject of a conference between us and Sir Frederick Bovenschen,[1] at the War Office. But your statement that on succeeding Lord Lloyd you found various points raised by me still outstanding, and that "negotiations never reached the final stage" conveys a quite different impression.

Here is your own letter of March 4th, 1941:

"My dear Dr. Weizmann,

I am very sorry to have to tell you that the raising of Jewish contingents has to be postponed. As you know, I was anxiously considering certain details with a view to the removal of minor difficulties, but the matter has now been shifted on to quite other ground, and the Prime Minister has decided that, owing to lack of

---

220. [1] (1884–1977). Deputy Under-Secretary of State for War 1936–42; Joint Permanent Under-Secretary of State for War, and member of Army Council 1942–45.

equipment, the project must for the present be put off for six months, but may be reconsidered again in four months.

Matters have, of course, changed very much in the last few weeks, owing to shipping and other difficulties, and I can assure you that the postponement is in no sense a reversal of the previous decision in favour of your proposal. I need not tell you how truly sorry I am that on the first subject that we have discussed together, events have made it necessary to reach a conclusion which will, I know, be so deeply disappointing to you. I shall, of course, be delighted to see you at any time, but it would be raising false hopes to leave you in any expectations that this decision of the Prime Minister can under present circumstances be reversed."

It was, as you see, the actual "raising of the Jewish Contingent" which was postponed for six months, not the further consideration of a scheme over which the two sides had failed to agree—the outstanding questions were rightly referred to by you as "details" and "minor difficulties." And we relied on your declaration: "I can assure you that this postponement is in no sense a reversal of the previous decision in favour of your proposal."

In the House of Lords on November 25th you went on to say:
"After Dr. Weizmann had returned from the United States, he informed me on September 1st that, owing to various reasons, it was no longer convenient to leave the matter open, and that he would prefer a definite refusal to any further uncertain postponement."

This extremely foreshortened account is hardly an accurate record of what happened. After my return from America, I saw you on August 1st and found you optimistic about the scheme—you said that you saw no objections to the formation of the Jewish Fighting Force, and encouraged me to see the War Office about it. I did so, and on August 19th, informed you of the results. But on August 28th I received the following letter from you:

"Dear Dr. Weizmann,

I promised to write to you again on the question of the Jewish contingent, about which you wrote to me on the 19th August; but I fear that you will find the letter I have to send you somewhat disappointing.

The position regarding equipment is little easier now than it was some months ago. The entry of Russia into the war has, of course, introduced a new and important factor. To illustrate this difficulty, I need only say that the shortage of equipment is one of the reasons which have so far prevented the War Office from agreeing to the raising of other combatant units within the Empire, for which there is a persistent demand.

I have consulted the Prime Minister; and in all the circumstances, I am afraid that we can only continue to leave the matter of the Jewish contingent in cold storage for the present. The situation may change, however, and in any case we propose that the question should again be considered in three months' time."

What had been a definite assurance was changing into something very much less certain and concrete. You omitted to tell the House of Lords about this second postponement. But it was this, coupled with the change in tone and attitude, which made me feel that the agreed scheme was being killed by degrees; and this caused me, on September 1st, to ask you for a definite reply. To be kept indefinitely in suspense, precluded from explaining the situation to our own people, put off on grounds which we could hardly accept as a full reason, and which we were never given an opportunity of discussing, was creating for us a painful, and indeed intolerable, position.

But the appeal which I made to the Prime Minister on September 10th gives evidence of the strength of our desire for a Jewish Fighting Force. You informed me on October 15th that this letter had been considered by the Cabinet, and that difficulties, mainly of shipping, precluded the carrying out of the original scheme. And here is the final paragraph of your letter:

"I am very sorry that this decision must be profoundly disappointing to you, and would much like to see you some day early next week to discuss various other possibilities."

This left me hoping that the "other possibilities" referred to the formation of the existing Jewish units in the Middle East into a Jewish contingent fighting under its own name and flag. But this was refused when Mr. Ben-Gurion and I saw you on October 23rd, and all that you offered was to employ some Jews as experts and technicians. This we could not accept as a substitute (though we are in fact supplying such men already, and are prepared to continue to do so).

I am at a loss to understand your remark in reply to Lord Strabolgi[2] that you cannot say "whether it would be of any use to reopen the matter." So far as we are concerned, we are now, as always, prepared to do our share to implement the scheme. May I call your attention to the concluding paragraph of my statement of November 9th,[3] in which I declared that "we do not lose hope, nor do we renounce our claim to a Jewish Fighting Force serving un-

---

[2] Formerly Joseph M. Kenworthy (Biog. Index, Vol. XV). Opposition Chief Whip, House of Lords 1938–42; strong Zionist sympathiser.

[3] See No. 201, n. 2.

der its own standard." And then, addressing myself especially to the
Palestinian Jews, I called on them to enlist in ever growing numbers,
and to "work and fight even if nameless."[4]

Yours very sincerely,

Ch. W.

221. To William C. Bullitt,[1] London.   *London, 2 December 1941*
English: Or. Copy. T.W.: W.A.

My dear Friend,

It was a great joy to me to hear that your work will shortly take
you to the Middle East and Palestine. I have had several talks with
Offey[2] lately, and both he and I were anxious that I should be in
Palestine during your own visit there. I have tried my best, and
am still trying, to get a passage, but it is extraordinarily difficult
just now. I have not entirely given up hope, but I would not care
to make any rash promises.

I need hardly tell you how much pleasure it would give me to
meet you in Palestine, show you something of what we have been
doing there, and discuss with you all our hopes and fears. In my
absence, there are, of course, a number of people who will regard
it as a great privilege to see you and show you round; in the midst
of all your pre-occupations, you must find a few days to visit Palestine. The Political Head of the Jewish Agency in Jerusalem is Mr.
Moshe Shertok, whom I would like most warmly to commend to
you. He is one of my dearest friends, a trusted worker and colleague
who is carrying the burden of responsibility in these troublous times
with great courage, devotion, and ability. He is a fountain of knowledge, and you can rely implicitly on his information.[3]

I have given Offey a copy of a long article of mine which is about
to appear in *Foreign Affairs*. It will, I think, indicate a number of

[4] Replying 5 Dec. 1941 (W.A.), Moyne claimed that he had made it clear that the scheme
had become impracticable due to the course of events; he could find no suggestion in his
speech that final failure had been caused by W.'s precipitate action. Any omissions on the
course of the negotiations had stemmed solely from the need to condense his arguments.
While aware that the terms of the scheme had been agreed in principle earlier than in Jan.
1941, Moyne had given this date as that on which the scheme had been given to W. in writing.
He denied that he had not done justice to the J.A. position in this matter, or that he had been
misleading, and he declined to issue a correction as W. suggested.

221. [1] 1891–1967. American Ambassador-at-Large, 1933–36, 1941–42; Ambassador to
France 1936–41.

[2] Bullitt's secretary.

[3] See also No. 222.

the questions which you may wish to raise with Shertok, who will, I am sure, be able to supply the answers. Above all, I would like you to look into the question of Palestine's absorptive capacity. It is this, which I believe, is a source of considerable worry to the President, who is under the impression that Palestine is too small to be able to take care of all those who will need homes after the war. I believe myself that, given proper development, and proper political and economic conditions, Palestine can absorb rapidly and satisfactorily at least three million more Jews, and that would be enough to relieve the pressure in the distressed areas. It is a question of paramount importance, on which your judgment, obtained at first hand and from your own observation, would go a long way towards solving a terrible problem.

In case you would care to stay for a day or two in Rehovot, and make that your centre for a study of the possibilities of Southern Palestine, you will I hope make use of my house there? I would be much honoured if you did so. I have telegraphed to Shertok requesting him to place everything at your disposal.

I am heartbroken that I shall probably not be able to see you in Palestine. I think it is perhaps pre-ordained that you should see for yourself our work there, and pronounce judgment on it in these critical days. Perhaps, even, it is better for you to do so in my absence! Though, personally, to have spent a day or two with you in Palestine would compensate me for many of the sad and anxious hours through which we have been living.

Wishing you every possible success, I remain

Affectionately yours,

Ch. W.

222. To Moshe Shertok, Jerusalem.   *London, 2 December 1941*
English: Or. Copy. T.W.: W.A.

My dear Moshe,

First of all let me thank you and Kaplan for your kind telegram of congratulations.[1]

Secondly, I would like to assure you that I have tried, and am still trying, my level best to get passage to Palestine. But the difficulties are very great—indeed they seem insurmountable. There is just a faint hope, but I would not build on it. Should it fail, we shall be leaving for America about December 29th from Lisbon. This is how things stand at present. After a comparatively short

---

222. [1] On his 67th birthday—27 Nov. 1941.

stay in the States, we propose to travel to Palestine. But you know how impossible it is these days to predict how things may shape a few months ahead.

From my statement, to which I see you referred at your Press Conference, you will have concluded what the result of all our endeavours has been: so far unfortunately nil.[2] The trouble is not so much in London, I believe, as in Cairo; you know the kind of difficulty we always have had to meet from that source.

I was particularly anxious to get to Palestine while Bullitt is still there.[3] As you may know, perhaps, he is a very old friend of mine, and is also a friend of the Movement. I think he is taking Harry Hopkins' place as Director of the Lend-Lease work. He is in very close touch with the President, and his opinion will carry weight. In his young days he was a great friend of Aaron Aaron-sohn,[4] and through him was acquainted with the Palestine problem. As you may have inferred, the main problem worrying both him and the President at present (so far as our affairs are concerned) is the question of Palestine's absorptive capacity. The President thinks that Palestine is too small to be able to absorb all the people from the distressed areas who will need a new start in life after the war. Any information you can give Bullitt which goes to prove our thesis on this matter will thus be of the utmost importance.

Bullitt travels with his secretary, Mr. Offey, who is also a friend of mine, and to whom I have given a copy of my article which is about to appear in *Foreign Affairs* (New York). I have had a few talks with Offey, and have asked him to get into touch with you when he arrives, which he will no doubt do. Perhaps you may meet them both in Cairo.[5]

This is really the most important point at present. I cannot tell you how sick at heart I am to be separated from Palestine for so long. Like you, I fully realise that it would be of great value both to me and to the work in America, if I were to visit Palestine first.

---

[2] In quoting W.'s statement of 9 Nov. at his Press conference (20 Nov., record in C.Z.A.), Shertok stated that the *Yishuv*, while not placing too much hope in future British agreement, should meanwhile join existing British units.

[3] See No. 221.

[4] Biog. Index, Vol. VII. Founder of *Nili*, the Zionist group engaged in espionage for Britain behind Turkish lines in W.W. I, and a confidant of W.

[5] They did in fact meet in Cairo, when Bullitt asked Shertok whether he agreed with Ben-Gurion that the main aim of Zionism at that time was the raising of a Jewish Army, and observed that Aaronsohn had been right during W.W. I in advocating the creation of a Jewish State in the whole of Western Palestine. Further meetings took place in Palestine, and Bullitt asked what the Jews wanted in Palestine after the war. Shertok replied: mass immigration under J.A. auspices, and impressed on Bullitt the need to convince Roosevelt of the Zionist case. (Shertok reports to J.A. Executive, 21, 26 Dec. 1941, Vol. 35, in C.Z.A.)

But unless we go by ship to the Cape, there seems to be no chance of reaching Palestine. And to go by ship would take at least six or seven weeks, a loss of time which I can ill afford just now.

I hope that you and your family, and Kaplan and all our other friends, are well. I wonder when we shall all meet again. But I am thinking of you and the burdens you have to bear almost every hour of my day here. It is a source of deep regret to me that I cannot be any use to you at present, but I do trust that in a few months' time we may meet. Should it become possible for me to come to Palestine, I shall of course let you know by cable at once.

With all my best wishes, and affection,

I am

Ever yours,

Ch. W.

223. To Aaron Wright,[1] London.   *London, 5 December 1941*
English: Or. Copy. T.W.: W.A.

Private

My dear Wright,
I am in receipt of your three letters dated 1st December.[2]
I am afraid that the Committee which you suggest in answer to my letter of the 28th November[3] is nothing less than a Court of Enquiry as originally desired by Professor Samson Wright.[4] As I have already explained, it is not within my competence to set up such a Court. The proper procedure would be for you to get into touch with the Chairman of the [Zionist] Congress Court of Honour, Dr. M. Smoira[5] (Rehov Rashba, Jerusalem), and place all the facts before him. If he finds that there is a *prima facie* case, he will make arrangements for some person or persons in this country to act on behalf of the Court. Another method would be for you to cable to the Chairman of the Court asking him to appoint some person in London to go into the facts submitted by you to find out whether there is a *prima facie* case for a Court to be instituted here.

As regards the suggested Committee to consider the whole mat-

---

223. [1] 1904–76. J.N.F. President in Britain 1942–50. He then settled in Israel as chairman of Keret Building Company.
   [2] Untraced.
   [3] Untraced.
   [4] D. 1956. Professor of Physiology, London University; Vice-President, Board of Deputies of British Jews, and J.N.F. in Britain. Brother of Aaron Wright.
   [5] Moshe Smoira (1888–1961). Jurist, settled in Palestine in 1922. Lectured on Civil Procedure at Mandatory Law School 1923–48. First President of Supreme Court of Israel 1948–54.

ter of the Farm City Scheme,[6] I am agreeable to the suggestions made by you for its membership, though I think it would be very useful to add Mr. Leonard Stein, since there will no doubt be a number of legal and tax matters to be considered. I am not quite sure whether he will be able to accept, as I know he is very busy.

Dr. Brodetsky and Mr. Locker have signified their consent to serve, and I take it that you have received the consent of Mr. Singer.[7] As soon as I hear from Mr. Sacher and Mr. Stein, a meeting of the Committee will be convened.[8]

Yours sincerely,

224. To Joseph Sagall, Beaconsfield.   *London, 9 December 1941*
English: Or. Copy. T.W.: W.A.

Dear Dr. Segal,[1]

Since discussing with you the subject of the proposed Anglo-Palestine Chamber of Commerce,[2] I asked Istorik[3] to see me, but I have not yet had an opportunity of discussing the matter with him fully. I have, however, had a talk with Singer, who tells me that we could probably count on the active cooperation of—for instance—Sir John Caulcutt,[4] if we could satisfy him that the various Palestine companies and institutions connected with Istorik, himself and others are actively backing the scheme. I have also seen a note from Lord Melchett[5] to much the same effect.

---

[6] The Farm City Scheme was initiated in Rumania in 1937, but had to be discontinued there owing to the war. It was re-activated in England by Fred Nettler of Glasgow. Under the scheme the J.N.F. was to set aside appropriate areas in Palestine for four 'Farm Cities', each divided into units on which the eventual settlers were to build their home and farm. Prospective settlers, against a minimum contribution of £250 to J.N.F., were to be granted an option on a plot of land, to be taken up after the war. Some 900 agreements were signed, but none of the signatories exercised his option. The project was abandoned.

[7] Paul Singer, 1893–1969. Then representative of Palestine Economic Corporation in England.

[8] Wright requested an enquiry so as to clear the Farm City Scheme of allegations of wrongful methods of advocacy. W. appointed a committee, which reported that the allegations were not supported by the evidence submitted—see Sacher to W., 12 Mar. 1942 (W.A.).

224. [1] *Sic* (1906–1967). An E.Z.F. Vice-President; chairman of European Executive of World Confederation of General Zionists; chairman, Editorial Board of *Zionist Review*.

[2] Record of discussion untraced.

[3] Leo Istorik (1887–1971). On Board of Jewish Colonial Trust from 1922, Anglo-Palestine Bank from 1933, Bank Leumi L'Israel from 1949.

[4] 1876–1943. Chairman, Barclays Bank D.C.O. from 1937; member Palestine Currency Board.

[5] Formerly Henry Mond (Biog. Index, Vol. XIII). Deputy Chairman Imperial Chemical Industries 1940–47; member J.A. Political Advisory Committee, London.

It seems to me essential that we should first secure the whole-hearted cooperation of all these various bodies, and for this purpose cable communication with Palestine is an indispensable preliminary. I shall ask Istorik to proceed with this as speedily as possible. Meanwhile, I am sure you will agree with me that no further action should be taken in the matter.[6]

Yours sincerely,
Ch. W.

225. To Lord Moyne, London.   *London, 10 December 1941*
English: T.W.: P.R.O. CO 968/39.

My dear Lord Moyne,

I have to thank you for your letter of December 5th.[1] In reca-pitulating the facts in detail, I did not mean to suggest that they should have been stated at length in Parliament, but meant to show why I considered (and still consider) the summary given by you on November 25th created a wrong, and for us damaging, impression. I did so by a letter to you rather than in a public statement, in order to avoid public controversy. But I fear it would hardly serve a use-ful purpose to pursue the general argument still further.

Still, there is one point which turns on clearly ascertainable facts. You say that of the modifications of the draft announcement sug-gested in my letter to Lord Lloyd of January 6th,[2] three "affected materially the substance of the project, i.e., those dealt with in paragraphs 5–7 of that letter." What were they?

Paragraph 5: The War Office considered 12,000 and not 10,000, the proper figure for the Jewish Fighting Force, and I called at-tention to this point which clearly had to be settled between the Departments concerned. As for the name, a compromise was in sight on a term such as "Jewish Fighting Force" or "Jewish con-tingent"; we were prepared to accept either. I note that in the subsequent correspondence you yourself referred to the "Jewish contingent" and not to the "Jewish units". This was one of the points I had in mind when saying in my letter of December 1st that "progress had been made in the meantime."

Paragraph 6: I stated clearly in my letter of January 6th our acceptance of the conditions to which it refers, and all we asked

---

[6] See No. 233.

225. [1] This letter was not despatched till 14 Dec., with a covering note to Moyne to the effect that the entry of Japan into the war had changed its significance, but it was nevertheless being sent as a matter of record. See W. to Moyne, 14 Dec. 1941 (*ibid.*). See also No. 220, n. 4.

[2] See No. 90.

was that "their substance should be secured without hurting the feelings, etc."

Paragraph 7: Even my original suggestion was worded tentatively: the point was not described as essential, nor pressed; I merely stated that such an announcement would be "pleasing to the Jews...and would greatly encourage recruitment." In the course of the further conversations with the Military Authorities, and with Mr. Eden at the Foreign Office on January 24th, this suggestion was explicitly dropped by us, and it can therefore hardly be quoted as outstanding when you assumed office.

To sum up: 5 a: a difference between the War Office and the Colonial Office;

5 b: a compromise term in sight;

6:    a question not of substance but of text;

7:    withdrawn by us.

I therefore submit that you were right, in your letter of March 4th, when you referred to three questions as "details" and "minor differences", but not in your statement of November 25th, when you treated them as sufficiently serious to justify your describing the negotiations as having never reached the final stage, or in your letter of December 5th, when you say that three of the modifications suggested by me "affected materially the substance of the project."

Yours very sincerely

Ch. Weizmann

226. To Oliver Harvey, London.   *London, 15 December 1941*
English: Or. Copy. T.W.: W.A.

My dear Harvey,

I attach a copy of a cable[1] which we have just received from Mr. Schwartz,[2] the Lisbon representative of the American Joint Distribution Committee, regarding nine Palestinian citizens who are stated to have been told that they could not be included in the plans which the British authorities in Lisbon are making for the evacuation of British subjects in case of need.

I am sure that there must have been some mistake, as Palestinians travel on British passports and are normally given protection by H.M. Consular Officers abroad. Such protection has been afforded

---

226. [1] Untraced.

[2] Joseph J. Schwartz (1899–1975). American communal leader; chairman, J.D.C. European Executive 1940–49; supervised relief and welfare programmes in 30 countries, involving over one million people. He was U.J.A. vice-chairman 1951–55; Vice-President, State of Israel Bonds Organization 1955–70.

in other countries, e.g., in France, where the protecting Power even provided financial relief; quite recently, too, arrangements were made for a number of Palestinian women and children from Germany to be exchanged for German women and children from Palestine.

I should be very grateful if you could possibly arrange for a cable to be sent to the Embassy and Consulate in Lisbon, so that these nine Palestinians should not be left behind there when other British subjects are evacuated.[3]

Yours very sincerely,

Ch. W.

227. To Lord Moyne, London. *London, 17 December 1941*
English: Or. Copy. T.W.: W.A.

After the Baghdad pogrom of June 1941, in which hundreds of Jews were butchered, a certain number fled to Palestine.[1] Non-Jewish fugitives from other countries are allowed to remain there— but when the Agency applied to the High Commissioner on behalf of these victims of Arab atrocities, they received a practically negative reply. (See the papers enclosed).[2]

I would add that the danger to some of these people of being returned to the tender mercies of an Arab Government is greatly enhanced by their flight, and their stay in Palestine, during which they may have talked freely about their experience.

Arabs have committed murder, and it is inconceivable that the refugees should now be handed back to Iraq by the Palestine Administration. Surely Jewish victims of Arab persecution have a double right to take refuge in Palestine.[3]

Yours very sincerely,

Ch. W.

---

[3] W. received reassurance in this matter from F.O. 19 Dec. 1941 (W.A.).

227. [1] This took place 1–2 June, with Rashid Ali's pro-Axis revolution against the British. Mobs massacred Jews and looted their property with the passive support of the army and police officers. Neither the Iraqi Regent, 'Abd Al-Illah, who had arrived in the city before the beginning of the riots, nor the British troops stationed outside the city, made any effort to intervene.

[2] Untraced—but presumably documentation from J.A. Executive, Jerusalem.

[3] W.'s letter was acknowledged 20 Dec. 1941 by Moyne's private secretary. In Apr. 1942, C.O. stated that deportation of Iraqi refugees from Palestine had definitely been stopped (Linton to W., 30 Apr. 1942, W.A.).

228. To High Commissioner for South Africa, London.
London, 18 December 1941
English: Or. Copy. T.W.: W.A.

Dear Mr. Waterson,
   Very many thanks for your note of yesterday, transmitting to me the text of General Smuts' most kind and encouraging message.[1] I need not tell you how deeply I appreciate it in these dark days.
Yours sincerely,

229. To Mikhail Weizmann, Haifa.   *London, 18 December 1941*
English: T.: W.A.

Am with you on day memorial mother's death. Hope come Palestine as soon as transport available, possibly from States. Love to everybody.[1]

Chaim Weizmann

230. To Lord Wedgwood, London.   *London, 22 December 1941*
English: Or. Copy. T.W.: W.A.

My dear Jos,
   May I offer you my heartiest congratulations on the occasion of your elevation to the Peerage?
   Well-deserved as this honour is if ever honour was, I cannot help feeling that the House of Commons will be very much the poorer for your absence, and that your voice, raised for so many years in defence of freedom and justice, will be sadly missed there, as well as by your innumerable personal friends. Of course, the Lords will gain a great deal—but I wonder whether that will be quite the same thing?
   I rejoice that it will mean less strain on you, and trust that we may continue, as in the past, to rely on your advice, assistance, and co-operation.
   With all affectionate good wishes, I remain

Ch. W.

228. [1] Smuts had thanked W. for his last letter with enclosure, probably referring to No. 170, which included a copy of No. 153 to Moyne. He asked W. to persevere with his good work, and to keep in touch with Churchill and Amery, both of whom were good friends and well-wishers (W.A.).

229. [1] For Rachel-Leah W., see Biog. Index, Vol. I.

231. To Anna Weizmann, Rehovot.   *London, 26 December 1941*
Russian: H.W.: W.A.

Dec. 26th. 41.
Dear Annushka,

I was so happy to hear from you,[1] even though it was a sad letter. Who can write "jolly" letters nowadays? I seldom write because it's difficult. The only thing that can be said is that we are alive and in good health. Otherwise, days and months pass in expectation of a gleam of hope. There's work, both Zionist activity and chemistry, but who can say on what foundation one should build now, when everything is so unsteady. It sometimes seems that the purpose of life has gone, and that we, of the older generation, shall not see better days.

That's why it is difficult to write. Of my small family there's not much to say. Michael is a pilot and works well; thank God, we see him from time to time, when he comes to spend his leave with us. Benji was in the army at first, but his state of health was not up to the strain and he is now free; he works very successfully at the laboratory. His wife is a wonderful woman, a physician, and they have a charming boy—David.

London and England have changed and keep changing. What these changes will lead to is difficult to say. The old is giving way to the new which is as yet unclear.

I did all I could to get to Palestine, but the question of transportation, especially for two, is almost insoluble. Perhaps; it can be done only if one goes by ship to South Africa and takes a plane from there. This may take months, and it is therefore easier to go to America and from there to Palestine, which I hope to do. We intend to go to America in 3½ weeks time. But, naturally, no one can say how the world will look in a month. Gates open today may then be locked. The only thing that can be done is to be patient, no matter how difficult it might be—and in such cases I always think of Michael, who flies every day and every hour over mountains and seas; our worries and dissatisfaction are nothing compared to his young life. I am already 67, while he is just starting, and he represents the young generation of which there are hundreds of thousands who are only embarking on life!

It was a shock to me to read about poor Feivel to whom I send my sincerest wishes for recovery. With mother's death he began to sink, but with God's help he may still recover. The first time I

---

231. [1] Untraced.

learned about him was from Moishey's[2] letter—a preposterous letter, a stupid one;[3] as though I was to blame for anything! Ah, well.

Bergmann and I are working hard. Whether anything will come of that work, i.e., whether it could be applied to existing conditions, is difficult to say as yet. Maybe, but I am not certain. But this work will mean something in the future! There is a vast body of scientific data for future development.

I am deeply grieved by the state of affairs at the Institute. I know nothing of what's going on there. I don't know what the staff, such as Hirschberg, Simon and some others, are doing. All my requests for regular reports have been ignored.

The only thing I know is that there's a shortage of money. I always took great pleasure and joy in seeing to it that the financial aspect of the Institute was kept in order. But since the scientific output has deteriorated so considerably, all these projects become senseless. I know the chemists are busy working, but the biologists and physical chemists are apparently doing nothing. I understand that times are tough now, yet it is easier there than it is here. I can't tell you how distressing all this is for me!

Please give my deepest regards to the whole family and Miss Gold-schmidt. Ask her to write to me.

With kisses and embraces,

Your brother,
Chaim

232. To John G. Winant, London.   *London, 31 December 1941*
English: Or. Copy. T.W.: W.A.

Dear Mr. Ambassador,

At the turn of the year I would like to send you my sincerest good wishes—both to you personally, and to your country which is now, together with the whole civilised world, passing through the ordeal by fire. I know that America, with the other free nations, will emerge victorious from this struggle, and her cooperation is the best guarantee for future freedom and a just peace.[1]

May I take this opportunity of expressing to you my grateful thanks for the kindness and consideration I have received at your

---

[2] I.e., their brother Moses.
[3] Untraced, but see No. 191.

232. [1] Japanese aircraft attacked Pearl Harbour 7 Dec. The U.S. declared war on Japan the following day, and Germany and Italy declared war on U.S. 11 Dec. 1941.

hands? It was a privilege to be able to speak to you so freely, and to find so much comfort, good advice and sympathy in these dark days.

For us it has been a year of frustration and deep disappointment—the more deeply felt because the greater part of the Jewish people is condemned to suffer passively, behind sound-proof walls. We are not allowed to take our place—however modest—as a people among the other peoples fighting for freedom; and it has been difficult to suppress the feelings of bitterness which this thought arouses. I was therefore very happy to hear from you that we may still hope for a Jewish fighting force in Palestine at some time in the not-too-distant future.[2]

As at present advised, I expect to leave for the States on the 20th January.

With very kind regards, and renewed good wishes for a happier 1942, I am[3]

Very sincerely yours,
Ch. W.

233. To Joseph Sagall, Beaconsfield.　　　*London, 2 January 1942*
English: Or. Copy. T.W.: W.A.

Dear Dr. Sagall,

I am in receipt of your letter of the 24th December.[1] I am somewhat surprised to find that, in spite of the concluding sentence of my letter of December 9th, in which I asked that no further action should be taken in the matter of the Chamber of Commerce pending a reply from Palestine, you have decided to make arrangements for an inaugural luncheon on February 4th.

The assumption that a reply from Palestine will be received before February 4th seems to me to be unwarranted. As I have already pointed out to you, I am deeply concerned that if a Chamber of Commerce is to be formed it should be very carefully prepared and organized. For its success and proper working it will need the co-operation of the responsible institutions in Palestine as well as of the bodies in this country connected with the work there. Until we have the views of Palestine no definite steps should be taken. In these circumstances, I can only repeat what I said in my letter of the 9th

---

[2] According to Blanche Dugdale, Winant had told W. to expect U.S. to urge the British to form a Jewish Army in Palestine (Rose, *op. cit.,*p. 189).

[3] W. sent a similar letter that day to Drexel Biddle, Minister at U.S. Embassy.

233. [1] Untraced.

December: you should not proceed any further with the scheme, and you should suspend any arrangements you may have put in hand for the inaugural luncheon, until you hear from me again.[2]

Yours sincerely,

Ch. W.

234. To Mikhail Weizmann, Haifa.   *London, 2 January 1942*
English: T.: W.A.

Am with you in our sorrow.[1]

Chaim Weizmann

235. To Viscount Samuel,[1] Oxford.   *London, 5 January 1942*
English: Or. Copy. T.W.: W.A.

You will, I expect, have seen from the papers the heavy news of Rutenberg's death, and will know how great is the loss which Palestine suffers by his passing.

We are arranging a small memorial meeting for him at this office on Thursday morning at 11.45, and we should very much appreciate it if you could attend and say a few words in his memory.[2]

With kind regards, I am

Very sincerely yours,

Ch. W.

236. To Arthur Lourie, New York.   *London, 6 January 1942*
English: T.: W.A.

Invitation to appropriate authorities [to] express adherence Washington declaration issued fourth January may open door for us. Sug-

---

[2] No reply traced. But J.A. wrote to Istorik 18 Feb. 1942 (copy in W.A.) questioning the purpose of an Anglo-Palestine Chamber of Commerce under circumstances of war, when trade had much decreased and was in any case directly controlled, leaving little scope for influence. The Agency saw the importance of such a body in the future, and indeed an Anglo-Israel Chamber of Commerce was formed 1950, with Israel Sieff as chairman and Istorik as treasurer.

234. [1] Their brother Feivel had just died.

235. [1] Biog. Index, Vol. VII. Liberal leader in House of Lords; first High Commissioner for Palestine. Samuel was chairman of the Palestine Electric Corporation, founded and directed by Rutenberg.
[2] Reply untraced. It is not known whether Samuel attended.

gest you consider matter with view action our part when I am in America. Meantime would suggest no steps be taken either by you or World [Jewish] Congress[1]

Weizmann

237. To Benjamin Bloch, Rehovot.   *London, 7 January 1942*
English: T.W.: W.A.

My dear Bloch,

At last I have two telegrams from you, dated 4th and 5th January, giving me some of the information for which I have asked[1]— though they still do not answer two questions on which I am specially anxious to be informed: What scientific work is now being done at the Institute and by whom? And are we still paying the Station £250 a year for the investigation of the soya problem?[2]

The last paragraph of your telegram makes me very uneasy indeed. It may be hard to have to reduce salaries, and I would be the last man to suggest it in normal times. But these are not normal times, and I fear the Institute should be no exception if it had to cut them. The financial stringency is universal, and everybody has his income cut down. However, I understand that if the Foundation contributes £13,000, and you can raise £1,300, the question of reduction of salaries will not arise. So far as I am concerned, I am anxious not to be responsible for more than £13,000—even that is a huge sum at present, and unless we exercise great economy we may find 1943 a very difficult year indeed.[3]

I resent the last sentence of your first telegram with its statement that you will effect reductions of salaries or staff only upon direct orders from me. I would not mind taking the responsibility provided that I were well-informed. But in spite of repeated questions, I know

---

236. [1] Britain, U.S., U.S.S.R., China and 22 other Allies pledged at Washington not to make separate peace treaties with the enemy. They also adopted the 'Atlantic Charter', signed by Roosevelt and Churchill 14 Aug. 1941, which re-affirmed the right of all peoples to choose their form of government, under the 'four freedoms.' See also No. 258.

237. [1] The telegrams (W.A.) informed W. that no chemists were as yet employed by Palestine Pharmaceuticals, since delays in transferring funds had held up the final installation of machinery; the factory was hampered also by lack of raw materials, and transport difficulties. Bloch dwelt also on the subject of the annual budget.

[2] Bloch replied 20 Jan. 1942 (W.A.) that he had never received instructions to pay the Agricultural Experimental Station £P.250 per annum—he had merely heard that W. had promised such an amount for 1939. W.'s dissatisfaction was due to the station's failure to produce results.

[3] See Nos. 265, 266.

nothing of what is going on in the Institute, of who is doing what, or of whether the work is likely to be useful or not. How on earth, in such circumstances, can I be expected to make recommendations for reduction of staff? It is grossly unfair to ask it of me. I confess to you that I would not mind closing the Institute completely, because I feel that the spirit must have gone out of it. But this again would be a drastic step to take without a full knowledge of all the facts, and this knowledge has been systematically withheld from me. I therefore propose to suggest to the Board that for 1943 only a skeleton staff be maintained until the end of the war. If we survive the war, we might reconsider the whole situation. You should address yourself to Green and Horowitz, and ask them to examine with you the whole situation at the Institute, both from the scientific and financial point of view, with a view to the preparation of a report on which we should be able to act. The terms of reference of the enquiry should be: (a) economies, and (b) reduction of staff. I shall do my best to come out to Palestine as soon as possible, but one can never be very certain these days of one's future movements, and meanwhile a re-examination of the whole situation by local people seems to me to be the only fair and appropriate way to handle such a delicate question.

We have no right to allow this state of affairs to continue next year. Why it should have developed at all remains an enigma to me. I am grieved more than I can find words to express. If you and your colleagues had made it an iron rule to send me regular monthly reports on the work, it might have saved a great deal of trouble and anxiety. We have asked for them, but without avail. The workers should have felt it their bounden duty to keep us informed; in this duty they have failed—lamentably. My repeated requests remain up to the present without response.

I am sorry to have to write in this vein. I feel compelled to do so only because of your omission to answer vital questions which might put me in a position to judge of what is going on.

With kind regards, I am
Very sincerely yours,
Ch. Weizmann

238. To Harold Davies, Rehovot.   *London, 7 January 1942*
English: Or. Copy. T.W.: W.A.

My dear Davies,

I have not heard from you for ages, and don't know anything of what you—or the Institute—are doing. I confess to feeling most uneasy about the whole situation—so much so that I am compelled to write to Bloch the letter of which I attach a copy.[1] I would be most grateful to you if you would let me know what has been happening. Why has the situation so deteriorated—at least, it seems to me to have deteriorated? I feel it is impossible to let things go on much longer in this way.

I have been trying to get out to Palestine myself, but the transport difficulties are so great that I have to go to America first, and try to find my way from there. But unless I hear within the next few months the full truth about the work which is going on, and have some rational proposals for effecting economies, I shall submit to the Donors that the whole situation must be completely revised—otherwise I cannot take the responsibility for next year's budget.

Nor have I any clear notion of what the Pharmaceutical Factory is doing, or who is working there: it is an intolerable state of affairs. Please let me know what you feel about it yourself.

I shall be leaving for America on the 20th of this month, and you can airmail letters direct to the States, so I look forward to having some correct information there.[2]

I hope all is well with you, and remain, as ever,

Affectionately yours,

Ch. W.

239. To Benjamin Bloch, Rehovot. *London, 9 January 1942*
English: T.W.: Photostat W.A.

My dear Bloch,

I would like to add a line to the main letter.[1] You know better than anybody how much trouble I have taken in the interests of the Institute. In spite of many preoccupations and anxieties, I have never for one minute lost sight of the Institute, and have done my

238. [1] No. 237.

    [2] Replying 18 Feb. 1942 (W.A.), Davies stated that W. had been misled in Apr. 1940: the Rehovot chemists were not then in possession of economic processes for the manufacture of the drugs required by the Genatosan Company, and the contract had fallen through. A new contract was being negotiated with Chemo-Orient, a subsidiary of Green Brothers, a Palestinian chemical company. Davies described the difficulties in completing installation of plant at the factory, but nevertheless advocated going ahead. He agreed that morale of staff was not high, and some members nurtured grievances about which they were consulting lawyers. Davies recalled that W. had previously over-ruled Bloch on staff matters; W., as Director of the Institute, must be responsible for decisions as to the projects justifying continuation in peacetime. See Nos. 265, 266.

239. [1] No. 237.

utmost to equip it in the best possible way; I have tried to establish it—so far as is possible in these difficult times—on a relatively sound financial basis; I have directed some of its scientific activities into channels which should lead to success, and whose results should enhance its good name.

The war has prevented me—much to my sorrow—from coming to Palestine. Although there is no satisfactory substitute for permanent personal contact with an institution, regular correspondence and reporting could, to some extent, enable us to follow developments in Rehovot, to make suggestions, and to help. But these reports the workers have omitted to supply. I regard this as a very grave omission indeed—as unpardonable as it is incomprehensible. What sort of people are they if they don't feel now that they must endeavour to do more than just ordinary routine work, and must impose upon themselves higher and more exacting duties and standards? After all, life in Rehovot has been much more comfortable and secure than in London, and they have had there far more peace of mind than we have had here. They are all grown men, who should know all this, and their lack of a sense of duty and responsibility causes me pain, and is a deep disappointment to me.

That is why I have decided on one of two courses: either there is going to be a radical change—which in my opinion will involve a considerable change in personnel, or I must withdraw from the whole thing, as I cannot countenance such a state of affairs.

I would like to go over once more the points which you will please fix in your mind as absolutely essential for future cooperation and for the conduct of the work:

I. *Budget:*

(a) You can spend £14,300, as indicated in my telegram of today's date,[2] but I can only take responsibility for £13,000, which will be made up as follows:

£5,000 from the [Marks and Sieff] Family;
£5,000 from the [Weizmann] Foundation;
£3,000 from other sources.

This I can guarantee, but no more. As already mentioned in my telegram, Mr. Sieff has withdrawn his subscription of £1,000, and this is why the Family contributes only £5,000.

(b) No money from the Foundation should be diverted to the Pharmaceuticals.[3]

(c) No outside loans should be contracted for the Pharmaceuticals. I hope, however, to make some arrangement in the U.S.A. which

[2] W.A.
[3] See No. 238, n. 2.

will help the Pharmaceutical Factory, but this can only be done by me personally when I am there. Until then it will, I am afraid, have to wait.

(d) Please let me know definitely how much more money you will need for the Pharmaceuticals to put you in a position to work normally.

(e) I understand the expenditure of £200 for the late Dr. Magasanik, and I think the Institute should bear part of this expenditure. But I also believe it is only proper that the Station should bear its share of it.[4]

II. *The Work in the Institute:*

(a) Before making any further reorganization, and before I can suggest any reductions of staff, I must be in possession of full information of what has been happening scientifically and what all members of the staff have been doing in 1941, and what they intend doing in 1942.

(b) Why have no reports come in since the beginning of 1941? The only exceptions are Felix Bergmann, B. Wilkansky,[5] and Miss Weizmann. The others have not thought it necessary to keep us informed of their activities. As I have said, this seems to me to be an unpardonable omission. Therefore, we must demand full reports for 1941 from everybody and regular monthly reports throughout 1942. On receipt of the reports for 1941, I propose to make some suggestions about reductions and changes—if necessary.

(c) The Station should give us a full report on the Soya and Ramie[6] question, and pending the receipt of such a report, you should discontinue the subvention—indeed, discontinue it until you get our decision on the basis of the report. It is ridiculous to refer me to the very unsatisfactory report on this subject sent to me by the Station at the beginning of 1941; apart from the fact that this report contained practically no information, there should have been some further development in the course of the year.

III. *Plan of Scientific Work for 1942:*

(a) This plan has to be drawn up and submitted to me at once. In view of the difficulty of obtaining chemicals and apparatus, subjects must be chosen for which materials and apparatus are still to hand. You will realise that we have here the same difficulty: conditions

---

[4] Reference to the Agricultural Experimental Station, established 1921, of which Isaac Wilkansky (Volcani) was director. It cooperated with Sieff Institute in research. Magasanik had been a soil chemist.

[5] Benjamin Wilkansky, b. 1915. Son of Isaac Wilkansky.

[6] A pure form of cotton for weaving.

of work here are certainly not better than in Rehovot; still we manage to carry on.

(b) Only after this information is to hand can suggestions for economies be made by us; you, on your part, should submit your own suggestions in the same direction.

(c) How many of the present staff will work in the Factory, and how many will remain on the payroll of the Institute? I want an answer to this question without further reservations.

(d) The junior members of the staff should be transferred to the Factory, and no new chemists should be employed. Here in England we have highly trained University men working as ordinary labourers in munition factories (men and women alike), and I see no reason why this should not be applied to the young men at the Institute. They, too, could work as ordinary workers. There is no humiliation in it: on the contrary, it is an honourable performance in time of war.

This last letter should be shown to Green and Horowitz, to whom please give my best regards.

As at present arranged, I shall leave here for America in just over a week from now. Should there by any change, I shall let you know. Your answers and telegrams should be addressed to America, and as there is a new airmail connection between Palestine and U.S.A. I should get your replies fairly quickly. Shertok can help you to expedite the despatch of letters.[7]

With kind regards, I am
Yours,
Ch. Weizmann

240. To Eliezer Kaplan, Jerusalem.   *London, 9 January 1942*
English: T.: C.Z.A. S53/215.

Cannot leave here without London budget settled. Linton entirely without money. Urge you arrange budget accordance his cable [to] Baharal 30th October. Regards.[1]

Weizmann

---

[7] Bloch replied 19 Jan. 1942 (W.A.), expressing distress at W.'s disappointment with the Institute. Though senior workers could have done better, he felt that the Institute had conducted much important work during the previous two years. Difficulty in obtaining raw materials had been principally responsible for delays in results. Chemists' reports had in fact been submitted during 1941, and W.'s dissatisfaction did not mean that he was not being informed on the Institute's scientific achievements.

240. [1] Linton's telegram untraced. London had submitted a budget of £20,000 for the year—£13,000 from the Agency (with K.H.) and £7,000 from J.N.F. (see letter of Linton

241. To Nevile Butler,[1] London.   *London, 15 January 1942*
English: Or. Copy. T.W.: W.A.

Dear Mr. Butler,

You have been so kind in helping me to arrange my journey to the States that I feel I owe you an explanation of the latest postponement—which is really no fault of mine. So far we have not, in spite of repeated cables, succeeded in getting our American visas, and time is getting very short. Moreover, in the last few days there have been some developments in my chemical work with the Ministry of Supply, which may involve me in chemical affairs in America. I am now awaiting a letter from the Ministry about this, and am told that I shall get it within a day or two.[2] A few days longer in London would therefore be of use to me on the chemical side, and this fact, combined with the absence of the visas, has led me to decide that it would be better to postpone the journey for a week or so.

I would have informed you earlier, but I had been hoping to get the visas in time, and the Ministry of Supply business only materialised in the last day or two. I have spoken to Mr. Winant about it, and we have also notified Pan-American Airways here. Mr. [E.G.] Taylor, of your Communications Department, has been in touch with me, and I am to-day sending him the letter, of which I attach a copy.

With kind regards, and renewed thanks for all your help, I am

and Brodetsky to Kaplan, 25 Sept. 1941, C.Z.A. S53/274). Kaplan proposed a total of £15,000, for the London and New York offices together. W. then demanded a £4,000 increase, and Kaplan finally concurred—Executive Minutes, 14, 19 Jan. 1942, Vol. 35, in C.Z.A. See also No. 100.

241. [1] (Sir) Nevile Montague Butler, b. 1893. British Minister in Washington 1940–41; Head of North American Department at F.O. from 1941; Assistant Under-Secretary of State from 1944; Ambassador to Brazil 1947–51, to Netherlands 1952–54.

[2] W. had that day learned from Harold Macmillan (letter in W.A.) that the Ministry of Supply accepted the feasibility of his process developed at Manchester Oil Refineries for manufacture of toluene, but that a final decision on manufacture in Britain must await Lord Beaverbrook's report, imminently expected, on 'pooling' arrangements with U.S. At the request of the American Embassy in London, W. sent a memorandum to Drexel Biddle, 19 Jan. 1942 (W.A.) on the production of toluene, aviation fuel and synthetic rubber. See also Nos. 247, 251. (W.'s toluene process also yielded butadiene and styrene, required for synthetic rubber, as by-products, a fact that W. was later to emphasise in U.S. when asked to help solve the rubber shortage.)

242. To Werner Senator, Jerusalem. *London, 20 January 1942*
English: T.: W.A.

Re cooptions concur Schocken's view his cable [of] eighteenth.[1]

Chaim Weizmann

243. To Richard Law,[1] London. *London, 21 January 1942*
English: Or. Copy. T.W.: W.A.

Dear Mr. Law,

With reference to the conversation which I had the pleasure of having with you on Monday, I would like to formulate briefly in writing the three main points discussed, which I hope you will find an opportunity of bringing to the notice of the Secretary of State:

1) The Jewish Units at present serving in Palestine should be given their own badge and organization;[2]

2) I am extremely worried and uneasy about the return of the Mufti's various collaborators and henchmen to Palestine;[3] in my opinion this will inevitably lead to trouble, and to anti-British as well as anti-Jewish activities. I need not dwell on this point; you know the spirit with which they are imbued, and it is hardly to be expected that they will remain inactive.

3) I am equally anxious about the general political position as regards Palestine—i.e., anxious that it should remain static and that no commitments should be entered into towards Arabs like Nuri Pasha[4] and others (who are now very active) which might prejudice the position in the future.

May I take the opportunity of thanking you for your courtesy in listening to my statement. I hope you may find time to glance at the documents which I left with you; they are not without interest.

---

242. [1] Schocken's cable (W.A.) informed W. of the Hebrew University's approval of the appointment of Horowitz, Smoira, and the poet Saul Tchernichowsky as new members of the University Executive Council.

243. [1] Later Lord Coleraine, b. 1901. Parliamentary Under-Secretary of State, F.O., 1941–43; Minister of State, 1943–45; Minister of Education 1945.

[2] Specific insignia for Jewish units were granted only with formation of the Jewish Brigade, Aug. 1944, while Jewish and Arab units serving in Palestine were organized into a 'Palestine Regiment' with common insignia.

[3] A group of 25 aides who had fled with the Mufti from Iraq when the Rashid Ali revolt was crushed had been arrested by British authorities in Iran, but had since been granted permission to return to Palestine. Some, including members of the Mufti's own family (the Husseinis), had already arrived.

[4] Biog. Index, Vol. XVII. Iraqi statesman. For his negotiations with Newcombe, see No. 59 and n. 2 there.

You may also like to see the enclosed copies of some messages sent to a Zionist Rally in Cleveland, Ohio, a day or two ago.[5]

My journey to the States has now been definitely fixed, and I shall be leaving here on February 2nd, and from Lisbon on the 6th. I shall be absent for some time, as it is my intention to go from America to Palestine if this proves possible. I would therefore like to introduce to you in writing two of my colleagues here, who will be carrying on in my absence. One is Mr. Berl Locker, a Palestinian member of the Zionist Executive, and of the Executive of the Labour Organization in Palestine, who is working with us in the London Office; the second is Professor L.B. Namier, whose name may be familiar to you. He is Professor of Modern History at Manchester University, and has been seconded to us by the University to help in our work here. I would be most grateful if you would extend to Mr. Locker and Professor Namier the benefit of your advice and assistance during my absence, as they will then be in charge of our affairs in London.

With kind regards, I am

Very sincerely yours,

244. To Anthony de Rothschild, London.   *London, 22 January 1942*
English: Or. Copy. T.W.: W.A.

Dear Mr. de Rothschild,

I would like to reply briefly to your letter of December 3rd, 1941.[1]

Careful study of the problems which you raise leads me to believe that a certain amount of agreement does exist between us on one or two questions; since these are the questions of paramount importance, I think that it will be better to leave aside for the time being those other questions whose formulation must lend itself to different

---

[5] Untraced.

244. [1] W.A. This argued the impossibility of foreseeing the political and economic position of post-war Europe, thus rendering unwise any assumption as to emigration on the scale W. envisaged. If all countries concerned accepted the Atlantic Charter, it would follow that Jews would be accepted as full citizens of the countries in which they lived prior to Nazi persecutions. De Rothschild admitted that some Jews in Central and Eastern Europe would wish to emigrate, and that Palestine was their obvious refuge; and that, were large-scale emigration to become necessary, Palestine should be able to receive considerable numbers. But this did not, in the opinion of Rothschild's group, create the necessity for a Jewish State, and a state formed on the basis of race or creed was fundamentally wrong. A Jewish State would also prove disastrous to the best interests of the majority of co-religionists throughout the world, especially those of Eastern Europe. De Rothschild advocated asking the Government for maximum possible immigration into Palestine, with changes in the constitution and administration of the country as required. His policy was economic and cultural, he said, while W.'s was political.

interpretations, and which are not really germane to the principal subject in which we are all interested.

1) You believe—and so do we—that "it is possible that emigration on a substantial scale will be desirable . . . Indeed, so far as the Jews are concerned, this is almost certain to be the case"—the more so since "the campaign of hatred against Jews which the Nazis have conducted will leave a mark which may be expected to take time to eradicate . . ." I fully share those views; perhaps I would even place rather more emphasis on them: not only in my view will it be "desirable" for many Jews from Central and South-Eastern Europe to emigrate; it may become a dire necessity for them—Atlantic Charter or no Atlantic Charter. My own conversations, and also the conversations which the British authorities have had with representatives of Czechs and Poles in this country, drive me to the conclusion that at least one-third of the Jewish population of these States cannot be re-integrated when the States are restored. The reasons given by the statesmen concerned are manifold, and they are not always due to hostile feeling towards the Jews (certainly not in the case of Czechoslovakia). So, for instance, of the 360,000 Jews who lived in pre-war Czechoslovakia, forming compact agglomerations mainly in Slovakia and Carpatho-Russia, roughly 120,000 cannot be expected to be re-integrated after the war. In other words, the Jewish population of Czechoslovakia will have to be thinned out to two-thirds of its original density. Taking into consideration Roumania, Hungary, Poland, and some of the Balkan States, one may assume that between 2–3 million Jews at least will find themselves homeless, and will have to be absorbed within a reasonable period of time. Of course, as you rightly say, much will depend on the attitude of Soviet Russia. I am prepared to assume that within Soviet Russia no problem will arise, but the size of the emigration problem will also depend on the frontiers of the new Poland; I have therefore mentioned a flexible figure of between two and three millions, which I fear is not an over-estimate.

It is equally reasonable to assume that the countries of the Western Hemisphere will not be prepared to re-open their doors to immigrants, at any rate for a few years after the end of the war. In that case, I think we must consider where these two or three millions from Central and Eastern Europe are to find homes. A problem of this magnitude cannot be shelved indefinitely, or it may aggravate to a dangerous degree the position both of the Jews and of the peoples among whom they live. I think it is thus no exaggeration to assume that at least 100,000 or 160,000 Jews a year will be seeking new homes after the war, and we must try to salvage out at least the younger people with their lives before them.

2) You acknowledge "Jewish ties with Palestine", and "recognise with pride and admiration the great pioneer work which has been done in that country, and which makes further settlement on a substantial scale possible." This is why we believe that Palestine is destined to play a prominent—if not the most prominent—part in the absorption of the mass emigration which is to be expected. I think we need not at this stage argue whether such absorption is possible; the experience of the last twenty-five years, supported by the practical evidence of experts who have laboured incessantly on the spot throughout that period, goes to reinforce our own conviction that, given certain political and economic conditions, it can be done. The main essential condition is administrative authority; irrespective of whether or not we desire it for its own sake, this is an indispensable prerequisite for the carrying out of a task of such magnitude. Such administrative authority would translate itself in practice into Jewish control of immigration, freedom to acquire land throughout the country, and the necessary measure of financial control. Naturally, none of this precludes a British overlordship; but Palestine can no longer be ruled by a Colonial Office bureaucracy which the last twenty years have shown to be anything but an unqualified success. From such a degree of administrative authority, some type of State would inevitably emerge, and I doubt whether any community outside Palestine would wish to interfere with so natural a process of evolution—or could so interfere, if it did wish—any more than it would wish to interfere in the development of self-governing institutions within the Palestine Jewish community today.

3) I confess to being a little puzzled by your argument that the eventual emergence of a "State" in Palestine may injure the position of the Jews outside Palestine. The creation of an Irish Free State after the last war does not seem in any way to have injured the millions of Irish in America. And there are other roughly parallel examples.

4) So far as is possible, one would naturally wish to achieve an agreed policy with the Arab population of Palestine, but it would be illusory to think that any such agreement can be quickly reached, even if the British Government were prepared to throw all its weight into the scales in favour of it—which at present it is not prepared to do and—to judge from past experience—is unlikely to be prepared to do in the near future. It might have done so with effect in the very early years of the Mandate (the Royal Commission shared this view), but for reasons into which it is better not to enter, it did not then do so. We must, therefore, beware of making our work in Palestine dependent upon Arab consent. But I believe that if the democracies—to whom the Arabs owe almost everything they have,

and from whom they may expect after the war considerable further territorial and political gains—would proclaim, perhaps also as a part of the Atlantic Charter, that the Jews have a right to build their National Home in Palestine, the Arabs might acquiesce in it in time. Such a declaration on the part of the democracies would open the way for direct negotiations between Jews and Arabs—and only such direct negotiations, without intermediaries, have any chance of success.

5)   A declaration on these lines from the democracies can be obtained if the Jews of the world, and particularly those of the Anglo-Saxon countries, ask for it. Their demand would be supported by all those European countries which have an acute Jewish problem on their hands, and can hope to solve it only by cooperation with us in drawing off a proportion of their Jewish population to Palestine.

6)   I assume that you, like us, are opposed to the White Paper policy for Palestine, which, in the light of past history, has neither legal nor moral sanction. I make this assumption on the basis of the unanimous vote passed by the Jewish Delegation during the Arab-Jewish Conference at St. James's Palace, when the proposals of the then British Government—embodying the White Paper policy—were rejected.

I have endeavoured in this letter to focus attention on those points on which agreement between us seems already in large measure to exist, and have eliminated from consideration all those "ideological" differences which have resulted in our reaching approximately similar conclusions by widely divergent routes. It is my hope that we may succeed by this means in finding a common platform on the basis of a common demand for free Jewish immigration, free acquisition of land, and the necessary measure of administrative and financial control vested in the Jewish authorities in Palestine.

As I am leaving for America on February 2nd, I should very much appreciate your early comments on this letter, as well as any suggestions for further procedure.[2]

Yours very sincerely,

---

[2] De Rothschild undertook to circulate W.'s letter to his friends; he would be unable to reply in full prior to W.'s departure for U.S. (letter, 23 Jan. 1942, W.A.). He wrote again 19 Mar. (W.A.) re-affirming that he and his friends were 'unalterably opposed to the establishment of a Jewish State'.

245. To English Zionist Conference, London.

London, 25 January 1942

English: Or. Copy. T.W.: W.A.

I am extremely sorry that a slight indisposition prevents me from attending the Conference of the English Zionist Federation today.[1] I would like to send you all my warmest greetings and good wishes for your work in the coming year, as well as to bid you goodbye before my departure for the United States and—as I hope—Palestine. I would have wished to join you in expressing our deep sympathy for our brethren now crushed beneath the Nazi yoke, and our determination to share to the fullest possible degree in the achievement of ultimate victory. I would also wish to join you in cordial greetings to the *Yishuv,* thousands of whose young men are already in the firing-line on all the Middle Eastern Fronts, and to assure them that we stand on watch and that we too will do our duty to the utmost of our ability.

Though I shall be away during the next few months, I shall follow with keen interest the progress of the work in England. You know as well as I do what that work must be and how urgent and vital it is. You will all have seen my statement of November 9 last; but the responsibilities devolving upon British Zionists, as members of one of the very great free Jewish communities in the world of today, are even greater in the light of that record of delays, disappointments and hopes deferred. The ultimate happy issue of our long struggle will depend upon our ability and readiness to act with complete determination and unity. The coming months will be vital in Zionist history. The whole future of our people may turn upon our ability to maintain, now, in the face of difficulties and delays, our courage and our faith undimmed, our unity of purpose unshaken, and our organization and practical work at its highest level of efficiency. That is a matter which concerns each one of us, and there can be no evasion of individual responsibility: "It all depends on me" is our slogan no less than it was Britain's in the dark days of 1940. And because I am sure that every British Zionist will realise this and act accordingly, I leave with confidence to undertake the work which awaits me in another great free Community across the Atlantic.

Chaim Weizmann

245. [1] W. was President of E.Z.F.

246. To Randolph Churchill,[1] London.   *London, 4 February 1942*
English: Or. Copy. T.W.: W.A.

Dear Major Churchill,
 It is my intention to see Lord Moyne before I go, and the enclosed aide-memoire has been prepared for him. But your kind efforts may make it unnecessary, and in any case if you feel that it might interfere with them, we shall hold our hand.[2]
 With kind regards, I am
                            Very sincerely yours,
                                    Ch. W.

247. To Harold Macmillan, London.   *London, 5 February 1942*
English: Or. Copy. T.W.: W.A.

Dear Mr. Macmillan,
 I write to congratulate you most heartily on your new appointment.[1] I hope that it may mean some rest for you after the strenuous life of the Ministry of Supply—though I am not sure whether such a change will please you.
 Among the various troubles and problems which you will find awaiting you in Downing Street there will be one with which I am intimately connected, but as I am going away for a quite lengthy period, I shall have no opportunity of worrying you much about Palestine, which is at present, as it were, lying dormant. I know you will keep a friendly eye on our affairs there.
 May I take this chance of expressing to you my very hearty thanks for all the interest you have shown, and the trouble you have taken, in my work while you have been at the Ministry of Supply? It is a pity that things have not yet reached the active stage—but perhaps all is not lost. For your own information, I enclose a copy of a personal letter which I have just sent to Sir Walter Layton.[2]
 With kind regards, and all good wishes for the future, I remain
                            Yours ever,

---

246. [1] 1911–68. Only son of Winston Churchill; author and journalist. M.P. 1940–45, but spent most of war overseas on special missions.
 [2] See No. 256. The nature of Randolph's assistance is not exactly known.

247. [1] As Under-Secretary of State at C.O., 4 Feb. 1942.
 [2] Later Lord Layton (1884–1966). Economist and newspaper proprietor; Director-General of Programmes, Ministry of Supply 1940–42. W.'s letter concerned the Ministry's refusal of a licence for the production in England of aromatics by W.'s process. W. challenged the reason given—shortage of shipping to transport the raw materials to England. Layton's

248. To Alice Ivy Paterson, Aberdeen.   *London, 5 February 1942*
English: H.W.: W.A.

                                                   5 February 1942.
My dear Ivy,[1]

Ever so many thanks for your telegram and letter and all the good wishes contained therein.[2] As you see we are still here. We were to leave last Monday and at the very last hour we had to postpone it by order of the Ministry of Supply. It was a waste of time after all, as all this chopping and changing has led to nothing. We are now going on Monday next the 9th and I hope there will be no further nerve-racking hitch.

From the States we shall try and go to Palestine, circumstances permitting. It again looks as if things are taking a dangerous turn in that part of the world, but I'm not losing hope.[3] It will be a different house to enter with dear mother gone and my elder brother Feivel as well. He died a few weeks ago.

We had an awful rush here and all sorts of excitements. Benji was laid up (like Orde); Michael was not well. Now all is clear, and the parting is difficult. However it is a hard and sorry world we are living in and it is to be hoped that something better will emerge of this welter.

I have just been speaking to Lorna. They are—I am happy to hear—much brighter. She too had a cross to bear and I hope it will go better from now onwards.

Let me wish you all the very best. When we meet again things will I hope look much brighter and victory nearer.

                                                   Yours ever,
                                                   Ch. W.

249. To Shalom Horowitz, Jerusalem.   *London, 5 February 1942*
English: T.: W.A.

Worried absence information from Institute. In spite repeated requests most workers not sending regular report. Also without reports

reply confirmed the negative decision 'while present conditions last'. The chairman of the Ministerial Council, Sir William Rootes, would be writing to the appropriate authorities in U.S. to recommend W.'s process there—exchange, 5, 7 Feb. 1942 (W.A.).

248. [1] She was Mrs. Moncrieff Paterson, mother of Lorna Wingate. In widowhood, she married the author Malcolm Vivian Hay.

[2] Untraced.

[3] Rommel's second offensive in the Western Desert began 21 Jan. 1942.

from Administration. Anxious that you and Green should go into Institute situation submit report following lines: first, technical activities answering my cable January 26th;[1] secondly, are all workers utilised full capacity; thirdly, which branches research continuable view supply position; fourthly, believe advisable reduce staff by dismissal unsatisfactory workers. Believe all negotiations regarding workers participation [in] industrial applications should be discontinued immediately till after war. Bloch and Committee must have full authority all administrative questions while workers concern research only. Grateful for your and Louis Green's full report on situation and proposals soonest and preliminary cabled reply my cable Bloch January 26th possibly within ten days as departure for States imminent. Rely on your good offices as neither Bergmann nor self able come owing transport conditions pressure work here. Regards.[2]

Chaim Weizmann

250. To Winston S. Churchill, London.   *London, 9 February 1942*
English: Copy. T.W.: W.A.

Dear Mr. Prime Minister,

On Thursday I am starting for the United States, and hope to proceed thence to Palestine. Before going I feel I must once more address myself to you personally on the question of the Palestinian Jewish participation in the war effort.

The ebb and flow of the Libyan battle has again brought the enemy nearer to Palestine. With the growing demands on British manpower from all parts of the globe, an additional twenty to thirty thousand Palestinian Jewish soldiers might be a far from negligible factor, which would still further increase in value were the fighting to approach their homeland. In spite of frustration and rebuffs from Whitehall, Cairo, and Jerusalem, the Jewish Agency has been doing its utmost to promote recruiting, though so far Jewish military service is not accorded a national character or public recognition. In spite of this, almost 12,000 Palestinian Jews have enlisted in the British forces. Does not this effort, on the part of a community of 500,000 which has experienced and is experiencing so much bitterness, deserve some response?

249. [1] This requested immediate information on progress in production of various drugs and the situation regarding applications of W.'s fermentation process, with questions on foodstuffs, artificial building materials and related matters.
   [2] No reply traced. See Nos. 265, 266.

But we should like to go much further in our war effort—to the very limit of our strength and even beyond it. To do that, national feeling and enthusiasm must be stimulated. Give the Jews their national name, emblems, and military organization, and enjoin on the authorities in Palestine a more sympathetic approach to our people. I venture to say this to you, as I know your own attitude towards us.[1]

Yours very sincerely,
Ch. Weizmann

251. To Lord Louis Mountbatten,[1] London.

London, 9 February 1942

English: Or. Copy. T.W.: W.A.

Dear Commodore Mountbatten,

You will find enclosed a short statement of the facts as they appear from the official correspondence. I am also enclosing our reply to Sir William Rootes'[2] letter dealing with the question of shipping and labour.[3]

I feel that all this speaks for itself, and would therefore ask you to use these facts only in any action you may wish to take, and not to bring in (as I understand Mr. Rollins[4] has suggested) extraneous matter like the small cost of the Laboratory, my own contribution in the form of apparatus and materials, or the fact that I have served in a purely honorary capacity. I venture to think that these minor points only obscure the main issue, and to that extent weaken our case.

I feel, too, that the only way in which anything can now be achieved is through the Prime Minister and his advisers—though

---

250. [1] Churchill replied 18 Feb. 1942 (W.A.): 'I understand the feelings of your people in this matter and I assure you that they are not overlooked'. He added also his 'heartfelt sympathy' on the news that W.'s son Michael was missing on active duty (see No. 255, n. 1).

251. [1] Later Earl Mountbatten, b. 1900. Naval Officer; Supreme Allied Commander Southeast Asia 1943–46. W. carried with him to U.S. personal letters for Mountbatten's daughter, then living in New York.

[2] Later Lord Rootes (1894–1964). Motor-car manufacturer, then at Ministry of Supply.

[3] Rootes' official letter (see No. 247, n. 2) giving the Ministerial Council's decision on W.'s process, was dated 5 Feb. W. replied 10 Feb. 1942 that the products yielded by his process would more than compensate for the amount of raw materials requiring shipment to England. Further, there would be a great saving of labour as contrasted with the existing toluene process—exchange in W.A.

[4] Robert Rollins, a staff member of the Grosvenor Lab. He died Aug. 1942.

without, of course, turning the matter into a *cause célèbre*. My name makes me too good a target and too bad a wicket for that!

Very sincerely yours,

252. To Sir John H. D. Cunningham,[1] London.

London, 10 February 1942

English: Or. Copy. T.W.: W.A.

Dear Vice-Admiral Cunningham,

I have received the enclosed papers and films from my friends in Palestine, with a request to do what I can to assist. Just what that is, I am rather doubtful, since I gather that the whole story has been sent to the Admiralty by the Haifa Naval authorities, and magnetic torpedoes are a very long way outside my field. I wonder whether you would be so very kind as to forward the enclosures a *qui de droit?*[2]

With apologies for troubling you, and many thanks for all your help in my affairs, I am

Yours sincerely,

253. To Leopold Amery, London.

London, 11 February 1942

English: H.W.: W.A.

11 February 1942.

My dear Amery,

I have not troubled you all this time knowing how preoccupied you must be. We are now leaving for the U.S.A. and possibly Palestine and so will be away for a considerable period. We are supposed to leave tomorrow, Thursday, afternoon (I hope there is going to be no more change!). Mr. James Malcolm of 25 Palace Gate will deal with my affairs in India if they develop into something practical.

Professor Namier and Mrs. Dugdale will be looking after the Zionist Office. I'm still anxious about cooperation between Palestine and India and I still believe that India can develop both explosives and synthetic rubber which will be needed badly and very soon. Should you wish to do something in this respect Malcolm and my chemist Dr. Bergmann in the Grosvenor Labs (Sloane 7214), 25 Grosvenor Crescent Mews, could give all information.

---

252. [1] 1885–1962. Vice-Admiral commanding First Cruiser Squadron 1938–41; Lord Commander of Admiralty and Chief of Supplies and Transport 1941–43; C.-in-C. Mediterranean and Allied Naval Commander 1943–46.

[2] Neither the enclosures, nor any further correspondence on this topic, have been traced.

I'm leaving this country with an aching heart. Both internally and externally things are very unhealthy and I'm hoping that this dark patch will clear.

To you and Mrs. Amery all our heartiest wishes go out—and our sincere thanks. We shall meet I hope in better days.

Ever yours,
Ch. Weizmann

254. To the Secretary, Jewish National Fund, London.

London, 11 February 1942

English: Or. Copy. T.W.: W.A.

Dear Sir,

I have pleasure in enclosing my cheque for the inscription of my parents' names in the Golden Book of the Jewish National Fund. The inscription can be quite simple: "In memory of Ozer Weizmann, who died on [31 May 1911] in [Pinsk, Russia]", and "In memory of Rachel Weizmann, who died on [31 July 1939] in Haifa, Palestine", and in the other column "Inscribed by his (or her) son, Chaim Weizmann".[1]

With sincere good wishes for the success of your great work in and for Eretz Israel, I am

Yours faithfully,

255. To Meyer W. Weisgal, New York.   *London, 15 February 1942*

English: T.: W.A.

Deeply grateful your telegram. Still some hope. Journey postponed week or two; shall let you know soon. Love.[1]

Chaim Weizmann

254. [1] Simultaneously W. sent a similar letter to the J.N.F. Secretary for an inscription for his late brother Feivel, who had died 31 Dec. 1941 in Haifa. The Golden Book was devised early in the history of the Zionist Organization as a method of honouring individuals and commemorating events. Entries are made against payment of a fee used by the J.N.F. for purposes of land reclamation. The various volumes are housed in Jerusalem.

255. [1] Weisgal's telegram, 13 Feb. 1942 (W.A.), expressed sympathy and hope following the news that W.'s son Michael was missing in action. Michael commanded a Whitley aircraft which had not returned from sea patrol during the night of 10–11 Feb. On 10 Feb., the eve of their departure for U.S., the parents had spoken with Michael by telephone. The following day, while awaiting their flight to Lisbon at Bristol airport, they were given the news and returned to London immediately. They resumed their journey some weeks later. See *T. and E.*, pp. 524–25.

256. To Lord Moyne, London.   *London, 18 February 1942*[1]
English: Or. Copy. T.W.: W.A.

AIDE MEMOIRE ON THE 'DARIEN' REFUGEES[2]

Having received further information from Palestine, we feel it our duty to draw your attention to the rising tide of intense bitterness among the Jews in Palestine over the continued detention of the passengers from the *Darien,* and to the consequences which would follow the carrying out of an attempt to deport them, as foreshadowed in Sir Cosmo Parkinson's letter to Mr. Namier of December 31, 1941.

2. Our correspondent writes:

"Keeping the refugees in a concentration camp creates a simply inhuman situation which neither the refugees nor the community can stand very much longer. Nervousness in the camp is extreme. There have already been attempted escapes, coupled with threats to the police. Policemen have tried to disperse gatherings in the camp, and there were some beatings-up and some broken bones as a result. Dozens of the internees were placed under arrest. After the Jewish Agency had with the greatest difficulty stopped a hunger-strike decision, there *was* a hunger-strike for twenty four hours as a protest against these beatings."

3. He further writes:

"These refugees have been kept in confinement for eleven months. Any attempt to send them away will produce unprecedented disturbance. There will certainly be determined resistance, leading to bloodshed. The result can only be clashes with police and military, whose repercussions on our military effort are incalculable. The effect on the outside world will be equally horrible."

4. Since the outbreak of the war the Jews have served and fought and worked and asked for nothing but more effective possibilities of doing so. In exchange, they have received little but violations of their rights and insults to their feelings.

---

256. [1] Though dated 4 Feb. 1942, this Aide-Memoire was sent on W.'s behalf on the date given, by Namier who was writing to Moyne on the subject of the *Struma* (see n. 3 below).

[2] The *S.S. Darien* had arrived in Palestine 19 Mar. 1941, with 793 illegal immigrants on board. All had been interned, and W.'s memorandum now argued for their release. Macmillan informed W. (15 Sept. 1942, W.A.) that all detainees from the ships, *Darien, Mihai* and *Mercia* had been released, apart from ten persons, in respect of whom further enquiries on security grounds had been found necessary.

The incidents accompanying the forcible deportation of the refugees in Athlit Camp filled the cup to the brim. The treatment of the *Darien* passengers, even apart from the threat that such scenes will be repeated, must make it overflow.

5. We solemnly adjure H.M. Government to consider what their own reactions would be if men, women and children of their own blood and race, very often their own kindred and friends, fleeing from torture and death, were herded and shipped like cattle from the shelter of the country which they have the right to call their National Home, or kept indefinitely in confinement, with their strength and willingness to serve unused, and their mental, moral and physical condition deteriorating. (Five men in the camp have already become insane.)

6. We ask again for the immediate release of the *Darien* passengers, and enclose a copy of our memorandum of December 1st, 1941.[3]

257. To Archibald V. Hill,[1] London.   *London, 19 February 1942*
English: Or. Copy. T.W.: W.A.

I wonder whether you will try to catch the Speaker's eye in the debate on the war situation which I understand will begin on Tuesday?

Recent events in the Far East,[2] as well as in the Libyan desert, have again focussed attention on the Middle East and on the vital role which Palestine can play in our war strategy. A Jewish fighting

---

[3] As to the *Struma*, stranded at Istanbul with broken-down engines since 15 Dec. 1941, the Palestine Administration and the C.O. refused to grant immigration certificates to any passengers except children under 16. But the Turkish authorities would not allow any of the passengers to land, and on 23 Feb. 1942 sent it back out to sea. It was towed through the Bosphorus and some miles further north sank as a result of an explosion, leaving only one survivor. The ship may have struck a mine or been torpedoed, but the opinion was also expressed that the passengers deliberately sank her, as had at first been implied of the *Patria* (see Bridgenote preceding No. 63). See also contribution by George Kirk in *The Second World War, 1939–1945,* London 1946, p. 244. Following the disaster, W. addressed a great demonstration of protest in London, laying responsibility on British Government—see *Jewish Chronicle,* 13 Mar. 1942; Barnet Litvinoff, *Weizmann, Last of the Patriarchs,* London and New York 1976, p. 224.

257. [1] B. 1886. Ind. Cons. M.P. for Cambridge University 1940–45; Member of War Cabinet Scientific Advisory Committee 1940–46; Nobel Prize for Physiology and Medicine 1922.

[2] Singapore surrendered 15 Feb. 1942.

force of some 50,000 men might have been an effective addition to the Allied strength in the Mediterranean. Even now, it is not too late, and if a Jewish fighting force were to be formed, some 30,000 more men could be recruited in Palestine alone, in addition to the 12,000 Palestinian Jews already serving with various units of the British forces.

I venture to hope that if you do take part in the debate you may be able to say a few words on this subject, as well as on the desirability of fully utilising the industrial and scientific resources of Palestine for the war effort.[3]

I am enclosing a little material[4] which you may perhaps find of use.

Very sincerely yours,

258. To State Department, Washington. *London, [?] February 1942*
English: T.: National Archives, Washington.

Jewish Agency for Palestine notes with satisfaction that American Government as repository declaration principles of United Nations invites support of all liberty loving peoples [for] principles this declaration. Am authorized by Executive Jewish Agency for Palestine, which was established and exists by virtue of Article Four of Palestine Mandate, to file with you statement [of] its adherence to principles that declaration.[1]

Chaim Weizmann, President

259. To A. J. Drexel Biddle, London. *London, 20 February 1942*
English: Or. Copy. T.W.: W.A.

My dear Mr. Ambassador,

It was a great comfort to have a talk with you this morning: you are always so very kind.

May I just sum up the practical side of our conversation?

1) You were kind enough to say that you would inform the President that I am delayed in England.

2) I really feel guilty about troubling Ambassador Winant's office again about a Clipper after all they have done, but it would be a great kindness if arrangements could be made for Mrs. Weiz-

---

[3] Hill spoke in the debate, but on another subject—see Hill to W., 27 Feb., C.Z.A. Z4/15145.
[4] Untraced.

258. [1] See No. 236, n. 1.

mann and myself to travel from Lisbon sometime in the first week of March.[1]

3) You were kind enough to say that you and Mr. Winant might be able to spend a short evening with me before I go to the States, so that we might have a talk about the various aspects of the problems which are at present exercising all our minds.[2]

May I again thank you and Mrs. Biddle for all your kindly thoughts of us in our sorrow: believe me it is no mere form of words when I say that you have been a great comfort to us.

With kind regards, I am
Very sincerely yours,

260. To Josef Cohn, New York.   *London, 20 February 1942*
English: T.W.: Photostat W.A.

My dear Josef,

This is just a line to say thank you for your kind message, which has been a great comfort to us both in our deep anxiety. There is no further news yet, and it may well be weeks—months even—before we hear anything definite.[1] Meanwhile, it seems to us that the only thing to do is to carry on, and we accordingly expect to leave within a week or two for the States. We look forward to seeing you soon, but I thought I would like you to know how deeply we appreciate your kind thought of us in our trouble.

Yours ever,
Ch. Weizmann

261. To Leonard Stein, London.   *London, 20 February 1942*
English: T.W.: W.A.

My dear Leonard,

This is just a line to say thank you for your and Kitty's[1] most kind message, which has been a real comfort to us both in our deep anxiety. There is no further news as yet—and we know that it may

---

259. [1] Drexel Biddle reassured W. of Winant's readiness to help with a flight, and agreed to a personal meeting—letter, 25 Feb. 1942, W.A.

[2] No record traced of a meeting of the three.

260. [1] Cohn's message was one of hundreds (from King George V and Churchill among them) expressing sympathy regarding W.'s son. On 4 Aug. 1942, after the mandatory wait of six months, R.A.F. authorities officially informed W. that Michael was now presumed killed in action (all in W.A.).

261. [1] Sarah, Stein's wife, formerly Kitay.

well be some weeks, or even months, before we hear anything definite. The tragic part of it is that we are only one among the many
families who must live out the coming months in suspense. But it
seems to us that the only thing to do is to carry on, and we accordingly expect to leave for the States as soon as we can re-arrange our
passage—probably within the next week or two. We wanted you to
know, now, however, how very deeply we had appreciated your
kindly thoughts of us in our trouble.

As ever
Yours,
Ch. Weizmann

262. To Viscount Cranborne,[1] London.   *London, 23 February 1942*
English: Or. Copy. T.W.: W.A.

Dear Lord Cranborne,
I should like to congratulate you on your appointment to the
leadership of the House of Lords, and to greet you at the outset on
the connection which your transfer to the Colonial Office estab-
lishes between you and the Jewish Agency for Palestine.

263. To Sir Philip Joubert,[1] Kent.   *London, 24 February 1942*
English: Or. Copy. T.W.: W.A.

Dear Sir Philip,
It was very kind of you to write to me.[2] It is a real comfort to
know that Michael's work was so highly thought of by his superior
officers.
To judge from the report which we have received from Wing-
Commander Richardson[3] there is still some hope that he may have

---

262. [1] Later Marquess of Salisbury (Biog. Index). He was Secretary of State for Colonies,
Feb.–Nov. 1942.

263. [1] D. 1965. Air Chief Marshal. Asst. Chief of Air Staff 1941; Commander-in-Chief,
R.A.F. Coastal Command, 1941–43.
[2] This described Michael W.'s work as 'outstanding for intelligence and scientific ability'
—20 Feb. 1942, W.A.
[3] Describing Michael's last flight, his squadron leader informed W. (14 Feb., W.A.) that
while leading an anti-U-boat patrol in Bay of Biscay Michael had reported engine trouble
some 100 miles south-west of St. Nazaire. Twenty minutes later, still the same distance from
the coast, he reported that he was alighting into the sea. A search party was organized, but
operations against the escaped German warships *Scharnhorst* and *Gneisenau* forced cancellation of the operation. Richardson entertained hope that the crew would reach land in
their dinghy or be picked up by fishing boats.

succeeded in getting to France—so that perhaps someday he may come back to the work he loved so much, and to us.

Though Michael was very keen on the scientific side and on his job in the Development Unit, I know that he was always most anxious to continue in the operational work: he felt strongly that it was only by a combination of scientific work and actual flying experience that one could get really valuable results: research work alone, in his view, made a pilot rather "stale".

With renewed thanks, I am

Very sincerely yours,

264. To Charles Glyn Evans,[1] London.   *London, 25 February 1942*
English: Or. Copy. T.W.: W.A.

Dear Sir,

I write to thank you for your letter of February 19th, informing me that my son, Michael, is missing as the result of air operations on February 11th, 1942, as well as for the Air Council's kindness in instituting enquiries so promptly through the Red Cross.

Judging from the report which we have received from his Wing-Commander, there is a chance that he may have succeeded in getting to France, so that he may one day return to the work he loved, and to us. But we know that it may well be weeks, even months, before we can hear anything definite. I shall, of course, inform the Air Council of any further news which may reach me.

I should like to take this opportunity of thanking you and the Air Council, on behalf of my wife and myself, for your kind expression of sympathy in our deep anxiety.

I am, dear Sir,
Yours faithfully,

265. To Benjamin Bloch, Rehovot.   *London, 2 March 1942*
English: T.W.: W.A.

My dear Bloch,

Your letter of December 31st last reached me today. You should know by now with what anxiety I am awaiting full and detailed news of what the Institute is doing, and especially about the ques-

264. [1] 1883–1961. Air Ministry official 1916–42.

tions raised in my letters of January 7th and 9th, which you should by now have received. There may not, of course, have been time for you to reply to them as yet, but an explanatory telegram would have been a great help to me. Your letter of December 31st, of course, says nothing of any of these matters, and deals merely with a few quite trivial financial points, which are really no concern of mine.[1]

There does not seem to be much point in asking further questions until I have answers to my earlier ones; but I would like to know what arrangements you have actually made with "Palestine Fermentation Industries", what are the said "industries", what are they doing, and on what scale? This affects me personally to some extent. I would also like to know whether my food products are being worked, and under what conditions? I would like answers to these questions, as well as to all those raised in my letters of January 7th and 9th.[2] (You may perhaps have written something to America, but I have heard nothing from there so far.)

I shall not address any further questions to you, since you seem so reluctant to reply. I would only mention that for two years past there has been no annual scientific report from the Institute—an unheard-of lapse for a scientific institution.

I would like to give you formal notice that as from 1943 the Budget of the Institute will be no more than £6,000 to £6,500,[3] so that you should begin to make the necessary arrangements to keep only a skeleton staff for the duration of the war. I certainly cannot countenance the state of affairs which seems at present to prevail at the Institute; nor have I the right to ask people to support something in which I myself no longer feel confidence.

Your reply to all these questions, whether by letter or cable, should be addressed to me in America, where we expect to arrive before the end of this month.

By now you should have received £3,000 from the Foundation; also £500 from me (accumulated from the legacy left to the Institute by Mr. Sieff, senior—Mr. Israel Sieff's father). I hope that the English Zionist Federation will send you a further £1,000 in the course of this month. By then you will thus have received £7,500 towards the £13,000 which I have undertaken to supply in 1942. From a telegram received from Josef Cohn I understand

---

265. [1] Bloch's letter (W.A.) related to payment of legal fees incurred.

[2] See Nos. 237, 239. In fact extended postal delays partly accounted for paucity of news. The orig. bears a handwritten marginal note, 'What about Kretschmer?' referring to the chemist Erich Kretschmer.

[3] The previous two budgets had been £12,000 annually. See No. 155.

that he is trying to secure the balance for the pharmaceuticals from some friends in Boston.[4]

> I remain, with kind regards,
> Very sincerely yours,
> Ch. Weizmann

266. To Harold Davies, Rehovot.   *London, 2 March 1942*
English: Or. Copy. T.W.: W.A.

My dear Davies,
I enclose copy of a letter which I have just written to Bloch, together with copies of letters addressed to him on January 7th and 9th.[1] I think they speak for themselves. I can scarcely tell you how deeply disappointed I am. It seems to me that everything at the Institute has deteriorated very seriously. I have therefore decided that we should, as far as possible, "cut our losses" without unnecessary delay, and that the Budget should be reduced, as from 1943, to between 40 and 45% of its present amount.

I know absolutely nothing of the scientific and technical work at present going on in the Institute. I hear some unpleasant rumours, but it is no use writing about them, because I have nothing definite or authentic, and Bloch has supplied me with no detailed information.

I await with impatience the letter announced in your cable,[2] and I shall be most grateful for your full support and advice. As things stand at present, it is impossible for us to come out to Palestine before the end of the summer.[3]

> With kindest regards, I remain,   Affectionately yours,

267. To Ivan Maisky, London.   *London, 2 March 1942*
English: Or. Copy. T.W.: W.A.

Dear Mr. Ambassador,
I must apologise for the delay in sending you the memorandum of which we spoke when I last had the pleasure of seeing you.[1] Unfortunately I have not lately been in a position to do very much

---

[4] Bloch cabled 21 Apr. 1942 (W.A.) that all points raised by W.'s letters in Jan. had now been covered. Scientific reports had already been despatched, and he was drafting the General Scientific Report. 'Palestine Fermentation Industries' would begin production in May 1942.

266. [1] W. had in fact already sent Davies a copy of No. 237.
[2] Untraced.
[3] Davies had written 18 Feb. 1942, but this had evidently not yet arrived.

267. [1] 'Memorandum on the U.S.S.R. and Zionist Aims' (undated, W.A.). This traced the origins of the modern Jewish problem, the need for emigration, the role of Palestine in a

work myself, and have had to put off writing it. The same reason has caused the postponement of my departure for America, though we expect to leave very shortly now.

To what is said in the memorandum I would only like to add the following few notes:

Three of the most fundamental aspects of the Soviet social philosophy are embodied in the national system which is being built up in Palestine by the Zionist Movement: collective welfare and not individual gain is the guiding principle and goal of the economic structure; equality of standing is established in the community between manual and intellectual workers; and consequently the fullest scope is provided for the intellectual life and the development of labour. There are no fundamental psychological barriers to mutual understanding, and the Zionist Movement has never felt antagonistic to the Soviet social philosophy. The Zionists, like the Soviets, construct their economy according to plan, for both have to build up in backward countries a fully developed modern society, and each has to transform the human material used in the work. The work of the Zionists is on a small scale, but their experience enables them to appreciate the work of the U.S.S.R. carried through on so enormous a scale. The vast majority of adherents of Zionism have close personal and family relations with the U.S.S.R., and a peculiar interest in, and special sympathy with, its people. The heroism and genius with which the U.S.S.R. has met the Nazi onslaught and defended the cause of civilisation have been hailed with admiration and understanding among Zionists.

In conclusion, may I express my firm hope and belief that the Soviet arms, which have already achieved such brilliant results, will succeed in freeing their country from the enemy, and will thus contribute to lifting the pall of darkness now hanging over a distracted world, and that the forces of progress and freedom will then unite in order to undertake the work of reconstruction which will lie before them. I have no doubt that the Soviet Government and people will show sympathy and understanding for the vexed Jewish problem which has weighed on us and on Europe for so many decades.

I would like to thank you personally for your kindness in receiving me, and in listening to our views.

Yours very sincerely,

Ch. Weizmann

solution, and a request for a new Soviet policy towards Zionism. W.'s diary shows an appointment with Maisky 30 Jan. 1941.

268. To Viscount Cranborne, London.   *London, 6 March 1942*
English: T.W.: P.R.O. CO 733/444.

Dear Lord Cranborne,

I enclose a Memorandum which will make clear to you the reasons why the feelings of Palestine Jewry towards the Mandatory Administration are as I described them to you in our talk.[1] In this I have confined myself to certain groups of facts, excluding major problems of policy as far as possible. But there are some fundamental considerations which I must put before you.

On the victory of the United Nations depends the survival of the Jews nationally, and even as individuals, for in the matter of exterminating the Jews Hitler is as good as his word; and traditional ties of deep moral significance bind our people to Britain's cause. The whole-hearted support of Jewry for Great Britain has therefore always been taken for granted, and British policy in the Middle East was based by the Chamberlain Government on the principle of trying to win over the Arabs at the expense of the Jews. But the moral loss involved has not, so far, been compensated anywhere by the political gains. We shall never waver in our conviction that the White Paper is a breach of Mandate pledges in which we can never acquiesce, and which has been publicly condemned by Mr. Churchill himself.[2] But even within the framework of the implemented two parts of the White Paper of 1939, the dignity and the feelings of the Jewish people might have received consideration. Instead, these have been trampled under foot.

Twice already in this war the battle front has approached Palestine, and it may well be that before this year is out the crucial battle of humanity will be fought there. Strategically, Palestine is a fortress no less important than Singapore, and what happens in Palestine resounds through the world. Palestine Jewry—one-third of the population—are bound to Great Britain—but is it wise to lower their morale, and to discourage their effort? Within the first week of the war 136,000 Jewish men and women in Palestine registered as volunteers for war-service. On December 1st, 1939, we offered

---

268. [1] The memorandum, dated 5 March 1942 (W.A.), reiterated Zionist grievances against the White Paper policy, with implementation of its land transfer and immigration clauses. Restriction of immigration meant governmental refusal to save children and youth from countries overrun by the Nazis, and produced such treatment of uncertificated refugees as was evidenced by the ships *Patria*, *Atlantic* and *Darien*. The Palestine Administration was attacked for its searches for illegal arms, for the continued imprisonment of the 43 *Haganah* members since 1939, and for the alleged police brutality towards those demonstrating against the Land Regulations in March 1940, when Menachem Prives had died. W.'s record of interview with Cranborne, 25 Feb., in W.A.

[2] I.e., in the Commons Debate of May 1939.

a Division to serve with the British Forces wherever desired. Our desire has been for a Jewish Fighting Force, to serve under our national name and flag; but we have already supplied 12,000 men— the pick of Palestine Jewry—to the British Forces, even though their service remains anonymous and unacknowledged, and the recruiting campaigns conducted by the Agency are hampered and thwarted by the British Authorities. In September, 1940, H.M. Government promised us a Jewish Fighting Force, extensive preliminary work was done, a British Commander was appointed— but on March 4th, 1941, the promise was put into cold storage, and rescinded half a year later. The entry of America into the war[3] has now deprived a Jewish Fighting Force of its main recruiting ground in the west; [there] remains Palestine. Status and national recognition for the 12,000 Jews already enlisted is a burning question there, and on it largely depends the further recruiting of some 30,000 Jews still available in Palestine. I spoke to Mr. Eden about this question, and he promised to examine it from his end. This matter is, I believe, shortly to be raised in the House of Lords, and in enclosures G and H I send you our precis of previous transactions and my statements about them.[4]

Palestine Jewry is asked to supply more men for the Army, and for military works and services of various kinds. This we try to do, and also to transform and develop our industries for war, and to intensify our agricultural production. For all this, labour is required; nevertheless, the immigration schedules sanctioned by the Administration have been of the most exiguous kind, and for nine months (October 1940 to July 1941) were refused altogether. This was justified on the ground that the "circumstances of international travel" made it most difficult for prospective immigrants to reach Palestine, and that by the time they did, conditions might have changed! (See Supp. No. 2 to *Palestine Gazette* 1065, p. 1827). The result of this neglect both of practical and humanitarian considerations is that tens of thousands of young Jews who were eager to fight and work on the British side have been left for the Nazis to kill or enslave.

I have not tried to describe the painful, hopeless, task of my colleagues in Palestine who have to deal daily, in matters great and small, with an Administration so unwilling to cooperate with us, so ready to injure us. From time to time I get flashes of insight into what happens behind the double curtain of Postal and Press Censorship, (how far this Censorship goes is evidenced by the fact that an Answer given by the Prime Minister in the House of Commons on

---

[3] Dec. 1941.

[4] No enclosures found. The statement was presumably that of the previous Nov., relating to rejection of the Jewish Fighting Force scheme.

July 20th, 1941, was not released in Palestine till September 7th). Thus, if from our side a first-hand picture of Sir Harold MacMichael's administration is to be obtained, it must be supplied from Palestine, and I am considering asking my colleagues there to lodge an official complaint with the High Commissioner against his Administration, for transmission to you. For my own part, I repeat what I said to you: that Sir Harold MacMichael has, in my opinion, proved himself unfit for the post he holds.

I fear that a vast bulk of enclosures accompanies this letter, and the Memorandum. We offer you these *pièces justificatives* in case you wish to examine the foundations of the statements I have made.[5]

Yours very sincerely,
Ch. Weizmann

269. To Jan Christiaan Smuts, Pretoria. *London, 12 March 1942*
English: T.: W.A.

Deeply grateful your intervention which hope may prevent recurrence such events.[1]

Affectionately yours,
Chaim Weizmann

270. To Eduard Benes, London. *London, 13 March 1942*
English: Or. Copy. T.W.: W.A.

Dear Mr. President,

May I invoke your good offices in a very worthy cause? You may, I think, have heard of the "Children and *Youth Aliyah* Organization", with headquarters at Woburn House, London, W.C.1. It is the Organization which takes care of the immigration of young children and youths into Palestine and it has been doing excellent work in saving our most precious heritage from the wreckage of the European Jewish communities, and training them for a new, productive, and happy life in Palestine. Included among its charges have been thousands of Czechoslovak Jewish children, and in this connection its work may perhaps already have come to your notice.

The *Youth Aliyah* Organization here is now undertaking some

[5] For W.'s subsequent interview with Cranborne, see No. 275.

269. [1] Smuts had presumably been asked to intervene to gain permission for the *Struma* passengers to enter Palestine. No record found of Smuts' intervention with the Government.

work among Czechoslovak Jews here, and for this purpose it would be of the greatest help if they could receive from you a brief letter or message of encouragement and approval. I know how busy you must be, but may I venture to hope that you will find this small request worthy of sympathetic consideration? I can assure you that the *Youth Aliyah* is deserving of all the encouragement we can give it. Should you feel able to write, the address is: Mrs. Eva Michaelis-Stern, Children and *Youth Aliyah,* Woburn House, Upper Woburn Street, W.C.1.[1]

With many thanks in advance, and kindest regards, I am

Yours very sincerely,

271. To Harold Macmillan, London.   *London, 13 March 1942*

English: Or. Copy. T.W.: W.A.

My dear Mr. Macmillan,

So far I have not worried you about Zionist affairs, nor would I wish to take up your time at present were it not for the fact that I shall be leaving next week for the States, on a visit of some months. I feel that it might be useful if, before I go, we could have a talk, at your leisure, when I could place the position fully before you. I am free any evening, during this week-end or afterwards, till next Thursday (we leave on Friday afternoon). If you could dine quietly with me here any evening before then, it would be a great pleasure.[1]

With kind regards, I am

Very sincerely yours,

272. To Ivan Maisky, London.   *London, 13 March 1942*

English: Or. Copy. T.W.: W.A.

Dear Mr. Ambassador,

We have recently approached the Foreign Office here with regard to a number of Polish-Jewish refugees in possession of Palestine visas, who are at present in Shanghai.[1] According to information

270. [1] Benes agreed—letter of 26 Mar. 1942 (W.A.).

271. [1] W.'s diary notes a meeting with Macmillan 18 Mar. 1942.

272. [1] The International Settlement in Shanghai received refugees without visa, and by 1941 their number had reached some 20,000, supported by J.D.C. and the British Council for German Jewry. Shanghai acquired significance as a stopover port for Jewish emigration, especially to Palestine. But new U.S. visa regulations of 15 July 1941, followed by Japan's entry into the war, frustrated plans for large-scale emigration from that part of Asia. See Mark Wischnitzer, *To Dwell in Safety* (Philadelphia 1948), pp. 205–06, 234.

which we have received, they could leave Shanghai for Palestine, provided they could obtain Russian and Turkish transit visas. In addition to those already having visas for Palestine, there are in Shanghai several hundred more Polish-Jewish refugees without such visas, for some of whom it may be possible to obtain immigration certificates, if the journey could be arranged and the necessary transit visas granted.

I do not yet know whether the Foreign Office has approached the Soviet Government in the matter of transit facilities through Russia, but in any case, if there is anything you can do to help it would be most deeply appreciated.[2]

Very sincerely yours,

273. To Wing-Commander Richardson, [Kent].
London, 13 March 1942
English: Or. Copy. T.W.: W.A.

Dear Wing-Commander Richardson,

I am writing to let you know that my wife and I will be resuming our trip to the States on Friday next, the 21st. We shall still be hoping for good news that may come through about Michael, and that he is safe somewhere.

Meanwhile, I suppose one must make some arrangements about his possessions, letters, etc. I do not know what the rule is, but what I should like would be to have the letters returned to me, and for you to keep the other things in your charge for the time being—till we are back in England.

Should you wish to communicate with someone here in my absence, I would like to give you the following two addresses:

Miss May (my secretary), at 77 Great Russell Street, W.C.1. (telephone Museum 3817), who always knows where to find me and how to reach me, and

Mr. Benjamin Weizmann, of Smallhythe, Godolphin Road, Weybridge, Surrey (telephone Weybridge 4056).

With kind regards, I am

Very sincerely yours,

---

[2] Maisky replied 18 Mar. 1942 (W.A.) agreeing to pursue the matter, but no further correspondence on this issue has been traced.

274. To Lord Rothschild,[1] Cambridge.   *London, 14 March 1942*
English: H.W.: W.A.

March 14th. 42.

My dear Victor,

We both thank you heartily for your kind words of sympathy.[2] We are still hoping that our Michael may one day return to us but it is an anxious and sorrowful time.

As you may have heard, the news has reached us almost at the aerodrome in Bristol before leaving for Lisbon. We turned back and intend to resume the trip on Friday next. I would be very glad indeed to see something of you before leaving.[3]

Affectionately,
Yours Ch. Weizmann

275. To Viscount Cranborne, London.   *London, 19 March 1942*
English: Or. Copy. T.W.: W.A.

Dear Lord Cranborne,

I am leaving tomorrow, and before I go I feel I must send you a word of thanks for the very kind reception you accorded me yesterday.[1] You know that I am not unmindful of the difficulties and complexities of the situation which we all have to face, but I leave in the hope that whatever it may be possible to do to improve matters will be done.

May I commend to you, in taking leave, the four colleagues who will be carrying on here in my absence? They are: Professor Selig Brodetsky, Mrs. Dugdale, Mr. Berl Locker, and Professor Lewis Namier.

Professor Brodetsky holds the Chair of Applied Mathematics at Leeds University, and is President of the Jewish Board of Deputies

---

274. [1] B. 1910. Biologist; Fellow of Trinity College, Cambridge 1935–39; F.R.S.; served W.W.II in Army Intelligence Corps, awarded George Medal; Chairman, Agricultural Research Council 1948–58, later Head of Central Policy Review Staff.

[2] His note, 9 Mar. 1942, in W.A.

[3] There is no record of such a meeting prior to W.'s departure for U.S.

275. [1] According to the record in W.A., Cranborne was personally against the 1939 White Paper, but did not think an early change was possible. W. asked that within the framework of the White Paper the Palestine Administration might adopt a more sympathetic attitude towards the Jews. Cranborne reassured W. that under himself there would be no repeat of the *Struma* disaster. W. expressed his concern over discussions then proceeding for a Federation in the Middle East, lest these prejudice the Jewish position. Cranborne undertook to watch the situation.

as well as a member of our own Executive; Mrs. Dugdale is well-known to you; Mr. Locker is a leading figure in the Palestine Labour Movement, at present seconded to us here as one of our political advisers and as liaison with Jerusalem; and Professor Namier is Professor of Modern History at Manchester University, seconded to us as Political Adviser.

I know you will accord to them the same courteous and sympathetic hearing as you have to me.

With kind regards and renewed thanks,

I am
Very sincerely yours,
Ch. W.

276. To Viscount Halifax, Washington.   *New York, 15 April 1942*
English: T.W.: Photostat W. A.

We have arrived here, finally, last night,[1] and I hope to be in Washington soon and have an opportunity of seeing you. I have most warm greetings to you from many of your friends, which I shall transmit personally.

I beg to enclose letters which were given to me for you and Lady Halifax. Of course they are rather old, because we were held up in Lisbon for three weeks.

With best regards to you and Lady Halifax, in which Mrs. Weizmann joins me, I am

P.S. I understand that some letters and documents were sent on to the Embassy for us by the Foreign Office. I should be most grateful if you would kindly instruct your secretary to send the correspondence here.

277. To Leib Jaffe, Buenos Aires.   *New York, 20 April 1942*
English: T.W.: W.A.

My dear Leib Jaffe,

It was with great pleasure that I learned that you are again about to undertake a visit to the Argentine on behalf of the *Keren Hayesod*. I am sorry that I just missed you on my arrival in America.

---

276. [1] The Weizmanns left England during the last week of March.

It is good to know that the many years of self-sacrifice and devoted service which you have given to the cause of our people and of Palestine have in no degree lessened in you the fervor of a poetic spirit or narrowed the breadth of human feeling and compassion with which you are so richly endowed, and I know that our friends in Argentine will greet you with the warmth which you deserve.

But it is for more than personal reasons that I hope and indeed know that your mission will be a success. For all mankind these are among the most critical days which modern history has to record. For much of the Jewish people they have been days of sorrow and grim tragedy. And the end is not yet. But throughout it all Palestine has remained as a token of hope and as a symbol of the redemption of a people. Our work there has given the lie to the slanders of our detractors. It remains as a beacon of faith for the future.

Today more than ever we must do our utmost to strengthen the *Yishuv* and give to it the means to continue both to play that vitally important part in the front lines of the free peoples of the world which it now occupies, as well as to prepare in due course to receive great numbers of Jewish immigrants in the future.

I send through you my warm greetings to Argentine Jewry and every wish for the success of your campaign.

Yours very sincerely,
Chaim Weizmann

278. To John G. Winant, New York.   *New York, 25 April 1942*
English: T.W.: Photostat W.A.

My dear Mr. Ambassador,

Let me first of all express to you my heartfelt thanks for the great kindness which you have shown, despite your extreme preoccupation, in receiving me in Washington. As promised, I am sending you a short statement on the Jewish Military Force. As the arguments are only too well known to you, I tried to make it as short as possible.

After my first visit to you I had the opportunity of talking to Mr. Sumner Welles.[1] I gathered the impression that there would be less difficulty in carrying this project through if one could begin by

---

278. [1] These meetings took place 22, 23 Apr. 1942 (W.'s diary).

simply organizing the companies which are already fighting into greater units like regiments or battalions, on the same footing as the Scots Regiment or the Welsh Regiment or the Irish Regiment— which form part of the British Army. They could obtain badges, names and commanders. It may prove subsequently of advantage to brigade one or two regiments into a larger unit and so on, and by a gradual process the Force would be built up without meeting very much resistance. I am informed that General Sir John Dill is not unfavourably disposed toward such [an] idea and he may have sent a message to that effect to the Cabinet in London.

As you know I am not a particular friend of the method which aims at exercising pressure on the British Government through a foreign government, however friendly; but we are allies now and it is in the interests of the common cause that the Jews should be fully mobilised in Palestine for reasons which are expounded in the attached memorandum. I believe that the present conditions are favourable to this idea. I think Mr. Eden would help in this matter. A word from here might, under the present circumstances, clinch it all.[2]

Thanking you once more for all you have done for us, I remain, dear Mr. Ambassador, with best regards and respect,

Yours v. sincerely,
Ch. Weizmann

Memorandum on Proposed Jewish Military Force in Palestine

It is respectfully submitted that the time has come for definite action on the part of the United States Administration, in cooperation with the British Government, to bring about the formation of a Jewish contingent as part of the British forces in the Near East. It is not necessary in this brief memorandum to present the moral or legal case for a Jewish military force based on Palestine. The fundamental right of the Jews to form such a military force is generally conceded. Therefore it is intended to deal here only with the practical aspects of the problem, which are as follows:

(1) The likelihood of an Axis thrust calls for the utilisation of all manpower available on the spot. To forego the full mobilisation of Jewish manpower in Palestine—by refusing to grant their legitimate demands—is to assume the responsibility of rejecting military aid at a critical time and place on rather insubstantial grounds and to repeat costly mistakes of a similar character committed in the Far East.

---

[2] Although various highly-placed members of the American Administration lent their names to the campaign in America for a Jewish Army, the Administration took no official initiatives with the British Government on this issue.

(2) In the war against Nazism, the Jews of Palestine have a special role to play in stiffening morale and pro-Axis [*sic*] sentiment. A Jewish contingent will not only keep abreast of other units, such as the Czechs, Free French, etc., but is likely to prove a pacemaker in military performance.

(3) The gap created by the withdrawal of Australian and New Zealand forces calls for replenishment. This fact has received recognition in the reported arrival of Polish contingents. Welcome as they are, it is intolerable to the Jews that while Polish units are brought from afar, Palestine Jewry should be precluded from making their own maximum contribution toward the defence of their homeland and Holy Land against a particularly odious enemy.

(4) The argument of inadequacy of equipment can no longer be taken seriously, in view of the progressive arming of other contingents. The contention that the steadily mounting pool of supplies falls short of equipping a relatively small Jewish force is obviously untenable.

(5) A long series of deplorable events, in and outside of Palestine, culminating in the *Struma* tragedy, has undermined the confidence of millions of Jews in British policy and depressed their morale. The insidious propaganda in this country directed against the British alliance makes it the more desirable and necessary in the interests of the common cause to stimulate rather than dampen the pro-ally sentiments of the Jewish masses, whose reactions are not an unimportant factor in the totality of American life. This can best be done by a recognition of the right of the Jewish National Home to participate in the struggle.

(6) The alleged danger of Arab opposition to a Jewish Force is vastly exaggerated; but as a gesture to the Arabs a simultaneous offer may be made to form an Arab contingent. There is a specifically Arab Legion in Transjordan; and other Arab States have armed forces which they are not, however, keen on throwing into the battle against the Axis. To strait-jacket one's friends for fear of offending actual or potential enemies, is the false logic of appeasement at its worst.

(7) The war can only be won by revolutionary fervor in the camp of the Democracies, matching in intensity the fanatical zeal of the Nazi hordes. The neglect of the Jewish people and the persistent denial of their claim to recognition and full partnership in the struggle is a moral contradiction whose effect is deeply hurtful to the cause of the United Nations.

(8) Furthermore, in facing the possibility of an invasion of Syria and Palestine by the Germans, allied statesmanship must take account of the incalculable effect upon public opinion, if all that has

been created in Palestine is exposed to the fury of the Nazis without the full opportunity having been given to the Jewish community to defend itself with all its strength and power.

(9) Opposition to the project of a Jewish force is on the wane in British circles and sentiment in its favor is on the increase. While opinions are still divided there is reason to believe that a positive step by the President of the United States may not be unwelcome and would settle the vexed question in the affirmative.

(10) In fine it is submitted that there are no insuperable obstacles. Such administrative inconvenience as may be involved in setting up a Jewish force under British command, will be more than compensated by considerable military and moral advantage to the Allied cause.

The plan may be implemented in successive stages as follows:

First: grouping existing Jewish combatant units (the companies of Buffs) into battalions and brigades, and simultaneously recruiting a Home Guard in Palestine.

Second: The recruiting and formation of additional Jewish battalions and brigades.

Third: The consolidation and rounding out of those units into a full–fledged division to be followed by a second.

A beginning should be made at once. There is urgent need for an immediate act signifying a change of attitude and policy, which will hearten the Jews of Palestine and of the world, stiffen allied morale in the Near East and throughout the democratic world.

Ch. Weizmann

279. To Stephen S. Wise, New York.   *New York, 29 April 1942*
English: T.W.: Photostat W.A.

My dear Dr. Wise,

From the many conversations we have had since my arrival here, I think one thing has emerged beyond all. It is this: The center of gravity for Zionism, no less than for world affairs today, is in the United States. It is therefore essential that the authority of the World Zionist Movement in this critical period be concentrated in this country. Accordingly, it is my intention—without weakening or prejudicing the position of existing organizations, but, on the contrary, [to] add strength and vitality to their activities—to create some visible instrument that will give expression to this authority.

I am proceeding, therefore, to set up, at once, what will be known as the Office of the President of the World Zionist Organization. This office will in no way replace or duplicate the work of any of the existing administrative organs of the organizations or the Emergency Committee. It will consist of a small staff of trusted workers whose primary functions will be—in addition to whatever limited executive or administrative duties it may have—to act as liaisons with the various agencies, Zionist, non-Zionist, governmental, scientific and otherwise, with which I shall have to deal in the months to come. It is neither possible nor desirable to detail here the various ramifications of this work. They cover a wide range of social, political and scientific activities impinging upon our present political tasks.

For this purpose a considerable fund will be needed to be placed at my disposal and to be spent in accordance with my own discretion. Such a fund will have to be raised forthwith in accordance with plans to be worked out. Whatever the method employed it will have to be done with great care and without the usual fanfare attending American fund-raising campaigns. This is a fund for political action and must be treated as such.

In order, however, to enable me to proceed with the work without any loss of time, I must ask that funds be made available to me at once to cover expenses already incurred and to meet foreseeable expenses during the next two or three months. Because of the urgency of the tasks involved, I ask that this be done on my authority as President of the World Zionist Organization and without reference to the usual committees and sub-committees and customary attending discussions. The same discretion that is expected to be used in the raising of larger funds should also be applied in this case. These are exceptional times requiring exceptional measures.

It is my desire to keep in closest touch with existing Zionist bodies, notably the Emergency Committee, representing as it does all Zionist groupings in this country. I shall want to meet regularly with the resident members of the World Zionist Executive and the senior officers of the Emergency Committee for exchange of views and information and formulation of policy and, from time to time, with the full membership of the Emergency Committee to render such reports on the progress of our political work as may be consonant with the interest of the Movement. Similarly, it is hoped, that you will keep me fully informed of the activities of the Emergency Committee, which, incidentally, should be increased rather than diminished, as a result of the work initiated by the Office of the President.[1]

With warmest regards, I am

Faithfully yours

279. [1] No reply traced. This proposal to establish a Presidential Office in New York led

280. To Abba Hillel Silver, New York. *New York, 30 April 1942*
English: T.W.: Photostat W.A.

I have your very kind letter of today's date.[1] It goes without saying that I am anxious to help the United Jewish Appeal, but I must warn you that I am at my worst in talking into a microphone. I have a natural aversion for the instrument, but if you think I shall be useful in furthering the campaign, I shall do my best.[2]

It was good to see you yesterday.

281. To Ernst David Bergmann, London. *New York, 8 May 1942*
English: T.W.: W.A.

Secret & Urgent

My dear Bergmann,

I have telegraphed to you this morning in accordance with the appended copy.[1] I believe that it is possible to send you a letter which may reach you quickly, and I would like to amplify the somewhat brief statements of my telegram.

Of the 3 weeks which I have spent here, I have worked about a fortnight in Washington, trying to disentangle the most complicated and confusing situation which exists here with regard to synthetic rubber. I have not yet had time to look into the problem of aromatic cracking and high octane fuel, but I believe that in that respect things may be a little better, but certainly not as good as people at home imagine it to be. I would like to give expression to my opinion that we shall be grievously disappointed if we build entirely on the facts and figures which are being published here from time to time. They have to be taken with a grain of salt, and not a small grain at that.

Up until about 3 weeks ago it was thought generally that the petroleum companies will supply all the synthetic rubber required,

to a clash between W. and Ben-Gurion, who wished to assert the primacy of the J.A. Executive in Jerusalem, and it seems to have been dropped as a consequence. W. adopted instead Wise's proposal to establish in New York an office of the Zionist Executive. See Nos. 292, 295, 298, 299; No. 304, n. 2.

280. [1] Untraced.
[2] W. broadcast a tribute to the work of U.J.A. and J.D.C. on a nationwide programme put out by N.B.C. 14 May 1942 (text in W.A.).

281. [1] The telegram (W.A.) explained that the war situation demanded all efforts to accelerate production of butadiene from butylene, through W.'s cracking process; Bergmann was to cable necessary data for the erection of a pilot plant in America, and was advised that he and his staff might be urgently required in U.S.

about 800,000 tons a year. The man who is responsible for impressing this view on the American Government and the public in general is chiefly Dr. Weidlein,[2] the mouthpiece of the great petroleum concerns. I have discussed the problem with him and have come to the conclusion that it would be extremely dangerous to rely on his statements. This fear is shared by Sir Clive Baillieu, the British Head of the Raw Materials Commission, who is as anxious about the whole situation as I am. In the last 3 weeks the possibility of making butadiene from grain, which means either from ethyl alcohol or from butyl alcohol, is being seriously considered, partly under pressure from me. At the beginning Dr. Weidlein opposed it violently, but the Vice-President, Mr. Wallace, and the Secretary for Agriculture,[3] and their chemical advisers, have supported my view energetically and so the matter is now being taken seriously.

This would explain to you why I have been urging upon you to send me the exact data regarding conversion of butylene to butadiene. Many processes are being discussed, but only those have a chance of succeeding and really helping the war effort which do give tolerably good yields, fairly pure butadiene and don't require complicated plant for the production. The last point is really a decisive one. There is a great shortage here—a shortage of copper and steel, and any plant which requires pressure needs a long time for its upbuilding, and therefore is practically ruled out.

The pretroleum companies will not produce any rubber before 18 months have elapsed, at least. This makes their effort unreal, as the shortage of rubber is extremely acute. The one process which seems to me at present to have any reasonable chance of supplying this country with a certain quantity of synthetic rubber, is the Union Carbide process, namely, ethyl alcohol-aldehyde-aldol-1-3 butylene glycol-butadiene. It is a simplified 4 stage process requiring complicated plant, although it gives good yields. How long it will take them until they produce appreciable quantities I cannot say, of course, and I don't believe that the Union Carbide can determine it exactly, but it is obviously the one thing which is promising and may yield results in about 8 months to a year.

I shall not dwell on the other matters, but it seems to me that the shortest way would be the conversion of butyl alcohol into butylene and the latter into butadiene. Before, however, expressing a definite opinion on it, it is essential to obtain an answer from you

---

[2] Edward Ray Weidlein, b. 1887. Chemical engineer; Director Mellon Institute, Pittsburgh 1929–51; adviser to Rubber and Research Group, National Science Foundation from 1941.

[3] Claude Raymond Wickard, b. 1893. Secretary for Agriculture 1940–45.

on the following questions:
1) What is the over-all yield in this process?
2) On passing butylene over our catalysts, one obtains naturally butadiene and hydrogen. In the first pass the conversion amounts to 20%. Do the other 80% consist of unchanged butylene or are any other gases formed? This is fundamental. If other gases are formed, how much of them are produced and is the recovery of the unchanged butylene easy?
3) How long is the life of the catalyst?
4) In view of the acute shortage of copper here, can it be replaced by silver? I hear on good authority that the petroleum companies have a catalytic method for the conversion of butylene into butadiene. There over-all yield is slightly over 50% on the butylene. I am naturally anxious to compare our yield with this. They tell me that there is slight carbonization in their case and formation of all sorts of by-products, *inter alia*, vinyl acetylene.
5) I would like to have, as soon as possible, the measurements and quantities of materials required for the erection of a pilot plant which would produce 100 kilograms of butadiene a day by our method, and would be grateful also for a sketch of the plant being transmitted to me by the quickest possible way, namely, in the same way as this letter.
6) The purification of butadiene also seems to be a problem. Our method is quite good and gives pure stuff, but I am informed that cuprous chloride is corrosive and if you do it in wooden tanks, attacks even the wood. But I believe this to be a question of secondary importance.

I have not had time yet to go into the question of cracking, but it seems to me, viewed from here, that it is most essential that this process should be put on, not on a 50,000 ton scale, but on a 100,000 ton scale in England. It would, in my opinion, not only give us a certain minimum of required important war materials, but would relieve the pressure here, which is very great. I wish you would impress this point of view on our friends at home.

The reliance on America that it will supply us with everything is extremely improvident, as they have to battle with their own problem and chemical production here is much more backward than anything else. I am saying so advisedly, and I am supported in this view by many competent Americans. Please point this out unhesitatingly to Lord Mountbatten and to Lord Cherwell.[4] If

---

[4] Frederick Alexander Lindemann (1886–1957). Personal Asst. and Scientific Adviser to Prime Minister from 1940; Paymaster General 1942–45, 1951–53. Bergmann made the required approaches—his letter to W., 28 May 1942 (W.A.).

we would have started our cracking process 8 months ago or 6 months ago, it would have greatly helped America and ourselves. As it is, so much precious time is wasted. I cannot emphasise enough how acute the shortage is in many directions chemically. Money is not so much of importance at present; time and materials are the limiting factors.

It is a great pity that Rollins has not come yet, and I am hesitating in speaking to the oil companies in his absence, but the pressure is so great that I shall probably be unable to await his arrival. The sooner he gets away the better for everybody concerned. It may become necessary either for you and Charlton or for Steiner and Charlton[5] to come over. I have spoken to Lord Halifax and he is quite prepared to arrange facilities for you to be transported in the quickest possible way. I am also making arrangements for production in Canada, if possible. In fact, there is more to do than I can possibly manage, and your presence here would be of incalculable value to me if we are to make any progress at all. But above all, I must have a clear answer telegraphically to the questions of yield and the composition of the gases after the first pass.

There is not too much butyl alcohol in this country either, but one can obtain a certain quantity, and there is also butylene obtainable from the oil companies, but it is not pure.

I hope that this letter and my telegram make the position clear and I shall await impatiently your answer. Please give my affectionate regards to Dr. Kind and his friends, and to Captain de Trafford,[6] and you will not hesitate to show this letter to them.

I would like to know how you and Benji are getting on, and I suppose that some letters are on their way.[7]

With affectionate regards,

Yours ever,
Ch. Weizmann

My love to the children.

---

[5] H. E. Charlton, staff member at Grosvenor Lab.

[6] Rudolph E. F. de Trafford, O.B.E., a Director of Manchester Oil Refinery Ltd.

[7] Bergmann's letter noted above stated that Cherwell had at Lyttelton's request independently investigated the W. cracking process, and had concurred with the Ministry's decision not to undertake production at Manchester Oil Refineries, where W. had done his preliminary work. See further, No. 291.

282. To S. Salman Schocken, New York.   *New York, 11 May 1942*
English: T.W.: Photostat W.A.

Confidential

Dear Mr. Schocken,

I would like to draw your attention to an article published in the *New Palestine* on March 27th by Dr. Walter J. Fischel,[1] "War and Research on Mount Scopus" and the sub-title "The Hebrew University Laboratories and Brain Trust put on Wartime Basis." Already the sub-title is in the worst possible taste, and can do no good to the University in the eyes of men of science. But turning to the text of the article, which is written in a florid style characteristic of a high-pressure salesman, it is full of inaccuracies. For instance, on page 9 "Remarkable discoveries have been made in extracting vitamin C from Oranges" seems ridiculous overstatement, because the preparation of vitamin C is the simplest possible thing and known for years to every chemist who has had anything to do with vitamins. Equally incorrect is the statement that the Hebrew University has found out that this vitamin neutralises the poison produced by many disease germs. What vitamin C can do, is again very well known, and the discoveries have certainly not been made in the Hebrew University exclusively.

It goes on in the same strain, and finally winds up with the statement that vitamin C is an antidote against inorganic poisons such as phenol, which is essentially an organic substance—and really, Mr. Schocken, statements like that make us look ridiculous. I could go on quoting more of the mis-statements, for instance, "As far back as 1934 a method was worked out for obtaining sugar from peel of citrus fruits" and then it goes on explaining what the sugar is, which explanation is (a) elementary knowledge, and (b) it happens to be wrong.

I shall not worry you with the enumeration of all the extraordinary statements accumulated in this article. He seems to have gone out of his way to mis-state every scientific subject which is being worked or is likely to be worked in the University. I understand that Dr. Fischel is by profession an orientalist. I wish he would stick to his job and not meddle in science. Incidentally, a good deal of the work he credits to the University has been carried out, particularly on fermentation and orange peel, in the Daniel Sieff Institute, but

---

282. [1] 1902–73. Orientalist, faculty member, School of Oriental Studies at Hebrew University, 1926–45; Professor of Semitic Languages and Literature at University of California from 1946.

I am glad he is not speaking about the Institute in that connection as it would only discredit it. So, for instance, I notice a statement in the J.T.A. Daily News Bulletin of Tuesday, December 2nd: "How the orange crop in Palestine is making a major contribution to the British war effort in the Near East was explained at the University of Chicago by Dr. Fischel"—this before a number of eminent scientists. All the work which Dr. Fischel describes so eloquently and so wrongly has been carried out by the Daniel Sieff Institute, and has been covered by patents taken out in the name of the Institute. It is, in the highest degree, discrediting to read such stuff, and have the name of the Hebrew University connected with it. I would be extremely grateful to you if you would kindly indicate to Dr. Fischel that he had better restrain himself and keep, in his propaganda, to the subject about which he knows something. I am sorry to trouble you with this matter, but I am sure you would not like to see the name of the Hebrew University connected with nonsensical propaganda of this kind, which can only do harm and no good.·

With kind regards I remain,

283. To Lazarus White,[1] New York.   *New York, 11 May 1942*
English: T.W.: Photostat W.A.

Dear Mr. White,

Permit me to thank you for your kind letter of the 5th[2] inviting me to attend the Annual Dinner Dance on May 14th, held under the auspices of the Hebrew Institute of Technology in Haifa, in honor of Dr. Karl T. Compton.[3] Unhappily I have an important engagement which prevents my joining you that evening in paying tribute to Dr. Compton, and in sharing in the celebration of this anniversary festival.

I should like to take this opportunity of saying that I have watched with close attention and interest, and with deep satisfaction, the development and growth of the Technikum since its inception in the year 1912. The Technikum has become an integral part of the cultural and economic structure of the Jewish National Home in Palestine and has also risen most creditably to meet the needs of the present war emergency period.

---

283. [1] 1874–1953. Civil engineer. President of American Society for Advancement of Haifa Technion (orig., Technikum).

[2] Untraced.

[3] 1887–1954. Physicist, noted for work on radar and related subjects.

The Annual Dinner is of happy significance because it will emphasise the fact that one of the chief requisites of the upbuilding of Palestine is the development of technological research, and that our Jewish students, to whom this privilege is denied in so many parts of the world, are successfully participating in this highly important constructive work.

Please convey my warm greetings to Professor Compton, together with my heartfelt thanks, for his active interest in the welfare of the Institute.

284. To Edward A. Norman,[1] New York.   *New York, 12 May 1942*
English: T.W.: Photostat W.A.

I am sorry to have missed you when you called on us a day or two ago, but I shall be hoping to see you soon. My time is rather divided between here and Washington.

I regret to have to trouble you again with the Montague Bell business.[2] I was under the impression that you were going to settle it. He is rather in great difficulties and it would be a pity if he were to nurse a grievance against us. I shall be very grateful if you can see your way to take care of the matter.[3]

With kind regards, I am

285. To Abba Hillel Silver, Cleveland.   *New York, 15 May 1942*
English: T.W.: Photostat W.A.

In the heat of the meeting, and after your excellent address, we had no time to have a talk.[1] I do not know when you will be in

---

284. [1] 1900–55. Financier, philanthropist; founding President of American Fund for Palestine (later Israel) Institutions; President, American Economic Commission for Palestine 1939–43.

[2] Henry Montague Bell (1873–1949). Former editor-in-chief, *The Near East and India*, he had offered in 1940 to work through his contacts in Iraq to persuade the government there to take in 100,000 Arabs from Palestine. The Z.O., with a contribution from Norman, sponsored him with £250 and travel expenses (see Brodetsky to Zionist Executive, 21 Nov. 1940, W.A.). Bell's mission was evidently unsuccessful. He had written to W. 15 Jan. 1942 (W.A.) for additional money. The Iraqi Government never agreed to absorb Palestinian Arabs. See also Vol. XXI, No. 117.

[3] No reply traced.

285. [1] Relates to Extraordinary Zionist Conference held at Biltmore Hotel, New York, 9–11 May, 1942, with Wise presiding and W. and Ben-Gurion as the principal speakers. The Resolutions formed what became known as the 'Biltmore Programme', and remained official Zionist policy throughout the war period. Its provisions were: that Palestine be opened at

New York again, and I am rather anxious to have a word with you now that I begin to understand the situation here. My movements are as follows: I shall be here all of next week, but shall probably have to leave for Washington on Sunday the 24th, remaining in Washington the best part of next week and then returning to New York. I shall be looking forward to an early opportunity of having a real quiet talk with you and would be grateful if you would let me know your plans for the next fortnight.[2]

With affectionate regards to you, Mrs. Silver and the children, in which Mrs. Weizmann joins me, I remain.

286. To Stephen S. Wise, New York.   *New York, 15 May 1942*
English: Or. Copy. T.W.: W.A.

My dear Stephen,

Although I have expressed very inadequately my thanks to you publicly for the wonderful and generous gift with which you have presented me at the conclusion of the Conference, I feel I ought to say a word to you personally. I realize deeply how much this ring means to you, and so it does, consequently, to me. But I feel certain that this ring should belong to the Jewish people, and that it should be placed in the custody of the Hebrew University Museum or the Tel Aviv Museum in Palestine, or in the Herzl Room of the Library. I hope that you do not mind, and possibly it may be your wish that I should hand this precious gift to one of these institutions at the next opportunity when I am in Palestine. I shall follow your instructions and, if God grants me the privilege of being present at the Peace Conference, and of pleading our cause, together with you, I shall wear this ring; but after that it should be given back to the Jewish people to whom it belongs, of right.[1]

I hope that this is in conformity with your wish, and that you will keep this letter, while I shall hold a copy here, so that this wish may be carried out should anything happen to either of us.

once to Jewish immigration; that J.A. be vested with control of immigration and with the necessary authority for developing the country; and that Palestine be established as a Jewish Commonwealth integrated in the structure of the new democratic world (Hurewitz, *op. cit.*, p. 158). See also Introduction.

[2] Silver's reply untraced. He offered to come to New York specially for a meeting, but W. decided that it could wait until 10 June, when a dinner in W.'s honour was due to be held— W. to Silver, 23 May 1942 (W.A.).

286. [1] Theodor Herzl's ring, presented to Wise in America on the occasion of his 65th birthday, had been given by Wise to W. during the Biltmore Conference. It does not seem to have been placed in any of the museums mentioned, and its whereabouts are unknown.

Permit me again to tell you how deeply moved I was by your great generosity, and that I shall always cherish the memory of this act as one of the most precious possessions.

In warmest friendship, and with deep affection, I am

As ever yours,
Chaim

287. To Stephen S. Wise, New York.   *New York, 16 May 1942*
English: T.: W.A.

I wish it were possible for me to join you in your deliberations.[1] After quarter of a century of valiant service in the defense of Jewish rights and for the ideals of Jewish National Home under your distinguished leadership the American Jewish Congress[2] enters today upon its most difficult task. You are meeting at a time of world crisis when our position the world over is threatened by dark and sinister forces pledged to its destruction. Today more than ever we are in desperate need of constructive, courageous and unfaltering leadership in American Jewish life. In these tragic yet also hopeful days the voice of democracy is ringing out in clear and historic words and must include the undimmed voice of Jewish democratic forces, of which you are so significant a part. It is my profound hope that this session of the Congress will make a substantial contribution to that unity of purpose in American Jewish ranks so essential in this grave hour. May wisdom and statesmanship guide your deliberations. My heartiest wishes for fruitful and successful conference.

Sincerely,
Chaim Weizmann

288. To Elena Margolis, New York.   *New York, 21 May 1942*
English: T.W.: Photostat W.A.

My dear Miss Margolis,[1]

I welcome the opportunity of joining with you in your celebration of the fifth anniversary of the establishment of *Kibbutz* Ain Ha-

---

287. [1] The American Jewish Congress was holding a 'War Emergency Meeting.'

[2] The Congress had first convened in Philadelphia, Dec. 1918, to formulate a post-war programme for the Jewish people. It was organized on a permanent basis under Wise's leadership 1928, and was active on the American scene as well as for Jewry in Palestine and elsewhere overseas. Since 1930s it was a leading force in the anti-Nazi movement and in aid for Nazi victims.

288. [1] She was a leader of *Hashomer Hatzair* (Young Watchmen), a Socialist-Zionist

shofet. The critical circumstances under which this outpost of Jewish settlement was founded have enshrined its achievements in the hearts of the entire *Yishuv*.

Ain Hashofet stands as a symbol of high Jewish courage, under fire. It is a monument to the late Justice Brandeis and to the intrepid American youths who struggled in the face of great danger to honor and redeem that immortal's faith in Zion.

The spirit of fortitude which was forged in the days of the disorders and disturbances has made lighter the burdens and responsibilities confronting the *Yishuv* in these momentous war months. I feel confident that the heroic exploits of the colonists of Ain Hashofet will find their counterparts in the courage and zeal with which the Jewish National Home will meet the challenge of the future.

With all good wishes, I am

Cordially yours,
Chaim Weizmann

289. To Angus Malcolm,[1] Washington.   *New York, 26 May 1942*
English: Or. Copy. T.W.: W.A.

Referring to the conversation which we had yesterday regarding the departure of Mr. David Ben-Gurion for Palestine, I would like to state that I have spoken about this matter to the Ambassador, who was kind enough to agree that arrangements should be made for Mr. Ben-Gurion to travel by air, if at all possible.

I realize that it is not an easy matter in view of the many claims for air-line accommodation via Africa, but my justification for asking you is the great urgency of Mr. Ben-Gurion's presence in Palestine as soon as possible. As you know we are at present engaged in the recruiting of, first, a group of 1,000 people for the Navy, who are to be organized as a guard on the Suez Canal.[2] Both the

---

Pioneering Youth Movement which aimed to educate youth for *kibbutz* life in Israel. Founded in Galicia 1916, the movement was established in North America 1923. The first American *kibbutz* of *Hashomer Hatzair*, established in the Hills of Ephraim 1937, was named Ain Hashofet (Well of the Judge) in honour of Louis D. Brandeis.

289. [1] B. 1908. F.O. official; Minister at British Embassy, Washington 1938–42.

[2] In Jan. 1942 J.A. Executive was approached unofficially by the Royal Navy to organize 800–1,000 Jews who would replace British sailors to guard the Suez Canal against mines dropped from the air. The Agency was promised that if the men on this mission proved themselves, they might later be employed on active service on warships. Shertok notified the Navy that he might raise some hundreds, not 1,000, provided the units were entirely Jewish and were organized by the J.A., and received the pay and conditions of British sailors. In Apr. 1942 the Palestine Administration organized a Palestine Coastal Patrol, composed of two-thirds Jews,

recruiting and other matters connected with it require the immediate presence of Mr. Ben-Gurion, whose cooperation in this matter is invaluable. I believe there are other recruiting operations going on, such as for the groups of experts in the auxiliary service in connection with the army.

I have had repeated requests from Palestine for Ben-Gurion's arrival as soon as possible, and would not have troubled you if I were not convinced that his early entry into the country would very substantially hasten the work in connection with recruiting and selection of the proper people—thus helping the war effort very considerably.

Should you require any additional information, I am always at your disposal.[3]

Thanking you in anticipation, I am

Yours very sincerely,
Chaim Weizmann

290. To Berl Locker, London.　　　　　*New York, 3 June 1942*
English: T.W./H.W.: W.A.

My dear Berl,

I am feeling rather guilty for not having written to you all this time. I have been spending a great deal of time in Washington, partly on our own affairs, and partly on matters connected with the war work. I have had an opportunity of seeing the Ambassador several times—General Dill, Litvinov,[1] Morgenthau, Sumner Welles, Bullitt, the Vice-President,[2] the Secretary for Agriculture[3] and Mr. Frankfurter and Mr. Ben Cohen repeatedly; also Winant, Donald Nelson[4] and others, including the Governor of New York.[5] Now arrangements are being made for me to see the President soon.

one-third Arabs. In May 1942 Shertok was informed by a Naval representative at Haifa that the original plan for the Canal would now be incorporated in a general plan of coastal defence. Shertok was informed that the Palestine Government had since insisted that Arabs also be mobilized for this task. See Shertok reports to Agency Executive, 1 Feb., 10 May 1942, in Vol. 35. C.Z.A. For recruitment of Jews for guard duties on airfields and strategic installations, see I.S.O. Playfair, *History of Second World War*, Military Series: The Mediterranean and the Middle East (London 1956).

[3] No reply traced.

290. [1] Maxim Litvinov (1876–1951). Soviet delegate to League of Nations 1934–38; People's Commissar for Foreign Affairs 1930–39; Soviet Ambassador to U.S. 1941–43.

[2] Henry Agard Wallace (1888–1965). Vice-President 1941–45.

[3] Wickard. See No. 281.

[4] 1885–1959. Chairman of War Production Board 1942–44.

[5] Herbert H. Lehman. See No. 138.

It is very difficult to give you anything definite, but on the whole there is a great deal of sympathy and understanding for the post-war Zionist claims.

Amongst the parliamentary people there is definitely a movement in favor of the establishment of a Jewish Commonwealth in Palestine, and it was manifested quite clearly during the political dinner which was given in Washington last week. A sensation has been produced by Wedgwood's speech which went fairly beyond the permissible and must have created some sort of stir in London as well as here.[6]

We are still negotiating with the non-Zionist Jews. These negotiations are protracted, but it is hoped that we may come to some sort of satisfactory conclusion soon. The difficulty is apparently the World Jewish Congress and the speeches which Dr. Goldmann is guilty of in the past.[7] However, it is more a matter of words than of actual principles. The Chairman of the non-Zionists, Mr. Maurice Wertheim,[8] is anxious to come to an agreement, but I fear that he is not carrying along his following and there may be a split in the ranks of the American Jewish Committee and similar groups when it comes to the acceptance of a formula satisfactory both to Zionists and to the negotiating committee. The workmen[9] and the *B'nai B'rith* are much easier to handle than the others.

The Zionist Organization of America and its new president[10] are a considerable improvement on the past, but I am afraid that they are neither strong enough nor sufficiently imbued with the importance and tragedy of the moment to expect from them much for the time being, beyond the ordinary activities.

Lourie is writing to you[11] about my last conversation with Lord Halifax, who for the first time since the publication of the White Paper asked for a memorandum on the future of Palestine and our aspirations.[12] I do not know the purpose for which he

[6] At the second Annual Dinner of the American Palestine Committee, Wedgwood proposed that U.S. take over the Mandate for Palestine from Great Britain.

[7] Relates to the conflicting philosophies of World Jewish Congress (in which Goldmann was a leading light) and American Jewish Committee.

[8] 1886–1950. President of American Jewish Committee 1941–43.

[9] 'The workmen' is a reference to the Jewish Labour group.   [10] Louis Levinthal.

[11] Letter untraced.

[12] At their meeting, 28 May 1942, W. asserted to Halifax that the White Paper offered no solution, and that the Government could not hand over 550,000 Jews to the Arabs. W. asked that no commitments be made in the Middle East that might create difficulties in the future. Halifax wished W.'s memorandum to propose a solution for Palestine, state how many Jews it could take after the war, on what the Zionists based their estimate of Palestine's absorptive capacity, and how many Jews would find homes in places other than Palestine, and where. Halifax also offered to help W. obtain an interview with Roosevelt (W.A.). For details of W.'s memorandum, see No. 296.

wishes to have it, but as he also offered to bring me to the President I believe that he may want to discuss our plans with him, possibly before my meeting.

Morgenthau is as sound as ever and he has told me that he had a talk with Churchill on Palestine and the latter has mentioned to him his "plan" about Ibn Saoud,[13] etc. The same was confirmed to me by Dill.

I am trying to get an audience with the President so as to enable me to have a talk with him on our problems—not in the rush of the office hours. This is not always easy, in view of the constant flow of visitors from England and the general war situation, which makes discussions on post-war problems rather academic just at present. However, I do not wish to postpone the meeting too long. The Vice-President, Mr. Wallace, who is becoming a figure of great importance here, is more accessible. I have seen him about three times on synthetic rubber, and he himself suggested a talk on Palestine at some time or another, and I intend to take him at his word rather soon.

I am grateful to you for all the papers and documents which you have sent me, and although there is a noticeable improvement in our relations with the Colonial Office as compared with Moyne's period, you are, I am afraid, having a hard time.

As you have heard, Ben-Gurion intends to leave for Palestine soon, and I have been trying to get a passage for him either via London or direct, and so far I have heard nothing definite; but the Embassy has promised to do its best. I believe that it is better that he should go to Palestine, and possibly return after a short stay there.

Will you kindly keep me informed of any developments in London, and I shall try from now onwards to send you, regularly, reports even though they are brief. I shall have something more definite to say after I have seen Sumner Welles again, and the President, and shall of course let you know at once.

Love to all of you.

Affectionately
Your Ch. Weizmann

I have found Litvinoff friendly and receptive.[14] Towards the end of the conversation he remarked: "We have no interest in the Arabs, they are all fascists". In his opinion 25% of Eastern Jewry will be destroyed.

---

[13] See No. 129.
[14] Postscript handwritten. No record of meeting traced.

291. To Ernst David Bergmann, London.   *New York, 6 June 1942*
English: T.W.:/H.W.: W.A.

My dear Friend,
As you may have heard in the press, Lord Mountbatten is here. He is staying a very short time, but still I had an opportunity yesterday to speak with him for a few minutes, and he is taking this letter to you. We again went over the whole situation and he has also told me about the new "discovery" which has been made in London—that there is a process here which is supposed to produce 20% of toluene. I have given him the facts as expounded in the short memorandum, of which a copy is enclosed. It speaks for itself. I do not think there is any truth in the whole story about a new process. It is the same hydro-forming process of which we knew, and as far as I know the Humble Oil Company is working it on something like a commercial scale—not a very large one. Both Ipatieff and the others inform me that there is no other process available. I am equally informed that the shortage of toluene may become very great, and that there is a shortage of benzene already. I don't know whether I shall have a chance of speaking to Lyttelton, but if I do I shall give him my view in no uncertain terms, and you will do well to inform Lord Cherwell that this story about some new secret process is merely a red herring.

I am most anxious to hear your results about butadiene, which is a burning and critical problem here. I would like to know exactly: (1) What the over-all yield is? (2) How pure is the butadiene which you obtain? (3) When will you be ready with a pilot plant experiment?—as time presses.

We are anxious to have you here as soon as possible, and if Charlton could join you it would be a great saving of time. Should Charlton not be able to come, then you will have to bring all the plans and sketches with you, so that the engineers here could build in accordance with the instructions.

It would take too long to give you a full account of the position here, but I have said enough in my statement to Lord Mountbatten, and I have tried to put it as mildly as possible. It is almost pathetic to see that in England we rely for the critical war material like toluene and rubber supplies from here, while they are battling here with the greatest possible difficulties and obstacles. However, if I have an opportunity I shall try to put it clearly to Mr. Lyttelton.

Sir Clive Baillieu[1] has been most helpful. He does realise the position and is anxious to remedy it.

291. [1] 1889–1967. Banker; Director of British Purchasing Commission in Washington, and British Raw Materials Mission there, 1941–43.

I am surprised that none of your telegrams, nor your last letter makes mention of Benji and his work. I am rather worried about it and would like to hear what the exact position is. Letters by airmail go much better now and so I hope to hear from you more frequently. I have received your letter of the 11th with all the interesting enclosures, which I have read with great attention and for which I thank you very much. I am dividing my time between New York and Washington, and shall go for a week to the Middle West to see some plants and some laboratories.

We are expecting the Blumenfeld family here in a few days.

Affectionately and greetings to all,

Yours ever,

Ch. Weizmann

What about Rollins? Is he coming and when?

1. PRODUCTION OF TOLUENE

The statement which was telegraphed over to me by Dr. Bergmann and to which reference was made by Lord Mountbatten in his conversation with me yesterday that there exists a process in America which yields 20% of toluene is incorrect.

There is one process which operates on a commercial scale at present in this country and which starts from naphtha. Naphtha on catalytic cracking by this process is supposed to yield 12% to13%, at the maximum 15% of toluene (the latter figure is considered very doubtful) and the rest of the product consists of low class gasoline. The process presents considerable technical difficulties, as the catalyst has to be changed every 5 to 6 hours. Assuming even the maximum figures of 15% to be correct, this process presents no advantage whatsoever over our aromatization cracking, because we obtain now 12.5% of toluene; but apart from toluene, 11% of benzene and 7.5% of ethyl benzene are produced, along with other useful materials—and our catalyst does not undergo any change even after working it for over 120 hours. We have not had any longer runs.

My attention was drawn, by persons competent to give judgment in this matter, that the engineering problems involved in the first process are very serious [and] costly and the setting up of plants takes a long time. In our case it is much simpler. The opinion is being expressed that there will be a shortage of toluene very soon in this country, particularly when large-scale military operations will begin, and if there won't be enough toluene to feed the military machine in this country, I fail to see where England is going to get its supplies when the need becomes urgent and great. There is already a shortage of benzene here. As for ethyl benzene, this is urgently required for making styrene, an ingredient for buna S. rubber.

303

2. RUBBER

The rubber position here is critical. Soon after Pearl Harbor, it was realized that large quantities of rubber will be required in the United States and for the United Nations. A program for the production of something like a million tons of rubber has been envisaged and the oil companies have undertaken this huge task. They are receiving a subsidy from the United States Government amounting to something like six hundred million dollars for this purpose, and in the opinions of experts, this sum will not be sufficient; but the most disturbing feature of the whole situation is that the oil companies, on their own showing, will not be able to produce any appreciable quantities of rubber until the end of 1943, and I doubt very much if this will happen even at that late date, as their method is complicated, their requirements in critical materials, like steel copper, etc., of which again there is a great shortage here, are very considerable indeed. Anybody who has looked through the Congressional Records of the last six weeks and the results of a searching inquiry made by the Senate, will bear out this statement. The heads of the British Raw Materials Commission, Sir Clive Baillieu and Mr. Clapp, with both of whom I have been cooperating throughout these two months, are keenly aware of the situation, and I am certain that they would confirm my view. The same applies to the situation in Canada, and the Canadian Minister of Munitions, Mr. Howe, has been apprised of it by the above-named gentlemen.

On arrival here two months ago, I have tried to press the view that one should not rely exclusively on oil as raw material for rubber, particularly as it would take such a long time to produce it, even if the question of cost is left out of account. The attention of the authorities here has been drawn to the fact that grain, of which there is such an abundance here (something like a billion bushels of wheat and corn) should be fermented and the products of fermentation should be converted into butadiene which is one of the main constituents of rubber. These ideas have received powerful support from the Vice-President, Mr. Wallace, and his technical advisers, with whom I have been in very close touch throughout. Styrene is the other constituent and is obtained as a by-product in the cracking process. Thus the combination of the cracking process and of the fermentation would yield rubber, benzene, toluene and some other essential war materials. I therefore venture to say that through adoption of these processes, a substantial contribution would be made to the present needs of America and of ourselves. In some degree we might meet the criticism which comes from various highly placed quarters, that we constantly ask a great deal from the American Government and are not in a position to give much in return. I do not share in this view, still it was indicated to me only yesterday morning by one who is the closest adviser to the Secretary of War.

At first the authorities (like Mr. Nelson and his advisers) were rather critical about the use of grain. Under the pressure of the facts, as elicited by congressional inquiry, this view has been completely changed. I am particularly anxious to begin the fermentation of the large quantities of wheat available in Canada, and Sir Clive Baillieu, who has been most helpful throughout, is trying to arrange with the Canadian authorities to increase their projected production of synthetic rubber from 40,000 to 100,000 tons, so that they could allocate one-half of it to the needs of Great Britain. They would need about 40,000 tons for themselves. It is at present generally admitted, after the discussions of the last two months, that the fermentation process would yield rubber in a comparatively short time, in about 6 to 8 months, and would not require any complicated plant, as existing distilleries and also existing refineries could be adapted to this process fairly quickly.

I do not propose to go into any further technical details in this short memorandum. I would only like to repeat that these matters have been thoroughly discussed with Sir Clive Baillieu, who, I believe, is aware of all the facts.

292. To David Ben-Gurion, New York.   *New York, 15 June 1942*
English: Or. Copy. T.W.: W.A.

Dear Ben-Gurion,

Upon my return from Washington yesterday, I found your letter of June 11th.[1] It comes to me—as you seem anxious to make me acutely aware—at a moment of great crisis in Zionist affairs both here and in Palestine. Although I am grateful for this reminder, I must, however, point out that the gravity of our position has not entirely escaped my attention nor even my thoughts. The moment,

---

292. [1] W.A. This notified W. that for all practical purposes Ben-Gurion no longer considered himself associated with W., whom he accused of having acted entirely on his own since he had arrived in U.S., consulting only with people of his own personal persuasion. Further, he was not convinced that W. was capable of conducting Zionist political affairs on his own; at this time of crisis the movement needed more than ever common counsel, concerted action and collective responsibility. Ben-Gurion warned that unless J.A. Executive and Emergency Council, with W.'s wholehearted support, could assure the necessary common and united action, he did not see how their work could be done properly, or how he himself could be of any use, or share responsibility.

too, makes it imperative that my answer be full, unreserved and not less candid than your "charges".

Two points stand out in this—I shall refrain from making any other characterization—rather amazing document. One, that I am carrying on alone, without consultation, the political affairs of the movement; and two, that if I pursue the course I am now following you cannot accept responsibility for the results nor associate yourself any longer with me.

As to the first point: I cannot defend my actions since I am not conscious of any guilt in that respect. On the contrary, on the record it can be shown that I have spent considerable time, during my brief sojourn here, in consultation with members of the Executive, the Emergency Committee and available members of the Actions Committee. Even the organizational form of my activities was decided upon after long and serious discussions with all our colleagues. If you, for reasons I am unable to comprehend, chose to absent yourself from some or most of these consultations, the fault is surely not mine. I am tempted to say that if any guilt attaches at all in that direction, it is rather with the accuser than with the accused. But what is infinitely more important than the fact of consultations, no action was taken by me without first indicating it to my colleagues and the officers of the Emergency Committee and then only when the course has met with approval. And in stating this I do not seek to avoid responsibility for what I have done in view of the fact that under any circumstances, contrary to your opinion, I am charged with the responsibility of conducting Zionist political affairs. I say it because it is the fact.

Whether or not what I have done has been wise or "helpful" cannot be the subject of discussion at this time, irrespective of your indictment that some of the things I have said and done have not been "very helpful to our cause". Perhaps. However, I think we can safely leave this for time to decide. My way of drawing nearer to our common goal has been fixed for many years and the Zionists have by their actions indicated many times that they believe their purpose is my purpose and my methods in consonance with that purpose. Surely you will not now, after so many years, select this moment to examine my motives—and this would be the only charge I would feel called upon to answer at this time.

From the moment I came to this country I have realized the great need for common counsel and collective action which, you will forgive me, you gratuitously stress in your letter. I think I have indicated in an unmistakable manner that the responsibilities of the Executive must be shared by the Emergency Committee. It is pertinent, I believe, to ask if during the five months preceding my arrival here and since, you on your part have always recognized this essential necessity? From all accounts this has not been the case. Nor is it irrelevant, I believe, to inquire whether this inexplicable document, so completely at variance with all the facts, is not aimed by indirection to cover up the failure of a mission, which was, I believe, rather nebulous in its nature and without set purpose. You did mention to me on several occasions that the Executive in Palestine has asked you to go to the U.S.A. It would never have entered my mind to question or to criticise their wisdom, or to take umbrage at the fact that neither my colleagues in London nor myself have ever been consulted in the matter. As you know, it has always been my conviction that your presence in Palestine, especially in these trying days, is of infinitely greater importance than anywhere else.

For this and other reasons, the second point of your letter gives me real anxiety. It indicates that while all other members of the Zionist Executive and the leaders of the Emergency Committee have come to appreciate the value of the collaboration I have established here, you come to the unfortunate conclusion that you cannot co-operate with me in the present crisis. I take it that this extends beyond the borders of the United States.

Before this fact, pregnant with so much meaning for our movement, I subordinate any personal feeling your letter might have aroused. And because I feel that there is no justification whatsoever for your letter, I reject *in toto* your conclusions as uncalled-for by the circumstances and regard the whole incident as merely the result of a temporary mood, dictated not by calm judgment but rather by an imaginary grievance caused undoubtedly by the many heartbreaking disappointments which all of us must face in this crucial hour.[2]

Sincerely yours,
Chaim Weizmann

293. To Morris Eisenman and Moses Feinstein, New York.

New York, 16 June 1942

English: T.W.: Photostat W.A.

Dear Friends,

I had hoped to be able to participate in the Commencement Exercises of the students of the Herzliah Seminary[1] and High

---

[2] See further, No. 295.

293. [1] Hebrew Academy and Teachers' Institute founded in New York 1921 by Feinstein

School, but much to my regret I was unable to do so as I was called away from the city.

From various sources I have been informed of the excellent work the Herzliah has accomplished, not without difficulty, in the twenty-one years of its existence. It is needless for me to say that advanced Jewish education, in the Hebrew language, is the best guarantee for the future progress of Zionism in America. I, for one, cannot conceive of Zionism without the Hebrew language and Hebrew culture. Herzliah, I know, has contributed greatly to the advancement of both.

I extend greetings to you, your Board of Trustees, your faculty, and above all the graduates and students of Herzliah. May we live to see happier days for our people and for Eretz Israel.

Cordially yours,
Chaim Weizmann

294. To Dorothy Thompson, New York.　　　*New York, 16 June 1942*
English: T.W.: Photostat W.A.

I should have written to you before, but I think I did mention to you that I was compelled to leave for Washington the morning after the dinner,[1] and I have been busy there ever since. I am now back for a short spell in New York and am going again to the Middle West tomorrow afternoon in connection with some chemical work, about which I hope to speak to you at the next opportunity. This should serve as an excuse in your eyes for the delay in writing to you.

I can scarcely put into words how deeply impressed and moved I was by your words at the June 10th dinner.[2] You seem to be endowed with the divine gift of giving expression to thoughts which are complex in their nature and require such a deep understanding of the Jewish people and their sore problems. To thank you for it

---

(1896–1964), who at this time was its Dean. Eisenman (1873–1948) was President of Metropolitan News Company, a founder of the Yiddish daily *Forward,* and active in Jewish cultural life.

294. [1] Held in W.'s honour in New York 10 June 1942. W. had spoken to a gathering of 2,000 guests there of the inevitability of a Jewish homeland in Palestine following Allied victory. He pledged full autonomy for the Arabs in a future Jewish State, with possibility of such a state joining an Arab Confederation. Roosevelt and Halifax sent messages—*New York Times*, 11 June, 1942.

[2] She had discussed W.'s work on acetone during W.W.I and hinted at his current work on the production of synthetic rubber from grain fermentation, drawing comparison between scientific method and political leadership (W.A.).

would be to "bagatellize" the effect of your presence at this dinner and your great utterances. But I would like, however, to say that personally I feel grateful to you as a friend who has come to our support in a difficult hour and has done so at great inconvenience and sacrifice to herself. May God bless you for all you are doing.

I do hope that it may be given to me to come and spend a few days with you, perhaps in the middle of July, if that time is still convenient to you.

With much love and affection, in which Vera joins me I am

295. To David Ben-Gurion, New York. *New York, 17 June 1942*
English: T.W.: Photostat W.A.

Dear Mr. Ben-Gurion,

I received your note yesterday.[1] In writing you before I had in mind not only your action here, but also in London.

Today I am leaving for a trip in the Middle West and I do not think that any useful purpose will be served by continuing our correspondence further.

Yours sincerely,
Ch. Weizmann

296. To Viscount Halifax, Washington. *Chicago,[1] 19 June 1942*
English: T.W.: Photostat W.A.

Private & Personal

Dear Lord Halifax,

You will recall that when I had the pleasure of seeing you last, you suggested that I should give you a short memorandum setting forth our views on the future of Palestine, and our desiderata. You stipulated that it should not be more than three or four pages. In trying to draft such a document I found that it was not easy to do it; however, I have tried to keep within the limits. I had to add to the main body of the memorandum, an appendix embodying both

---

295. [1] Replying 16 June 1942 to No. 292, Ben-Gurion claimed to be unaware that he had absented himself from consultations and challenged W. to specify dates and occasions when he had ignored invitations to be present. He disputed W.'s claim to be solely entrusted with responsibility for Zionist affairs, which in his view would not be in the best interests of Zionism and Palestine (W.A.). See further, No. 298.

296. [1] Besides scientific work, W. was that week fulfilling speaking engagements in Chicago.

the arguments and certain data on which the statements in the memorandum are based. That is the best I could do.[2]

I am here in the Middle West inspecting some factories where I believe synthetic rubber could be manufactured quickly. I am still to visit some places in the vicinity and hope to be back in New York on the 25th or 26th. I plan to be in Washington on Monday, the 29th, where we are to have an important conference with Sir Clive Baillieu, Mr. Newhall[3] and others, at which conference I shall have to make a report.

I see from the press that the Prime Minister has arrived in this country. I do not know how long he is going to stay. Neither do I know whether he would care to see me, if he is still in Washington on the 29th. You remember, when you were in London last you suggested that he should see me and he has promised to do so; thus far the interview has not taken place. Knowing how preoccupied he is, I did not, of course, press the matter in any way. I believe that at the present stage I should tell him a few things which might be of considerable interest and importance to him. I am wondering whether I am not asking you too much in suggesting that you might use your very good offices to arrange for such an interview.[4]

I do hope that I shall still find you in Washington towards the end of the month, and that you will allow me to come and see you before your contemplated visit to England. A message will find me here at the Drake Hotel until Tuesday morning, and then in Peoria at the Pere Marquette Hotel Tuesday afternoon and Wednesday morning. I plan to be back at the St. Regis Hotel in New York after the 26th or 27th.

Thanking you in anticipation, I remain, with very kind regards,
C.W.

---

[2] The memorandum tentatively estimated the number of Jews who would wish to leave Europe after the war at between two and three million; Palestine west of the Jordan, given industrial and agricultural development, could absorb an additional three million people. In order to facilitate the necessary migration, the future regime of Palestine would have to be given to a suitable Jewish authority; mass immigration would result in an early Jewish majority and the establishment of a self-governing Jewish commonwealth. In the meantime, the memorandum advocated, both Arabs and Jews in Palestine should be granted a larger measure of municipal self-government, with educational and religious matters entirely left to the respective communities (W.A.).

[3] Arthur Newhall, British 'Co-ordinator of Rubber', stationed in Washington.

[4] W. did not meet Churchill in U.S. See No. 305.

297. To Lord Halifax, Washington.   *Chicago, 21 June 1942*
English: T.: Copy. W.A.

In view of the recent emergency in the Middle East[1] I respect-fully reiterate our ardent wish to take a greater part in the struggle against the invading armies and to participate more directly and effectively in the defence of Palestine. This, as you know, can only be achieved by the organization of a Jewish military force out of the existing units and their augmentation through further enlistment in Palestine to fight under its own flag under British command. I would like to submit this request through you to the Prime Minis-ter whose mission I trust will be eminently successful and who, as a result of the long discussions on the subject, is familiar with every aspect of the plan. More than ever I am convinced that now is the time to implement the promise made more than a year ago. For it will not only contribute substantially to the defence in the critical area but will also have an enormous effect on the morale of American and world Jewry. I am equally convinced that without in any way disturbing the situation in the Middle East such an act of simple justice and prudence at this time will go a long way towards creating that goodwill towards the British cause in this country so essential at this crucial moment.

Chaim Weizmann

298. To Stephen S. Wise, New York.   *Chicago, 20 June 1942*
English: T.W.: Photostat W.A.

Private

My dear Stephen,

The last meeting of the Emergency Committee at the Astor Hotel[1] has left me with a rather painful impression, and I hear from Meyer [Weisgal], who has arrived here this morning, that you share this view with me. Since that evening I have been thinking a great deal about our position here, and what one can do to remedy it.

Meyer has outlined to me here a sort of plan which apparently meets with your approval, and which would, if implemented, pos-sibly lead to some definite action. Without entering into details, I would like to say that the Emergency Committee is an unwieldy

---

297. [1] Rommel's offensive in the Western Desert forced British withdrawal from Libya to the Egyptian frontier 19 June 1942. The garrison at Tobruk surrendered 21 June. (This telegram reproduced out of sequence.)

298. [1] Held 16 June 1942. This witnessed a further altercation between Ben-Gurion and W., who had dwelt on and condemned the continued strife within American Jewry.

body; it should be limited in its activities to Zionist affairs in America; it should be kept informed about the general political position, but not itself direct political policy. This can be done by the Executive and some senior members, who should be co-opted by the Executive.

I was puzzled to hear the long disquisition on federation by our friend Szold.[2] He presented a very clear and concise case and did it extremely well. But he has put up a target to shoot at, at a time (a) when the question of the federation is not at all on the *tapis*, and (b) he pictured federation on the pattern of the United States. Arab Federation, if it ever comes to pass, would be something quite different, and the entry of the Jewish State into such a Federation would only turn on the one fundamental fact: that our life as a State should be autonomous and should not be majorized by the other Arab States within the Federation. However, the whole problem is academic; it seemed to me singularly out of place to start a discussion on federation at a time when we wanted to discuss the making of public opinion, literature, political fund, and the things that have to be done in Washington—practical problems of this nature, of which the Emergency Committee, it seems to me, is fighting shy. Unless these practical things are brought to a speedy realization, I do not see what there is for me to do here.

You remember that during the period preceding the Balfour Declaration, you and your friends here, and the small circle of friends in London, were ploughing up the ground for almost two years before we obtained results. We may not have these two years now: the more reason for concentrating on intensive work without much more delay. One gains the impression that the Emergency Committee does not wish to grapple with the problem and would rather indulge in interesting but, for the moment, futile discussions.

All this is complicated by the peculiar attitude of our friend Ben-Gurion, who has been grumbling and grousing, really, ever since he came to London, and has continued to do so successfully here. This grumbling finally culminated in a letter which Meyer has given to you.[3] I think the real cause of his unhappiness is the failure in persuading the British to agree to our plans for a Jewish fighting force. But nobody is more unhappy about it than I; and I would reject the suggestion that my colleagues in London and I have not done everything in our power to bring this plan to fruition. The suggestion that I have not been energetic or "strong" enough in

---

[2] Szold's actual words not recorded. For the idea of Arab federation, see bridgenote preceding No. 44.

[3] See No. 292, n. 1.

pressing this matter is exactly the same sort of futile and unjustified argument which the Revisionists are now using, and have been using for the past 20 years, and which Ben-Gurion himself has been combatting so energetically. Here in the United States, it is difficult for me to use "strong" language. As a British subject I have to be exceedingly careful not to contribute to the strain in Anglo-American relations. Perhaps Ben-Gurion does not feel it, but I do, and chiefly for one reason: We have one great friend in England, the Prime Minister. Just as you would be extremely careful not to alienate the sympathies of the President, I find myself, especially on foreign soil, in an extremely delicate position. I must be doubly careful not to do anything which might possibly make Mr. Churchill's task more difficult. This naturally places a limitation on my public utterances. It does not in the slightest affect my conversations with friends, or would-be-friends in Washington or elsewhere. There is a time and place for everything. I did press Mr. Winant several times here, and General Dill, both of whom promised to do their best to help us. I may still have an opportunity of talking to Halifax about it; he is, in spite of Mr. Ben-Gurion's view to the contrary, not unsympathetic to this project.

This state of affairs cannot go on very much longer. I hear from Meyer that you wish to call a small meeting in your house. All I would like to say is that I would be most happy and grateful if you would do so. Please do not delay it beyond the 26th or 27th.[4] These are the only two days when I shall be tolerably free in New York (except for a luncheon appointment on the 26th). I think it would be useful to have the attendance of Mr. Szold as well, so that we may clear up everything; and on the outcome of this meeting would depend my decision either to continue my stay here or to go back to London.

In accordance with your suggestion to Meyer, I got in touch with Silver, and he was kind enough to consent to make the trip to Chicago in order to have a full talk with me. This should be followed up by a more or less official talk between Silver, Lipsky, Goldmann and yourself, so that the effort to bring him into more active collaboration may meet with success.

I remain, with much love,

Yours ever
Chaim

---

[4] See No. 304.

299. To Stephen Wise, New York.   *Chicago, 20 June 1942*
English: T.: W.A.

Just received your letters with enclosure—Ben-Gurion's astounding enclosure.[1] Wrote and dispatched letter to you prior receipt your communications. Suggest no action re proposed meetings until Weisgal returns New York Monday noon. He will communicate my views to you.

Affectionate regards.
Chaim

300. To Winston Churchill, Washington.   *New York, 25 June 1942*
English: Copy. T.W.: W.A.

My dear Mr. Prime Minister,

On learning of the news of the fall of Tobruk, which reached me while I was in Chicago last week, I took occasion to send a telegram to Lord Halifax, the contents of which I hope may have been brought to your attention.[1] I attach a copy and should like to add a few words of amplification on one or two points.

The new and critical developments in the military situation in the Middle East impel me to put before you again, as a matter of extreme urgency, the proposal for the organization of a military force, composed primarily of Jews from Palestine, to fight in the Middle East under British Command. Your express approval in September 1940 of a similar proposal, which I then had the honour to submit to you, was for various reasons not acted upon. Today again, the Jews of Palestine are facing a period of supreme danger. It is not only the annihilation of our work but the actual physical existence of nearly 600,000 Jews in Palestine which is at stake.

Approximately 14,000 Jews from Palestine are at present enrolled in various British military and airforce formations. For the most part they are organized in auxiliary technical and pioneer units, in the ground forces of the R.A.F., and in a number of infantry companies stationed in Palestine. These diverse and scattered units

---

299. [1] Ben-Gurion to Wise, 19 June 1942 (W.A.), advising that W.'s actions in U.S. were jeopardising the political objectives of Zionism, and undermining the unity of the movement. Ben-Gurion warned that, unless some remedy was effected, he would request J.A. Executive and the Actions Committee in Palestine to call for W.'s resignation. But he first wished Wise to call an informal meeting of American Zionist leaders and members of the Executive in New York to discuss the situation.

300. [1] No. 297.

fail altogether to meet the claim of Palestine Jewry to defend themselves through a single, organized military force of their own, fighting under their own flag alongside the armies of the United Nations. At least two and probably three divisions could be raised in Palestine in this way for immediate service.

If I may repeat what I said in the critical days of June 1940, if we go down in Palestine, we are entitled to go down fighting. The Mandatory Power is in duty bound to grant us this elementary human right. I know that I speak for the great mass of Jews everywhere when I say that the refusal to grant this right will never be understood. I most earnestly urge that you, who perceived the wisdom and justice of this claim nearly two years ago, should now see that it is implemented without delay. Speed may make all the difference between life and death for us.

With sincerest good wishes for the success of your mission,[2]

I remain
Yours very sincerely,
Ch. Weizmann

301. To Lewis Namier, London.   *New York, 27 June 1942*
English: T.W.: W.A.

My dear Friends,

I have asked Arthur [Lourie] to send you short reports, from time to time, about happenings here but I really do not know whether he has done so. He seems to me to be desperately busy here, and rather remote from London and its worries. I would like to continue my previous letter.[1]

My work hitherto consisted chiefly in reconnoitering and in finding out what methods are required in order to systematize the work, so as to build up some organization in Washington particularly, which would watch over the events and initiate the necessary activities. The Emergency Committee in its present composition is, in my opinion—and this is shared by a great many others—not fit to do this highly important work. They are busy with day to day routine, and although the burdens of collecting money are much easier now, they still have, somehow, a great deal to do, hold interminable meetings, and the Committee, being unwieldy and very

---

[2] This letter did not reach Churchill before his departure from U.S., and was forwarded to London (Martin to Namier, 7 Aug. 1942, W.A.).

301. [1] See No. 290.

numerous, and in its entirety concentrated in New York, is really not in a position to watch over events in Washington, which is a very complicated and difficult city. One therefore has to make the members of the Executive present, who are Lipsky, Goldmann and Ben-Gurion, responsible for the political work, and they may co-opt certain members of the Emergency Committee, like Wise and above all Dr. Silver, and perhaps one or two others. Of all the personnel in American Zionism, Silver seems to be the most suitable, if he could be induced to take a leading part in the general political activities of the movement. I was in Chicago last week to speak on behalf of the National Fund, and I took the opportunity of inviting Dr. Silver to come over from Cleveland and spend a few quiet hours with me. We have reviewed the situation in American Zionism, and I think Silver would be prepared to take the part assigned to him, if it can be done with dignity and without friction, which is, I confess, not altogether easy to achieve. One would then establish an office in Washington with an appropriate secretariat and really begin systematic work. I have also raised repeatedly the question of a political fund, both for here and London, and recently we have made some progress in the following direction: It is difficult to add to the many fund-raising activities by creating another fund, and a new collection runs the risk of a failure. One can, however, achieve two things: (1) The *Keren Hayesod* and *Keren Kayemeth* would be, I believe, willing to contribute a certain percentage of their income for the purposes of political work. That might give a quarter of a million dollars. (2) Apart from that, it is not impossible to obtain sums of money from good wealthy Zionists, who understand the urgent necessities. There are not many such people, but, nevertheless, it should not be too difficult to add to this quarter of a million another sum which might increase the power of such a fund. After numerous discussions and repeated urgings, this matter seems to be in a fair way of realization. Incidentally, the National Fund gave me $10,000 for my trip to Chicago. Five thousand has been paid up, and I was thus in a state of sending $4,000 to Linton. The other $5,000 will follow in due course.

Washington:

I have mentioned before that Washington is not an easy place. It is terribly over-crowded. Its population has increased three-fold in a very short time, and the usual amenities of life there are difficult. Moreover, it is a regular whispering gallery, combining all the disadvantages of a great capital and a small village. One has to be meticulously careful of what one says, because rumor and gossip are carried on invisible wings, with speedy and lightning rapidity, and in most cases distorted. Everybody is working there, and the deafening noise caused by the grinding of so many axes is most unpleasant to the ears.

The Arabs are quite active there, and with the sending of American commissions to the various parts of the Middle East, there are a good many people now in Washington who are likely to be affected by Arab propaganda, particularly by the Iraqis. The officials in the State Department, as I have already pointed out on several occasions, are of the same frame of mind as many gentlemen in the Colonial Office, whom we know so well.

The Embassy still considers the White Paper as their Bible, and are not likely to take the initiative in the direction of any change of policy. Halifax is benevolently neutral and something must have stirred in him recently, as he has asked me, without the slightest suggestion on my part, to give him a short memorandum on our views of Palestine. I enclose a copy of the document as presented to him, and a copy of his reply to my letter.[2]

I am going to Washington next week for a somewhat longer stay, and am again seeing all those people whom I mentioned in my first letter. Whereas my first visit was merely a visit of politeness, I propose to go a little more deeply into our questions now, at the second encounter. I am seeing Mr. Morgenthau on Wednesday, also Mr. Welles, and some of the important press people. I shall try to see the Vice-President, who is accessible, and arrangements are being made for a visit to Mr. Roosevelt himself. On my return to New York I shall be able to report more accurately regarding views and ideas prevailing in the political circles in Washington.

I am not writing about my chemical work; perhaps you hear, from time to time, from Bergmann how this is proceeding, and I don't wish to burden you with a lengthy account.

As of course you know, I have found Ben-Gurion here. I have repeatedly urged him to return to Palestine, but he seems to take his time over it; besides, means of transport are difficult. The Embassy has promised me to arrange for this journey, but so far I have had no definite results. Ben-Gurion has been extremely difficult, grumbling and grousing, most secretive, always wandering off on tangents of his own—and complaining that I do not cooperate with him. As to the last, I think the reverse is true. He has been here for 5 months previous to my arrival, and it is extremely difficult to determine what he has been doing and what he has achieved, aside from repeating the same speech about the army which we have heard so often at our various meetings in London. I have tried,

[2] See No. 296 and notes there.

two or three times, to have a quiet talk with him, but I have obviously failed in my task. At the last private talk he announced to me, among many complaints, that in London he came to the meetings merely out of courtesy, as he did not think them important enough; but he did not attach any value to anybody's opinion except Namier's. He put it in a quaint way by saying that I am holding court every morning, and this is why the meetings have no value in his eyes. I was aghast when I heard that. It was perfectly useless to try and argue with him as I think the man suffers from some mental aberrations. These conversations were soon followed by letters,[3] copies of which I enclose, and which speak for themselves. I do not propose to offer any comment on them, and am only communicating it to you by way of information. Whether he will be going soon or not is difficult to judge, as his ways have become very erratic. I would like to add that I have never taken any step, or tried to see anybody here, without discussing it previously with the members of the Emergency Committee and without reporting fully to them such conversations. I hope to be able to write you either from Washington or soon after my return.

I have just received your letter of June 18th,[4] and I was very happy to read it. We shall, of course, do all we can to draw attention to the book.[5] Knickerbocker[6] is away in Australia; but as for Dorothy Thompson and John Gunther,[7] they are quite accessible and I am sure they will do what we ask them to.

I am glad you have received my letter to Berl,[8] and I hope that this present script will put you wise to affairs here. It is my present intention to stay over until about the second half of August. I shall then be thinking of returning home.

Vera sends her love. She is keeping her courage up, which I am afraid is not easy for her. We are expecting any hour now the arrival of her sister and her family, and that might make life somewhat easier for her.

> Affectionately,
> Ch. Weizmann

---

[3] See Nos. 292, 295.

[4] Untraced.

[5] Namier's book *Conflicts*, essays published by Macmillan in New York 1943 (the Z.O. contributed to publication costs).

[6] Hubert Renfro Knickerbocker (1898–1949). Journalist and author.

[7] 1901–70. Author, journalist, broadcaster.

[8] No. 290.

302. To Bernard A. Rosenblatt,[1] New York. *New York, 28 June 1942*
English: T.W .: Photostat W.A.

I am much obliged to you for your kind letter of the 18th,[2] and am glad that you think the last meeting of the Emergency Committee was useful. I was somewhat disappointed that we did not come to any real grips both in the direction of defining a policy to be followed within the next period, and the political steps to be taken in order to give effect to such a policy. I am, however, happy to hear that you did discuss the question of a political budget, and that you seem to have come to some positive conclusions.

I am going away to Washington for a period of about eight to ten days, where I hope to have the opportunity of seeing some people and of obtaining a more concrete idea of the views prevailing there on our subject. As soon as I come back I shall try to follow up your suggestion of a second meeting, when we might take the opportunity of defining our policy more accurately.

With regard to your remarks concerning the enlistment of American boys, you are probably right as far as the legal side of the question is concerned, but I was given to understand that there was a chance, and that we have somehow missed it. However, I thank you for your explanation; but the matter is, at present, of academic interest.

With kind regards, I am

303. To Joseph Blumenfeld, S.S. Guine, Staten Island.
New York, 29 June 1942
English: T.: W.A.

All awaiting impatiently your arrival. Shall meet you on landing.
Affectionately
Chaim Vera Weizmann

304. To Stephen S. Wise, New York. *New York, 30 June 1942*
English: T.W.: Photostat W.A.

Dearest Stephen,
I share wholly your view that this unfortunate controversy with B-G. is both untimely and unnecessary.[1] Likewise I am sure you

---

302 [1] Biog. Index, Vol. X. K.H. President in U.S. 1941–46.
[2] Untraced.

304. [1] See Wise to W., 29 June 1942 (W.A.), requesting W. to write to Ben-Gurion with-

will agree with me that the whole thing is not of my making. I have brought no charges against Mr. Ben-Gurion; I have not refused to cooperate with him. It is he who, in my opinion, has raised an entirely non-existent issue. It would be folly to pretend that any of us is infallible. Least of all do I claim that for myself.

If what I said on Saturday seemed to you too sharp, I hope you will, my dear Stephen, concede to me that the provocation was responsible for whatever bitterness may have crept into my remarks.[2] Of course it was not my intention to cast any reflection on Ben-Gurion's personal integrity in any of the remarks that may have passed between us.

It is my deep conviction that a continuation of this unfortunate controversy will only lead to further misunderstandings and result in untold hurt to the movement. Even if colleagues do not always see eye to eye, it is possible to work together if it is believed that all of us have our minds fixed on the same goal. The only way out of this whole difficulty is to normalize the situation here, establish the authority of the Executive here as was suggested and, in the course of the work, I am hopeful that whatever differences may exist will eventually be removed. That, I believe, is the only course open to us. Let us then not nurse any grievances, and let us think of the task which lies ahead of us.[3]

Affectionately yours

Chaim

drawing disparaging remarks he had made during an informal meeting at Wise's home the previous Saturday, 26 June. Wise had also pleaded in vain with Ben-Gurion to drop his charges and avoid splitting the movement.

[2] At the meeting, Ben-Gurion reiterated to W., Wise, Goldmann, Greenberg, Levinthal, Lipsky, Szold and Weisgal his accusations against W. He questioned W.'s constitutional right to act on his own, claiming that this was rendering incalculable harm to the movement; W. did not always grasp realities when faced with a new situation, and still adhered to the Ahad Ha'am school of thought (which had envisaged the establishment of a 'spiritual centre' for the Jews in Palestine). He accused W. of having compromised with the British over the Jewish Army scheme, and warned that he was wrong to trust Halifax as a friend and confidant. He demanded to join all meetings with Halifax, and warned that if W. continued working as hitherto, he, Ben-Gurion, would recommend his resignation to the Executive. W. denied that he had initiated any 'personal regime', and rejected Ben-Gurion's insinuation that he 'could never say no to any Englishman'. W. stated that he was leaving the country at end August, and was perfectly willing for others to continue his work. If J.A.'s members in Executive shared Ben-Gurion's view, he would abide by their decision. He concluded: 'I am not going to be subject to the particular strictures or whims of a man, or men, who are trying to frame up a case out of imaginary grievances for political assassination'. Wise pleaded with W. to strike from the record the words 'political assassination', but apparently to no avail. Wise proposed that their political work be placed on a formal basis in U.S. through an office of the Zionist Executive independent of the office of the Emergency Committee. The meeting ended inconclusively (Minutes in W.A.).

[3] See No. 317.

305. To Viscount Halifax, Washington. *Washington, 1 July 1942*
English: Or. Copy. T.W.: W.A.

This is a short note to thank you for your very friendly reception accorded to me this morning, and for the sympathy which you have shown in the present difficult situation in which we find ourselves. I do beg of you to use your good offices with the Prime Minister, that something should be done in the last moment to organize the Jews of Palestine both for the defence of the country itself and as a Jewish force to fight in the field. You may in that way acquire, in addition to those already engaged, another thirty or forty thousand men who would fight to the last breath—and this is not a negligible quantity in this present emergency. What it would mean to public opinion generally, and to Jewish public opinion particularly here, I think you appreciate, and I need not dwell on this subject.

The other idea which just occurs to me, and I am merely throwing it out, is to form the Jews into a sort of desert corps under the leadership of a man like, say, Col. Wingate. I believe they would be very valuable. At any rate Mr. Shertok has discussed the various possibilities with the Commander-in-Chief, who is, I believe, both well-informed and sympathetic.[1] Everything really turns on the Prime Minister's giving his decision at the last moment.[2]

Wishing you a very safe trip, I am, with kind regards to Lady Halifax and yourself, and to our friends in London, like Victor [Cazalet] and the others,

Yours very sincerely,

---

305. [1] On 17 Apr. 1942 Shertok had addressed a memorandum to Gen. Sir Claude Auchinleck (C.-in-C. Middle East, 1941–42), asking for the general mobilization of Palestinian Jewry, to defend the country in the event of Axis invasion. A suitable frame already existed in the Jewish Settlement Police and its reserves of special constabulary. The memorandum reiterated the plea for a Jewish Fighting Force, to participate directly on the current field of battle. Auchinleck promised an early decision, following consultation with London, but had as yet received no definite reply (Shertok to Linton, 25 June 1942, W.A.).

[2] W.'s approaches to Halifax and to Churchill bore fruit. Following the onward despatch of No. 300 to Churchill, Halifax advised F.O. that in view of the great agitation in U.S. for a Jewish Army—led mainly by the Revisionists—it might be advisable for the Government, if they were going to make a concession, to make it to W. the moderate, rather than to appear to concede to the 'extremists' (Halifax to F.O., 27 June 1942, in P.R.O. F.O. 371/31379 E4028/6/31). Churchill himself advised that some concession be made: 'Now that these people are in direct danger, we should certainly give them a chance to defend themselves. . . Wingate should not be put on one side, but given a fair chance and proper authority' (Churchill to Cranborne, 5 July 1942, in P.R.O. Prem. 4/51/9). These initiatives led the Government to announce formation of a 'Palestine Regiment' 6 Aug. 1942. See also No. 321, n. 3.

306. To Berl Locker, London.   *Washington, 1 July 1942*
English: T.W.: W.A.

My dear Berl,

I have received Linton's cablegram today.[1] It was transmitted to me from New York but before having read it I saw the Ambassador, who is leaving for London tonight. In fact, he is carrying this letter. I have made the strongest possible representations to him about the necessity of a Jewish fighting force. I can say at this moment that he fully understands both the gravity of the situation there and the effect which the attitude of the British Government is having on the Jews here. He knows that something must be done. What can be done in a hurry now is difficult for me to say. Of course if instructions were given to Auchinleck to use the Jews in the best way possible as a fighting force, they might be organized in Commandos or as a desert corps. Not knowing exactly the technical side of the question, I have just merely thrown it out as a suggestion. Of course, if they wish to do it properly they can do it. Halifax has promised definitely that he will speak to the Prime Minister as soon as he comes, and we have agreed that I am to telegraph both to him and to the P.M. as soon as he reaches London, which may be in a day or two. This [is] all I have done this morning, but I am seeing Mr. Sumner Welles this afternoon, and possibly some other people tomorrow, and I am going to press the point as hard as I can. I have informed the Ambassador that I shall speak to the American friends on this subject.

You will have received the lamentable correspondence between Ben-Gurion and myself. I shall not go into details, but only say that there was a meeting last Saturday[2] at which he made all sorts of charges, which could easily be made by Jabotinsky. I was really furious, and if it were not for the critical situation, the best thing one could do is to leave the whole thing alone and let those who can do better try and do it; but unfortunately one is a prisoner.

He wants to return to Palestine. I have tried at the Embassy to get him passage, but if he wants to go on a plane he may have to wait for two months. They can guarantee passage on a boat, and they all think that in the end this would be the quickest way. Whether he will take it, I doubt. At any rate, if he stays on here I feel I would like to return to London as soon as possible. I don't wish

---

306. [1] This, 25 June 1942, recapitulated the information about Shertok's initiative, as given in No. 305, n. 1.

[2] See No. 304.

to worry you with his statement at the Saturday meeting, and my reply. You will probably get it some time, in due course. It is not edifying. To all the troubles and complications, this has come as an unexpected difficulty for me, at any rate; but all that really does not matter as compared with the seriousness of the military situation, which I do trust may clear up before long.

With much love to everybody,

Yours ever
Chaim Weizmann

Dictated by Dr. Weizmann. Signed by
Blanche J. Shepard, Secretary.

307. To Blanche Dugdale, London.   *New York, 4 July 1942*
English: H.W.: W.A.

July 4th, 42.

Baffy dearest,

I hope you are not angry with me that I did not write specially to you. I'm sending letters to the office and I take it that you all read them. I shall now be writing in turn to everyone.

The last few days were more than hectic, reminiscent of those which have preceded the fall of France. Linton's telegram to B.G. and myself[1] has reached me while in Washington where I have to spend a good deal of my time. On receipt of the message I had a conference with Felix Frankfurter and the following steps were taken:

1) I saw Sumner Welles and have asked him to arrange for an interview with the President, which he has done. The interview will take place next Tuesday 7th.[2] He has also telegraphed to the American Consul in Jerusalem asking him to get in touch with the Agency and obtain from them their views regarding all needs for the defence of the Nat. Home. The Consul will report to the State Department and I shall no doubt hear more from Welles.

2) I saw Dill, on whom I have urged most strongly the formation of a fighting force and that such a force should be placed under Wingate. He has promised to telegraph home about it.

3) I then went to see Morgenthau yesterday (for lunch) and explained to him the idea about Wingate, etc. He at once rang up General Marshall (Chief of Staff), who has asked me to come and see him, which I did at 2.45. Marshall knows Wingate by name and

307. [1] No. 306, n. 1.
    [2] Nos. 310, 312.

thought it is a good idea and promised to discuss the matter at once with Dill so as to elaborate a practical plan (perhaps Jewish Commandos).

4) After having reported the result of the interview with Marshall to Morgenthau, the latter telephoned to the President who has telephoned to Dill suggesting that Wingate be brought to Palestine. I am returning to Washington on Monday the 6th and shall know what has happened meanwhile. Today is Independence Day and tomorrow is Sunday. On Monday I shall be back in Washington.

5) Felix has made strong representations to Stimson[3] whom he has found very receptive.

6) I have seen Halifax before he left for home. He is carrying a letter of mine to the office.[4] I think I have succeeded in impressing him with the seriousness of the situation here as far as Jewish and non-Jewish public opinion is concerned. He has promised to speak to the P.M. soon after arrival in London and has suggested that I should telegraph to him and to the P.M. about Monday next.

In the last 3 weeks B.G. has just gone off.....You can judge from the correspondence how he is behaving. He says he wants to go to Palestine, but there is no possibility for him to go by air. Whether he will decide to go by boat I really don't know. Meanwhile the whole thing is a perfect nuisance.

I am terribly worried and overworked. Vera is keeping as well as she can under the circumstances, more like a wounded bird trying to fly. I may soon be able to let you know our plans concerning our return home. I hope that all is well with you and your family. My best love to you, Lewis, Berl and the others in the office. My love to Walter.[5]

Affectionately
Chaim

308. To Sumner Welles, Washington.   *New York, 5 July 1942*
English: T.W.: Photostat W.A.

I would like to express to you my deep gratitude for the great interest you have shown in our troubles when I had the pleasure of seeing you.[1] May I also thank you most warmly for having so

---

[3] Henry Lewis Stimson (1867–1950). Secretary of War 1911–13, 1940–45; Secretary of State 1929–33.

[4] No. 306.

[5] Walter Elliot (Biog. Index, Vol. XIII). Former Cabinet Minister, close friend and confidant of Mrs. Dugdale.

308. [1] See No. 307.

kindly arranged the interview with the President, and for your valuable cooperation in connection with the other matters about which I have spoken to you—all of which caused me to feel greatly encouraged.

It is my intention to be in Washington Monday evening (at the Wardman Park Hotel) and, as arranged, I propose to telephone you between 10 and 10.30 o'clock Tuesday morning, that I may know the hour for the interview with the President.[2]

With very kind regards and renewed thanks I remain

309. To Stephen Wise, New York. *New York, 6 July 1942*
English: Draft. T.W.: W.A.

My dear Dr. Wise,

It is generally agreed that the most important field of our political efforts lies in the United States and that the Zionist Executive under its responsibilities is called upon to devote itself to the best of its ability to the development of the resources of that field.

After a number of conferences with my colleagues on the Executive, we have come to the conclusion that it is for the best interests of the movement that for the duration, we establish here an authority or agency of the World Zionist Executive which shall consist of the members of the Executive sojourning or resident in the United States and such other leading Zionists here whom the Executive will invite to share in this responsibility on the pattern of the London Political Committee.

Accordingly, I have taken steps to set up an office of the Zionist Executive, which shall function for the World Zionist Organization in the political field. This authority or agency will meet regularly, twice or three times a week. It will invite to its meetings from time to time American Zionist leaders without regard to party representation or position, to participate in its discussions and decisions.

It will also invite, as may be required, representatives of the organizations cooperating in the American Emergency Committee. Periodically, of course, a representative of the Executive will report on the progress of the political work to the American Emergency Committee at its sessions. Needless to say, the functions of this authority or agency will be in the political field and not assume responsibility in matters covered by the over-all activities of the American Emergency Committee.

The intention is to set up a small and compact machinery which,

[2] See No. 310.

practically, we already have, and which shall be capable to handle the essential needs of such an office. It is our hope that the larger administrative tasks arising out of the decisions of the Executive, the American Emergency Committee or the individual organizations directly concerned may be in a position to execute. The limited budget required for the administration of such an office should be part of the larger proposed budget now under discussion.

It is hoped that the setting up of such an office of the Executive will help to regularise and direct into one channel all Zionist political activities in the United States, and that it will make for a more effective and harmonious all-around collaboration at this critical juncture.

I have come to the conclusion to take this step only after long and serious consideration of the difficult problems we have to face. I trust that our decision will meet with general approval.[1]

With best wishes, I am

Sincerely yours,

Chaim Weizmann

310. To Franklin D. Roosevelt, Washington.   *New York, 8 July 1942*
English: T.W.: FDR. Lib., Hyde Park, New York, P.P.F. 8084.

Dear Mr. President,

One can deeply appreciate your difficulty in getting any satisfactory picture of the synthetic rubber situation. While one might have some definite ideas on certain aspects of the situation, it is difficult for any one to speak with complete assurance without the real knowledge of what is being done or attempted. There is clear need for the pooling and appraisal of all readily available knowledge.

It is for that reason that I ventured to suggest to you in our talk on Tuesday,[1] and that I renew the suggestion now, that it would probably save time in the long run as well as contribute to the shaping of a more satisfactory program if you were to name someone of unquestioned standing, such as a Supreme Court Justice, to review quickly but thoroughly the whole synthetic rubber program and the various plans proposed in connection therewith and to report his findings and recommendations to you within a fortnight.[2] The

---

309. [1] Apparently W. did not send this letter, the first draft of which was written 3 July 1942. W. evidently discussed the issue in person with Wise (see further, No. 312).

310. [1] For transcript of interview, see No. 312.

    [2] W. received a letter of introduction from the President to Vannevar Bush, head of War

person chosen for this important task should have attached to him a small panel of distinguished and completely disinterested scientists who have not participated in such decisions as have already been made. He and his scientific aides should of course confer not only with the corporate officials who have presented the plans of their companies, but with the real scientists who are advising these companies on their respective processes.

They should also, I think, avail themselves of the knowledge of three distinguished European scientists who are now living in this country, who are familiar with the European experience in this field. These scientists whose integrity and expertness I can vouch for are: Professor Ernst Berl, Carnegie Institute of Technology, Pittsburgh, Pennsylvania; Professor V. N. Ipatieff, (Professor Emeritus, Northwestern University) care of Universal Oil Products Company, Chicago, Illinois; and Professor H. Mark, Brooklyn Polytechnical College.[3]

Again thanking you for the time you have given me, I am

Yours sincerely,

Ch. Weizmann

311. To Paul Uhlmann,[1] Kansas City.   *New York, 14 July 1942*
English: T.W.: Photostat W.A.

My dear Mr. Uhlmann,

I appreciate more than I can tell you your prompt response to my plea.[2] All of us today are confronted with enormous respon-

Research, and found himself in a tug-of-war between the big oil concerns and the Farmers' Union, each seeking the lucrative contract to produce rubber synthetically. W. put his proposal officially to William Clayton, Asst. Secretary of Commerce. The Administration did in fact appoint a committee, but the Supreme Court Justice nominated by the President, Justice Stone, refused the appointment (according to W. this was due to some 'administrative blunder'). Bernard Baruch took the Justice's place at the head of the committee, which also included Prof. J.B. Conant (President of Harvard) and Prof. Jack Compton. Compton had made unsuccessful experiments in the same field, and was sceptical from the beginning. The committee returned a negative report. Col. Bradley Dewey, Assistant Director of the Rubber Board, expressed interest, but was against setting up the huge plants needed for mass production. Finally, W. handed his process over to a private firm in Philadelphia, which began to manufacture during the war, and continued afterwards (*T. and E.*, pp. 527–29).

[3] Herman Francis Mark, b. 1895. German chemist; Professor at Brooklyn Polytechnic Institute 1940–44.

311. [1] President of Uhlmann Grain Company, Kansas City; made substantial contributions to Sieff Institute and Weizmann Institute at Rehovot.

[2] Untraced. Evidently W.'s plea for support of his 'political fund'.

sibilities which we must meet with courage and sacrifice. I know I can always count upon you and a select few who will come forward with their aid to me.

As for the other situation you touch upon in your letter, as the matter stands today I have reached the point where I believe it is no longer necessary to depend upon conversations in Washington or elsewhere.[3] Commercial Solvents has begun to work on a pilot plant and I believe that within a reasonable time definite results will be available. It has always been my conviction that the person who will deliver the first hunk of rubber on the President's desk, will play the tune.

I hope I shall have more news for you in a short while.

With warm personal regards, I am

Cordially yours,

312. To Berl Locker, London.   *New York, 15 July 1942*
English: Copy. T.W.: W.A.

My dear Berl,

I have just concluded a fortnight of very strenuous work both here and in Washington, and I need a few days respite after this. The strain is increased twofold—1, the work itself; 2, the normal or rather abnormal aggravation with which some of the work is accompanied. But about this later on.

However, before I leave New York for a few days, I am anxious to bring you up to date with some of my activities, and perhaps a bit more comprehensively touch upon some of the things briefly reported hitherto. In my letter to you of July 1st transmitted through the Ambassador,[1] I hinted briefly on some of the subjects discussed in Washington with the various Government officials, etc. I propose to make this account somewhat fuller, and if there is some repetition and over-lapping from previous correspondence, I hope you and our colleagues won't mind.

Lord Halifax: The day before the Ambassador's departure for home, we had quite a lengthy talk. The Ambassador was considerably worried about the rising anti-British feeling in this country. I told him, and I think he agreed, that the Jews in this country are the only influential group which is sympathetic to the British cause, but that their anger too is rising in ever increasing degree because

---

[3] I.e., in manufacture of synthetic rubber.

312. [1] No. 306.

of the many rebuffs. The Ambassador realised and admitted that I am the only person standing, as it were, against this possible tide. My position, I pointed out to him, has become increasingly more difficult because to date there has been not the slightest indication, either by gesture or deed, on the part of His Majesty's Government, towards an improvement in our position.[2] This is grist for the mill among our extremists who always thrive on our difficulties. The Ambassador promised that he would convey all this to the Prime Minister upon his return, and asked me to cable him as a reminder. I have not done so yet, but may do it within a day or so.

General Dill: Had two conversations with him. He has been and still is sympathetic to the idea of a Jewish Military Force. He expressed himself in favour of Wingate in case it is decided to form Jewish commandos. He wants to be helpful, and I think is trying to be so, but undoubtedly he is blocked by London and Egypt.

General Marshall: Through the good offices of Henry Morgenthau, I met with General Marshall. He makes an excellent impression, is a man of considerable stature, alertness of mind. From the brief conversation with him, I carried away the impression that he is sympathetic to our cause. I presented to him all the arguments in favour of a Jewish Military Force, and took the occasion also to mention to him the name of Wingate. He knew of Wingate, it seems, and in quite a favourable way. He thought that the matter of Wingate's transfer to Palestine should be brought to the attention of the President. This was done immediately by Morgenthau, as you will see from a later conversation with the President.

Sumner Welles: My two interviews with Sumner Welles were productive of several results: 1) He made the appointment for me with the President. 2) He contacted the American Consulate in Jerusalem on our behalf. In my interview with Welles, I took occasion to present to him the general precarious position in the Middle East and especially the intolerable position in which we are being placed in Palestine as a result of the appeasement hangover from which we are still suffering in that sector of the world. Mr. Welles, insofar as it is possible to judge, evinced interest, and I might say, sympathy, for our cause. I believe also that he agreed with my analysis of the situation in Egypt and the whole of the Near East. Specifically, I asked him for the two things mentioned above, both of which he attended to with great dispatch. In addition to the ap-

---

[2] Negotiations with C.O. were then in train. Cranborne informed Melchett 7 July 1942 (W.A.) that the Regular Forces in Palestine already afforded sufficient opportunities for any Jews who still wished to enlist. Further, taking into account the large number already serving, the number of Jews still available for service was considered limited.

pointment with the President, which was made within a few hours'
time after my interview, he cabled the American Consulate in
Jerusalem asking him [*sic*] to call in the members of the Executive
to enquire from them what, in their opinion, they feel is needed in
Palestine in order to strengthen our position. Whether our people
have been called in or not and what the results of the meeting have
been, I do not yet know, but I believe we should have some information shortly on the subject.[3] Parenthetically, I might add that
at a dinner party the same evening, Mr. Welles took occasion to
tell F[elix] F[rankfurter] that he was greatly impressed by the pre-
sentation of our case.

The Vice-President: From previous correspondence you know
that I had occasion to meet with the Vice-President several times
on the rubber situation. Because of his high moral standing and
intellectual vigour, the position of Vice-President, unlike the usual
run of Vice-Presidents in this country, is rising to a very considerable
extent. I believe—and that seems to be the opinion also of the *cog-
noscenti*—that the Vice-President will occupy a central position
in the post-war settlements, and it is therefore important that he
should be thoroughly and completely familiarised with our views.
Although I did not speak to the Vice-President about our affairs
(this I did intentionally) he is, I know, prepared to listen to me, and
to listen sympathetically. Through Dr. Wise yesterday, he sent word
to me of his "high appreciation of Dr. Weizmann's enormous contribution toward the solution of a very difficult problem." I hope
he is right. The next time I am in Washington, which will be within
a week or ten days, I expect to meet with him and have a comprehensive talk on all ramifications of our own problem.

The President: I met with the President on Tuesday, July 7th.
The interview was friendly, cordial, and conducted in that spirit
of informality for which he is known. I think the best way of conveying this interview is to quote herewith a transcript which my
secretary made immediately following my return from the White
House.

"When I came in he said: How are you? You seem to be working
very hard, and I said: Yes, I am trying to understand what the
position is in this country.

"He said: What do you think about the rubber position? I said:
It is very confused, and you, the Chief, cannot know the truth. He
said: I agree; I do not know the truth; how am I to get at the truth?

"I said: The only way is to appoint one man perfectly capable
of weighing and testing evidence—a Supreme Court Judge—and

[3] No further information traced.

also he should work with two distinguished independent scientists. We should all come in and give them the evidence; everyone should lay his cards on the table, all resources pooled, and out of this should come a report on which there should be predicated the decision. He put this down on paper. He said: Is that your opinion? I said: Yes. I said I have been trying now for two or three months to get the truth, and I know only the partial truth. I said: My opinion is that if you would have to start your programme again you would have to begin with grain, but the critical materials have been pre-empted by the oil companies. I am not criticising them; that is my opinion, and now it has to be adjusted.

"He said: What do you think of setting up a pilot-plant and producing, and I said: That could be done in five weeks. He said: The Commercial Solvents could do it. I said: They are my children, and that is why I have pushed them forward.

"Now, I said, Mr. President, you will throw me out soon, because I know you are behind your schedule. He said: I wanted to have a very long conversation, but you will come again in ten days or a fortnight, will you not? I said I shall always be glad to come.

"Now, I said, what about Palestine? He said: I always wanted to make a statement about the Jewish Army, which I think is a good thing, but the situation in Egypt is so dangerous that the British are frightened of the Egyptian Army turning against them, and therefore I think I would like to wait ten days or a fortnight.

"I told him this appeasement of the Egyptians is just nonsense; that you might just as well try and appease a rattlesnake. He said (rather explosively): Is that what you think? I said: Yes. If we are strong, the Egyptians will obey; if we are weak, they will stick a knife into us. Did he know that there are so many Jews fighting? He said: Yes, he knew. I said: The only way to get the maximum of Jews to fight is to organize a Jewish Force and bring Wingate down. He said: Wingate's a wonderful fellow. I said: But the British won't bring him down. (I didn't tell him that I had already tried through Dill, nor that I am seeing him tomorrow.) He said: How long will you be staying in this country? I said: I would like to have achieved something before leaving. He said: Don't go away until we shall have finished; to come and see him again.

"When I saw his secretary, MacIntyre, he said: All right; I will put you down again for an appointment in a fortnight."

Our conversation lasted about 25 minutes.

The general impression which I carried away from my interview with the President is that although he is sincerely sympathetic and desires to be of help, he is worried by the situation in Egypt. He gets his information from the usual channels, and they are not always, to say the least, favourable to our side. It is essential that the President be thoroughly and impartially informed about the position in the Middle East, the double dealings of the Egyptians, the chicanery of the Arabs, and the continued stupid appeasement policy of His Majesty's representatives both in Egypt and Palestine. He should know all the facts about Miles Lampson[4] and I cannot do it from here. My information is somewhat inadequate on that subject. I am making an effort to get the latest information about Egypt from one who has just arrived from Cairo and who is, I believe, in a position to know the facts. I am meeting with him this Saturday. He may be helpful. In any event, a comprehensive memorandum on the political currents and cross-currents in the Middle East ought to be prepared in London and sent to me as quickly as possible, so that I may be in a position to apprise the President of what is really happening. I realise, of course, how difficult it is to keep up with events. Things move so swiftly these days, and before one is able to communicate with one another, a situation which seems of transcendental importance one day, loses all value a day or two later. However, these are the conditions under which we must work, and we must make the best of them.

Washington in General: I think a word or two should be said about the work in Washington, in general. All these contacts and conversations are important but they lose their value unless the work is pursued continuously and systematically. We are constantly breaking ground, but that is not enough. The ground must be tended and watered almost daily. That requires a machinery and an operation similar to what we had in London in the years preceding the Balfour Declaration. We must have a home in Washington to which people can be invited. The social aspect in Washington is of considerable importance. I have discussed this matter with some of my colleagues here, and I am hopeful that some action will follow. Morgenthau, Felix, Ben Cohen, with whom I am in constant touch, are trying to be helpful. Rosenman, who is perhaps closer to the President than any other individual is, I believe, becoming more and more sympathetic. While waiting in the President's ante-room I had occasion to have a fairly long talk with him. He expressed himself in favour of a Jewish Military Force, and asked me to provide him with all the arguments so that he could, in turn, convince the President. Incidentally, he is also a key figure in our negotiations with the American Jewish Committee. Morgenthau, who is remaining steadfastly friendly, does not yet completely understand our problem. For instance, he cannot see why the Jews in Palestine

---

[4] Biog. Index. British Ambassador to Egypt and High Commissioner for Sudan 1936–46.

should not enlist in the British Army without necessarily forming into a special force. It took me quite some time to explain to him the difference. I am not sure whether he is convinced or not, but I am sure he will not do anything that will be injurious to our interests.

I have made these few observations merely as an indication of the enormity of our task here. This task, in Washington alone, requires men, money, organization, unity of purpose, and above all teamwork. This brings me to the next subject of my letter.

The Internal Situation: There is not much that I can add to what I said in some of my previous communications. When we speak of the internal Zionist situation, we must be careful to distinguish between the internal machinery and the Zionists in general. The one creaks; the other is acutely aware of the momentous days in which we live. We have had several manifestations of it. First the Biltmore Conference two or three weeks following my arrival. That was an extraordinary event of considerable importance, well organized, and served I think a very useful purpose. It required a well-regulated machinery to follow up and bring to full fruition the results of that conference. That, I am afraid, was not completely done. The dinners at the Waldorf Astoria, in Washington, Chicago, and Philadelphia, and the meeting at the Astor only three days ago— all are manifestations of tremendous interest on the part of the general, as well as the Zionist, public. I think I am not exaggerating when I say that never before during my many visits to the United States has the authority and the prestige of the World Zionist Organization been so thoroughly and universally recognised as it is today. All this is to the good. It represents political capital of an intangible character which must find expression in practical utilisation by the internal machinery. The Emergency Committee, a well-meaning but heterogeneous body, does not seem to possess either the power of decision or the galvanising forces to translate decisions into acts. I am saying this without any desire to criticise or castigate anyone. It is unfortunately a situation which has developed through the years, and it is not an easy task to wrench the machinery from its normal ponderous grooves. To do this, central authority and central leadership is required. This the Emergency Committee is lacking. No one seems to be willing to accept the authority of one person. I have been aware of this situation almost from the day I arrived here. I am enclosing here a copy of a letter to Dr. Wise which was to have gone off finally last week, but is still on my desk. The letter is self-explanatory, and needs no comment. It has been my intention to establish some sort of collective authority either of the Executive plus a select few of the American leadership or of the President of the Zionist Organization plus the Executive and a number of American leaders. This has not yet been achieved for a variety of reasons, notably the attitude and general incomprehensible behaviour of our friend, B.G... Of course I realise that the best solution of the problem would be to send him back to Jerusalem. That is involved with great difficulties. I am trying my best to get him transportation. Failing that, I am trying to make every possible effort to establish the collective authority of the Executive. Whether it will work or not I cannot tell. With Moshe [Shertok] or another member of the Executive here it would be a different story. With B.G. in his present mood the whole outcome is unpredictable. However, one must try, no matter how trying it may be.

On the outcome of this attempt will depend a number of things.

1. The duration of my stay here.
2. The initiation of a number of activities.
3. A visit to Canada.
4. The time of my return to England.

With regard to (1), I should like to have your views and the views of our colleagues in London. There can be no question about the importance of work here provided the conditions are created for such work. Therefore, my return to England must be weighed very carefully. Not in the light of my personal convenience, but in the light of the interest of the movement. (2) In response to a cablegram which B.G. and I received from Palestine, a meeting was held the other day at which plans were laid for a campaign for one million dollars.[5] Discussions are now going on regarding the method to be pursued. It has not yet developed to a stage where I can give you any intelligent account. Within the next week I believe plans will be worked out. The present decision is that we approach the U.J.A. for the allocation of an extra million dollars. If we fail in our plea, we shall seek the consent of the U.J.A. to go out on a special campaign for that sum or perhaps a larger amount. In any event, we are determined to get this extra million for Palestine defence as well as for political work which needs to be done both here and in London. (3) I am being pressed to go to Canada to attend a meeting in the Fall. I am not inclined to do it unless Canada is prepared to undertake a large action in connection with our political work. Freiman[6] is coming to New York next week to discuss the whole matter. I may combine my trip to Canada with a little vacation. In

---

[5] Shertok had wired on the urgent need for funds to increase the *Yishuv's* preparedness should Rommel capture Egypt and invade Palestine (see Ben-Gurion to Shertok, 8 July 1942, W.A.). A figure of £250,000 above the regular K.H. budget till end 1942 was specified in cable of 13 July (Ben-Gurion Archives).

[6] Archibald Jacob Freiman (Biog. Index, Vol. XII). Zionist President in Canada.

that event I shall remain in New York until the beginning of August, and from wherever may proceed to Winnipeg where the meeting is scheduled to be held. (4) Upon the receipt of this letter, I would request that you discuss the whole programme of work and secure an objective reaction regarding the timing of my return to England. I should like you to cable me your opinion so that whatever activities may be in the offing here they should be co-ordinated with the plans in London if it should become necessary for an early return.[7]

I think I have given you a fairly comprehensive account of the situation here. I must confess that I am a bit tired. Give my love to all our friends, and convey to them our warm affections, in which Vera joins me.

As ever,
Ch. Weizmann

Since writing this letter the Office of the Executive has been set up.[8] But with B.G.'s antics, I doubt whether it will last long. Our next meeting is Friday.[9] I shall write you again after that about plans. Please telegraph on receipt of this letter. All the best.

Ch.

313. To Albert S. Goldstein,[1] Sioux City.   *New York, 17 July 1942*
English: T.: W.A.

It gives me real pleasure to send greetings to your State Conference. I know that all of you gathered at this time feel keenly the grave seriousness of the moment, but the steadfastness and resolution of the *Yishuv* in these days of crisis and danger are a reflection of the undying faith of Israel in its imperishable destiny. It is the duty of everyone of us to strengthen the hands and the hearts of the *Yishuv* by doing our maximum. With all good wishes for a successful meeting I am with warm Zionist greetings

Chaim Weizmann

---

[7] See No. 317.

[8] Despite opposition of Ben-Gurion to establishment of a branch of J.A. Executive, W. had formed an *ad hoc* body consisting of himself, Goldmann, Lipsky and Wise, as a central 'political group' in U.S. W., on his own authority, established a branch of the World Zionist Executive early Oct. 1942 (see No. 331, n. 1; No. 365).

[9] For this meeting, see No. 317.

313. [1] Rabbi, President of Z.O.A. in Iowa.

314. To Aaron Rosmarin,[1] New York.   *New York, 17 July 1942*
English: T.W.: Photostat W.A.

My dear Dr. Rosmarin,

I am pleased to have your letter of July 13th informing me of the establishment of "Youth and Education Department" by the *Mizrachi* Organization of America.

Such a department at this time having for its purpose the organization of various forms of Jewish groups in this country is, in my opinion, of considerable importance. The *Mizrachi*, because of its special religious appeal to Jewish youth, may be instrumental in galvanising the scattered and disorganized elements among the youth for Palestine and Zionist work.

I can only wish you the best of success in your endeavours confident in the belief that such a department will make a real contribution to the intensification and strengthening of Zionism in this country.

With Zion's greetings, I am

Cordially yours,

315. To Chona Modzevitzki,[1] New York.   *New York, 20 July 1942*
English: T.W.: C.Z.A. K 12/39.

Dear Chona,

I have heard from various sources that you would like to have a token from me signifying my acknowledgement of your value to the human race, not to mention the Jewish people and the Zionist Movement.

I hasten to give you that sign in the hope that it may, if nothing else, ease some of your burdens during the hot summer days.

With best regards, I am

Cordially yours,
Ch. Weizmann

314. [1] B. 1898. Educator. Founder of *Jewish Spectator* and Yiddish weekly *Der Yid*. Later, settled in Israel.

315. [1] 1888–1966. B. Poland, spent the years 1909–12 in Palestine, thereafter in America. Settled in Israel after establishment of State. For this well-known character of the New York East-Side, and journalist *manqué*, see Weisgal, *op. cit.*, pp. 69–71.

316. To David Ben-Gurion, New York. *New York, 27 July 1942*
English: T.W.: Photostat W.A.

Dear Mr. Ben-Gurion,
You were informed of the meeting which was called of the members of the Executive of the Zionist Organization resident or sojourning in the United States, scheduled to be held at the St. Regis Hotel on July 24, 1942, Room 703 at 3.30 p.m.

The meeting was held as scheduled and we regret that it was not possible for you to attend. We are enclosing here brief minutes of the meeting.[1]

Another meeting will be called shortly after Dr. Weizmann's return from Washington and we hope you will favour us with your presence.

Yours cordially,
Ch. Weizmann
Louis Lipsky

317. To Berl Locker, London. *New York, 27 July 1942*[1]
English: T.W./H.W.: W.A.

Dear Berl,
Nothing really of any great moment has been happening here since my letter to you of July 15th.[2] The weather here has been extremely hot and in this country it means a paralysis of all activities. Most of the Zionists seem to be scattered here and there. However, I did manage to get in a few licks of work. This will be a rather brief account since I am anxious to keep you *au courant* and not allow too much time to elapse between letters.

Met with Ben-Gurion and Nahum Goldmann at the latter's office at the Emergency Committee on the 16th, the day following the dispatch of my letter. During that meeting we had an exchange of views. I came away more or less encouraged, hoping that the ground work had been prepared for cooperative action. Apparently, I was mistaken. In line with what we had discussed at Goldmann's office, I called a meeting of the Executive for last Friday, July 24th, which was the day when I returned to New York after a three days

---

316. [1] Untraced, but see No. 317.

317. [1] From the handwritten portion, subjoined, it will be seen that the letter was delayed to 2 Aug. 1942.
 [2] No. 312.

absence. To my great surprise, I was advised by Goldmann that Ben-Gurion would not appear at the meeting because it was held at my office. Frankly, the only reason it was held here was because it is air-cooled and quite convenient to meet. After the last meeting at Goldmann's office, I was incapacitated for the rest of the day because of the heat and the noise. Everybody had agreed that this was the most convenient and comfortable place to meet, but Ben-Gurion apparently had come to a different conclusion. If, on account of such a triviality the chairman of the Executive refuses to attend a meeting, the whole thing becomes rather annoying and inexplicable. However, the meeting was held. The minutes are enclosed here as well as the notice for the meeting and a copy of the letter which Goldmann, Lipsky and I sent to Ben-Gurion.[3] Another attempt will be made to persuade the gentleman to fall in line with our work here but if that fails, well, I shall cease all further efforts. We shall proceed the best way we know how with the others who are apparently ready to cooperate regardless of Ben-Gurion's decision in the matter.

From the brief and rather sketchy minutes of the meeting, you will observe that we are endeavouring to undertake a systematic piece of work. I hope we shall succeed. Since the meeting, I had another talk with Goldmann in the course of which a certain plan of action has been evolved which, if carried out, would establish the authority of the Executive on a more or less firm basis. I shall write to you more fully about that as the plan will unfold itself.

I am waiting to hear from the President with reference to our second appointment. It may come off this week or perhaps next week, following which it is my intention, as you already know, to go away on a holiday. My future plans here will then depend on the conditions that will be created during my few weeks absence for a continuation of fruitful work in the Fall and Winter. If these conditions are created we shall, of course, remain here. If not, we shall return to England sometime in September.

As I wrote you in my last letter, there was talk of my going to Canada. This is now definite. I shall be in Winnipeg the 6th and 7th of September. Mr. Freiman was here last week and definite arrangements were made for my visit. During my conversation with Freiman, I asked him to send £1,000 to the London office for our political work. This he agreed to do and I presume that you shall have it within the next few days.

Mrs. Archie Silverman came in to see me last week and brought me regards from everyone of you, for which I was grateful. She seems

---

[3] No. 316, not signed by Goldmann.

to be eminently pleased with her visit to England and I think we too have every reason to be pleased with her accomplishments.[4]

I shall write you again as soon as I return from Washington. In the meantime, please convey my affectionate greetings to all our friends.

As ever,
Yours,
Ch. Weizmann

2 Aug. 1942

My dearest Berl,

Isaiah Berlin[5] is leaving for London today and I have given him all sorts of messages. As his memory is good he will no doubt transmit it correctly.

1. B.G. We shall have tomorrow a meeting of the "Executive"— Lipsky, Goldmann, B.G. and myself and we shall decide who is to be invited from the American side.[6] There is not very much choice. B.G. has stiffened on formalities and constitutional punctilios. At this time it seems somewhat strange but here it is. There will never be any more cooperation between us and I'm quite certain that he is developing fascist tendencies and megalomania coupled with political hysteria. I'm awaiting replies to my letters. We are worried that Baffy has never written to us. I hope she is well.[7]

2. Bowman's book and Freda White's article.[8] Although the meeting referred to was held 21 years ago I remember well what has happened. The statement imputed to me is a lie. Sir W. Deedes was sponsoring the meeting and he might remember more.

---

[4] Ida M. Silverman (1882–1973), wife of Archibald Silverman (1880–1956). She was Vice-President of Hadassah 1926–30, of Z.O.A. 1926–28 and Young Judea 1926–28. During the war years she visited Britain on Zionist fund-raising tours.

[5] Biog. Index. Attached to British Ministry of Information, New York 1941–42; British Embassy in Washington 1942–45.

[6] See No. 323.

[7] Blanche Dugdale in fact wrote to W. 21 July 1942 (W.A.) but the letter had evidently not yet reached him. It discussed *inter alia* the appointment of Cranborne, her cousin, as Colonial Secretary, and stated that due to her influence he was more favourably inclined to the Zionists.

[8] Relates to a review in *New Statesman* by Freda White of *Middle East Window*, by Humphrey Bowman (1879–1965), former Director of Education in Palestine. The book alleged that W. had stated to Mandatory officials in Palestine that 'Palestine was to be handed over to the Jews'. The account proceeded: 'One of us asked him what he intended to do with the Arabs. "Those who wish to remain here, of course, can do so", was Dr. W.'s reply. "But for those who do not wish, there is Egypt, there is Syria, and" (pointing with a significant gesture to beyond the horizon of the Moab hills visible from the window) "there is the great desert from which they originally came".' W. wrote that he would ask Sir Wyndham Deedes to confirm his own assertion that this alleged conversation had not in fact taken place (see Lourie to W., 31 July 1942, W.A.). See also Vol. XI, No. 411.

3.   There is something which I would like you to consider with Albert Cohen[9] very carefully. It concerns André Blumel[10]— Blum's secretary. I have seen his sister yesterday—a very charming and most intelligent woman and she gave me the sad history of this case. Although Blumel has had opportunities to leave France he did not avail himself of it because he wanted to remain near Léon Blum. He has applied repeatedly for permission to visit B. but this was refused to him. In the end he has decided to leave with his son (who is a young airman). He crossed the Pyrenees in the winter, had both his feet frozen and nearly lost his life. His friends succeeded in saving him and brought him to Lisbon. There he was seized and forcibly delivered to Spain, imprisoned and gone through hell for 7 weeks. He was then released and brought to France, imprisoned again. Now he is free and lives in Formiguares (Oriental Pyrenees) about 40 km. from Perpignan. It is essential and urgent that he be brought to England. The Free French or the English could do it. She has very little confidence in the Free French and fears that they might not try properly. She would prefer to do it through the English or if it is to be done by the French, the English must know about it and indicate that they are interested in the matter. I thought that perhaps you could take it up with Mr. Bevin or Mr. Creech Jones.[11] Blumel must be saved. His position in France is not secure. I have forgotten to add that just before leaving he has received permission to see Blum and although all was ready for his departure he gave up everything and went to see Blum. After having seen him he left but through this postponement he missed his opportunity and that is why he was caught in Lisbon.

I don't know yet what my plans will be. We shall be heading for a short holiday soon. There are several things pending and America is a slow country.

My love to Baffy, Lewis and Brod and give our love to Malka.[12] You will receive £1,000 from Canada these days. I shall be in Winnipeg in September and hope to send you some more.

Affectionately,

Chaim

Vera sends her love. She is keeping up her courage but at a very heavy cost.

---

[9] B. 1895. French novelist. Formerly a Zionist representative at League of Nations, he was then J.A. representative to Allied governments in London.

[10] 1893–1973. French attorney, *Chef de Cabinet* of Prime Minister Léon Blum 1936–37. Prominent in Left-wing politics, he participated in Jewish communal life after the war and became President of French Zionist Federation in 1955.

[11] Arthur Creech Jones (Biog. Index, Vol. XXII). Lab. M.P. Colonial Secretary 1946–50.

[12] Locker's wife.

318. To Samuel Rosenman, Washington.   *New York, 7 August 1942*
English: T.W.: W.A.

My dear Judge Rosenman,
First of all, let me thank you for the time you were good enough to accord to me while in Washington.[1] I was greatly pleased to have had the opportunity to have your views on the various subjects we discussed.

The memorandum which I promised is now in preparation and will be handed to you by Mr. Ben-Gurion, who is seeing you next week in Washington.[2]

I found on my return from Washington the enclosed memorandum of a conversation between one of our most trusted and intelligent representatives in Palestine (who, incidentally is an American) with Field Marshal Smuts.[3] It was delivered to me by hand from Cairo by one who left there only a week ago. Although rather lengthy, I think it will be worth your while to peruse it carefully. You might, if you consider it wise, since the views come from such a high source, pass on an extract of this memorandum to the President.

With kind personal regards, I am
Cordially yours,
Ch. Weizmann

---

318. [1] On 4 Aug. 1942. Rosenman advised W. not to negotiate his rubber process via the Secretary of Agriculture, Wickard, as the President himself would shortly make a statement. They also discussed the negotiations in train between Zionists and non-Zionists, and possible modifications to the Biltmore programme in order to achieve a broad political consensus. Rosenman requested a memorandum on the defence needs of Palestine, so that he could discuss the Jewish Army scheme with the President.

[2] Copy in W.A.

[3] Record of a discussion 17 July 1942 with Gershon Agronsky, editor of *Palestine Post* (W.A.). Smuts had been most emphatic that Britain intended to make a stand in the Middle East, and would not withdraw, as some thought, further into the Empire. He thought the only solution for the Palestine problem would be its absorption into a Middle East Federation of Arab States, in which the Jews would have a guaranteed place. Having studied the White Paper of 1939 carefully, Smuts stated, he had decided it was not a workable document, and would not affect future policy. Further, it was imperative that the Jews 'stopped the fighting in Palestine', i.e., ceased opposition to the Mandatory Administration. He informed Agronsky that he had discussed the question of the Jewish Force with the authorities in Cairo, who were not opposed on principle. But there was a limit to the people one could draw on without disrupting the regular war organization. Smuts thought that the Jews in Palestine were doing well in the war effort, but the Jewish Army scheme was fraught with too many difficulties.

319. To Susanne Blum, New York.   *New York, 9 August 1942*
English: T.W.: Photostat W.A.

Dear Mrs. Blum,
   I should have written to you earlier, but I was out of town. This is to let you know that I have written to London urgently and have sent them an extract of the documents, which you left with me.[1] The matter is in good hands there and I hope to hear of some results very soon. I shall, of course, communicate with you immediately. My movements for the next week are as yet not certain and as soon as I know I shall get in touch with you.
   Meanwhile I remain with kindest regards,
                                   Very sincerely yours,
                                   Chaim Weizmann

320. To Benjamin Bloch, Rehovot.   *New York, 11 August 1942*
English: T.W./H.W.: W.A.

Dear Dr. Bloch,
   Your letter to Mrs. Weizmann of May 24th has been received, and I note with regret that it took 6 months to give us the information regarding the upkeep of the garden and the orange grove.[1] Our main concern is that the grove should be kept, as we do not want the trees to perish. It has to be done, however, at the lowest possible cost, and I would ask you to advise us by cable as to the minimum required expenditure for wages, manure and irrigation. When we gave the General[2] the use of our house, we naturally assumed that he would pay:
   a)   For rent of the telephone, and not only for the actual calls made.
   b)   For the water and electricity he is using, and that he would also contribute to the
   c)   Minimum upkeep of the garden.
We are now faced with a bill which we really cannot afford to pay, and with the painful dilemma either of paying a large sum of money for things which we do not enjoy or letting the garden perish, and

---

319. [1] She was the sister of Blumel, and left with W. documents on his predicament—see No. 317.

320. [1] Details given here were furnished by Bloch at V.W.'s request in a letter dated 17 Dec. 1941 (W.A.).
   [2] Gen. George Clark, former G.O.C. Palestine.

lose the expenditure made over the last 3 years, which amounted to something like 1,500 Pounds. If the military authorities would have requisitioned my house, they would have had to assume responsibility for everything, and no costs would have been incurred by me. On the contrary, I would have been entitled to compensation. Now that I have placed the house at the disposal of the General, free of charge, I can certainly expect that he would make himself responsible for the upkeep of the garden and for the guarding of the house. His soldiers could easily do it. In that case no workmen should be paid by us except Epstein[3] as, naturally enough, the General may not want to look after the orange grove. This, Epstein can do with the minimum of expense, and we can pay for. As to the water-pump, I cannot understand why its repair should cost 150 pounds when the purchasing price amounted to only 100 pounds.

Despite the troubles and anxieties with which I am beset, I have never for a moment ceased to think of and work for the Institute and the comfort of its staff, and therefore I have the right to claim that the Administration of the Institute should look after my property. I have also received your letter regarding the dismissal of Haber.[4] I have the suspicion that he has been treated harshly because he is not a member of the *Histadrut*. He has been a faithful servant for many years, who has never failed in his duty and worked to the satisfaction of everybody.

In view of the suggestion that the general would take care of the guard of the estate and of looking after the garden, there is no necessity for Abrasha,[5] in my opinion, to live on the premises, and no doubt the *Histadrut* could find another job for him. As for Haber, I can do nothing from here except to appeal through you to Eisenberg[6] that he should be treated fairly.

With kind regards,
Yours sincerely,
Ch. Weizmann

Thanks for telegram re pharmaceuticals.[7] I'm surprised that the sodium has not yet come.

---

[3] Foreman of the orange grove.
[4] Moshe Haber, W.'s gardener, was in fact given another post at Sieff Institute that year.
[5] A domestic watchman.
[6] Apparently a staff manager.
[7] The factory had begun production May 1942.

321. To Moshe Shertok, Jerusalem.   *New York, 12 August 1942*
English: T.W.: Photostat W.A.

Dear Moshe,

I am taking advantage of George Britt's[1] departure for the Middle East to send you these few lines and to enclose here a copy of a letter to Berl of July 15th,[2] which I believe will give you some fair idea of the situation here. Since then I have been in Washington again and have seen various people and there is really nothing of any great moment to add. The main purpose of my repeated visits to Washington is to keep the interest alive and see the people that matter most.

With regard to Ben-Gurion, nothing material has changed except that we had one meeting of the members of the Executive here and in due course of time you shall probably receive the minutes. I understand he is now making arrangements to return to Palestine shortly and no doubt he will tell you his own story, whatever it may be worth. All I can say is, neither here nor in London has he been an unqualified blessing.

I was glad to see the attitude you have taken in the new developments concerning the Jewish Force.[3] My view, all along has been, on the basis of conversations I have had with various people, that some such development will take place sooner or later.

As for our personal situation, there is nothing, unfortunately, that I can say. We are still wavering between hope and despair. We have made no plans for the immediate future. I am expecting to see the President again, following which, some definite plans will be made.[4]

Give my love to Kaplan and other friends,

As ever,
Yours,

---

321. [1] Unidentified.

[2] No. 312.

[3] On 6 Aug. 1942 the Colonial Secretary announced formation of a Palestine Regiment, based on units of the Palestine Buffs already serving in Palestine. The Regiment was to be normally employed in Palestine or adjacent countries for the defence of Palestine (see statement in *House of Commons Debates, 5th Series,* Vol. 382, col. 1271). Wingate was debarred from command of any Jewish Force due to his professed sympathy for Zionism (Sir James Grigg to Ismay, 20 Oct. 1942, in P.R.O., Prem. 4/51/9), though the reason given to J.A. was that he could not be spared from his work of training guerillas in India (Linton cable to W., 30 July, Ben-Gurion Archives). The J.A., taking the view that the Regiment was to become a combat unit, initially gave its full support to further mobilization. Disillusion followed on realisation that the British intended the Regiment to fulfil static guard duties only.

[4] The meeting took place only at the end of W.'s stay in U.S., May 1943.

322. To Leon Gellman,[1] **New York.**   *New York, 13 August 1942*
English: T.W.: Photostat W.A.

My dear Mr. Gellman,

Before I embark again on my daily grind, I feel impelled to express my deepfelt appreciation to you, Rabbi Gold[2] and Mr. Bublick[3] for the manner in which you made it possible for me to join in prayer with our fellow-Jews and give expression to our oneness and solidarity in these days of trial.

I was deeply moved by the dignity and simplicity of the services and felt at one with all of my fellow-Jews wherever they may be and however they may be suffering. It gave me inner strength, as I know it gave you and Jews throughout the world who joined with us on this day of fast and prayer.[4]

I was so completely recaptured by the atmosphere of genuine Jewishness, that I felt moved to pen these words to you. Please accept again my thanks to you, Rabbi Gold and Mr. Bublick.

In the hope of Zion restored,

         Cordially yours,

323. To Berl Locker, London.   *New York, 18 August 1942*
English: T.W./H.W.: W.A.

Dear Berl,

Within a few hours I shall be leaving for a holiday. As usual, it has been delayed beyond all reasonable time. However, I have the satisfaction of knowing that the work has been more or less cleared up and that I had an opportunity to spend a few days with Bergmann.

Although my holiday ends on September 3rd, for all intents and purposes, I shall not be back in New York until the 9th or 10th of September as I am leaving for Winnipeg on the day I return to the city.

Since my last writing, I have been to Washington several times,

---

322. [1] 1887–1973. Executive Secretary American *Mizrachi* 1914–17; its National Vice-President, then President, 1930–39; moved to Israel in 1949 as chairman World *Mizrachi* Organization.

[2] Wolf Gold (1889–1956). President American *Mizrachi* 1932–35. Settled in Palestine 1935, represented *Mizrachi* on J.A. Executive from 1945; on Jewish delegation to United Nations 1946.

[3] Gedalia Bublick (1875–1948). Yiddish journalist, among founders of American Jewish Congress and of *Mizrachi* in U.S., served on Executive of W.Z.O. 1919–26 and J.A. Council from 1929.

[4] The Orthodox rabbis of U.S. and Britain had proclaimed the day preceding the month of Ellul (12 Aug.) as a Day of Fasting and Supplication for Jews in danger of extermination.

primarily in connection with chemical matters. I, of course, utilized my presence in the Capital to see several people, notably, Rosenman and Morgenthau, with both of whom I had long and interesting conversations. I dictated a memorandum on these conversations when they were still fresh in my memory. A copy is being enclosed here.[1]

During my last visit to Washington, at the invitation of the Baruch Committee,[2] I also had occasion to meet Eugene Meyer.[3] You will remember him from the early Brandeis days when he was active and helpful. Although a Republican, he is rather influential in Washington, being a publisher of an important paper there. We had quite a friendly chat. He indicated a willingness to be of help. I am to meet him soon again.

The rubber situation has kept me quite busy the last few weeks. What with the confusion here and going to and fro, it has not been a very easy task. What it will all come to, it is difficult to say. The whole problem has been canalized into the Baruch Committee with Professors Conant and Compton, as the scientific experts. My advice has been sought on various aspects of the situation. I hope it will prove valuable. Whatever else happens, the scientific work has opened many avenues for me which, as you will probably gather, I am not neglecting to use for our own affairs. They may prove decisive at the opportune time.

Concerning our own internal affairs, there has been very little change since I wrote you last. There was one meeting of the Executive with B.G. present. The minutes are not yet available but they will be sent to you in due course of time.[4] I am sending you, however, a copy of a letter which I wrote to Goldmann following the meeting.[5] Perhaps before I leave for Canada, we may have one more meeting, although it is not certain. There is a possibility of

---

323. [1] For the meeting with Rosenman, see No. 318, n. 1. At a meeting 5 Aug. 1942, Morgenthau advised W. that he had had a most unsatisfactory talk with the President regarding the Jewish Force. The President felt that so long as the military situation in the Middle East did not improve, any statement on his part would only make matters worse. Morgenthau stated that the American military experts did not believe the British were using their forces correctly in the Western Desert, and confirmed the British claim that there was a shortage of equipment (record in W.A.).

[2] For the Baruch Committee, see No. 310, n. 2.

[3] 1875–1959. Banker, Government official. Owner of *Washington Post* and *Times-Herald*; first President of International Bank for Reconstruction and Development.

[4] Untraced.

[5] Dated 11 Aug. (Ben-Gurion Archives). This requested insertion of an addendum to the Minutes of the Executive meeting to the effect that W. repudiated Ben-Gurion's assertion that W. 'had kept him in the dark'. W. cited many examples of his reporting to Ben-Gurion, either at meetings attended by others or alone. Ben-Gurion had also alleged that London was being neglected, and W. wished a cable of 9 Aug., received from Locker, to be inserted in the Minutes stipulating the importance of W.'s remaining in U.S.

B.G.'s leaving for Palestine soon. I hope nothing interferes with these plans. *Dai lachkimo beremizo.*[6]

The conciliatory atmosphere in the Revisionist camp, both in Jerusalem and London, and the statement by Moshe,[7] are having their repercussions here. Several editorials have already appeared in the Yiddish press greeting the imminent outbreak of "peace". It has been suggested that it might be useful to have some talks here with that group. The suggestion has come from our side as well as from the Revisionists. The present head of the Revisionists in the United States is Natanyahu, the son of the late Rabbi Millikofsky,[8] whom you probably knew. Natanyahu, I am told, is a very able and reasonable young man and a fine writer. Do you think it would be worth while my meeting with these people and exploring the situation here?

At the first opportunity, I shall take up with the Emergency Committee the matter of the distribution here of Namier's book. Mrs. Weizmann received a copy of the book only a few days ago. No one seems to have it here although Lourie is expecting a couple of copies shortly. I wish you would see to it that a number of copies are sent to me forthwith.

For an "erev"[9] holiday letter, I think this will do. Unless something of moment occurs between now and my return from Canada, you shall probably not be hearing from me until then.

Give my love to Baffy, Lewis and other friends.

My affectionate regards to Brod. I propose to write to him soon.

Ch. W.

324. To Ellis Island Immigration and Naturalization Service, New York.

New York, 24 August 1942

English: T.W.: Photostat W.A.

Gentlemen,

Please be advised that on Thursday, September 3rd, I am leaving via Trans-Canada Airlines for Toronto and thence to Winnipeg to

---

[6] 'A hint to the wise is sufficient.' (Aramaic; *Midrash*).

[7] Shertok had on 9 Aug. 1942 issued a call to the *Yishuv* to pray for the victory of the Allied armies (the Western Front had stabilized at El Alamein, end June 1942), and to enlist into the Jewish units of the British Army, into the Women's Service, the Auxiliary Police, and for security duties. Shertok's statement had closed with a general call to the *Yishuv* to mobilize all its manpower and materials (W.A.).

[8] I.e., Benzion Netanyahu, b. 1910. Executive Director, New Zionist Organization in U.S. 1941–48; Editor-in-chief *Encyclopaedia Hebraica*, 1948–62; professor at Dropsie College, Philadelphia 1957–68, later at Denver and Cornell. His father, Nathan Mileykovsky (1879–1935), a well-known preacher in Poland, settled in Palestine.

[9] Hebr.: 'eve of'.

fill several speaking engagements. I shall stay in Toronto overnight on September 3rd and take the plane for Winnipeg on September 4th and return to the United States the 9th or 10th of September.

Will you please be good enough to send my Form 257, which you have in your possession, to the American Consulate in Winnipeg so that I may pick it up there in order to return to the States.

Yours very truly,

[In January 1942 the Nazi regime had decided to implement its 'final solution' to the Jewish problem, the systematic slaughter of the Jews. The first reliable and accurate information about the new policy seems to have reached the West in Aug. 1942, sent by Gerhard Riegner, representative of the World Jewish Congress in Geneva, to Stephen Wise. Eye-witness accounts from exchanged and escaped prisoners, and fugitives, especially from Poland, endorsed the reports. On 17 Dec. 1942 the fact was officially accepted, and the Allied Governments issued a formal condemnation of 'this bestial policy of cold-blooded extermination'.]

325. To the Zionist Review, London.   *New York, 4 September 1942*
English: T.: W.A.

In world at war sufferings European Jewry at hands of dictatorship unexampled for cold-blooded and ruthless savagery continue write terrible chapter in history man's relations with man. Nazis foredoomed [to] extinction but leaving in wake horror and misery untold. For great masses our people Palestine still remains only light in present and only hope for future. We shall continue our struggle for regeneration *Eretz Israel* confident in victory of forces [of] freedom, justice, and determined that out [of] chaos shall come new and worthy life for Jewish people in own land.

Chaim Weizmann

326. To Abba Hillel Silver and Meyer Weisgal, New York.
New York, 7 September 1942

English: T.: W.A.

Deeply touched by your kind telegram[1] and encouraged by successful outcome great conference. My warmest congratulations and thanks to you both and to all friends.

Affectionately,
Chaim Weizmann

326. [1] Silver and Weisgal had, on behalf of a Zionist Conference in Michigan, transmitted a message that it 'appreciates your great leadership for the cause of Jewish liberation and wishes you a speedy recovery and a long life.' The conference resolved to establish a colony of 1,000 dunams in Palestine (6 Sept. 1942, W.A.). On 25 Aug., W. had been admitted to Mount Sinai Hospital, New York, suffering from nervous exhaustion. After some two weeks, he went for convalescence to Grossingers, the resort centre in the Catskills founded 1914 by Jennie and Harry Grossinger, noted Zionist supporters.

327. To Abraham Granovsky,[1] Jerusalem.

Greenwich, Conn., 11 September 1942
English: T.: W.A.

In solidarity with *Yishuv* join in tribute [to] Menahem Ussishkin.[2] The call of the land summons us. Dunams of good earth is most fitting memorial imperishably written in *Eretz Israel*. To the *Keren Kayemeth* that he served and loved most, entire movement dedicates itself to the great unfinished task. Let us resolve not to rest until a free Jewish people established on free Jewish land. I send through *Keren Kayemeth* my greetings best wishes, happy New Year. My heart is with *Yishuv*.

Chaim Weizmann

328. To Felix Frankfurter, [? Washington].

Ferndale, N.Y., 25 September 1942
English: T.W.: Photostat W.A.

My dear Felix,

Forgive me for answering so belatedly your letter of September 2nd.[1] You may have heard perhaps that I was laid up in the hospital and I am now here trying to recuperate.

Many thanks for sending me the cutting from *The New Statesman and Nation*. The Bowman story is certainly distorted. Fortunately Sir Wyndham Deedes was present at the meeting to which he refers and I have sent him a note asking him to correct the Bowman statement.[2]

Much love from both of us.

P.S. I am afraid the Baruch report is disappointing.[3]

---

327. [1] Later Granott (1890–1962). Economist, settled in Jerusalem 1922; Managing Director of J.N.F. from 1941, Chairman from 1945, President from 1960. Founding-chairman, Progressive (Independent Liberal) Party in 1948 and member of First *Knesset*.
   [2] It was first anniversary of Ussishkin's death.

328. [1] Untraced.
   [2] See No. 317, n. 8. Deedes confirmed W.'s denial in a letter to Namier 2 Sept. (W.A.).
   [3] See No. 310, n. 2.

329. To Louis Lipsky, New York.   *Ferndale, N.Y., 27 September 1942*
English: T.W.: Photostat W.A.

Meyer brought me a copy of your letter to Kaplan.[1]
My person apart, I think you have stated the case clearly and co-
gently. That has been our policy for more than 20 years and is now
in danger of being disturbed by a contemplated action—whatever
its effect upon me personally—which I cannot describe as other but
utterly irresponsible.

The place here is lovely. I am making considerable progress in
regaining my health and strength. I hope it will be possible for you,
Wise and Goldmann to come up here real soon, perhaps next week-
end or a few days later. Be in touch with Meyer and he will make
the necessary arrangements.

With warmest regards to Mrs. Lipsky and yourself,

As always,

330. To Benjamin V. Cohen, Washington.
Ferndale, N.Y., 28 September 1942
English: Or. Copy. T.W.: W.A.

My dear Ben,
You will find at the head of this letter our new address. We have
been here now about four days and have really enjoyed it. The
weather has been, with the exception of yesterday, quite good and
invigorating. It is dry and although it is a purely Jewish district we

---

329. [1] This, 23 Sept. 1942 (W.A.), warned J.A. Executive in Jerusalem that Ben-Gurion's
activities in U.S. had impaired W.'s leadership and caused the breaking-up of the Zionist
front there. Whereas Lipsky had the impression that W. represented official Zionist policy,
Ben-Gurion had given the impression that he himself represented J.A. Executive in U.S. for
political purposes. This had created a confusion of authority. Ben-Gurion's strange behaviour
had reached its climax, according to Lipsky, in the development of the fixed idea that W.
could not be trusted to conduct political negotiations and should be asked to resign. Moreover, Ben-Gurion had communicated his views, both officially and informally, to various
groups in the Zionist movement, and had thus become a rallying point for all who nursed
grudges against W. In Lipsky's opinion, W. was indispensable in U.S., and no real substitute
leader had yet emerged. Despite American Zionists' pleas to Ben-Gurion that his complaints
could be remedied by the establishment of an Executive of members resident in U.S. with
whom W. could cooperate, Ben-Gurion had left the U.S. evidently determined to propound
W.'s resignation to the Executive and the Actions Committee. Lipsky considered that this
step did not enjoy the support of any U.S. Zionist group, and would be disastrous. Ben-
Gurion's activities were not only bringing to life the old anti-W. group, but might well revive the sleeping antagonism towards Labour Zionism. Ben-Gurion had left U.S. 18 Sept.
1942.

have been living in seclusion as the people here have given us a cottage to ourselves and have made us comfortable in every respect. I am beginning to take mild walks and feeling fairly well. Perhaps when you come for your week-end to New York you might find a possibility of paying us a visit here. We shall put you up and you will be more than welcome.

Before leaving New York I had a visit of a certain Mr. Patton and his friends. He is the President of the National Farmers Union and anxious to manufacture butadiene from grain. I have seen them for only a short while, but they stayed in New York for several days and dealt with my brother-in-law Mr. Blumenfeld, to whom they wrote a letter, of which copy is enclosed.[1] I would be most grateful to you if you would let me know what sort of people they are and whether cooperation with them would not involve us in a political controversy, which I would not like to face.[2]

With affectionate regards,
Yours very sincerely,

331. To Meyer W. Weisgal, New York.

English: T.W./H.W.: W.A.   *Ferndale, N.Y., 6 October 1942*

Meyer dear,

Very many thanks for your note of October 5th. I have read all the enclosures with the greatest interest and am returning them to you as you may want them all for your files.

I think the memorandum of Saturday's meeting renders correctly the decisions which we have taken and does not require any further corrections on my part.[1]

I have never said anything in the American press about the Com-

---

330. [1] Untraced.
   [2] No reply traced. W. did not enter into any agreement with this group.

331. [1] Weisgal's note of 5 Oct. enclosed the record of a meeting held Saturday 3 Oct. at Ferndale, when W., Wise, Goldmann, Lipsky and Weisgal decided to establish a branch of the World Zionist Executive in U.S., consisting of W., Goldmann and Lipsky. Shertok was to be invited to join the Executive in New York for several months. Approval of this move would be sought from Jerusalem (see following letter). It was decided to co-opt Wise, Silver and Levinthal, and to send an American delegation to Palestine, consisting of Silver, Levinthal and Monsky. Wise, as Zionist co-chairman of the negotiating committee with the non-Zionists, was to seek a meeting with Wertheim, finally to determine the current status of their negotiations, and should the negotiations collapse, the Zionists should immediately organize a united front on a wider and more democratic basis. The meeting decided to reconvene at regular intervals (W.A.).

mandos, to which Linton refers in his cablegram.[2] The only man who might know something about this is either Adamic[3] (who, as you may remember, spoke to us about such a possibility) or Ciechanovsky, the Polish Ambassador. We might inquire from these two people and see what can be done.

It might be useful, perhaps, if you would make inquiries from William Hard[4] about an article in the *Reader's Digest*[5]—but you know how difficult it is for me to write at present.

I was very much interested in the interview between Shertok and Willkie[6] for two reasons: (a) His notions about immigration which, curiously enough, are identical with mine; (b) he found it rather difficult to present to Willkie a plausible case with regard to the Arabs. It might be that Willkie does not understand very much about our business, but I believe he is not quite satisfied with the answer, that we shall get a majority and then we shall treat the Arabs well. It may be that this is the right answer and the only answer we can give, but we might make up our mind that it won't go down easily, even with a great many people who are friendly to us. And supposing the Arabs are not prepared to give up their claim to one small corner—who is going to force them to do so? I am quite sure that Mr. Willkie felt the weakness of the situation here. We shall find it out when he comes back.

We have had bad weather the last two days here, but it seems that there may be a hope for improvement tomorrow. Still, we were able to take walks, even in this unsatisfactory weather.

We expect the Blumenfelds will come here during this week—and

---

[2] Untraced. Evidently relates to the commando scheme to be led by Wingate. The J.A. was then considering a plan for parachuting Jewish commandos into Poland for resistance and rescue work. W. proposed co-ordination with the Polish Government-in-Exile, which was itself in contact with the Polish resistance. No further correspondence on this issue traced.

[3] Louis Adamic (1899–1951). Slav-American author.

[4] Unidentified.

[5] Weisgal had proposed in his letter that W. write an article for *Reader's Digest*, which had a readership of several millions.

[6] Wendell Willkie (1892–1944). Lawyer. Republican candidate for Presidency of U.S. 1940. Shertok had met Willkie in Palestine 1 Sept. 1942. In reply to a question on immigration, Shertok stated that he hoped for an annual immigration of 100,000 to continue for 'many years', and although he foresaw a link with the Arab States, it would not necessarily be through federation, for in the early stages of its development a Jewish Palestine would not be able to transfer its sovereignty to a federation. Willkie asked about the Zionists' relations with the Arabs, and was told that while everyday relations on the local level were good, Shertok did not expect the Arabs to agree initially to large-scale Jewish immigration into Palestine. Shertok's impression of Willkie was that he was well-disposed and good-hearted but with a primitive approach (Shertok report, 15 Sept. 1942, in Vol. 36 of J.A. Executive Minutes, C.Z.A.).

in that case you might possibly ask Naiditch to come next week.
Much love to you and Shirley[7] from both of us, I am

Yours ever

Ch. W.

I have written to Judge Levinthal.[8]
I think the telegram to Palestine[9] is alright.

332. To the Jewish Agency Executive, Jerusalem.

Ferndale, N.Y., 6 October 1942

English: T.: W.A.

Concurrence [of] Wise have determined in best interest movement
[to] establish here branch Executive. Request your approval. Wise,
Silver, Levinthal or Szold will be asked to join in deliberations
and decisions. Earnestly request that as soon as possible and practicable Shertok join us here for at least several months. Cable
decision immediately.
Chaim Weizmann, Nahum Goldmann, Louis Lipsky.[1]

333. To Maurice Hexter,[1] New York. *Ferndale, N.Y., 9 October 1942*
English: T.W.: Photostat W.A.

Thank you very much for your kind note.[2] I hope to be back in
New York at the end of this month, and I shall not fail to get in
touch with you almost at once, so that we might have a talk. Meanwhile, we have heard from Palestine about the effect which Ben-
Gurion's reports have produced there.[3]

---

[7] Weisgal's wife.
[8] This, 5 Oct. 1942 (W.A.), regretted that W.'s health was unlikely to permit him to attend
the Zionist Convention, but he would send a message. He invited Levinthal to visit him.
[9] See following letter.

332. [1] In reply, J.A. Executive cabled 19 Oct. urging W. to make an early visit to Palestine. He had been absent for three years, and a visit was essential for the co-ordination of their
efforts in London, U.S. and Palestine. Further, it was important for W. to obtain a first-hand
impression of Palestine's war-time achievements. (For text, see Weisgal to London Executive,
8 Jan. 1943, W.A.).

333. [1] Biog. Index, Vol. XIV. Non-Zionist member of J.A. Executive 1929–38; executive
Vice-President, Federation of Jewish Philanthropies of New York from 1941.
[2] Untraced.
[3] Transferring his battle against W. to Palestine, Ben-Gurion submitted to J.A. Executive

Thanking you once more for your great kindness, I remain
Affectionately yours,

334. To Benjamin V. Cohen, Washington.

Ferndale, N.Y., 12 October 1942

English: T.W.: Photostat W.A.

I have missed reading the announcement in the press to the effect that you have a new and very important appointment,[1] but I was informed about it by various people, who have been talking to me since. I do not know what the scope of the new work is, but I understand that it is very important and I am quite sure that it is certainly good for the Government to have a man like you in a post of this significance. I do sincerely trust that it will give you some satisfaction, and that it will make you feel that you are pulling your weight in this time of emergency. On the other hand, I am saddened by the thought that we shall see less of you than we did in the past, and that you may not be able, perhaps, to come over here as you thought before. Please let me know.

I understand that you are meeting with some friends of Israel Sieff's tomorrow, Tuesday, and I hope that this meeting will inaugurate the creation of a small group who might be helpful to us in Washington in these critical times. I feel that it is most important, as our representation in the capital is very weak now.

You will be interested to hear that our experiments in Terre Haute are going on very satisfactorily indeed, and I reckon that in a month's time from now we shall have demonstrated the feasibility both of making butadiene by our method, and of producing isoprene quite easily.[2] When Bergmann comes over next, you might per-

a comprehensive report on his activities in U.S., and on the Biltmore Programme as he understood it. A majority of the Executive endorsed his position, and brought the Biltmore resolutions before the Smaller Actions Committee 15 Oct., and for final approval 10 Nov. 1942. As sole authoritative interpreter of the Programme at these meetings, Ben-Gurion stressed the need to transfer two million Jews, in which assistance from U.S. would be decisive (Yehuda Bauer, *From Diplomacy to Resistance*, Philadelphia 1970, pp. 242–43). See also Introduction. Ben-Gurion pressed the Executive severely to restrict W.'s political freedom, and this occasioned extended controversy between Jerusalem and New York (see Nos. 340, 341). Shertok visited New York early 1943 in an attempt to smooth out relations between the two leaders—see Vol. XXI.

334. [1] Director of Office of Economic Stabilization.

    [2] W.'s process was being tested by Commercial Solvents (a company with which W. had been associated for some 20 years) in their plant at Terre Haute, Indiana.

Deportation of Jews
to the death camps.

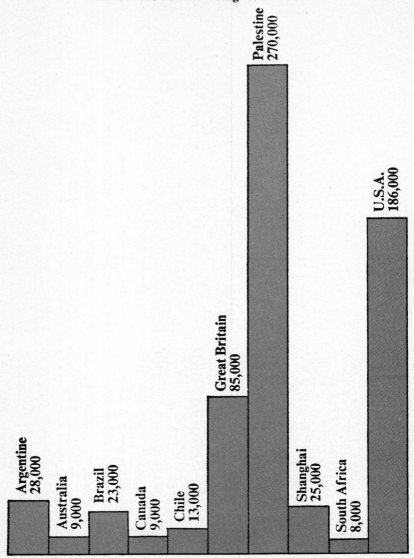

Note: No figures are given for the U.S.S.R., as many fleeing from Eastern Europe were either overtaken by the German invaders and perished or returned subsequently to their homes, mainly Poland and Rumania. The Palestine figure excludes 'illegals', about 100,000. Peak figures for U.S.A. were in 1939-42. Figures for France are not available, as many refugees were either in transit or perished in deportation. The British total includes about one-third who moved to other countries. Shanghai admitted Jews without visa, but the total includes some 3,000 deported there by Japan.

haps care to meet him, and I shall let you know in time when this happens.

With affectionate regards from both of us, and all good wishes for your new work, I am

335. To Morris Eisenman, New York.

Ferndale, N.Y., 12 October 1942

English: T.W.: Photostat W.A.

My dear Moishe,

May I again call on you for a favour, which I know you will be glad to do with your usual kind cooperation. Next Friday a rather important gentleman in the service of the British Government will come, with his wife, to spend the week-end with us here.[1] I should be very grateful if you could lend your car to bring them here, and I am asking Meyer Weisgal to get in touch with you to learn whether this can be arranged. Meyer has the information as to where these people are to be picked up.

This place is really wonderfully good for us. I feel stronger daily, and look forward, early in November, to return to my activities.

With affectionate regards, and thanking you for your kindness, I am

336. To John G. Winant, London.

Ferndale, N.Y., 19 October 1942

English: T.: W.A.

As President World Zionist Organization and Jewish Agency for Palestine [I] warmly second invitation cabled you by Wise and Neumann deliver brief radio address connection 25th anniversary Balfour Declaration as was done last year by Prime Minister Smuts. I venture to suggest your address may serve to cement Anglo-American friendship. To the Jewish people now suffering wholesale massacre at Nazi hands any message which your sympathy will dictate on this occasion will come as a gleam of hope for a better future.[1]

Chaim Weizmann

---

335. [1] This was Col. Wren. It is not known for what purpose he was visiting W. He carried back correspondence from W. to London.

336. [1] See Winant to W., 31 Oct. 1942 (W.A.), regretfully declining the request; his sentiments regarding the persecution and sufferings of the Jewish people had been made public on several occasions.

337. To Arthur Lourie, New York.   *Ferndale, N.Y., 20 October 1942*
English: Or. Copy. T.W.: W.A.

I thank you for your note of the 19th, and for sending me the
Zionist Review.[1] There is very little which I would like to add to
my statement as reprinted in the *Review*. Perhaps it might be useful to insert in the speech some remark with regard to Lowdermilk's
article about the Jordan Valley project.[2] Unfortunately, I do not
have the article before me, but I think you can get it in the office,
and something like the attached insertion might be added to my
speech in the *Zionist Review* on Page 10, following the sentence
"The mind of the Arabs became confused." You might edit it
slightly, and I think it would form a valuable addition to this article.

I am gradually improving and hope to be back in New York the
first week in November.

C.W.

338. To David Weizmann, Walton-on-Thames.
Ferndale, N.Y., 20 October 1942
English: T.: W.A.

Dearest David, love and kisses to you on second birthday. All good
wishes from Grandma and Grandpa

Vera Chaim Weizmann

339. To Stephen S. Wise, New York.   *Ferndale, N.Y., 21 October 1942*
English: Or. Copy. T.W.: W.A.

My dear Stephen,
I am most grateful to you for your dear letter of October 19th,
but am very sorry to hear that Louise[1] has not been in good health

---

337. [1] Weekly organ of E.Z.F. This contained W.'s speech to the Biltmore Conference,
which the London office intended reprinting as an introduction to a book of essays commemorating 25th anniversary of Balfour Declaration—see *The Jewish National Home 1917–
1942*, ed. Paul Goodman, London 1943.

[2] Walter Clay Lowdermilk (1888–1974), world authority on soil reclamation and conservation; chief of U.S. Agricultural Department's soil conservation service. He had investigated irrigation and soil reclamation projects in Palestine 1938, and his findings were
published in *Palestine, Land of Promise,* a book that argued that Palestine might one day
support three million people. His recommendation for a National Water Carrier (based on
his own experience as Director of Tennessee Valley Authority) was later implemented by the
Israel Government. He lived in Israel 1955–58 as head of Agricultural Engineering Department at Haifa Technion.

339. [1] Wise's wife.

and had to keep to her bed for a week. I am afraid that my report about Vera is not very satisfactory either. She has given us a great deal of anxiety of late, but I hope she is on the road to improvement.

Your report about the Convention is most gratifying, and it is a real milestone on the road of Zionist development in this country, that the Hadassah had to feel the moral strength of Zionism and that the leadership of this organization had to take the orders of the rank and file.[2] I do hope that the effect of it will be lasting and find expression in its actual performance in Palestine.

You were most kind in suggesting to the Administration to send me a message, and also to speak about me, and I am deeply grateful to you for having given proof of your friendship to me on so many occasions during my stay in this country, and particularly at this time.[3] It does one's heart good to feel the warm atmosphere of friendship, particularly during times when one's moral and physical state is somewhat low.

I did not realize that you have to go to Mexico, and of course I understand that you will not visit me tomorrow together with the others, and we shall miss you, but with such a heavy schedule before you, you had better not put yourself out too much.

The Libman dinner is causing me some heartache, as he has personally asked me to come and take part in it.[4] I would have loved to do it for many reasons: first, I have a warm regard for him as a scientist and as a friend, and he has been extremely good to me during these difficult days—but it would mean cutting short my stay here, and if I speak at the Libman dinner I could not possibly ignore the second of November function[5] in New York, and I really do not feel equal to it. I shall therefore be only too happy to send you a message[6] which you will be good enough to read for me.

I have never feared that B.G.'s antics would make any serious impression on Zionist opinion in this country. He has behaved so

---

[2] Wise wrote (19 Oct. 1942, W.A.) that the extraordinary Convention of Z.O.A. with Hadassah, 16 Oct., registered a 'real revolution in Hadassah', in that it had become much less intractable and much more cooperative with the official Z.O.A. line, particularly in regard to Hadassah's past connection with Judah Magnes' *Ihud* movement and its undertaking to oppose *Ihud* policy in future. As to Magnes and *Ihud*, see No. 358 and ns. there.

[3] Wise has asked the newly-elected Zionist administration, as its first act, to send W. a message of affectionate goodwill—done with 'utter enthusiasm and by a rising vote'. Wise also reassured W. that Ben-Gurion had made 'no dent whatever, indeed not even impacted upon, Zionist opinion in America'.

[4] Emanuel Libman (Biog. Index, Vol. XVI). Physician, chairman of American Committee for Medical Development of Hebrew University. W. was under his professional care.

[5] To mark the 25th anniversary of Balfour Declaration.

[6] W.A.

foolishly that, regardless of whatever opinion Zionists may be, he has simply shocked the common sense of the people. I am not so sure about his influence in Palestine in certain circles. That does not worry me either, but it does introduce an element of disharmony and disunity at a time when all should be on deck and pull together. I had read his statement made before the Office Committee in my absence.[7] He has mostly repeated the charges which he made at the meeting in your office; but he has added a few more. The curious fact which strikes one about it all is this: All my sins, which he has enumerated, were committed in London during his stay there. Why did he not ever raise all these points in London, where all the facts could be verified and tested and where there were many witnesses to my performance? He has never as much as mentioned, during his lengthy stay there, one syllable, and he brought it all up suddenly here where I have neither the correspondence nor the minutes of our meetings, nor is there anybody else, apart from myself, who could disprove the distorted statements which he has been making. But leaving this part of his speech alone, I was appalled to read his views on the future immigration policy. And here it seems strange that he should have kept a matter of such fundamental importance to himself all the time and blurted it out in a few hysterical sentences just several hours before he had to leave the country. Here is the central point of the whole Zionist program—Immigration. B.G. has some revolutionary ideas about it, and he has not chosen to discuss it with his friends in America, of whom he expects primarily the carrying of the burden in carrying out this program, excepting at the very last moment, when nobody had a chance of going into the matter a little more carefully.

As to his views about the role of the Jewish Army, of which I heard so much recently, he seems to have gone much further than Jabotinsky ever dared to go. I have no doubt that he and his friends in Palestine are not hiding their light under a bushel, and are probably making their views known; and this explains to me the curious statement made by one of the generals to Shertok in Cairo—that the Jews want the army for political purposes after the war, and which has been also repeated by Moyne in his famous (or infamous)

---

[7] On the eve of his departure from U.S., Ben-Gurion had called a meeting of the Office Committee of the Emergency Committee, and announced that he would be calling for W.'s resignation, both from J.A. Executive and the Actions Committee. He remained silent on the Americans' proposal to form a smaller, more efficient executive in New York. He also attacked W.'s 'gradualist' philosophy, and indicated that the movement needed to obtain governmental support to transfer some two million Jews, in one great operation (Lourie to Brodetsky, 18 Sept. 1942, W.A.).

speech in the House of Lords.[8] B.G. always emphasized that he is giving expression to the views of the Executive. Are these really the views of the Executive? In Shertok's conversation with Willkie he seems to have spoken of immigration at the rate of 100,000 a year, and not of the one-time transfer of two million, which Mr. Ben-Gurion is discussing at present. All these mock-heroics are disquieting, most harmful and demoralizing.

By the time you return from Mexico, I hope to be back at my post in New York, and I shall be looking forward to a thorough discussion of plans for the immediate future. I have had time to think about this in my solitude, and I hope to get the benefit of your advice.

With all best wishes for the good health of your wife and yourself, and for a successful trip, I remain, with love from both Vera and myself,

As ever yours,
Chaim

340. To Jewish Agency Executive, Jerusalem.

Ferndale, N.Y., 22 October 1942

English: Draft. T.W.: W.A.

[Second Draft]

I am most grateful to you for your telegram, conveying your invitation to come to Palestine.[1] It has been my ardent wish ever since the war broke out to go and to take part in the life of the country, but fate has decreed differently. Last year, when we had definitely decided to go, I tried in every possible way to obtain passage for Mrs. Weizmann and myself, but failed. You were informed of it at the time. Then disaster came upon our family just at the moment, on February 11th, when we were in Bristol trying to catch the plane for America. We were so overcome by the news which reached us there that we could not continue our trip and returned to London, and two months later Mrs. Weizmann and myself decided to come to this country, where there was a chance for us to do a certain amount of useful work, both for the movement and for the war effort. We have, from time to time, been considering travelling to Palestine from here, but suddenly, about two months ago, a serious breakdown occurred in my health and this imposes, for the time be-

---

[8] Moyne made his speech Aug. 1942.

340. [1] See No. 332. This letter was not in fact sent.

ing, very strict limitations on my work and my movements in the near future. I have been in the hospital for about a fortnight, suffering from trouble in the lungs as a result of a sorely neglected cold, have been ordered to take a strict rest for something like six weeks to two months, and am at present here trying to recuperate, and shall no doubt have to go very slow in the course of this winter. This, and all we have lived through, has also affected Mrs. Weizmann's health, and so, from a purely personal point of view, we have had our share. It is out of the question that I could undertake a long flying trip to Palestine at a time when I am not even allowed to see many people, or attend any meetings, and it would be folly to risk the journey now. I therefore, much to my regret, cannot accept any invitation, although I see the force of your arguments. In fact, I do not need any convincing at all, that this journey would be valuable and important from every point of view. But it is, at present, a case of *force majeure* to which I have reluctantly to submit.

I do not know whether apart from general considerations, which I appreciate very much, you are not urging me to come because of Mr. Ben-Gurion's attitude and behaviour towards me, which I can assure you has come as a shock and a surprise to me, as it must have been to a great many other people who had an opportunity of acquainting themselves with the situation. I have no desire in this letter to expatiate at great length on the arguments and "facts" which Mr. Ben-Gurion has chosen to array against me. I am supposed to have prevented the mobilisation of the *Yishuv*. I have of my own volition changed the character of our military projects. I can never say "no" to an Englishman and therefore must never go alone to see people, must always be accompanied by a strong man who would keep watch over me. If I accept his own statement that things have gone wrong with me since the beginning of the war and that my sins and shortcomings are primarily concerned with the work for the army, which matter I handled obviously carelessly and high-handedly, the place for arguing this point out and clarifying the situation was naturally London. My activities in that respect were chiefly centered there; Ben-Gurion spent many months in London, he participated in all the meetings and shared all the disappointment with us; there were, apart from him, other people equally interested in the problem and equally keen to bring it to a successful conclusion, and if Ben-Gurion had something to criticise, and he obviously had a good deal, he should have had the courage and courtesy to bring it up then and there. He might have possibly rendered a service to the whole cause by doing it, but he has chosen to say nothing, and only when we met in New York he surprised me by remarking that he used to come to the meetings in London "merely out of courtesy", because he attached no value to the opinions of the people there with the exception of those held by Mr. Namier. "You were simply holding court", he said, meaning to convey that I have surrounded myself with yes-men and did just as and what I liked. Even if it were true, which certainly it is not, it was his duty to raise this question in London. It was perfectly useless to make these remarks to me *post factum* in New York, where I could do nothing to change or remedy the situation. So much for his accusations, which are incorrect in fact and which are always torn out of context and twisted, but there is no use in wasting your or my time in elaborating this lamentable subject. The records of our work are all in London, the minutes of the meetings at which every step was discussed are in London, anybody can see and read them, and I am perfectly willing to stand by the facts as recorded there. To the best of my recollection he only mentioned once at our meeting having heard from Greenwood[2] that I agreed to parity between Jews and Arabs in recruiting. I have not the slightest idea where Mr. Greenwood, whom I have not seen for years, has got that information, which was utterly false. I have told Ben-Gurion and the others that Greenwood must have been misinformed.[3] Subsequent events should have proved to Ben-Gurion the truth of my contention. Still, he keeps bringing this somewhat trivial matter up in spite of my denial. Here again he is true to form. He believes in reiteration of the same thing at every occasion. The idea of bringing it up in America suddenly and discussing it with people who could not possibly have known the facts except in very rough outline, after having been silent for months and months in London—this careful choosing of the ground for the delivering of a blow at a time when I was trying to grope in the maze of America-at-war, was nothing short of an attempt at political assassination, carried out deliberately, calculated coolly, and with a zeal and energy worthy of a better cause. I have watched Mr. Ben-Gurion carefully during his stay here. His conduct and deportment were painfully reminiscent of the petty dictator, a type one meets with so often in public life now. They are all shaped on a definite pattern: they are humorless, thin-lipped, morally stunted, fanatical and stubborn, apparently frustrated in some ambition, and nothing is more dangerous than a small man nursing his grievances introspectively. Mr. Ben-Gurion is in a constant state of exaltation and tension, obsessed by a mission in life which is bending down his shoulders. He alone, apparently, is the self-appointed

---

[2] Arthur Greenwood (1880–1954). Lab. M.P. from 1932; member of War Cabinet and Minister without Portfolio 1940–42; Lord Privy Seal 1945–47.

[3] See No. 10, n. 9.

guardian of pure Zionist principles. He alone knows and represents the views of the Executive. He alone has the solution to the Zionist and Jewish problem, he alone is conscious of the tragic plight of our people. He is utterly intolerant of anybody else's views. Anybody who is unfortunate enough to question some of his statements is simply jumped upon and shouted down and he terrorizes his audience by interminable ranting speeches in which these remarks constantly recur: "I have been sent here to place the position before you; I know what the Executive wants; I know what has to be done"—and this is being repeated systematically, at every occasion. He attempted to do the same thing in London, but there it did not go down so well. First of all, his audience was too small, we were only five people in a small room, and such modest surroundings do not lend themselves to histrionic display. You cannot thunder at us. Moreover, after we had heard him speaking once or twice, he certainly must have felt that the tirades do not produce the desired impression. The same is true for America. This had the following effect: Ben-Gurion must have felt at times that this activity and fictitious dynamism lead nowhere, achieve nothing except irritation and this only increased his sense of frustration. His tension grew and so did his self-righteous indignation. When I arrived in America two years ago I initiated conversations with the non-Zionists, chiefly with representatives of the American Jewish Committee. Before leaving, a mixed committee consisting of Zionists and non-Zionists had been formed, which would continue these discussions. When Mr. Ben-Gurion arrived on the scene, he took a great interest in the matter and sometimes conducted negotiations ignoring the existence of the committee. These negotiations have so far led to nothing. It is not perhaps Mr. Ben-Gurion's fault, but this failure so far did not improve Mr. Ben-Gurion's temper. He had nothing to show by way of achievement after having spent in America the best part of the year. He became trapped in a vicious circle out of which he could not extricate himself. While I was ill he delivered himself of two statements, one before the Emergency Committee and the other before the Executive of the Zionist Organization. In the speech before the Emergency Committee (I do not know how many hours it lasted) there are two distinct parts:

First he deals with his grievances against me and with the reasons why he is demanding my resignation. I do not know how many people were present at this performance, but he apparently did not meet with much response on the part of anyone present, not even his own party friends, with perhaps the possible exception of Mr. Szold, who, I think, has since recanted. (Incidentally, there is another feature which is not unfamiliar to anyone who has studied the behaviour of dictators. He is seeking political alliances and friendships in circles which represent just the opposite of what he and his colleagues are supposed to have been standing for all their lives.)[4]

The second half of his speech before the Emergency Committee, and the main part of his oration before the Executive of the Zionist Organization of America, were devoted to a programmatic statement of Zionist aims. After reading it, it became clear to me that there is a connection between his onslaught on me and this so-called new revolutionary program. Ben-Gurion well knew that I would not countenance all these fantastic utterances. It was therefore necessary to discredit me in the eyes of American Zionists, and thus render them more receptive to his grandiose ideas. It was necessary for his purposes to create a gulf between my "minimalist" Achad-Ha'amist ideas and his conception of modern Zionism. This programmatic statement is a knot of contradictions. Out of this tangle it is possible to isolate certain leading ideas which are, and I believe I am not doing him an injustice, as follows: It is no use to wait until the end of the war. We have to do things now. The sort of constructive work which we have been doing in the last 20 years has been valuable in its time, but now it is of secondary importance. Matters of primary importance are political. I was searching in vain as to what the policy is, and all I could find in reading the minutes of his statement is that the minds of the Zionists have to be attuned to revolutionary activity instead of evolutionary, as has been the case hitherto. So, for instance, one cannot rely on governments. Governments do not keep any promises. Of course the British Government will play only a secondary part in the future settlement, and the American Government, however, is the prop on which one has to lean (in spite of the fact that it may not keep its promises). We should aim at convincing the American Government that immigration has to be carried out on a very large scale, with Governmental support, and as soon as he reached Palestine (I am quoting him) "I am going to ask Dr. Ruppin to work out plans for a one-time transfer of two million Jews, which in my opinion can be done in a matter of a year or two; see the example of the exchange between the Greeks and Turks."[5] All this has to be prepared and worked for now, and this transfer might have to be undertaken as soon as the concentration camps are open.

---

[4] While in U.S. Ben-Gurion had quarrelled with *Poalei Zion* (whose policy he castigated as 'anti-Zionist and anti-Socialist'), as they had opposed his attempts at uniting American Jewry. He then allied himself to opposition groups within Zionist Emergency Committee.

[5] Exchange effected 1923 under League of Nations auspices.

As to Ben-Gurion's ideas about the necessity of an army, I can only say that Jabotinsky's views were merely milk and water as compared with his, excepting that they were more gracefully put and couched in more attractive terms. All I am saying is not merely hear-say; I have studied the shorthand reports of these two meetings, and I am again asking myself, why didn't Mr. Ben-Gurion give us the benefit of his views in London? He apparently did not think us worthy enough to even discuss it with them [*sic*].

As I am still hoping that my health may permit me, in a few months, to come to Palestine, I am anxious to know whether these policies, as adumbrated in this letter, represent the views of the Executive, and whether the "co-ordination" you are speaking of in your telegram means a desire on your part to adopt such views as the aims of the Zionist movement. This is clearly a matter of supreme importance for everybody concerned and your colleagues here and in London must be enlightened. This is one of the reasons why we have asked you to send Shertok here, even if his stay is not going to be long. As far as I know, up to the present there has been no discrepancy between the views as laid down in my speech before the Biltmore Hotel Conference and in my article in *Foreign Affairs* and the remarks which the political officer of the Zionist Executive made to men like Willkie and others.

It is true that we have no possibility of exchanging views on every detail, but the great lines of policy were more or less clear, until Ben-Gurion revealed his views and signified his intention to reshape the Zionist world in his own image. Now this is a serious situation which cannot be glossed over, and which may be fraught with fateful consequences. We have battled against revisionism for years under the leadership of Jabotinsky. It would be a calamity to have to fight a new and more dangerous brand of fascism under the leadership of Ben-Gurion.

My personal controversy with B.G. is of no importance. But he is the Chairman of the Executive in Palestine, he stands at the head of a great and important organization and therefore his views can be easily construed as those of the movement. Clarity in the matter is of the utmost urgency.

341. To Jewish Agency Executive, Jerusalem.

Ferndale, N.Y., 22 October 1942

English: T.: W.A.

Would be most happy come Palestine renew personal contact *Yishuv* consultation colleagues unfortunately physicians forbid strain such trip for several months.[1] Strongly urge again Shertok come immediately who, after full exchange views, may return Palestine together with Nahum Goldmann, whose presence Palestine brief period as you suggest most valuable, especially for American purposes. Fullest cooperation, harmony resident Executive members and Wise, Silver propose setting up collective authortity Executive here for effective prosecution our political activities. Assume concurrence. Inform Senator[2] Biltmore resolution has my unequivocal endorsement.

Chaim Weizmann

342. To Samuel J. Rosenman, Washington.

Ferndale, N.Y., 26 October 1942

English: Or. Copy. T.W.: W.A.

Dear Judge Rosenman,

I am writing from a secluded cottage here in the Catskills, whither I have been ordered by my physicians for a six weeks' rest, following a breakdown in my health about two months ago. I am beginning to feel much better now, and look forward to resuming my normal activities early in November, and to a visit to Washington during the latter part of that month.

I am greatly interested in a recommendation by Dr. Lowdermilk, expert on soil conservation for your Government, concerning the construction of a Jordan Valley Authority along the lines of the Tennessee Valley Authority here in America. Dr. Lowdermilk is, unfortunately, out of the country now, having been sent to China on an official mission, but he has left a manuscript dealing with the matter, and Mr. Emanuel Neumann has had many conversations with him on the subject. I believe it is a thing of supreme importance which may have a great influence on the future of Palestine, and I

341. [1] Reply to Jerusalem Executive's telegram, 19 Oct. 1942. Responding 26 Nov. (W.A.), the Executive doubted the advisability of establishing a branch of J.A. Executive in U.S., but agreed to consider the matter further, together with an American delegation, preferably to include W. himself, in Palestine. Shertok would not be able to come to U.S. (In fact, while in London Shertok decided on his own initiative to visit U.S., principally to cut short negotiations then under consideration with Ibn Saud, for he regarded any such agreement as utopian; but he also sought to mediate between W. and Ben-Gurion—see Vol. XXI).

[2] Senator, a non-Zionist member of J.A. Executive, opposed the Biltmore resolutions.

would be most thankful to you if you could find time to receive Mr. Neumann, who would place the matter before you.[1]

Ch. Weizmann
Ross Cottage
Grossingers
Ferndale, N.Y.

343. To Paul Henri Spaak,[1] London. *Ferndale, N.Y., 28 October 1942*
English: Copy. T.W.: W.A.

On the occasion of the twentyfifth anniversary of the Balfour Declaration issued by His Majesty's Government on November 2nd, 1917, I have the honour, as President of the World Zionist Organization and the Jewish Agency for Palestine, to send this message of greeting and gratitude to your nation, whose Government endorsed and supported the purpose of that Declaration: the establishment of a National Home for the Jewish people in Palestine. To the Jewish people, now threatened with annihilation throughout Nazi-occupied Europe, the Balfour Declaration, and the sympathy and support of civilised mankind, are beacons of hope for a brighter future. I trust that you will accept this expression of our profound esteem, and of our complete solidarity with the cause of the United Nations; and that you may, through me, favour our suffering people with words of encouragement on the occasion of this memorable anniversary.

Chaim Weizmann[2]

344. To David Wertheim, New York.
Ferndale, N.Y., 1 November 1942
English: Or. Copy. T.W.: W.A.

My dear Wertheim,
I have already expressed to you personally my deep regret at not being able to be present and participate in your convention.[1] In a

342. [1] Rosenman replied 29 Oct. 1942 (W.A.) that he had received the Lowdermilk study from Neumann, whom he would contact after he had read it.

343. [1] 1899–1972. Belgian Minister for Foreign Affairs 1939–45; President U.N. General Assembly 1946; Secretary-General NATO, 1956.
    [2] This message was despatched by Linton in London to the several Governments-in-Exile there. Replies (from all except the Belgians) were relayed to W. for use at a public meeting in New York.

344. [1] The Convention of *Poalei Zion-Zeire Zion*.

sense, I feel the disappointment perhaps even more keenly than you and the other assembled delegates. Had I been able to attend your convention, meeting as it does in a crucial period in world history, I would have availed myself of the opportunity not to deliver a speech, but rather [for us] to take counsel with each other. For though not a member of your wing of the Zionist Movement, I believe that I have earned for myself the right to address you as *Chaverim*.[2]

In the midst of this global conflagration, when continents and peoples are in the grip of destruction, all of us must perforce feel that we have reached the end of a period; indeed, it must be said, a very fruitful period of more than a generation of cooperation between ourselves and Labor Zionism.

The war and all its attendant consequences will undoubtedly result in enormous changes, political, social and economic, which will vitally affect the future course of our work in Palestine. Save for victory, it is difficult to foresee what the end of the war will bring in its train, both for ourselves and the world. Yet there are already certain signs, certain indications, clear and unmistakable, which may serve us as guide-posts. These guide-posts are marked with the words: "The era of the common man". These words have a profound meaning for us and our work in Palestine. For the "common man" implies neither partisanship nor sectionalism, but the greater good for the greatest number. It has been implicit also in the very basic principles of the Zionist Movement as expressed in the constructive program of work which we, in partnership with Labor Zionism, have engaged in [in] Palestine for the past twenty-five years. This partnership, productive of the greatest results in and outside of Palestine, must not be allowed to be disturbed or marred by dissident forces, from whatever source, attempting to create a cleavage within the totality of our Movement. If anything, it is necessary at this time, and during the post-war period, to intensify this partnership, making it productive of even greater results.

In this commonalty of interest, Labor Zionism has an enormously significant role to play. This role carries with it also an enormous responsibility. A British statesman once remarked: "All power corrupts, and absolute power corrupts absolutely".[3] Fortunately, this has not been true of Jewish Labor in Palestine. Having acquired great strength and vast power from the common effort of all of us, our Labor organization in Palestine has remained singularly free from this corruptive influence. *It must remain so.*

[2] Hebr.: comrades.
[3] Lord Acton.

It has been my considered policy for more than a generation that only through such common effort shall we be able to build the national props upon which a future Jewish Palestine will rest securely. From this policy we shall not deviate; from this road we shall not depart, firmly rooted in my conviction that the "common man" in Palestine means the overwhelming majority of the *Yishuv*, whatever the party label, whatever the shade of opinion. None must be crushed between the hammer and the anvil; all must be given the opportunity to share fairly in the fruit that we shall bring to bear upon the sacred soil of the future Jewish Commonwealth. In the society which we hope to build in this Jewish Commonwealth, there shall be neither oppressor nor oppressed, neither a dictatorship of capital nor of labour, but a common heritage for all who have had a part in laying the foundations of the Jewish future in the Jewish land.

Toward the fulfilment of this ideal, I hope that the deliberations of your convention will make a substantial contribution.

In the hope of Zion redeemed,

Ch. Weizmann

345. To Jewish Agency Office, London.

Ferndale, N.Y., 2 November 1942

English: T.W./H.W.: W.A.

Dear Friends,

It is again a long time since I have written to you. Neither have I heard very much from your side. My silence is to be explained partly by the fact that August and September are, from the point of view of New York, more or less months of stagnation, and partly, because I fell ill, had to spend about a fortnight in the hospital, and then was sent away to the country here, where I have been for six weeks. I was not able to do very much the first four weeks, and now I am preparing to return to New York and set to work again, as my health has improved considerably. I shall have to go slowly and cut down most of my public speaking engagements and travelling, but I shall be able to attend to things in Washington, and this is perhaps the most important part of one's work. I am worried by the very indifferent state of health of Mrs. Weizmann, who has been suffering of late, but again I am hopeful that she may soon recover and be herself again. All this has not been conducive towards strengthening one's morale, but now the real season of work begins, and I am, in a sense, looking forward to it, as the enforced idleness is something to which I am not accustomed.

I was glad to receive yesterday the telegram from Berl about his satisfactory conversation with Mr. Talboker,[1] whom I hope to see in due course and hear his impressions.[2] You have probably heard that Isaiah Berlin, through whom you sent me some messages, fell ill on arrival in New York, was taken from the airport straight to the hospital and there was laid up for almost 4 weeks. He has now joined us here for convalescence, and he has told me a little of his meetings with some of our friends in the office. We hear very little from Palestine, except the news which is reported in the Palcor. The organization here has invited Shertok to come over, but thus far there was no reply and I doubt very much whether Mr. Ben-Gurion will allow Shertok to come here after his own somewhat curious exit from America.

Apart from ordinary routine Zionist work, there is nothing much happening at present but the season has only begun and I hope that this winter may bring some developments, of which I propose to write to you later.

We are doing what we can with regard to Lewis' book, and Mac-Millan[3] is supposed to make some proposals in the course of the next week or so.

I shall be very grateful to hear from you all, and I propose to write to you more regularly, now that I can commence my activities again. I am not writing separately to anyone, but my affectionate regards to Baffy, Lewis, Berl, Brodetsky, Miss May and to the others, including Bakstansky and Linton.

Affectionately,
Ch. Weizmann

Mrs. W. has not been at all well these last weeks and hope she will now begin to pick up a little.

---

345. [1] Hebr.: 'Morning Dew', i.e., Morgenthau.

[2] See further, Nos. 349, 352. Locker was told by Morgenthau, 27 Oct. 1942, that he believed Churchill to be a good friend of the Jews, but that their friends could not do much for the present; they would have to wait until all danger passed from the Middle East. Roosevelt was also their friend, and with two such friends, the Jews could be confident of the future. Locker expressed his fear of a *fait accompli* before they were prepared to act, and raised the question of Jewish participation in the war. Morgenthau said that he knew the British had no equipment, but agreed with Locker that even if they had, it was not certain that it would be given to the Jews. Locker asked Morgenthau to impress upon British statesmen (especially Eden) the strength of American feeling on the Jewish question. Morgenthau stated that he had never sought to hide his own Jewishness, he helped whenever possible, and was interested in Palestine. He was grateful to American Jewry for not trying to embarrass him. He endeavoured to make a good job of his post, because his success was important not only for himself, but for the Jewish people also (note by Locker, 29 Oct. 1942, W.A.).

[3] The publishers.

346. To Jewish Agency Office, London.

Ferndale, N.Y., 3 November 1942

English: T.W.: W.A.

Dear Friends,

I have received the cablegram, which appears below, from the Prime Minister yesterday.[1] As far as I know it is a spontaneous expression, as I have not been in touch for a long time with him or with any member of the Government.

Ch. Weizmann

347. To Viscount Halifax, Washington.

Ferndale, N.Y., 7 November 1942

English: Or. Copy. T.W.: W.A.

I would like to thank you for transmitting to me the Prime Minister's message.[1] May I ask you to be good enough to arrange for the following reply to be sent to the Prime Minister.

"Deeply grateful for your important message. Am particularly encouraged to have received it at this auspicious moment for us all.[2] Heartiest congratulations and greetings."

Chaim Weizmann

348. To Israel Sieff, Washington.

Ferndale, N.Y., 8 November 1942

English: Or. Copy. T.W.: W.A.

My dear Israel,

I have read the first draft of the intended announcement,[1] and would like to make some remarks about it, and also take the liberty

---

346. [1] The message, occasioned by the 25th anniversary of the Balfour Declaration, was forwarded by Halifax, who asked that it be treated as private. It read: 'My thoughts are with you on this anniversary. Better days will surely come for your suffering people and for this great cause for which you have fought so bravely. All good wishes. Winston Churchill.' (Israel State Archives, Weizmann File 1, 105/1/4)

347. [1] No 346, n. 1.
[2] The Eighth Army began its attack on Rommel's forces 23 Oct. 1942. By 4 Nov. Rommel was in full retreat, and by 10 Nov. Egypt was cleared of German troops. Tobruk was retaken 13 Nov.

348. [1] Sieff was on an extended visit to U.S., first in connection with British exports, then in secondment to Office of Price Administration. On W.'s behalf, he was seeking to orga-

of putting down on paper certain views regarding the formation of a group of persons interested in a New Deal for Palestine.

1. It is clearly important that there should be constituted in Washington a group of United States Government officials and experts interested in the social, economic and political development of a Jewish Palestine.

It is assumed that the American interest in the settlement of the Middle and Near East will grow, and it is essential that there should exist in Washington a group of pro-Zionists able and willing to draw up, present and work for the realization of an enlightened social and economic scheme which should do justice to the National Home and enable it to develop on a large scale.

This group should observe and report trends in Washington likely to affect the future of Palestine.

2. The chief purpose of this group should be to achieve an agreed attitude on all problems concerning Jewish Palestine, to give expression to this attitude from time to time in writing, and to secure for it the adherence of circles and individuals most likely to influence decisions regarding Palestine.

It is therefore, in my opinion, somewhat premature to develop at present a large-scale educational or publicity campaign for its aims, because: (a) the group has not yet been able to define such aims and it must not lose itself in the sort of propaganda which is really the domain of the Zionist Organization; (b) it must avoid even remotely to compete with the kind of general political agitation already carried out by the official Zionist bodies; (c) because of the official position and character of the majority of the members of the group, they would be precluded further from political Zionist activity. The group consists, for the most part, of persons who hold responsible positions in the United States Government, and would quite naturally wish neither to make, nor to be regarded as making, extra-governmental propaganda of any kind. This very proper and justified attitude should be scrupulously respected, and the meetings should therefore be made informal and private, and no guests should be introduced. Such informality has great advantages, cer-

nize a committee, from members of Roosevelt's inner circle and other leading Democratic Party figures, in order to obtain a 'Palestine Declaration of the Second World War', with a view to having Palestine awarded to the Jews. The committee, to be completely independent of official Zionist bodies, was intended as a political instrument to be placed at the sole disposal of W., and would create its own 'Political Fund.' The work would include study of the Jordan Valley Authority plan and would also establish a Research Foundation in Washington. The draft announcement (untraced) was for publication in the first issue of the bimonthly bulletin of the body, tentatively called 'Palestine Charter Committee'. See Cohn to W., 25 Oct., 4 Nov., 1942.

tainly in the early stages. It gives the members of the group an opportunity to become fully acquainted with each other's point of view, and therefore to achieve a degree of cohesion which is the essential pre-requisite for the good functioning of the group activity. It is quite certain that unless it achieves a strong and distinctive quality of its own, its work is likely to be desultory and ineffective.

While publicity will be required later, the group can work successfully, in its early stages, avoiding undue publicity or the upbuilding of any formal organization. Of course it may be very important to keep a record of its meetings and discussions.

3. The preservation of the private character of the group has the very important additional advantage of guarding its activities from being misunderstood by the official Zionists on the one hand, and by ill-informed and/or antagonistic Jewish and non-Jewish bodies on the other.

If the group becomes, at the outset, an official public body, the Zionist Organization may quite reasonably seek to exercise authority over it, demand conformity and object strongly if this is not accepted. This would either rob the group of its independence or involve it in unnecessary acrimonious controversy, which should be avoided at any cost.

4. If it is deemed necessary, at some later stage, to make an appeal either to the general American public or to select sections of it, and to educate public opinion as opposed to small groups and individuals with regard to the aims of the group, that might be done by an *ad hoc* organization consisting of persons able to devote themselves to such propaganda and in cooperation with the Zionist Organization, advised and stimulated by the Washington group, but not identical with it. The qualifications for public educational work are different from the detailed and specialized and often personal activity which the group of government and expert officials is alone fit to perform, and these two functions should be carefully kept apart.

Unless there is something genuinely new of importance to say, it is better for this new group to remain silent. I would therefore venture to advise that the group would have to perform a good deal of preliminary work. All the energy and enthusiasm should be directed at present to the organization of a small compact and devoted group of serious persons, intellectually, morally and politically qualified, to act both as observers of the relevant portions of the Washington scene and as protagonists in the right quarters of the social and economic ideas of the New Deal in its special application to Palestine and the Middle East.

5. The group should begin, in my opinion, by a careful study of

the relevant documents pertaining to the position of the National Home at present: (a) all the material collected by the Peel Commission and the evidence on all the problems presented by the Jewish Agency. It is valuable material, giving a complete picture of the state of Jewish Palestine as it presented itself in 1936; (b) the war gave a new stimulus of peculiar developments, both industrially and agriculturally, and the Agency must be requested at once to give a full report of these developments; (c) I would also recommend a study of the legal position created by the MacDonald-Chamberlain White Paper;[2] (d) I would devote some time to Stein's Gray Book,[3] which we have presented to the Peel Commission, also to (d) the report of the Woodhead Commission[4] and (e) to the debates on the White Paper, both in the Commons and Lords and to (f) all the reports of the Mandates Commission. Recently the Chatham House in London has been collecting some material, and I think it can be obtained either in the Congressional Library, or certainly in the British Library in New York. The group should enter into contact with Dr. Ruppin and his statistical institute,[5] and might obtain valuable information from him, and also with Leonard Stein, Namier, Isaiah Berlin and George Backer. Berlin has kindly offered to give us the necessary bibliography.

Forgive please, the length of this letter and the liberty which I have taken in offering advice. But I believe that a very great deal depends upon the first steps which you will take.

Affectionately,
Chaim Weizmann

349. To Doris May, London.　　　　　*New York, 13 November 1942*
English: Or. Copy. T.W.: W.A.

I returned from my country retreat a day before yesterday, and was happy to find your note of Oct. 23rd.[1] Meanwhile we have received telegrams and a letter from the children.[2] I have already

[2] Legality of the 1939 White Paper (see Vol. XIX) had been challenged by the Permanent Mandates Commission in Geneva, July 1939.

[3] Presumably Stein's memorandum on the Passfield White Paper of Oct. 1930 (see Vol. XIV), which followed investigation of the 1929 disturbances. Stein's pamphlet, published Nov. 1930, has a grey cover.

[4] The Woodhead Commission was appointed late 1937 to study the various partition schemes for Palestine. Its Report (Nov. 1938), dismissing any plan of partition as impractical, was accepted by the Government—see Vol. XVIII.

[5] Presumably the J.A. Institute of Economic Research, established 1935.

349. [1] Untraced.
　[2] Untraced.

heard something from Henry Morgenthau,[3] who wanted me to come over and lunch with him, but I am not yet fit to travel at short notice from here to Washington, and I have therefore had to postpone seeing him.

A few days ago I sent a letter to the office saying really very little, as I have been more or less out of everything for some time.[4] I intend now to take up the threads again, but it will be a few days before I can think of going to Washington. Mrs. Weizmann's health is not too good at present and she would not be able to travel, and I don't care to leave her alone. You might be so kind and point it out gently to the children. I know you would not upset them too much, but Mrs. Weizmann's health has not been satisfactory, really, all these months, and I dare say that my illness has upset her a great deal. All we have gone through since February has left its mark on both of us, but she is less robust than I am. She is making a recovery, but it is very slow. If I could only influence her that she should not fret constantly, she might recover more quickly, but as you understand, it is not easy.

With regard to my chemical work, that will be finished very soon, and on the whole it has gone very well, although we may still have to fight the vested interests in order to get it adopted by the Government. However, we have the satisfaction that all our experiments have come off extremely well on a large scale. Bergmann has been a tremendous help. He has been away of late in the Middle West, but he is coming back next Sunday.

We are naturally greatly interested about the military events which may have far-reaching consequences; and the thought that Palestine is safe once more, and that possibly the route to it may be considerably shortened is rather comforting and encouraging.[5] There is not very much to be done just at the moment politically here, but in view of the great changes in the Middle East the time for action is quite near and I intend, if at all possible, to go to Palestine and stay there for a period, perhaps in a fortnight's time.

Will you please give my love to everyone in the office, and also please convey my affectionate regards to Sigmund [Gestetner] and to Simon [Marks] and to Melchett also, and thank him for his telegram[6] which I appreciated very much. Please write to me as often as you can. We both send our love to you and all our friends.

P.S. Very many thanks for the calendar for 1943, which has duly arrived.

[3] For their meeting in Dec., see No. 352.
[4] No. 345.
[5] Reference to Rommel's retreat.
[6] Untraced.

350. To Emil Flesch,[1] New York.   *New York, 16 November 1942*
English: Draft. T.W.: W.A.

Dear Dr. Flesch,

I beg to thank you for your note of November 12th[2] and for so kindly sending me your *Jewish Family Almanac*. I have not yet had time to look through it properly, but it seems to contain a variety of subjects, some of them of considerable interest. I would like, however, to say after reading through the little note which you are so kindly publishing about myself, that I am not the inventor of TNT and that I never had anything to do with it. I have repeatedly pointed this out to the press, but somehow this mis-statement crops up again much to my annoyance. I would be very glad if, some time when you publish the second edition, you would correct it. Neither is it correct to say that I am helping the Government solve the rubber situation. The little which I have done does not merit such a flattering characterisation. These statements only do harm. It always saddens me to see that we indulge in unnecessary exaggerations, when a modest statement of facts would do. I hope you do not mind my pointing this out, as you have asked for my candid opinion. I am exemplifying this opinion on my own case, which of course I know best.[3]

Sincerely yours,
Chaim Weizmann

351. To the Va'ad Leumi, Jerusalem.   *New York, 2 December 1942*
English: T.: C.Z.A. Ji/1366.

Conference of leading Jewish Organizations including American Jewish Congress, World Jewish Congress, American Jewish Committee, *Bnai Brith,* Jewish Labour Committee, *Mizrachi, Agudath Harabonim, Agudath Israel,* Synagogue Council of America, *Poalei Zion,* have accepted and strongly support proposal [that] Wednesday December second be solemnly observed by Jews throughout world as Day of Mourning, Fasting, prayer for Jewish victims greatest crime against humanity. Facts concerning horror directed against

---

350. [1] President, FFF publishers, New York.

[2] W.A.

[3] The *Jewish Family Almanac*, publ. New York, an annual survey of the Jewish world. The note on W. read: 'Won high honours from his adopted country, Great Britain, for his discovery of TNT and the synthetic acetone during World War One, when Britain was threatened with a total cut-off of her rubber import.' The note added that the Balfour Declaration was part of W.'s 'reward'.

Jewish people unquestionably appeared [in] your local papers now have confirmation [in] Hitler's order to exterminate all Jews [in] Nazi occupied countries by December thirty first nineteen hundred forty two. Almost two million already massacred. Sending you full report.[1] In the meantime urge that you, in cooperation with all your organizations, observe December second as memorial day; [also] to secure cooperation [of] non-Jewish community and Press comments on these atrocities.

Stephen Wise, President American Jewish Congress and
Chairman Executive Committee World Jewish Congress;
Dr. Chaim Weizmann, President World Zionist Organization.

352. To Henry Morgenthau, Jr., Washington.

New York, 6 December 1942

English: Draft: T.W.: W.A.

May I be permitted to tell you and Mrs. Morgenthau how greatly we enjoyed the evening spent at your home last week.
I also feel that the discussion was fruitful and may bring some practical results.[1] I was particularly pleased with the news you told me privately before I left your home.[2]

---

351. [1] Replying 3 Dec. 1942 (W.A.), Isaac Ben-Zvi (chairman of *Va'ad Leumi*), informed W. that the entire *Yishuv* had united in three days mourning, ending with the fast. The *Va'ad Leumi* had cabled Roosevelt, Churchill, Stalin and Smuts, demanding the rescue of children, the exchange of German internees for Jews, and the opening of gates of all free countries to Jewish refugees. Ben-Zvi requested information on the steps taken by W.Z.O. In England, Zionist delegations lobbied Ministers, and in U.S. the Z.O.A. lobbied members of the Administration, with a view to having Allied leaders issue a statement condemning Nazi atrocities. In England Christian and Jewish deputations sought meetings with Churchill or Eden (see Linton to Melchett, 8 Dec. 1942, W.A.). On 2 Dec. 1942 the State Department published details of some two million Jewish victims who had been deported or perished since 1939 in Axis-controlled Europe.

352. [1] Among others present were Rosenman, Benjamin Cohen and Weisgal. Rosenman had asked for an exposition by W. on the relations between the Zionist movement and the Mandatory Government in Palestine. W. reviewed the progress of the *Yishuv* and of the obstacles it confronted; the main problem now was immigration, and he believed Palestine had room for three to four millions without disturbing the Arab population. Some 400,000–500,000 Jews in most urgent need could be brought in immediately, but this could only be achieved under J.A. control. W. stated that every Jew should have the right to enter Palestine if he wished, and the absorptive capacity of the country should be determined by the Jews themselves (see Weisgal to London Executive, 8 Jan. 1943, W.A.).

[2] Morgenthau had told W. that he had seen the President that same afternoon, and the latter had approved of the meeting, and asked him to inform W. that the Zionist cause had his full sympathy and support (note in W.A.).

You will be interested to know, I am sure, that I had, what I regard, a satisfactory conversation with Mr. Welles on Friday.[3] Among other things, I took up with him two major issues: 1. That no commitments of any kind should be made to the Arabs at this time which would in any way conflict with our interests in Palestine. 2. The appointment of a representative of the State Department under Mr. Welles' guidance who would discuss with us now in a practical way all the questions concerning Palestine. Mr. Welles agreed to appoint such a person under his guidance and I venture to hope that the person appointed will be sympathetic and understanding of our interests.

I hope I will have an opportunity to see you soon again.

With warmest regards to Mrs. Morgenthau and yourself, I am

Very sincerely yours,

Chaim Weizmann

353. To Chaim Nahoum,[1] Cairo.   *New York, 8 December 1942*
English: T.: W.A.

In common we pray for the utter defeat of our enemy and the deliverance of mankind and our suffering people.[2]

Chaim Weizmann

354. To Henrietta Klotz,[1] Washington.   *New York, 9 December 1942*
English: Or. Copy. T.W.: Photostat W.A.

Dear Mrs. Klotz,

Colonel Victor Cazalet, who is attached to the Sikorski mission, recently arrived from London, requested me to recommend him for an appointment with Secretary Morgenthau. Colonel Cazalet, who is a close friend of Lord Halifax, with whom he stays at the Embassy while visiting here, and is also a close personal friend of mine, has been a most valuable friend to us in London, and I would appreciate your advising the Secretary to that effect. I might add that he is also a member of Parliament.

---

[3] See No. 356.

353. [1] 1872–1960. Chief Rabbi of Cairo 1925–60, member of Egyptian Senate from 1931. Previously Chief Rabbi of Instanbul.

  [2] Nahoum had cabled 5 Dec. 1942 (W.A.) that a solemn fast had been proclaimed throughout Egypt for that day.

354. [1] B. 1901. Morgenthau's secretary 1930–55.

In accordance with your suggestion to Mrs. Shepard, I am writing Colonel Cazalet that he apply for an appointment following the routine procedure of requesting one through a Department secretary, but I did want to convey the above facts to you.

It was a pleasure to see you last Friday, and I would like to thank you for all you have done.

355. To Count Edward Raczynski,[1] London.

New York, 9 December 1942

English: T.: W.A.

My profound thanks to you behalf myself and Jewish people for your words of sympathy and genuine friendship in this hour of travail.[2] May the blood of our martyred peoples bind us in eternal friendship and in common prayer for the utter defeat and prostration of our enemy. When the day of deliverance will come to the Polish nation and to the Jews on its hallowed soil in Palestine we shall I hope be privileged to work together and make our contributions towards a better world.

Chaim Weizmann

356. To Sumner Welles, Washington.   *New York, 9 December 1942*
English: Or. Copy. T.W.: W.A.

Dear Mr. Welles,

This is the first opportunity I have had on my return to New York, to express to you my sincere thanks for the time you were good

---

355. [1] B. 1891. Polish Ambassador to Great Britain 1934–45; Acting Minister for Foreign Affairs 1941–43.

[2] On 3 Dec. 1942 Raczynski had cabled the following telegram to W.:

'The Polish Government receives almost daily reports on the untold atrocities perpetrated by Germans on the people in Poland. From these sources they have recently obtained the confirmation of the monstrous slaughters carried on by Germans on Jews in Poland. These terrible crimes afflict both the Polish Jews and the large number of Jews from other countries whom the Germans have deported to Poland in order to exterminate them. The Polish Government and the Polish nation have pilloried with horrified indignation these mass murders committed on the soil of Poland by the German authorities of occupation. Profoundly affected by these horrible reports I hasten to convey to you, the most eminent representative of the Jewish national idea, the expression of my heartfelt compassion with the martyrdom which the German barbarians have inflicted on the Jewish nation. I can assure you that the Polish Government is determined that the dehumanized perpetrators of these dreadful deeds shall receive a punishment commensurate with their crimes.'

enough to accord to me while on my recent visit to Washington.[1]

I am happy that you could agree to my request to designate some-body from your Department who, under your guidance, would discuss with us the problems of Palestine. [2]

Thanking you again, I am

Very cordially yours,
Ch. Weizmann

357. To Benjamin Bloch, Rehovot.   *New York, 12 December 1942*
English: T.W.: W.A.

My dear Dr. Bloch,

I was very glad to have received your letter of November 18th and to get at last some authentic information with regard to the budget of the Institute and the manufacturing program, but I was literally staggered to read that you are contracting a loan of £17,000 and paying 6% to Mr. Green.[1] I believe it is a fatal policy which has always been pursued in Palestine, and which I have been combatting all my life. People over-extend and force the pace, and contract loans lightly, and then find themselves in great diffi-culties. Times are difficult at present. You do not know whether

---

356. [1] W. was accompanied by Goldmann at the meeting, 4 Dec. 1942. He stated that the White Paper could not now be allowed to obstruct large-scale immigration into Palestine, the main source of which was now the half-million Polish Jews existing in deplorable con-ditions in Russia. The Zionists wanted more immigration certificates from the British and more exit permits from the Russians. Welles replied that he was certain that there would be an improvement in the status of Polish Jews in Russia. Roosevelt had sent a personal letter to Stalin, and had received assurances to this effect. Arrangements were being made for 16,000 to go to Kenya, 5,000 to South Africa, and some to Mexico. W. expressed concern lest the U.S. Government made commitments to the Arabs during the war. Welles promised that there would be no commitment without first consulting the Jews, and, if possible, gaining their consent. Regarding post-war plans, W. stated that even by conservative estimates Pales-tine could take in another three millions. Welles agreed to his request to appoint a special State Department official to discuss details with the Zionists, and asked whether the Zionists were thinking of a transfer of Arabs from Palestine. W. stated that the Arabs might sponta-neously leave, but the Zionists would not tell them to do so, for with development on a large scale, there was enough room for all (record in W.A.).

[2] Welles appointed Wallace Murray, Adviser on Political Relations in the State Depart-ment, to discuss the Zionists' plans in detail (letter to W., 21 Dec. 1942, in State Department Archives, 867N.01/1831).

357. [1] Bloch had listed the drug manufacturing programme of Palestine Pharmaceuticals since production began 1 May 1942. Production had been handicapped by a shortage of minerals and raw materials, and the loan incurred was needed in order to cover initial outlay on stock. W. cabled additionally 13 Dec. 1942 disapproving strongly of the terms of the loan, and urging Bloch to cancel it (W.A.).

you will be able to manufacture as much as you propose to do now—and supposing you can't produce all the material, where are you going to get the money with which to meet your obligations? I therefore request that you must cancel this loan. We shall simply have to go slow during the war, and expand afterwards, when normal conditions are re-established. I presume that Mr. Horowitz and Louis Green have been informed of your transaction, but you are really morally bound to keep Mr. Marks informed, although formally it may not be necessary. But knowing Mr. Marks, as I do, I am sure he would object most energetically to such a procedure. Will you let me know at once whether you have informed him, although I am now sending him a copy of this letter.[2]

Under the circumstances I do not propose to send you the residual £1,200 which we still owe you as a loan to the factory; I think I had better keep this money in reserve in case you get yourself into difficulties.

With kind regards I am

Yours sincerely,
Chaim Weizmann

358. To S. Salman Schocken, New York. *New York, 16 December 1942*
English: Or. Copy. T.W.: Photostat W.A.

Thank you for sending me a copy of Dr. Magnes'[1] letter to Rabbi Lazaron of October 6, 1942.[2]

It does not make a particle of difference to me whether the sentence reads "terrorists in the best style of Eastern European nationalism" or "terrorists in the best style of European nationalism". I think, if anything, it makes it worse because Roumanian and Hungarian fascism is, if anything, worse than the German or Italian

---

[2] Bloch wired 21 Dec. (W.A.) that W. had mis-apprehended his condensed report. The loan was £5,000 only, the remainder being an advance on goods ordered by Green's own company. There was no risk, as Green was himself a member of the Pharmaceuticals Board. Provided the raw materials arrived on time, Bloch anticipated repaying the loan within one year. He regretted W.'s disapproval, but there was no other source of finance. W. was presumably assuaged, for he took the matter no further.

358. [1] Judah Leon Magnes (Biog. Index, Vol. IV). Chancellor, then President, Hebrew University 1925–48. A pacifist, he had founded *Ihud* (Unity) in 1942, to foster better Jewish-Arab understanding.

[2] Morris Samuel Lazaron, b. 1888. American Reform rabbi, of Baltimore Hebrew Congregation from 1915; compulsorily retired 1948, due to his active identification with anti-Zionist American Council for Judaism, of which he was founder and Vice-President. Magnes' letter (published by Lazaron in *Baltimore Jewish Times*) advocated establishment of a bi-national state in Palestine, and strongly criticised official Zionist policy—see No. 365.

brand. Besides, he might have also had in mind Germany, which is more eastern than western.

The other points in Magnes' letter, like his encouragement given to Lazaron, a deadly enemy of the Zionist movement, are equally repugnant. I therefore abide by my decision, to which I have given expression yesterday.

I shall call in the members of the Board [of Governors of the Hebrew University] again next Tuesday, the 22nd, at 3 o'clock, to which meeting a formal notice will be sent you.[3]

I assume that you have sent copies of this letter from Magnes to the members of the Board who attended the meeting here Monday.[4]

Sincerely yours,
Chaim Weizmann

359. To Selig Brodetsky, London.   *New York, 23 December 1942*
English: T.: W.A.

Calling meeting Board [of] Governors University re Magnes situation which becoming increasingly disturbing view irresponsible statements. Would you [and] other friends on Board cable me your proxies. Met with eleven Board members here, and there is general agreement on course of action. Also cabling Sacher.[1]

Chaim Weizmann

[3] The meeting of 22 Dec. decided to call a general meeting of the Board to consider a resolution expressing its views on the Magnes letter, this to be cabled to the London and Palestine members, asking their views. W. stated that he would not call for Magnes' resignation, but would have to consider his own resignation from the Board, and warned that he could do nothing for the University while Magnes remained President. The meeting felt, however, that they should avoid a public furore that could threaten the University's fund-raising campaigns. See Warburg–W. exchange, 17, 23 Dec. 1942 (W.A.).

[4] This had been a meeting only of Zionist members of the Board of Governors, 15 Dec. 1942, when action was postponed pending sight of the actual letter, so as to avoid a scandal or play into Magnes' hands. W. claimed that whatever standing Magnes possessed was due to his position as President of the University. Further, Magnes' letter was not a question of political views, but of defamation, which he could not tolerate. He was prepared to take the advice of the Board, but would do nothing for the University while matters stood as they did (record in W.A.).

359. [1] Both Brodetsky and Sacher were on the Board of Governors. They jointly cabled 2 Jan. 1943 (W.A.) advising that the Governors of the University issue an instruction to members of the University that political statements or activism had to be specified as personal, and were not in the name of the University. They deprecated action beyond this.

360. To Israel Goldstein, New York.   *New York, 24 December 1942*
English: Copy. T.W.: C.Z.A. KKL 1941/43.

My dear Dr. Goldstein,

I regret more than I can tell you that I am not in a position at this time to undergo the strain of a long journey. This is the only reason which prevents me from travelling to Detroit to participate in the National Conference of the Jewish National Fund.

Ever since I arrived in this country, on my present visit, and many times before, I have given utterance to my deep conviction that the acquisition of land in Palestine through the *Keren Kayemeth* is a primary responsibility which rests upon all of us at a time when we are engaged in a desperate struggle for survival. It is not merely because land, in its broader social, political and economic implications represents the foundation of our national existence, when—it is our fervent hope and belief—the gates of Palestine will be opened to the surging Jewish masses; their settlement and integration into the economic fabric of the country will be impossible without this primary requirement.

There are today in Palestine hundreds of thousands of dunams of land unoccupied, untilled and undeveloped, waiting for the fructifying touch of the anxious tens of thousands who are ready to give to the soil of Palestine their life-blood, the blessing of their labor and the vitality of their renaissant spirit. Far from injuring our neighbors, the redemption of these vast stretches of uncultivated land will be of enormous benefit to all the inhabitants of Palestine, both Jews and Arabs.

What is needed at this time is not only the good will of the Mandatory Government to permit us to acquire this land, but also, and primarily, the will and the determination of the Jewish people in this and other free countries to perceive the wisdom of such a constructive program. In our Zionist work we are dependent always on these two factors: the goodwill of the world at large and the will of the Jewish people to do the job. The Mandatory Government and the United Nations have it in their power to make our task easier or more difficult, but the task of redeeming the land of Palestine for the hundreds of thousands of Jews who must need go there lies with us, and with us alone.

What is needed is vision, daring and determination. Indeed, the *Keren Kayemeth Leisrael,* the *Emek*[1]—the brightest jewel in the crown of our colonization achievements in Palestine—have been built up because of that vision and daring. He who possessed that

---

360. [1] The Plain of Jezreel.

vision—Menachem Ussishkin—will always be enshrined in our memory.

There was a time when the Jewish National Fund of this country played a secondary role in our Zionist activities. That day is gone. Guided by devotion and farsighted leadership, the Jewish National Fund, during the past ten years, has carved out for itself a place in the heart of the Jewish community in America which is today secure and permanent. For this, my dear Dr. Goldstein, not only the Zionist movement but the Jewish people everywhere, must be deeply indebted to you.

You are meeting at a time of great tragedy for our people. In our despair, in our deep sense of mourning for those who have fallen under the brute force of the enemy of mankind, we must steel our hearts in high resolve to go on with our work, undeterred and unremitting in our efforts. For in work alone can we find consolation— that perhaps a better day will come for those who will survive this holocaust. In this spirit, in the spirit of *Am Yisrael Chay*[2] you will and must go forward for the redemption of our people and the redemption of the land of Israel.

In the hope of Zion reborn,

Cordially
Chaim Weizmann

361. To Chaim Tchernowitz,[1] New York.

New York, 30 December 1942

Hebrew: Or. Copy. T.W.: Photostat W.A.

My dear Rav Tzair,

I hope you will forgive me for the delay in answering your letter of November 29th.[2]

My enforced absence from the city for these many months has caused the accumulation of a tremendous amount of work and correspondence and even to this day I have not as yet been able to clear all the decks.

The problem that you present to me is one which affects me rather deeply. I have seen several copies of the *Bitzaron*[3] and have

---

[2] Hebr.: 'The people of Israel lives'.

361. [1] Pseudonym *Rav Tzair* ('young rabbi'), 1871–1949. Talmudic scholar, Hebrew author; taught at Jewish Institute of Religion at New York from 1923.

[2] Untraced.

[3] 'Stronghold', Hebrew monthly founded 1939 and published in New York; designed to serve as an organ for original Hebrew scholarship and literature.

been greatly impressed by the literary as well as the physical appearance of the magazine. It certainly represents a fine contribution to the achievements of Hebrew culture and a worthy successor to *Hashiloah*.[4] The modest budget required for its maintenance certainly ought to be met by the Zionists of America and I shall endeavour to do what I can to impress my Zionist friends on the necessity of helping you in this splendid piece of work. Like yourself, I am primarily interested in the thing that is being done and the cause for which the thing is done although I am not at all unmindful of the high quality of the person behind this great piece of cultural work.

The enclosed letter to Judge Levinthal is self-explanatory.[5]

> With best wishes,
>
> Cordially yours,

362. To Albert K. Epstein, Chicago.   *New York, 31 December 1942*
English: Copy. T.W.: W.A.

My dear A.K.

I would not like 1942 to pass without replying to your letter of December 28th which has just reached me.[1] Hence the unusual speed.

I must confess that your letter is somewhat puzzling to me. Its implication, although I am sure it is not intended as such, is that Dr. Goldman is "anxious" and "eager" to do Zionist work and that he is being frustrated in this eminently commendable desire. I know of no person or group of persons who have directly or indirectly made any such attempt. On the contrary, I am aware of the innumerable efforts that have been made to spur Dr. Goldman on to greater activity on behalf of our movement. I myself, as you know, unsought and unsolicited by Dr. Goldman, and, I may add, not without some reluctance on his part, made a serious attempt, on my last visit to Chicago, to secure his fullest cooperation. He promised such cooperation; he denied the existence of any differences between himself and myself. At least I am not aware of any. As

---

[4] Hebrew literary monthly, founded in Russia 1896. Ahad Ha'am was first editor. It was published in Jerusalem 1920–26, then ceased to appear.

[5] This, 30 Dec. 1942 (W.A.), requested Z.O.A. to grant Tchernowitz the $5,000 budget he required to continue his paper, and stressed the important role it filled. But Tchernowitz had already been informed that Z.O.A. could not increase its subvention of $1,500 (Levinthal to W., 4 Jan. 1943, W.A.).

362. [1] Untraced.

a token of his assertions he promised to appear at our meeting in Chicago on that day. Not only did he not appear as promised, but he mysteriously became a *ne-elam*[2]—never to be heard from again. Not even a word of explanation.

Believe me, I too would like to withdraw from all activities. What is more, you will concede me that I am entitled to a bit of rest. I too am not pleased with everything that is being done nor with everybody who is doing it: but I do not use this as an excuse to withdraw from the work which is at hand. No one has a right to do it now regardless of personal opinions or differences. Least of all Dr. Goldman, whose talents are universally recognised but whose strange behaviour is equally universally deplored. Ours is a democratic movement. Leadership and service in the movement demand responsibility, steadfastness and ability to take it "on the chin" as you Americans would say.

Our movement today is in such a perilous condition that everyone of us, regardless of previous conditions of servitude, ought to be able to pull together, and by pulling our weight together, we might perhaps achieve what we seek to achieve. Outworn prejudices, old animosities, ought to be relegated to the limbo. There is a place for everyone and certainly there is a place for Solomon Goldman, but he must make up his mind that a movement is made up of people and people have opinions and that their opinions have a right to a hearing and that not all the wisdom and sagacity is concentrated on Chicago's North Side. Once he has made up his mind to that, he will become a great and valuable asset to our movement. We need people of imagination, of daring, of ability to lift themselves above the daily grind and dust of small organizational affairs. Solomon Goldman at one time I thought possessed that, but it seems to have fled. You, as a devoted friend of Goldman, will make a substantial contribution if you would help to recapture it.

One last word and I shall conclude. If the same letter had come to me signed by Rabbi Solomon Goldman, it would have been an index to the "clarification of his thinking", not to say *Chozer B'teshuva*.[3] That your own mind is clear on the subject, I have never doubted for a moment.

With warm regards to Harris[4] and the other members of the *mishpoche*,[5] I am

Affectionately yours,

---

[2] Yidd.: i.e., 'he vanished'.
[3] Hebr.: 'his repentance'.
[4] Benjamin R. Harris, b. 1896. Brother-in-law and partner to Epstein.
[5] Yidd.: family.

363. To Isaiah Berlin, Washington.   *New York, 1 January 1943*
English: Or. Copy. T.W.: Photostat W.A.

I hear you are having guests shortly, and I am wondering whether Martin is coming as well. If so, will you kindly give him my best love, and would you be so good and tell him that I am anxious to see him. I would even be prepared to go over to Washington, if he is not coming to New York.

As for his chief,[1] I know that there will be difficulty, and I am wondering whether you should not write to the Ambassador about it. I shall be guided by your advice. If you have time, please drop me a note regarding the other matters which we discussed when you were here. If it is more convenient, you can telephone me. I shall be at home Monday evening for dinner.[2]

Affectionately,

364. To Blanche Dugdale, London.   *New York, 8 January 1943*
English: T.W./H.W.: W.A.

Baffy dearest,

I am taking the opportunity of Victor's [Cazalet] departure for London to send you a few lines. Of late, communications have become very bad indeed. Letters seem to take an interminable time and are often held up by the censors both ways. Telegrams are equally bad, and this is one of the reasons, at any rate, why one feels that writing is almost a useless task. By the time a letter reaches its destination, the situation has changed so much that everything which one did write about has become obsolete. But this is a good opportunity, and you will get a full report which is being drafted now, on the few things which matter. These are just a few personal notes, which I would ask you to kindly read to the entire Executive, as it is almost impossible to write people individually.

THE POLITICAL SITUATION: I am not very happy about it generally. Since the last elections,[1] there is a trend in politics here which reminds one of what happened after the last war. Iso-

---

363. [1] Churchill. (Martin was a Principal Private Secretary.)

[2] There is no record of further contact between W. and Berlin on this subject. W. did not obtain an interview with Churchill in U.S.

364. [1] Roosevelt had been re-elected President Nov. 1940.

lationism is raising its head, anti-British feeling is rather strong, and these two things go together. It has found expression in the number of Republican candidates who have been returned to Congress, in the whole Darlan business,[2] in the departure of Leon Henderson[3] from the Office of Price Administration, and in many other matters of that kind. This is weakening the hands of the President and of the administration to a considerable degree, and one feels that there is no firm line at present. (Witness the muddle in North Africa.[4]) Such happenings are not good for our cause. It may change! I would not like to say any more at present, except to let you know it as a warning, which is the more necessary in view of the nonsense which Ben-Gurion has been talking both here and in Palestine. As far as I can gather from the scanty reports, he attaches a decisive importance to America, in contradistinction to Great Britain, repeating the slogans which one hears occasionally here—that the British Empire is doomed; that the greatest force which will emerge out of the war is America, and therefore we have to rely primarily on what can be done here. Of course no one can foretell what shape the British Empire will take, but it certainly won't disappear, as it would be a disaster if it would. It is quite true that America will arise as a very great force in the world, I hope for the good; but whether the United States, after the war, will take an interest in Middle East politics, or whether it will again retire from continental and European entanglements—that is a very moot question, and in view of the present tendencies which I have adumbrated earlier in this letter, it would be a great mistake to discount Great Britain and to overemphasize the importance of America for our cause. I think both are important, and our work must go on with equal fervour on both sides of the Atlantic. What I have been trying to do here, you will see from the report which Weisgal, who has been a tower of strength, is now drafting for the office, and which you will read carefully.

My activities culminated in the arrangement which is being made now for conversations   between us and the State Department, and I believe these conversations will begin on the 17th of this

[2] Jean François Darlan (1881–1942). Admiral of French Fleet 1939; C.-in-C. French Military Forces (Vichy) 1942. Darlan had collaborated with the Germans in 1940, was violently anti-British, and had resisted the Anglo-American landings under Eisenhower in North Africa, Nov. 1942. But he was subsequently accepted by the Americans and made High Commissioner in Algiers, to the displeasure of the British. He was assassinated in Algiers 24 Dec. 1942.

[3] Leon Henderson, b. 1895. Economist, administrator of Office of Price Administration 1941–42.

[4] I.e., Anglo-American differences in political and military assessments there.

month.[5] The man who has been assigned to us by Mr. Sumner Welles is a certain Wallace Murray, who is a glorified Shuckburgh. He is not a friend and he is not imaginative, but Welles could scarcely eschew him as he is the head of the Department, but the conversations will be carried on further with Welles himself. We have his assurance for it. This will be the first time that we might really get to know what is in the mind of the American Government. From all one hears, there is a disposition in the higher reaches of the administration to go a long way with us, but the lower strata and the bureaucracy are, as usual, opposed to us.

On this occasion, I would like to say a word about the Biltmore Declaration, of which such a fuss has been made by Ben-Gurion on his return to Palestine. It has become, as far as I can see, a new Decalogue, or certainly, a new Basle Program, and one would have thought that it has emerged out of deliberations which occupied months of serious study. Let me tell you that it is nothing of the kind. The Biltmore Declaration is just a resolution, like the hundred and one resolutions usually passed at great meetings in this country, or in any other country. It embodied, in somewhat solemn terms, the chief points as laid down in my article in *Foreign Affairs*. But Ben-Gurion, after his stay here of 8 or 9 months, had absolutely nothing to show by way of achievement, and so he stuck to the Biltmore Resolution, more or less conveying the idea that it is the triumph of his policy as against my moderate formulation of the same aims, and he injected into it all his own extreme views, such as: an immigration of two million people in three years, or something to that effect; and the building up of a great defence force to fight either the Arabs or the British or both or goodness knows whom, and many more adornments of that kind, of which the Biltmore conference never thought and would certainly have rejected had such a meaning been imparted to these resolutions. The word "commonwealth" was introduced because (a) it is more popular in America than the word "state", and, (b) it is considered more flexible. Whether it should be a commonwealth attached to the British Empire or under the trusteeship of the United Nations is, I think, immaterial to people here, and either opinion would largely depend upon the form which the whole political structure in the Middle East will take. I have certain ideas about it which I would like to put briefly to you as follows:

It is, of course, entirely speculative as to what will happen to the Far Eastern parts of the British Empire—like Malaya, Singapore, Hong Kong. I am quite certain that India will acquire a new polit-

[5] See Vol. XXI.

ical status after this war; therefore, the whole of the Far Eastern structure will have to be remodelled. I think British Colonial enterprise will concern itself with Africa, where Great Britain has consolidated its position, and where it is a paramount power. What with the Italian possessions now falling within the British orbit, and probably some of French North Africa, in spite of talk of the restoration of the French Empire. Through cooperation with the Belgians in the Congo, practically the whole of the African Continent, with the exception of the Portuguese Dominions and a few other pieces, will be under British influence. But colonial policy of the future can only be based on development, and not on exploitation, and if Great Britain develops its African dependencies, it can easily make up for its losses in the Far East. The vicinity of Palestine, just across the Suez Canal, may prove a great boon in this system of development, and I see here a possibility of cooperation which might give most beneficial results to both parties. I have discussed it here with one or two important people, and they seem to be very much taken by this idea. Equally, we ought to take the stand that if Palestine is developed to the full, room can be created for at least four million people there soon. You remember the name of Dr. Lowdermilk, the gentleman who travelled in the Middle East to study the problems of erosion, and who passed through Palestine on his way. There he was struck by what we have done and by the manner in which we have stopped erosion. He has been interested in our problems ever since. I saw something of him, and he is about to publish a book on Palestine which, coming from an authority of that calibre, will prove very valuable. There is a chapter in this book entitled "The Jordan Valley Authority", which described a project for development of both banks of the Jordan along the lines of the Tennessee Valley Authority here, which, from a technical, agricultural and particularly, social, point of view, is a model performance under the aegis of the central federal authority. I enclose an extract of this chapter. Now this is taken very seriously here by men like Vice-President Wallace and other authorities, and we are studying carefully the TVA project, for which a special committee has now been set up. We believe that it is possible to prove that the principles governing the TVA can be applied to the Jordan Valley, and thus we can assert: (a) that Palestine can hold a vast population; (b) and we can dissipate the fears of the Arabs lest they will be ousted, also (c) we would set an example of how to develop empty spaces for the benefit of oppressed populations, and such a plan could not be held up by chauvinistic tendencies of fascist Arabs. Liberal opinion in this country would favor us as against the chauvinism of the Arab leaders. I therefore consider

389

the JVA project not only as eminently important in itself, but as a great weapon to combat opposition. I believe, as I always did, that our fate is again bound up with England. They will have to develop Africa to the maximum, just as we would have to do the same in Palestine, and here both sides meet. From that point of view, just as from many others, I deplore the departure of Cranborne,[6] who probably would be the one who could understand and appreciate such a line of thought, but he is still in the Cabinet and possibly you might find it useful to talk to him about it. I know that Lord Hailey[7] is here, and it would have been useful to speak to him, but I thought I would first put it to you and possibly he can be seen on his return to London.

ZIONIST–NON-ZIONIST NEGOTIATIONS: I see from the very short reports about Moshe's statements in London that he is optimistic with regard to the outcome of the negotiations between the Zionists and non-Zionists. I don't share in this optimism at all. It is again one of the chimeras of Mr. Ben-Gurion, who tried to handle these negotiations here, and did not carry them very far. At present they are, to speak mildly, in a state of suspended animation, or, a little more brutally, practically broken up. There is going to be a unilateral statement issued by the American Jewish Committee about January 31st, which I am told is going to be couched in friendly terms, but it certainly is not the formula which we would have liked them to agree to. What will happen afterwards I do not know. Meanwhile, the anti-Zionist elements, apparently encouraged by some personages in the American Jewish Committee, partly spurred by Dr. Magnes from the Mount Scopus, are girding their loins to combat the idea of a Jewish state and Zionism generally. You have no doubt read the resolution of the 90 reform rabbis and the various utterances of their leaders.[8] These Priests of Baal do not represent anything. They are an infinitesimal fraction of the general body of reform rabbis, which is either Zionist or certainly not unfriendly, but they do have an oligarchy of Jewish millionaires behind them,

[6] Cranborne left C.O. Nov. 1942 to become Lord Privy Seal.

[7] William Hailey (1872–1969). British delegate on Permanent Mandates Commission 1935–39; Chairman, governing body of School of Oriental and African Studies, London University 1941–45.

[8] A conference of American Rabbis at Atlantic City, 1–2 June 1942. It issued a 'Statement of Principles by Non-Zionist Rabbis', which read, *inter alia*: 'But in the light of our universalistic interpretation of Jewish history and destiny, and also because of our concern for the welfare and status of the Jewish people living in other parts of the world, we are unable to subscribe to or support the political emphasis now paramount in the Zionist program.' Some 92 Reform leaders endorsed the statement, and were dubbed by their Zionist colleagues 'The Goy (Gentile) Nineties' (Samuel Halperin, *The Political World of American Zionism*, Wayne State University Press 1961, pp. 84–85).

men like Roger Straus, Ittelsohn,[9] probably some of the Warburgs, and no doubt Hexter plays with them; also several smaller groups in Chicago, and San Francisco, and in other places. It is all like 1917 in England.[10] They represent to the American Government an "important section of Jews". Our opponents in the State Department seize upon them and this strengthens their obstructionist tendencies, and I know that Mr. Welles, who is friendly, is constantly warned by his subordinates that the Jews are not at all united on the subject of a state in Palestine, that there are powerful groups in American Jewry violently opposed to it, and Lazaron and his friends are constantly quoted as crown witnesses. Magnes is trafficking with these people at this period in Jewish history. His article in *Foreign Affairs,* which has appeared in the January number and is more or less a reply to mine, is something which caused great annoyance, and is definitely harmful.[11] I see from the utterances of MacMichael a sort of veiled agreement with Magnes' point of view.

So the line-up is quite clear, and history repeats itself once more. And this is why we here are trying to meet this challenge by organizing a democratic referendum of American Jewry. It won't be a referendum in the ordinary sense, because that is too difficult and too vague, but we are calling an all-Jewish American Congress for the beginning of April, and the delegates to this Congress are to be definitely elected in each Jewish community on a Zionist platform, to be outlined and determined. So that it really will be a democratic representation of American Jewry as opposed to the self-perpetuating group of plutocrats of the American Jewish Committee. This should strengthen the hands both of ourselves and of our friends in the administration. I would like to say that this will be, I hope, my last act in this country, as we intend to leave in April, immediately after this conference.[12] From now on I am concentrating on: (1) The negotiations or the conversations in the State Department; (2) The preparation of this conference. It therefore seems

---

[9] Roger Straus (1893–1957): Head of American Smelting and Refining Company (owned by Guggenheim family); vice-chairman, Republican National Campaign Committee 1944; founder, National Council of Christians and Jews 1928; and of World Council of Christians and Jews 1947. Henry Ittelson (1871–1948): Banker; hon. chairman U.J.A.; on Executive of American Jewish Committee.

[10] Ref. to opposition from assimilationist Jews, among them the Secretary of State for India, Edwin Montagu, to Zionist aspirations—see Vol. VII.

[11] The article, Jan. 1943, contended that only U.S. was capable of imposing a suitable compromise in Palestine, based neither on a Jewish nor an Arab State.

[12] A conference of American Jewry was finally convened later that year, after W.'s return to England—see Vol. XXI.

impossible to leave here before the middle of April, and, incidentally, from the point of view of health, it would be very risky for both Vera and myself to travel by air during the winter months. We have both made progress, but as Victor will tell you, we have still to be very careful. Lord Halifax is informed about the forthcoming negotiations.

The reason why we have been so insistent on Shertok's coming here is primarily connected with the conversations in the State Department. We would naturally want to have a man fresh from Palestine, and with Moshe's experience. I realize that it is not easy for him to give us much time, but I believe it is just as important a mission as anything he might want to do in Palestine. I am not optimistic about Mr. Ben-Gurion's letting him come here, for reasons on which I need not labor too much, but still I think he should disregard it and devote a fortnight to a stay here which might prove invaluable under the circumstances. He has to go to Lisbon and from Lisbon to West Africa in any event, so that he would be halfway to America as it is, and we have arranged for his priorities. I cannot but repeat insistently that his presence here is very necessary.

MAGNES: I do not know whether you are acquainted with Magnes' performance, which has been very much publicized here. A letter from Magnes, addressed to Rabbi Lazaron, has been published by the latter. Lazaron, as you know, is the head of the anti-Zionist rabbis. In this letter, Magnes makes the following statements:

"I am opposed to the political content of that program, not because it is political but because I think the content under present conditions likely to provoke civil war in Palestine and confusion abroad."

. . . .

"It is true that Jewish nationalism tends to confuse people, not because it is secular and not religious, but because this nationalism is, unhappily, chauvinistic and narrow and terroristic in the best style of Eastern European nationalism."

Now that has naturally caused great indignation in this country and rightly so, and the Board of Governors of the Hebrew University is being pressed to take some action. I find myself in considerable difficulty, as it is impossible to get a full meeting of the Board, and, moreover, it is impossible to communicate with both the people in Palestine and in London, and give them the contents of Magnes' statement. It is not desirable to let everybody read it. I believe that the Palestine censor has probably suppressed all reference to it. Here, of course, it is widely known. A meeting of the Governors present here is going to take place soon, and I have asked Brodetsky and Sacher to give me their proxies,[13] but I did not give them the statement of Magnes. They probably thought that the Board will discuss Magnes' *Ichud* and other political activities. That, of course, is not the case. In his letter to Lazaron, he went far beyond anything he has ever done or said before, and he is gradually becoming a terrible nuisance. People here are always frightened that if Magnes is thrown out of the University the financial support will not be forthcoming. This is a mistake. I think the U.P.A. could include the University in its program, produce the $225,000 which America is giving to it, and integrate the University into the system of Palestine education, as has been done with all other educational institutions. It would not have to depend on a few rich anti-Zionists. However, I shall be glad to hear your opinion about it very soon, and perhaps you will show Sacher my letter.

NAMIER'S BOOK: With regard to Lewis' book, we have arranged with Macmillan for the publication in the Spring. We are going to see to it that proper reviews are forthcoming. I think we have done, on our side, everything which could possibly be done under the circumstances to further this enterprise, and I have spoken to a great many people about it. We are looking forward to the appearance of the book here.

ZIONIST AFFAIRS IN AMERICA: I have not said very much about the state of affairs in the organization here. There is a good Zionist atmosphere in this country, and there are quite a number of Zionist personalities, but the central organization, as embodied in and represented by the Emergency Committee, is, I am afraid, utterly inadequate to deal with the complexities of the situation. It is a bulky, unwieldy body, always hampered by party interests, can take no definite decision on anything, and all the important matters have to be taken out of their hands. This was the reason why I wanted to form a branch of the Executive of the Jewish Agency here, and although the Palestinians, chiefly Ben-Gurion, have opposed it, Dr. Nahum Goldmann, Lipsky, Dr. Wise and myself have formed a sort of central group with whom some of the American members of the Emergency Committee are cooperating, and will cooperate with more in the future, and which will get something done as far as the political field is concerned. The fund-raising is in order, but everything else sinks into the morass of interminable discussions and you know how distasteful these things are to me. I am, therefore, a very rare visitor to the meetings of the Emergency

---

[13] See No. 359.

Committee. They are, however, kept well informed of the steps which we are undertaking.

WASHINGTON ZIONIST GROUP: In Washington, which is a particularly important center, we have formed a small group consisting chiefly of high government officials who are experts in their respective fields, and they are being organized into a sort of council by Israel Sieff, who is doing it very well. All these enterprises need special funds. Well, I am getting some of them, but it is not enough for the task; and although the Emergency Committee realizes the necessity of such funds, they have not yet got up sufficient steam to take some steps towards the realization of that project. Mr. Ben-Gurion has a great share in the demoralization of the Emergency Committee, to which he used to come every day with some new ideas and wild-cat schemes.

My affectionate greetings to all of you, and I am beginning to look forward to the time when I shall see you in our little office.

Love,

Yours ever,

Chaim Weizmann

OMITTED LETTERS

Items of minor significance or of a repetitive nature, as detailed below, are available for reference at the Weizmann Archives in Rehovot. Some names and dates are conjectural.

1940   *July*   Aliens War Service Dept.; Leopold Amery (two items); Benjamin Bloch (three items); Joseph Blumenfeld; Brendan Bracken (two items); Bristows, Cooke & Carpmael (three items); R.A. Butler; E.M. Clover; R. Clover; Lady Colefax; W.D.H. Danby; F. Demuth; Christopher G. Eastwood; Augusto d'Esaguy; Lucio T. Feteira (three items); Fitzpatrick, Graham & Co.; Archibald Freiman; Nelly Friedberg; Nathan Nachman Gesang; H.J. Gough; Hans Halban; O.A. Harker; Charles Hearson & Co.; A.C. Jessup; Franz Kind (two items); Helen Kirkpatrick; Nicolai Kirschner; Lord Lloyd; Harold Macmillan; Manchester Oil Refinery Ltd.; Marks & Clerk; W.M. Marshall; D.C. Martin (two items); Naldi; Lewis Namier; H.L. Nathan; National Provincial Bank; Osbert Peake (two items); Lord Victor de Rothschild (four items); Ian Roy (two items); Rabbi S. Schonfeld; Oswald Scott; R.H.P. Senhouse; Leon Simon; Sir Archibald Sinclair; H.W. Turner; Albert Wasserman; W. Waterson & Sons Ltd.; Meyer W. Weisgal (two items).

Aug.   Leopold Amery; R.D. Andrews; Brendan Bracken (two items); Cambridge University, Vice-Chancellor; Henry Channon (two items); Therese Clay; Sidney Clive; Josef Cohn (two items); Lady Colefax (two items); Courtice; W.D.H. Danby; Lucio T. Feteira; Nahum Goldmann; C.J. Goodwin; Charlotte Haber (two items); C.R. Hinds Howell; Mrs. V. Jabotinsky; Siegfried Kramarsky; Harold Laski; Miss Len-Festy; Harold Macmillan; John M. Martin; Osbert Peake; Alexander Pekelis; Chaim Raphael; J. Roffey (two items); M. Rosin; Miriam Rothschild; Harry Sacher; P.B. Seal; Sir Franklin Sibley (two items); Sir Archibald Sinclair; Major Thomas; Albert Wasserman; Meyer W. Weisgal (seven items); Stephen S. Wise.

Sept.   Aliens War Service Dept.; Brendan Bracken; W.A. Burton; J. Cameron (two items); David Dainow; Eliahu Dobkin; Lucio T. Feteira (two items); Jean Fischer; Fitzpatrick, Graham & Co.; S.J. Fox; R.H. Haining; George Halpern; Nicolai Kirschner; Lord Lloyd; Harold Macmillan; Ministry of Supply, Establishment Officer; Herbert Morrison; Isaac Naiditch (two items); William Paley; Osbert Peake (two items); Alexander Pekelis (two items); Petrocarbon Ltd.; J. Roffey (four items); Lauchlan Rose; Paul Rosin (two items); Lord (Victor) Rothschild; W. Watson & Co.; Meyer W. Weisgal (eight items); Michael Weizmann; Stephen S. Wise (two items); Daniel Wolf.

Oct.   Walter Baer; Pierre Bigar; Benjamin Bloch; Joseph Blumenfeld; Louis D. Brandeis; J. Cameron; Ben V. Cohen; Josef Cohn; Reginald Coupland (two items); W.D.H. Danby; Edwin Guthrie & Co.; Hans Halban; Jacob Hodess; Barnett Janner; Franz Kind; Nicolai Kirschner; Arthur Lourie; John M. Martin (two items); H. Moss-Morris; Osbert

Peake; Chaim Raphael; J. Roffey; Joseph Sagall; Moshe Shertok (two items); Leon Simon; Sir Archibald Sinclair; E.B.B. Speed (two items); F.A. Voigt; Yizhak Volcani; Meyer W. Weisgal (seven items); Vera Weizmann (three items).

Nov. Werner Baer; Josef Cohn; Cooper, Bake & Co.; W.D.H. Danby; Israel Goldstein; E.I. Kaufmann; R.T.E. Latham; A.W. Lee; Lord Lloyd (two items); Arthur Lourie (two items); D.C. Martin (four items); John M. Martin; Vincent Massey; Henry Montor (two items); National Labour Committee; J.M. Pearson; Joseph Sagall; Leon Simon; Roland F. Slade; H.W. Turner; Meyer W. Weisgal (three items).

Dec. Walter Baer; Benjamin Bloch (four items); Joseph Blumenfeld; Selig Brodetsky; D.M. van Buuren; Josef Cohn; W.P. Crozier; Sir John Dill; Lady Fitzgerald; R.H. Haining; Oliver Harvey; J.J.W. Herbertson; Nicolai Kirschner; Walter Loeb; Julian W. Mack; John M. Martin; Herschel Meyer; Order of Ancient Maccabeans; Charles B. Parker (two items); Emanuel Rosen; Leon Simon; E.B.B. Speed; Meyer W. Weisgal (five items); Miss E.A. Wilson; Stephen S. Wise.

1941   *Jan.* Leopold Amery (two items); Walter Baer; Bank of England, Foreign Exchange Control; Benjamin Bloch (two items); Leon Bloch; Kurt Blumenfeld; Brendan Bracken (two items); Selig Brodetsky; Josef Cohn; P.S. Crickett; Sir Wyndham Deedes; Duke of Devonshire; Walter Elliot; Augusto d'Esaguy; S.J. Fox; Leopold Greenberg; R.H. Haining; Hans Halban; O.A. Harker; Sir Cuthbert Headlam; Sir Edmund Ironside; Frederick H. Kisch; Lord Lloyd; D.C. Martin (two items); Jan Masaryk; Lord Melchett; Gilbert Murray; National Provincial Bank; Gaston Palewski; Osbert Peake; Jesse Schwartz; Leon Simon; M. Stephany; George Trenter; Meyer W. Weisgal (two items).

Feb. Leopold Amery (two items); Benjamin Bloch (eight items); Brendan Bracken (two items); M. Chenciner; Josef Cohn; P.S. Crickett; Harold Davies; Fitzpatrick, Graham & Co. (four items); Jacob Gitlin; H. Goldstein; George Hall; Home Office, Under-Secretary of State; Earl of Jersey; Arthur Lourie; James A. Malcolm; Simon Marks; D.C. Martin; Ministry of Labour and National Service, Secretary of State; Henry Montor; Emanuel Rosen; Miriam Sacher; Werner Senator; Abba Hillel Silver; Ludwig Tell; Mona Wainright; Meyer W. Weisgal (five items).

Mar. Ernst D. Bergmann (three items); Joseph Blumenfeld; Ben V. Cohen; Christopher G. Eastwood; Federacion Sionista; Fitzpatrick, Graham & Co. (three items); Harry Friedenwald; Joseph Garfinkel; Rev. J.K. Goldbloom; I.M. Golden; J.J.W. Herbertson; J.B. Hobman; R.R. O'Reilly Kabalkin; George Katona; George Liebrecht; James A. Malcolm (four items); Estelle Mark; D.C. Martin; Doris May; Desmond Morton; Lord Moyne (two items); Muhlstein; H.L. Nathan; Harold Nicolson; W.H. Pettersen; J.H. Retinger; J. Roffey; Emanuel Rosen; Paul Rosin (two items); Lord (Victor) Rothschild; Lewis J. Ruskin; Joseph J. Schwartz; Meyer W. Weisgal (four items); Garfield Weston.

Apr. Naomi Bakstansky; E.J. Barnsley; Ernst D. Bergmann (four items); Adolphe A. Berle; Bruce Bliven (two items); Benjamin Bloch (three items); Joseph Blumenfeld; Raymond Leslie Buell; Clarence R. Decker; Fitzpatrick, Graham & Co.; Bruno Foa; Daniel Frisch; L.

Germain; Sigmund Gestetner; Israel Goldstein; Harry Grayer; Benjamin Halpern; Robert A. Hess; Leo Istorik; Ada H. Land; Anka B. Landau; David A. Legg; Levin; Berl Locker; Arthur Lourie; Simon Marks; Doris May (five items); Henry Monsky; Edward A. Norman; Tamar de Sola Pool; Bernard A. Rosenblatt; Paul Safro; William B. Schloss; Seaboard Zionist & Hadassah Regions, 19th Annual Conference; Count Sforza; Lawrence Shaughnessy; M. Simons; Nathan Straus; Meyer W. Weisgal; Chilik Weizmann; Stephen S. Wise; Alex S. Wolf.

May Harry Batshaw; Ernst D. Bergmann (three items); Benjamin Bloch (three items); Leon Bloch; Joseph Blumenfeld; D. Dunkelman; Archibald Freiman; Rev. J.K. Goldbloom; Harry Hollzer; Stanley J. Kann; Paul Kronacker; Doris May (four items); Lord Melchett; Henry Montor; William Paley; Meyer L. Prentis; Charles Ress (two items); Morris Rothenberg; Knowles Ryerson (two items); H.B. Speakman; Chilik Weizmann; Stephen S. Wise (two items); Samuel Zemurray.

June Ernst D. Bergmann (four items); Ernst Berl (two items); Jacob Billikopf; Benjamin Bloch (three items); Edward Bransten; Ben V. Cohen (two items); I.M. Golden; Paul Kronacker; Louis Lipsky; Arthur Lourie (two items); Louis Lourie; Isaac D. Magnes; Doris May (two items); André Meyer (three items); Mrs. W. Paley; H.J. Prebluda; Leo J. Rabinowitz (three items); Miss V. Roney; Abba Hillel Silver; H.B. Speakman; Sol M. Stroock; Dorothy Thompson; Meyer W. Weisgal (three items); Stephen S. Wise.

July D.F. Anderson; Ernst D. Bergmann; Ernst Berl; P.E. Bewshea; Benjamin Bloch (four items); Bonn; J. Cameron; Louis F. Fieser; Fitzpatrick, Graham & Co.; Joseph Goldberg; Israel Goldstein; Lord Halifax; Shalom Horowitz; The Jewish Advocate; Stanley J. Kann; Emanuel Libman; Fred Mann; Doris May (two items); André Meyer; Henry Montor; Isaac Naiditch; Charles Ress; Bruno Rosenfeld; Jules Sax; Lorraine Shaughnessy; Abba Hillel Silver; Mrs. Archibald Silverman (two items); Major Thomas; Dorothy Thompson (two items); Meyer W. Weisgal (two items); Stephen S. Wise (two items); Herbert Young.

Aug. Alec Alexander; Paul Baerwald; Lavy Bakstansky; Benjamin Bloch (five items); Brendan Bracken (two items); Josef Cohn (three items); Reginald Coupland; P.S. Crickett; W.H. Crickett; Nicolai Kirschner; Miss Leibell; Mrs. Alfred Lyttelton; Walter Monckton; Desmond Morton; Raistrick; Lewis J. Ruskin; Daniel Sieff Research Institute; Morris Troper; Georg Tugendhat; H.W. Turner; Meyer W. Weisgal.

Sept. Leopold Amery; Ernst D. Bergmann (four items); Benjamin Bloch (two items); Joseph Blumenfeld; Josef Cohn; A. Felix; Fitzpatrick, Graham & Co.; Guaranty Trust Co., New York; Jewish Agency Executive; Eli Kahan; Anna Kallin; Sir Walter Layton; Louis E. Levinthal; D.C. Martin; John M. Martin; André Meyer; Lord McGowan; Fred Nettler; Arthur Newell; Anthony de Rothschild; Moshe Shertok; Daniel Sieff Research Institute; Israel M. Sieff (two items); Meyer W. Weisgal (three items); Stephen S. Wise.

Oct. Hamilton F. Armstrong (two items); Benjamin Bloch (three items); Victor Cazalet; Josef Cohn; The Financial Adviser; Lord Greene; S.E. Kark; Franz Kind; Frederick H. Kisch; H.L. Nathan; J.H. Retinger; Hubert Ripka; Lord (Victor) Rothschild; Lewis J. Ruskin (two items); Blanche Shepard; Moshe Shertok (two items); Sir Archibald Sinclair; Yizhak Volcani; Sir Robert Waley-Cohen; Meyer W. Weisgal (five items).

Nov. Leopold Amery; Norman Bentwich; Benjamin Bloch (five items); Brendan Bracken; William Croft; Alfred A. Eibschutz; Albert K. Epstein; Fitzpatrick, Graham & Co.; Esther Hellinger; Inter-American Jewish Conference; Nicolai Kirschner; A.W. Lee; Lord Luke; S.E.V. Luke; Harold Macmillan; John M. Martin; Edward A. Norman; Palmer; A.J.K. Pigott; V.E.A. Pullin; Emanuel Rosen; Miriam Rothschild; Lord (Victor) Rothschild; Salman Schocken; Moshe Shertok; Spenceley; Sir Charles Tegart; H.W. Turner; Sir Frank Waterson; Meyer W. Weisgal (five items); Wise, Lipsky and Goldmann; Mrs. I. Zangwill.

Dec. Aegis Assurance & Trust Co.; Leopold Amery; Norman Bentwitch; Benjamin Bloch (eight items); Brendan Bracken; Nevile Butler; S. Costa; P.S. Crickett; William Croft (two items); Lord Davies; F. Demuth; A. J. Drexel Biddle (two items); Albert K. Epstein; Eliahu Epstein; O. Frey; Oliver Harvey; Keren Hayesod; V.G. Lawford; A.W. Lee; Hugh R. Leech; Louis E. Levinthal; B.A. Levinson; Harold Macmillan (two items); Lord McGowan; Ministry of Labour and National Service, Secretary of State; Eugen Mittwoch; Alphonse Nahum; H.L. Nathan; Louis Nissen; C. Offey (two items); Charles Peat (three items); S. Ravidowicz; Emanuel Rosen; Paul Rosin; Leopold Schen; I. Schwarzbart; Werner Senator (two items); Moshe Shertok; Leonard Stein; Marjorie Stephenson (two items); Gustave Tuck; Meyer W. Weisgal (eight items).

1942   *Jan.* F.W. Bain; Jacob D. Beam (three items); Benjamin Bloch (four items); Nevile Butler; Randolph Churchill; A.J. Drexel Biddle (two items); A. Gavronsky; Oliver Harvey; Sir Cuthbert Headlam (two items); Eliezer Kaplan; A.W. Lee; Harold Macmillan (five items); Arnold Minnis; Lord Louis Mountbatten (three items); National Provincial Bank; Lord (Victor) Rothschild (two items); Hadassah Samuel; Schwartz; Werner Senator; Moshe Shertok; Sir Archibald Sinclair; Sweet-Escott; E.G. Taylor; Meyer W. Weisgal (five items); Zionist Federation, England.

Feb. Isaiah Berlin; Benjamin Bloch (three items); Nevile Butler; P.S. Crickett; Shlomo Eisenberg; Israel Goldstein; Harold Hartley; Leo Herrmann; Leib Jaffe; Jewish National Fund, Secretary; Jewish Telegraphic Agency Bulletin; Sir Cecil Kisch; Sir Walter Layton; Louis E. Levinthal; Geoffrey Lloyd; Judah L. Magnes; André Meyer; Lord Louis Mountbatten (three items); William Rootes; Cecil Roth; Anthony de Rothschild; Moshe Shertok; Charles Solomon; Sweet-Escott; Meyer W. Weisgal; Harold Wernher; Zionist Federation, South Africa.

Mar. Benjamin Bloch (three items); Nevile Butler; P.S. Crickett; W.L.M. Dunlop; Emin Erkul; Joseph Fisher; Sami Gunzberg; Sir Cecil Kisch (four items); Lord Louis Mountbatten; Marquis of Reading; T. Ronsheim; Harry Sacher; Hadassah Samuel; Jan C. Smuts; Sir Ronald Storrs; Dorothy Thompson; Yizhak Volcani; Meyer W. Weisgal (five items); Stephen S. Wise (two items).

Apr. Ernst D. Bergmann (two items); Jacob Billikopf; Maurice Bisgyer; Benjamin Bloch (two items); Joseph Blumenfeld (two items);

Fitzpatrick, Graham & Co.; Harry Friedenwald; Lazar Frisch; Leon Gellman; Rev. J.K. Goldbloom; Gottlieb Hammer; Joseph C. Hyman (two items); Max Kabatznick; Maurice J. Karpf; E.I. Kaufmann (two items); Georgette Mayer-Harari; Miss Mountbatten; James N. Rosenberg; Bernard A. Rosenblatt; Edward V. Sahek; Eugene F. Saxton; Joseph Schlossberg; Jesse Schwartz; Joseph J. Schwartz; Lorraine Shaughnessy; Rebecca Sieff; Leonard Stein; Rabbi Milton Steinberg; Eliahu D. Stone; Nathan Straus; Joe Weingarten; Benji and Maidie Weizmann; David Wertheim; Russell Young.

May Ernst D. Bergmann (three items); Jacob Billikopf; Jacob Blaustein; M.H. Blinken; Benjamin Bloch; Alexander Brin; Felix Frankfurter (two items); Paul Gaiser; Rev. J. K. Goldbloom; Henry Goldschmidt; Israel Goldstein; E.I. Kaufmann; Mrs. M.R. Lichtstern; Robert J. Longuest; Arthur Lourie (two items); Angus C. Malcolm. Mrs. Simon Marks; Zvi Hirsch Masliansky; Abraham Mazur; Jacques Mercier; Tamar de Sola Pool; Charles Rosenbloom; Samuel Schulman; Abba Hillel Silver; Judah L. Steinglass; Genevieve Tabouis; Benji and Maidie Weizmann (four items); Saul E. White; Stephen S. Wise; Col. T.W. Wren.

June Lavy Bakstansky; Ellen Ballon; Ernst D. Bergmann (four items); Morton Berman; Benjamin Bloch (three items); Ben V. Cohen (two items); Albert K. Epstein; Simon Federbusch; Mrs. Abe Goldberg; Israel Goldstein; Harry Grayer; Ralph Gustafson; Philip W. Ireland; Ivor Joseph Linton; Samuel Lipkovsky; James McDonald; John F. McCabe; M. Pritzker; Bernard G. Richards; Robert Rollins; James L. Rosenberg; Martin Rosenblueth; Rudolf Samuel; Samuel Schulman; Abba Hillel Silver; A.H. Sulzberger; John Tatelman; Abe D. Waldauer; T.P. Walker; Benji and Maidie Weizmann; Maidie Weizmann.

July Lavy Bakstansky; Ernst D. Bergmann (five items); Benjamin Bloch (four items); Nevile Butler; Ronald Campbell; Elias Charry; Winston Churchill; Simon Federbusch; Fitzpatrick, Graham & Co.; Israel Goldstein; Benjamin R. Harris (two items); Kenneth Hoover; Philip W. Ireland; E.I. Kaufmann (three items); Henrietta Klotz; Fiorello LaGuardia; Richard Lichtheim; Angus C. Malcolm; Ruth E. Martin; Doris May; Henry Montor; Emanuel Neumann; Edward A. Norman; Louis Rimsky; Franklin D. Roosevelt (two items); Henry Rosenbaum; Louis Rosenbaum; Bernard A. Rosenblatt; Mrs. Carola Rothschild; Lewis J. Ruskin; Alfred Sachs; Morris Sendar; Mrs. Adolphe Sieroty; Archibald Silverman; Robert Silverman; Eliahu D. Stone; Theodore Strimling; Ezra Teubel; T.P. Walker; Charles K. Webster; Aaron Weiss; Benji and Maidie Weizmann (three items); Stephen S. Wise; Young.

Aug. Paul Baerwald; Bernard Baruch; Ernst D. Bergmann (two items); Frank S. Cohen; James Conant; Kenneth Hoover (two items); Eliezer Kaplan; Louis E. Kirstein; Lord Lytton; Ralph W. Olmstead; W.H. Oppenheimer; Emery Reves; Morris Rothenberg; Jesse Schwartz; Louis Segal; Chilik Weizmann; Zionist Record.

Sept. Walter Baer; Benjamin Bloch; Miriam Cohen; John Gunther; Rabbi I. Herzog; Eliezer Kaplan; R.J. Kimmel; Ivor Joseph Linton; Simon Marks; Leopold Schen; Blanche Shepard; Moshe Shertok; Benji and Maidie Weizmann; Chilik Weizmann (two items); Stephen S. Wise .

Oct. Walter Baer; Maurice Bisgyer; Kurt Blumenfeld; Mendel Fisher; Fitzgerald, Graham & Co.; John Gunther; Maurice B. Hexter; Jewish Agency Executive; Siegfried and Mrs. Kramarsky; Louis E. Levinthal (two items); Arthur Lourie (two items); Abraham Mazur; Nathan Ratnoff; Morris Rothenberg; Guy de Rothschild; Lorraine Shaughnessy; Mrs. Maurice Silverman; Robert Szold; David Wertheim; Stephen S. Wise; Zionist Executive.

Nov. Clive Baillieu; M.H. Blinken; Benjamin Bloch; Joseph Cohen; Ashley Cole; Albert K. Epstein; Israel Goldstein; George Greenbaum; John Gunther; Salomon Herenroth; Mrs. Edward Jacobs; Dept. of Justice; Abraham A. Neumann; Ralph W. Olmstead; Morris Rothenberg; Michel I. Samuelson; Salman Schocken; J. Edward Stern; Dewey Stone; Max Sulzbacher; Robert P. d'Voren; Maidie Weizmann; Sumner Welles (two items); Stephen S. Wise; Col. T.W. Wren.

Dec. P.B. Blasbalg; Benjamin Bloch; L. Boyd-Hatch; Mrs. Frank S. Cohen; Morris L. Ernst; Leon I. Feuer; Lazar Frisch; Gottlieb Hammer; D. Heineman; Nathan D. Kaplan; Louis E. Levinthal; Ralph W. Olmstead; Harry Sacher; Alexander Sachs (two items); Max Schloessinger; T.P. Walker; Edward Warburg; Israel Wechsler; Sidney N. Weitz; Maidie Weizmann; Sumner Welles; Maurice Wertheim.

1943   *Jan.* Selig Brodetsky; Mrs. Frank S. Cohen; Fitzpatrick, Graham & Co.; Doris May (two items); Harry Sacher; U. Schäcter; Lorraine Shaughnessy; Israel M. Sieff; Maurice D. Waldman; Sumner Welles.

BIOGRAPHICAL INDEX

For abbreviations see p. xxix.

BAKSTANSKY, Lavy (1904–71). B. Russia, graduate of Herzlia High School, Tel Aviv, and London School of Economics. General Secretary Zionist Federation of Great Britain from 1930; director Joint Palestine Appeal; on Executive, Foreign Affairs and *Erez Israel* Committees, Board of Deputies of British Jews.

BENES, Eduard (1884–1948). Czechoslovak President 1935–38, and from 1945 until forced to resign in 1948 due to Communist demands. Professor at Prague Academy of Commerce 1909–12, and sometime Professor of Sociology at University of Prague. General Secretary, Czechoslovak National Council in Paris 1917; Minister of Foreign Affairs 1918–35, Premier 1921–22. Following Munich, 5 Oct. 1938, he became visiting professor at Chicago University. Headed Czech Government-in-Exile in London during W.W.II. As a champion of rights of small nations, he warmly supported Zionism.

BERLIN, Sir Isaiah. B. Riga, 1909. Order of Merit 1971. Brought to England as a boy, he became a lecturer in philosophy at New College, Oxford, 1932; Fellow of All Souls, Oxford 1932–38, Research Fellow 1950–57; Fellow of New College 1938–50. Served with British Information Service in New York, and with British embassies in Washington and Moscow during W.W.II and subsequently. Chichele Professor of Social and Political Theory 1957–67; first President, Wolfson College, Oxford 1966–75; President, British Academy from 1974; formerly President, Jewish Historical Society of England; on Board of Governors, Hebrew University. Editorial Board, *Weizmann Letters and Papers.* Author, *inter alia,* of *Karl Marx* 1939, *The Hedgehog and the Fox* 1953, *Life and Opinions of Moses Hess* 1959.

BEVIN, Ernest (1881–1951). Began career in trade union movement as national organizer of Dockers' Union 1910–21; General Secretary, Transport and General Workers' Union, 1921–40; Minister of Labour and National Service 1940–45. As Secretary of State for Foreign Affairs, 1945–51, his Middle East policy based on major role of the Arabs there and the assumption that Palestine could not solve the Jewish problem, led him into conflict with, and hostility against, Zionist Organization, and ultimately to submission of Palestine question to United Nations, 1947.

CRANBORNE, Viscount (Robert Arthur James Cecil, 5th Marquis of Salisbury, 1893–1972). Cons. M.P. 1929–41; Parliamentary Under-Secretary of State for Foreign Affairs 1935–38; Secretary of State for Dominion Affairs 1940–42, 1943–45, for Colonies 1942; Lord Privy Seal 1942–43, 1951–52; Leader of House of Lords 1942–45, 1951–57; Chancellor Liverpool University from 1951; Secretary of State for Commonwealth Relations 1952; Lord President of Council 1952–57.

GESTETNER, Sigmund (1897–1956). Chairman and managing director of Gestetner office equipment concern from 1920. His friendship with W. brought him to chairmanship of K.H. in England, and to J.N.F. as treasurer 1949, President from 1950. Active in Joint Palestine Appeal and hon. President Weizmann Institute Foundation. He lent his farm to Zionist movement for training agricultural pioneers.

HAINING, Sir Robert Hadden (1882–1959). Professional soldier, served European War 1914–18; barrister-at-law Lincoln's Inn 1919–27, at Imperial Defence

College, then Aldershot and Colchester Commands, 1927–31; at W.O.1931–34, 1936–38; commander British forces in Palestine and Transjordan 1938–39; G.O.C. Western Command 1939–40; Vice-Chief Imperial General Staff 1940–41; Intendant-General, Middle East 1941–42.

HULL, Cordell (1871–1955). U.S. Secretary of State, 1933–44. Lawyer, member Tennessee House of Representatives 1893–97; judge in Tennessee 1903-07; Congressional Representative 1907–21, 1923–31; Senator for Tennessee 1931–33. He belonged to the international school of thought in American diplomacy as opposed to isolationists.

KOLLEK, Theodor (Teddy). B. Vienna 1911. Israel public figure. A student Zionist and youth leader in Austria, Czechoslovakia, Germany and England, he settled in Palestine 1934; founding-member of Kibbutz Ein Gev 1937. In J.A. Political Department 1940–47; representative of *Haganah* in U.S. 1947–48; Israel's Minister Plenipotentiary in Washington 1951–52; director-general, Prime Minister's Office 1952–64; chairman Israel Government Tourist Corporation 1956–65; Mayor of Jerusalem from 1965. Founder of Israel Museum, Jerusalem, and its chairman from 1964.

LAMPSON, Sir Miles (1st Lord Killearn, 1880–1964). Entered F.O. 1903; served Tokyo 1908–10, Sofia 1911, Peking 1916; Acting British High Commissioner in Siberia 1920; Minister to China 1926–33; High Commissioner for Egypt and Sudan 1934–36; Ambassador to Egypt and High Commissioner for Sudan 1936–46; Special Commissioner in South-East Asia 1946–48.

LEVINTHAL, Louis Edward (1892–1976). Judge, on Philadelphia Court of Common Pleas, 1937–59. President, Jewish Publication Society of America 1949–54, chairman of its Publication Committee 1939–49, 1954–62. President Z.O.A. 1941–43; Special Adviser on Jewish Affairs to Gen. Lucius D. Clay and U.S. European Command 1947–48. Settling in Israel, he was chairman of Board of Governors of Hebrew University 1962–66. His *Credo of an American Zionist* publ. 1942.

MASARYK, Jan Garrigue (1886–1948). Son of first President of Czechoslovakia, Thomas Masaryk. In 1918 he entered Ministry for Foreign Affairs in Czechoslovakia, serving in Washington and London 1919–22; Secretary to Foreign Ministry 1922–25; Czech Minister in London 1925–38, resigning after Munich. Foreign Minister of Czech Government-in-Exile from July 1940, and again after liberation of his country, May 1945–48. Following Communist coup d'état of 25 Feb. 1948 he apparently committed suicide by jumping from his window at the Foreign Ministry.

MORGENTHAU, Henry Jr. (1891–1967). Secretary of Treasury 1934–45. Son of Henry Morgenthau Sr. (Biog. Index, Vol. VII). An agronomist, he was publisher of *American Agriculturist* 1922–23; appointed 1928 by Governor Franklin D. Roosevelt as chairman, Agricultural Advisory Commission, and in 1930 Conservation Commissioner, State of N.Y. Head of Federal Farm Board and Farm Credit Administration in Washington 1933. In 1943 he obtained State Department approval to transfer private U.S. funds to Europe to rescue French and Rumanian Jews; and at his suggestion Roosevelt established War Refugee Board Jan. 1944. His 'Morgenthau Plan' proposed post-war partition of Germany and its conversion into an agrarian area. He was U.J.A. general chairman 1947–50, honorary chairman 1950–53; chairman, American Financial and Development Corporation for Israel and Israel Bonds, 1951–54.

MOYNE, 1st Lord (Walter Edward Guinness, 1880–1944). Served in South Africa 1900–01; in W.W.I. Cons. M.P. 1907–31; Under-Secretary for War 1922–23; Financial Secretary to Treasury 1923–24, 1924–25; Minister of Agriculture 1925–29; chairman, Royal Commission on Durham Univ. 1934, on West Indies 1938–39; Colonial Secretary 1941–42; Deputy Minister of State, Cairo 1942, Minister 1944; assassinated by members of *Lohamei Herut Israel* (Stern Group) 6 Nov. 1944.

PHILBY, HARRY ST. JOHN BRIDGER (1885–1960). Explorer and Orientalist, b. Ceylon. Indian Civil Service 1908–15; served in Mesopotamia W.W. I; led British political mission to central Arabia 1917–18; crossed Arabian peninsula 1920; chief British representative Transjordan 1921–24; became a Muslim in 1930 and lived in Jidda as representative of Sharqieh Ltd., 1926–55. Conducted extensive exploration of Arabian peninsula 1930–40. Close adviser of King Ibn Saud. Author, works on Arabia.

THOMPSON, DOROTHY (1894–1961). U.S. writer. In Europe following W.W. I as free-lance newspaperwoman with syndicated column on international affairs called 'On the Record'. Head of Berlin Bureau of New York *Evening Post,* expelled by Nazis in early 1930s. President of American PEN Club 1936–40. Her second husband was the novelist Sinclair Lewis. Until 1948 she wrote and lectured extensively on behalf of Zionism and plight of European Jewry, but subsequently supported the Palestinian Arab cause.

WAVELL, ARCHIBALD PERCIVAL, 1ST EARL (1883–1950). Served in India 1903–10, with Russian Army 1911–12, in France 1914–16, in Palestine 1917–20. Commanded 2nd Division Aldershot 1935–37, Forces in Palestine 1937–38, Southern Command 1938–39. In July 1939 he formed Middle East Command, of which he was G.O. C.-in-C. until July 1941, when he became C.-in-C., India; Supreme Commander, South West Pacific Dec. 1941–43. Viceroy of India 1943–47. Author, *Palestine Campaigns* 1928, *Allenby* 1940, *Allenby in Egypt* 1943.

WELLES, SUMNER (1892–1961). U.S. career diplomat from 1914; in State Department's Division of Latin American Affairs 1920–22, later serving in Dominican Republic, Haiti, and Honduras. Assistant Secretary of State 1933–37, Under-Secretary 1937–43; retired 1943.

INDEX

Cross-references to other volumes are given where appropriate.